The
Mexican
American
Orquesta

GG Orchestra Dance Poster

MANUEL PEÑA

The Mexican American Orquesta

Music, Culture, and the Dialectic of Conflict

UNIVERSITY OF TEXAS PRESS

Austin

First edition, 1999

Requests for permission to reproduce material from this work should be sent to Permissions, University of Texas Press, Box 7819, Austin, TX 78713-7819.

⊗ The paper used in this book meets the minimum requirements of ANSI/NISO Z39.48-1992 (R1997) (Permanence of Paper).

Library of Congress Cataloging-in-Publication Data

Pena, Manuel H., 1942–
    The Mexican American orquesta : music, culture, and the dialectic of conflict / Manuel Pena. — 1st ed.
        p.   cm.
    Includes bibliographical references, discography, and index.
    ISBN 0-292-76586-x (hardcover)
    ISBN 0-292-76587-8 (pbk.)
        1. Mexican Americans—Southwestern States—Music—History and criticism.   2. Mexican Americans—Southwestern States—Social life and customs.   3. Popular music—Political aspects—Southwestern States.   4. Dance orchestra music—History and criticism.   I. Title.
        ML3481 .P44   1999
        781.64′089′6872079—dc21

                                                        99-6098

In memory of my mother,

Agustina Jasso, for all the

talents she bequeathed.

Here and now, music can do no more than to present, in its own

structure, the social antinomies which, amongst other things,

carry the responsibility for music's isolation. It will succeed all the

better, the more deeply it manages to form, within itself, the force

of those contradictions and the need to resolve them in society,

and the more precisely it expresses, in the antinomies of its own

language and forms, the miseries of the status quo, emphatically

calling, through the ciphered language of suffering, for change.

THEODORE ADORNO

Contents

CONTENTS

Illustrations

Acknowledgments

Many people have contributed to the consummation of this long-planned project. First and foremost, I wish to thank all of the musicians—some colleagues, some "informants" (some both)—who shared with me their time and their notions of what orquesta music represents. Some of them may think my interpretations bizarre, others as perhaps interesting, and yet others might agree with me on many points. I can only assure them that I have thought about our music for a long time, and, given my own twist on the order of things, this is the best I could do.

The names of all the musicians who collaborated with me, as well as a few other collaborators, appear at the end of these acknowledgments. All of them, as unique individuals, mean a great deal to me, and they share equally in this polyphony of voices whose collective wisdom informs the pages of this text. I am, in a sense, merely the "midwife" (to borrow a term from George Marcus) who has delivered their musical progeny—mediated as it may be by my own intellectual insemination. For the orquesta was their artistic creation, an aesthetic form of great power that they and I took for granted—until its strains disappeared, swallowed up by the music of a new era.

I also wish to thank the following academic colleagues, who took time out from their own busy schedules to critique earlier versions of the various chapters: Mario García, Alex Saragoza, and Steve Feld. I owe special thanks to Doug Foley, who read the entire manuscript and was, as usual, the merciless heckler when he spotted inconsistencies and bad writing. Of course, neither Foley nor the others mentioned can be held accountable for any wrong-headed conclusions (or bad writing). Those are mine alone.

A tip of the academic hat is in order to Theresa May, Assistant Director and Executive Editor of the University of Texas Press, for her steady encouragement and expressed conviction from early on that the manuscript was worth publishing.

I shall always be indebted to my mentor, don Américo Paredes, who opened my sluggish eyes to the endemic, deeply rooted conflict of races in the Southwest. No doubt, his spirit hovers over the pages of this book.

Gracias also to my son, Daniel Peña, who transferred my pencil transcriptions onto the music-writing program Finale. Finally, I want to acknowledge María's infinite patience and good cheer, even as I spent all of that eternity away from home. To her I also dedicate this book, as partial compensation for all those lonely moments.

Herewith (in no particular order), a list of my primary collaborators:

René Sandoval	Carmen Moreno
Gibby Escobedo	Lydia Mendoza
Sunny Ozuna	Rubén Ramos
Carlos González	Pedro Bugarín
Manuel Contreras	Moy Pineda
Lalo Guerrero	Delia Gutiérrez
Beto García	Roberto Pulido
Paulino Bernal	Carlos Villegas
René Ornelas	Ventura Alonzo
Little Joe Hernández	Frank Alonzo
Tony "Ham" Guerrero	Sylvia Winton
Manny Guerra	Jimmy Edward Treviño
Darío Pérez	Freddie Martínez
Eloy Pérez	Isidro López
Bobby Galván	Anselmo Martínez
Ricky Díaz	Oscar Hernández
Chico Sesma	María Delgado
Don Tosti	Octavio García
Beto Villa	Alfonso Ramos
Armando Marroquín	Martín Rosales
Arnaldo Ramírez	Reymundo Treviño
Oscar Lawson	

The
Mexican
American
Orquesta

PRELUDE

Music, Culture, and Dialectical Interpretation

The seeds for the production of this book may have been sown by the early 1960s, when, as a fledgling *orquesta*[1] musician, I first became aware of the musical differences that existed among the Mexicans of my native Rio Grande Valley. To be an aficionado of orquesta music, with its brassy trumpets and lambent saxophones, was to move in the better social circles of Mexican American society. Luis Arcaraz, Carlos Campos, and Pablo Beltrán Ruiz, "El Millonario," were the orchestral names local musicians invoked with a tone of reverence in their voices, though great respect was shown as well toward American bands such as those of Stan Kenton and Duke Ellington. Such names, Mexican and American alike, evoked glittering ballrooms filled with tuxedoes and gowns dancing gracefully to the strains of the bolero, *danzón, cha cha cha,* or the foxtrot. Indeed, playing with local orquestas like that of Oscar Guerra, I found myself in the midst of such elegant ambiences.

To think everything historically, that is Marxism.

PIERRE VILAR (1994: 41)

But there was another side to the musical culture of the "Magic Valley," as the Chamber of Commerce dubbed this fertile delta bordering on the northeastern corner of Mexico. In the seedy cantinas of Weslaco, Donna, Mercedes, and other Valley cities, a different music played, and a different clientele danced. Proletarians, hardened by arduous toil in the fields and in other menial jobs that barely sustained them, danced the *polca* and *canción ranchera* (country song) to the thumping beat of *conjunto* music—accordion and *bajo sexto*—celebrating with abandon their sense of liberation, however fleeting, from the daily grind awaiting them outside the walls of the cantina. Conjunto and its *música ranchera* (country music), so dear to these proletarians, had been in development for the better part of one hundred years (Peña 1985a), and, disparaged as it might be by orquesta musicians and their partisans, it was deeply entrenched in Valley culture, forming a dynamic opposite to the more sophisticated orquesta in an in-group dialectic that pitted Mexicanized proletarians against Americanized affluents.

I witnessed the musical and social disparities but could not then understand the ideological dynamics involved nor the contradictions present. Why were orquesta musicians, disdainful as they were of conjunto music, so adept themselves at playing ranchera music? Why did Mexican American socialites display such exhilaration when Oscar Guerra's orquesta played an occasional *polca ranchera,* in the style of that master of *lo ranchero,* Beto Villa? For that matter, why did Beto Villa, easily the most popular orquesta in the Hispanic Southwest during the 1940s and '50s, exploit *música ranchera* so freely, when he was just as capable of performing its opposite—what people used to refer to as *música jaitona,* or "hightone" music?

I gave much thought to these seeming contradictions in the intervening years, witnessing the same interplay between ranchero and *jaitón* when I moved to my adopted city of Fresno, California, where I continued my career as a weekend orquesta musician. In Fresno, I saw Beto García y sus GGs, the orquesta with which I played for over twelve years, undergo a subtle transformation from ranchero to jaitón, and I noticed the subsequent change in clientele—from a predominantly working-class audience to a decidedly more affluent one. Meanwhile, orquesta music was evolving, and I was taken aback when I first heard on the radio what I now see as the culmination of the orquesta tradition in the Southwest—Little Joe y la Familia playing the landmark song "Las nubes" (The clouds). I instinctively realized that something unique had taken place: "Las nubes" was a breathtaking fusion of both ranchero and jaitón, Mexican *and* American styles. I headed for the nearest shop, bought the record I had just heard, and pleaded with Beto García to let me copy the arrangement for the GGs.

"Las nubes" became a virtual emblem of a "Chicano" musical aesthetic; indeed, the style it represented, known as La Onda Chicana, attained deep and widespread support among the members of my generation, or what is now known as the "Chicano Generation." But it was only later that I came to understand the importance of La Onda and the whole orquesta tradition, and to articulate what had been, in the fifties, sixties, and seventies, but a dim awareness of what conjunto and orquesta signified in the complex cultural system of the Mexican Americans. I expressed my thoughts on the former in a previous work, *The Texas-Mexican Con-*

junto (Peña 1985a). After several years of further research and reflection —and having witnessed the orquesta's peak and decline—I now offer this interpretive history of the orquesta, thus completing the diptych "in the form of a pair" I had envisioned some years ago on these two ensembles (Peña 1985b).

It is by now a truism that we are all ideologically constrained by the social position we happen to occupy—more specifically, our class position—which sets limits on the "values" we embrace and the discourse we engage in. Few, it seems, can transcend such ideological constraints. Born into the harsh world of Mexican American proletarians, I experienced the life of that world in all its economic violence, and I imbibed all of its cultural values: its glorification of *machismo;* a certain cynicism toward wealth and power; a romantic attachment to *lo mexicano,* especially *lo ranchero;* and, in the absence of an effective political voice, its recourse to the *gritos por abajo*—our muffled rage at what the gringo *patrones* (bosses) did to squeeze every ounce of exploitation they could from our overworked bodies.

But, like many of our contemporaries, we were proud Mexicans, stubbornly believing we could overcome an unfair fate and someday claw our way out of misery. A few of us did. At considerable family sacrifice, I transcended the world that gave me birth. Through my association with orquesta musicians, I overlaid my rough proletarian grain with a smoother veneer of middle-class gloss. I even made it to the university, and as a student, first of literature and music and later of anthropology, I absorbed the culture of the academy—especially Marxist culture, for which I developed a strong affinity. I embraced its tenets, in particular its notion of class struggle and the dialectic, which I have reworked to fit my own idiosyncrasies.

It is especially the latter aspect of Marxism—the notion of a materialist dialectic—that informs the writing in the present instance. Ever the romantic, perhaps, I am animated by the ultimately optimistic conception of humanity conveyed by a dialectical approach. Despite its unrelenting critique of capitalism, the Marxist dialectic sees it as a necessary stage in the progression of humanity from an existence driven by the force of blind necessity to one in which a true "realm of freedom" is finally carved out.[2] More than that, this progression is not explainable as a random phenomenon; rather, it consists in the logical, though for the most part unconscious, movement of the human collectivity through a series of maturational stages, each defined by its own productive arrangements, and each inexorably driven by internal contradictions toward its own dissolution.[3] But the movement is always "forward" in the sense

3

that the realm of necessity is continually being pushed back (though hardly eradicated!) by an ever-improving technology and the expanding social consciousness that each stage of social evolution introduces, as we humans instinctively drive toward the Utopia perhaps awaiting us in some "Star Trek" future.

Meanwhile, our expressive culture very much articulates the contemporaneous state of material development at any given stage of social evolution: animism for the Bororo, commodity fetishism for the Americans. In the historical juncture that produced the cultural activity described in this work, economic imperatives, driven by the logic of an expanding capitalist system, clashed with (prematurely) Utopian notions of a society of free and equal citizens, giving rise to a dialectic of conflict that suffused the expressive culture of the Mexican Americans. In some instances, that culture represents an unmediated response to the clash of material and ideological forces, as in the case of the *corrido,* or ballad, which often pits one noble Mexican hero against an army of Anglo[4] lawmen. In other instances, such as that of the orquesta, the cultural message is highly mediated, filtered by the thick layers of ideology masking the politically unconscious content that ultimately gives orquesta its aesthetic grace and symbolic power.

However articulated, the dialectical thrust, like time, is irreversible: the economic and ideological structures regnant today cannot be replaced by yesterday's. Unlike time, however, these structures are subject to retrogressive "warps" that can momentarily arrest or even set back the process of social evolution while contradictions are resolved and new social arrangements await their implementation. Such is the context in which the orquesta emerged, flourished, and declined—a context marked by conflict, followed by mediation, then contradiction, then followed again by a new cycle of conflict, mediation, and contradiction, until the social and material forces that spawned the orquesta evolved beyond its capacity to articulate their ideological content. In short, orquesta was the product of a particular moment in what I refer to throughout this work as the "dialectic of conflict" that governs Anglo-Mexican relations in the American Southwest. Responding to economically driven realities encumbered by race and class, and the ideological articulation of these, the orquesta delivered its symbolic load, only to be replaced in the end by other artistic vehicles more suited to the changing material and ideological circumstances of their social base.

It is my hope that this book on the Mexican American orquesta will complement the previous one on the conjunto (Peña 1985a), and that, in combination, they will enrich what at first glance appear to be artistic forms of incidental cultural significance, and portray them for what they in fact are: powerful (if dialectically opposed) artistic expressions embedded in the deepest fibers of Mexican American social life. At the same time, the dialectical interpretation offered here diverges from the more static "us-versus-them" approach, which my friend Alex Saragoza (1987) has correctly faulted for its simplistic treatment of Anglo-Mexican relations in the Southwest. Much as we Chicanos may find satisfaction in demonizing the Anglo—and there is plenty of justification for that—the historical record reveals enough nuance in the interethnic relationship to confirm a dialectical dynamic, especially for the twentieth century.

Finally, for conjunto purists who might dismiss orquesta as the bastardized expression of a misplaced ethnic identity, I would remind them of its great power to synthesize disparate cultural experiences and make of them a unique bicultural—that is to say, Mexican American—expression. In this sense, the Mexican American orquesta is truly an organic artistic form, one that sprang from the richest humus of cultural soil to give full aesthetic bloom to the complex material and ideological forces cross-fertilizing Mexican American society during a critical period of its evolution.

On Dialectical Interpretation

Before proceeding further, a few additional comments are in order on the critical theory that both informs and motivates this study of the orquesta. I have turned to the Marxian-Hegelian metatheory of the dialectic or, more precisely, the Marxian concept of dialectical materialism because I see it as the best tool to obtain a synthesizing interpretation of music, culture, and what I refer to as the dialectic of conflict. In most Marxist writing, however, this dialectic is couched in highly abstruse and metaphysical terms. I have tried to give it a more empirical grounding in an effort to demonstrate its articulation in and through lived historical events. My preference for a dialectical interpretation stems from a conviction that the sociohistorical forces driving the development of the orquesta are not the result of random occurrences. Rather, they follow a logical pattern of social evolution flowing from the equally logical development of capitalism in the Southwest.

As conceptualized by Marx and others (e.g., Habermas 1975; Jameson 1981; Lukács 1971), the capitalist system, as a particular mode of production, is fundamentally structured by the antagonism between the dominant owner classes and the subordinate laboring classes. Structural antagonism gives rise occasionally to overt class conflict, but it mostly simmers as latent class struggle (Habermas 1970), or what Fredric Jameson (1981) has called "the political unconscious." Most important, the systemic pressure to maintain and legitimate class disparity generates a host of antinomies, unconscious for the most part, but expressible in terms of contradictions between the professed ideals ("theories") and the actual practices of the antagonist classes (Habermas 1975). Given those contradictions—for example, the reality of class domination vis-à-vis the belief in equality for all individuals (what Balibar has called "equaliberty" [1994: xii])—the built-in antinomies continually invade consciousness, where they come to a crisis and are "resolved" (or mediated) through the ideological adjustment of sociocultural patterns (e.g., normalization of the shortened workday; the workers' right to paid "vacation time"). The new patterns are eventually overcome by the systemic antinomies, creating new contradictions and new attempts at resolution. This cycle of conflict and its "resolution" (or, in more Hegelian terms, the movement from antithesis to mediation to synthesis) constitutes the empirical expression of the dialectic.

In the Southwest, the dialectic takes on an enhanced form: *overt* ethnic conflict converges with *latent* class struggle to augment but also complicate the basic contradictions of capitalism. I call this enhanced form the dialectic of conflict. Conceived in such terms, the course of ethnic-class relations in the Southwest conforms to the logic of the dialectical cycle that keeps the global capitalist system in perpetual motion. Here, too, renegotiated sociocultural arrangements are inevitably undermined by tensions and contradictions, as long as the productive relations remain predicated on unequal access to material wealth and power. Finally, in its peculiar manifestation in the Southwest, that is, in its conflation of ethnic-racial and class disparities, this dialectic and its cycle periodically introduce new forms of interethnic communication, so that the relationship between Anglo and Mexican necessarily changes over time. Qualitatively, the conflict present in the 1990s differs from that of, say, the years 1910–1919.[5]

A dialectical approach to the anthropological study of culture may seem outmoded in this era of "late capitalism" and its "postmodernist" moment, especially since post- and anti-Marxist paradigms have come to predominate, in particular the postmodernist/poststructuralist one. The discipline of anthropology itself is increasingly influenced by the tide of postmodernist (and poststructuralist) thought (Clifford and Marcus 1986; Kottack 1992). To delve into the ongoing debate between Marxism and postmodernism is well beyond the scope of these comments (but see

Agger 1992; Kellner 1994; La Cappra 1983); however, the influence of post-modernism on contemporary cultural analysis is undeniable. A contrastive sketch of the two positions may clarify my preference for Marxism.

Fredric Jameson has summed up the challenge that postmodernism poses for key elements of Marxist theory, such as that of class-as-historical-subject: "We no longer believe in political or historical teleologies, or in great 'actors' and 'subjects' of history—the nation-state, the proletariat, the party, the West, etc." (1984: xii). The notion of human agents involved in class struggle, which is crucial for Marxist thought, is rejected by postmodernists, for whom class struggle has been eclipsed by such postulates as the "end of ideology" and contestation (D. Bell 1960; Lyotard 1984), the triumph of the political economy of the sign (Baudrillard 1975; 1981), and the dispersion of power and domination by "apparatuses" and "machines" (Grossberg 1992).[6] Their senses dulled by the "hyperreality" of massive commodification, their social selves dissolved "into a host of . . . contradictory codes and interfering messages" (Jameson 1984: xviii), the subaltern classes (or masses, since real classes have now been problematized [Balibar 1994]) are rendered powerless—captives of a world beyond ideology, beyond struggle, beyond contradiction.

Not only have classes as active agents been effaced, but so has the very notion of autonomous, stable subjects. We are, all of us, contingent egos, constantly dissolved and reconstituted on the slippery terrain of our shifting social identities. Fragmented, as well, is social history, which is marked by breaks and discontinuities, rather than some grand logic of cultural progression. "Grand narratives," or totalizing theories of history, are therefore inapplicable; they fail to account for the "decentered" and fragmented fabric of life in the postmodern world. In an extension of the Frankfurt School's theory of "one-dimensional" society (Marcuse 1964), in which "the crushing forces of capitalism, state socialism, sexism, [and] racism" (Agger 1992: 10) foreclose the possibility of challenge against a hegemonic system (see also Habermas 1970; Horkheimer and Adorno 1972), postmodernist theorists deny even the prerequisite for a counterhegemony: an integrated human agent capable of rational action. Human agency is reduced to "an incoherent welter of sub- and trans-individual drives and desires," buffeted, as it is, by the "fragmentary, heterogeneous and plural character of reality" (Callinicos 1989: 2). In short, "the individual is an illusion" (Horkheimer and Adorno 1993: 41).

This postmodernist view of the world, spearheaded by French intellectuals since the 1960s (but adumbrated by the Frankfurt School), has had an increasing impact on anthropological thought in the United

States. To be sure, its most extreme postulates—the effacement of the subject and human agency, for example—have met with some resistance, perhaps because these constitute the very core of fieldwork among real people. But other staples of postmodernism—the contingency of the self and the crisis in representation—are very much problematized among postmodernist ethnographers (e.g., Clifford and Marcus 1986). In fact, however, some aspects of the postmodernist critique of positivist empiricism have had a salutary effect on anthropology—the challenge to representation, for example, the notion that an ethnographer can unproblematically portray the social life of cultural beings far removed from his own world of experience (see Paredes 1977). "Reflexivity," anthropology's contribution to postmodernism, has effectively put to rest the notion that an ethnographer utilizes some kind of theoretical alchemy to transmute social analysis into objective science. Ethnography, as we now know, is as much "true fiction" as it is scientific description (Clifford 1986); "writing culture" involves the politics and poetics of the ethnographer as much as it does the social reality she sets out to describe.

Despite—or perhaps because of—the reflexive preoccupation with the act of writing culture, postmodernist ethnography faces the same crisis as its counterparts in other fields of cultural study, namely, its reluctance (or inability) to historicize, to draw the bold strokes required in the analysis of epic struggles that pit races, classes, and genders against each other.[7] For me, the postmodernist obsession with "endless difference" (Nicholson 1990: 8) and its microcosmic particularism (what Stuart Hall called the "gospel of absolute diversity" [1988: 52]) can miss the global action, the universal struggles of subaltern groups to wrest a realm of freedom out of oppression—struggles inescapably grounded in long-playing cycles of history and the *grand récits* inscribed in their grooves.[8] By denying the power of such metanarratives, postmodernist theory disconnects expressive culture from its historical-materialist wellsprings; it strips it of its power to articulate the global struggles carried on in the trenches of racial, gender, and class struggle.

Thus, in sliding toward the postmodernist mode, we ethnographers may unwittingly throw out the contextualized baby with the now-contaminated bath water of grand theory. In our haste to apply the antiseptic balm of postmodernist particularity, we may deny ourselves the powerful tonic of universal theories, such as Marxism and radical feminism, which dare to grapple with the totalizing effects of class and gender oppression. And, while anthropologists seem loathe to strip their subjects (objects?) of a redemptive agency, in at least some instances they are wavering between the emancipatory thrust of a properly humanist (i.e., Marxist) stance and the nihilistic tone of the most extreme postmodernist voices.[9]

In my interpretation of the orquesta I have stood fast to a Marxian position, first, because the evidence I will lay out strongly suggests that its genesis is linked to the highly active and purposeful struggle of a real community to impose its will on history. Second, the emergence of orquesta was grounded in a context rich in class and ethnic struggle and contradiction (the dialectic of conflict), and, third, the history in which the orquesta is embedded is itself a chapter in a narrative writ large over the course of capitalist development on the American continent. Thus, if the postmodernist turn in "late capitalism" (Jameson 1984) has affected Mexican Americans, it is only during what I refer to here as the post-Chicano era (see the Coda), and then in the drift toward a cultural and political fragmentation that inevitably followed the demise of the Chicano movement of the 1960s and '70s, with its strongly synthesizing thrust (see Chapter 6). Yet, out of this fragmentation has risen a geographically limited but highly potent musical form, *banda*, which, despite its commoditized encumbrances, has already proven that at least the potential exists for strongly focused ethnic/working-class expressions to emerge, even in this postmodernist age.

In generating a dialectical interpretation of the orquesta, I have found it useful to "periodize" the sociohistorical setting in which it develops.[10] To this end I have partially adopted the generational scheme worked out by Rodolfo Alvarez (1973) and Mario García (1989). Alvarez, in particular, divides the course of Mexican social history in the Southwest into four more or less discrete historical blocs: the "Creation Generation," the "Migrant Generation," the "Mexican American Generation," and the "Chicano Generation." Each of these blocs encounters its own unique problems within the social system as it evolves in the American Southwest. Taking my cue from the implicit recognition of periodic stages in the generational approach to Mexican American history, I have superimposed a dialectical framework over the last two stages, in particular, as these respond to the dialectical cycle that governs the various generations in their relationship to the dominant Anglos. In sum, the dialectic of conflict commences immediately after the triumph of the United States over Mexico in the Mexican American War of 1846–1848, when the Southwest became part of the United States. Thereafter relations between the two groups conform to a dialectical motion, wherein the cycle of conflict and mediation repeats itself (always, of course, in dynamic and transformative ways).

Finally, while the interpretation that informs this historical ethnography has a dialectical bent, it is nevertheless grounded within the empirical field where musical action is generated—at least as this ethnographer has observed it. The empiricist orientation no doubt veers the description in a "linear" and "realist" direction that might appear contrary to the "reflexive" or "experimental" turn espoused by postmodernist ethnographers (the "stream-of-consciousness" effect), for whom writing about culture becomes a compromise between politics and poetics, a statement as much about self as about the "Other."[11] Yet, in many ways, this account of the orquesta represents just such a reflexive compromise, one forged out of the multiplicity of voices heard throughout the text. Of course, in the end it is my voice that transposes the basic themes and creates the final cultural score. But those themes were there to begin with; my task has simply been to orchestrate them.

Mexicans and Anglos in the Southwest
The Dialectic of Conflict

Properly speaking, the type of orquesta described in this book is neither a Mexican nor an American music. It is a synthesis of the two. Although relying on both the Mexican orquesta and the American swing band for repertorial and stylistic cues, the ensemble, as it evolved in the southwestern United

The gringos come not to share, but to possess.

Pío Pico, Governor of Alta California (quoted in Bell 1930: 262)

States, differs from both in its musico-cultural development. As a musical expression with its own cultural charter, orquesta speaks to, and in critical ways symbolizes, the deepest ideological structures of the population it historically represents. Its cultural significance cannot be fully appreciated unless we ground our study within the social context in which it flourished. This Exposition surveys that social context. It is intended as a thematic summary of the various sociohistorical motifs that form the basic topics for later chapters, where the relationship between music, culture, and the dialectic of conflict is more fully interrogated.

Although this is not by design a history of the orquesta, history necessarily enters into the discussion, since it is in its diachronic setting that the ensemble embeds itself within the web of social, economic, and ideological forces it symbolically addresses. It is within the confluence of those forces, which themselves are driven by the conflict defining Anglo-Mexican relations in the Southwest, that the orquesta materializes and is ultimately transformed into a powerful musico-symbolic form. The aim of this book, then, is not only to describe the musical style of the orquesta, but to go the full ethnomusicological distance—to enmesh the orquesta's development within a historical-materialist matrix and thus achieve a real synthesis between musicology and anthropology, that is, between musical description and cultural analysis.

INTERCULTURAL CONTACT
AND THE LEGACY OF CONFLICT

People of Spanish-Mexican descent have been in what is now the American Southwest for several centuries. Not surprisingly, given their long history in a region so closely linked to Mexico, the Mexicans—whether descendants of the original settlers or more recent immigrants—have never entirely lost their identification with the mother culture. There is, of course, considerable variation in the rate of "acculturation." Depending on region, generation, and social class, the extent of contact with and absorption into the dominant Anglo-American society varies widely among the different segments of Mexican American society in the Southwest.

Social class and acculturation (the degree of "Americanization," or the absorption of a broad range of American practices) serve as the most important variables in determining what symbolic equipment Mexican Americans use to express their most basic sense of group identity. Class functioned as a marker for social difference during the Hispanic period (until 1848, when the Americans took over), but the nature of the economy, relative isolation, and a harsh frontier environment (which included conflict with hostile Native Americans) mitigated the effects of class formation on social relations (De la Teja 1988; Paredes 1958).[1] These conditions imposed a need for close-knit communities, where the division between classes was never as pronounced as it was in more developed regions of New Spain (or Mexico, after 1821) (Camarillo 1979; León-Portilla 1972; Paredes 1958). Class-induced cultural fragmentation did not appear until the twentieth century, when Mexican Americans were integrated into the American social-class structure.

By the same token, the wholesale Americanization of Mexicans of the Southwest is predominantly a twentieth-century phenomenon, and even more recent is their "structural" assimilation into the dominant society—their integration as fully enfranchised citizens (see Gordon 1964; McLemore 1980). Anglo-American control of the Southwest, which began in Texas in the 1830s and culminated in the annexation of the total area after the Mexican War of 1846–1848, immediately marked the native Mexicans as aliens in the new order, and by the end of the nineteenth century, most of them, with the exception of a few elites, had been reduced to the status of peons and proletarians. Facing intense racial-cultural prejudice, with little chance for upward mobility or acculturation, these Americans-by-default had no choice but to cling tenaciously to their Mexican way of life as they struggled to survive in a social order in which they were now the foreigners.

When the Anglo-Americans arrived in the Southwest, they encountered more or less stable Spanish-Mexican communities scattered throughout the present states of Texas, New Mexico, Arizona, and California. These communities never evolved much beyond a subsistence economy and folk culture prior to their annexation to the United States. Moreover, although a uniform set of cultural practices prevailed, each enclave was relatively isolated, autonomous, and structured along the principles of the "inorganic democracy" outlined by Romero for other regions of Latin America (cited in Burns 1980: 87ff.). Each community thus evinced a socioculturally homogeneous organization and a general tendency to live according to orally transmitted traditions rather than codified laws. When the Americans gained control of the region, native Spanish-Mexican society experienced considerable destructuration as the inorganic democracy was shattered and replaced by a whole new set of rules that contributed to the breakdown of the old order (Barrera 1979; Camarillo 1979). This breakdown was never complete, however. The marginalization of the Spanish-Mexicans within the larger Anglo-American social order, reinforced by the ranching and agribusiness industries they were predominantly employed in, allowed for a certain continuity of life: still rural, still based on oral traditions.

Given their marginalized and subordinate status in the new order, the Mexicans of the Southwest—whether descendants of the original settlers or the new immigrants who began to flood the area at the onset of the Mexican Revolution—continued to resemble the folk communities that existed in the Hispanic period. Like the folk societies described by Redfield (1947) and Foster (1953), Mexicans in the Southwest continued to live in relative isolation, to share a more or less homogeneous culture, and to evince only minimal socioeconomic diversification (Barrera 1979; Camarillo 1979; De León 1982). This state of affairs did not change appreciably until the 1920s.

As we might expect, open conflict between Anglos and Mexicans was most pronounced during the earlier period of interethnic contact, beginning with the Anglo drive for independence in Texas during the 1830s and continuing until the early part of the twentieth century. Especially after their victory in the Mexican American War of 1846–1848, the Anglos held every advantage, militarily, economically, and culturally. This was a time when the conflict was barely mediated by the American ideology of "equaliberty," and the Mexicans were still treated as a vanquished and despised minority. Expressive culture that communicated the interethnic conflict could be explicitly blunt. The Anglos early on developed a litany of handy stereotypes that defined the Mexicans as inferior; the latter were considered everything from thieves and profligates to savages (Paredes 1958; De León 1983).

For their part, the Mexicans, as the subordinate group in the relationship, spent even more symbolic energy in defining the interethnic encounter. While they too invented stereotypes about the Anglo, a good deal of effort was expended on more elaborate forms of ethnic resistance. This resistance is best embodied in a vibrant tradition of epic-narrative ballads known as corridos, in particular those Américo Paredes (1958, 1995; see also Peña 1982) has labeled corridos of intercultural conflict. These ballads represent a strong symbolic reaction by the Mexicans of the Southwest to their subordination. Corridos written prior to 1920, in particular, forcefully articulate the stage of interethnic relations that Paredes (1966) has called the period of "open hostility," a time when conflict between the two groups was sometimes bloody, always intense. Of course, the Anglos held the upper hand, and it was precisely this recognition of dominant Anglo power that the corridos so eloquently addressed.

But corridos could only address one side of the Anglo-Mexican relationship; they were one-dimensional expressions most suited for the climate of unremitting hostility between Anglo and Mexican that marked the early period of interethnic contact. As this work attempts to demonstrate, the groups evolved with time, as they struggled in progressive stages toward more accommodative methods of intercultural communication (Foley 1990; M. García 1989; Montejano 1987). The changing relationship was best captured by forms of expressive culture other than the corrido, such as the orquesta and certain kinds of humor (Paredes 1966).

In fact, the long history of intercultural contact in the Southwest is most profitably interpreted within the framework of a dialectic of conflict that moves progressively from inequality toward equality, conflict toward accommodation, exploitation toward reciprocity, hate toward love—in short, a dialectic that oscillates between economic imperatives and Utopian, liberal-democratic notions of a society of equal and unfettered individuals. The various forms of expressive culture (in particular the orquesta) that mediate this dialectic of conflict will be examined later. For now I wish merely to point out that in the intercultural drama unfolding historically in the Southwest, the corrido functions as the absolute antithesis between Anglo and Mexican—the symbolic epitome of the most conflictive stage of the dialectic.[2]

DOMINANCE, SUBORDINATION, AND THE MEDIATION OF CONFLICT

Interethnic conflict, with increasingly more complex attempts at its mediation, is the key to Anglo-Mexican relations in the Southwest. However, any study of Mexican Americans must also take into account another factor: *intra*ethnic, or in-group, differences induced by class divisions present since the initial colonization but especially evident in the twentieth century. Moreover, these class divisions must always be seen in the context of the continuous immigration of Mexicans. Beginning with the period of the Mexican Revolution, the latter have gravitated to the Southwest in ever increasing numbers, particularly since World War II. In the second half of the twentieth century, this immigration reached tidal proportions, as Mexicans continued to escape the chronic economic problems that afflicted Mexico.

The influx of largely impoverished Mexican immigrants into the Southwest has had enormous consequences, both for interethnic relations between Anglos and Mexicans and for intraethnic relations between Mexican Americans and immigrants. For the former, the presence of such dispossessed people reinforces long-held prejudices toward Mexicans by constantly recasting the Anglo-Mexican relationship in the old terms of dominant Anglo–subordinate Mexican. For the latter, the flood of immigrants replenishes Mexican working-class culture in the Southwest, thus accentuating the social distance between increasingly affluent and acculturated Mexican Americans and the newly arrived carriers of a stigmatized ancestral culture (Browning and De la Garza 1986; Rodríguez and Núñez 1986).

These twin factors—interethnic conflict and intraethnic class difference—play a decisive role in charting the direction that Mexican American society takes, as each exerts its now-polarizing, now-mediative influence on the cultural impulses that engender such expressive forms as the corrido (Paredes 1995; Peña 1982), the dynamic Texas-Mexican conjunto (Peña 1985a), and the orquesta (Peña 1985b). Finally, to ethnic and class conflict we may add complementary processes such as acculturation and assimilation (as well as cultural resistance) as factors shaping the expressive culture of Mexican Americans.

But fundamentally, ethnic and class conflict, as well as mediative processes such as acculturation and hybridization, are best conceived within the framework of a historical-materialist dialectic that governs the evolving, conflictive relationship between Anglos and Mexicans in their epic struggle to coexist in the Southwest. A dialectical approach, grounded in the realities of productive life and its symbolic articulation, best captures the dynamic give-and-take between conflict and cooperation, progress and retreat, and equality and inequality that defines the evolving field in which the two contending groups collide. More important, a dialectical-materialist theory enables us to anchor empirical practices within a "grand narrative," one that privileges material production as among the most fundamental acts (along with human reproduction) upon which human communication and survival are predicated.

The general history of Anglo-Mexican coexistence in the Southwest can be described in such theoretical terms. Fundamentally driven by ecological-economic imperatives pitting a dominant group against a subordinate one, the relationship between Anglo and Mexican is inevitably shaped by those imperatives. Moreover, given the disparity between the two people's economic and cultural systems at first contact—one capitalist, the other essentially subsistent—the gap between economic practice and its cultural articulation widened in the Southwest after the U.S. conquest. Words could not hide actions. The Mexicans' oppression was too stark for ideological cover. Thus, the always precarious nexus between economic "base" and its "superstructure" assumed a more transparently conflictive form in the Southwest than in areas where capitalist development was more deeply entrenched and less culturally contested, such as the Eastern Seaboard.[3] In regions such as the latter, where capitalism and its cultural hegemony had long since eradicated competing cultural economies, the rift between economic and cultural structures was not as exposed as it remained on this contested border long after the U.S. conquest. It was this rift that gave impetus to such antagonistic forms of expressive culture as the corrido.[4]

Such was the situation in the American Southwest from the mid-nineteenth century until the 1920s, with ascendant capitalism and its hegemonic social relations clashing with, but eventually rooting out, the native economy and its associated culture. Although a primitive form of capital accumulation existed in the Southwest when the Anglos arrived (mainly in the form of land), much of the economic activity was still at the level of subsistence and its web of reciprocal social relations and their obligations—a major reason why the formation of true social classes remained incipient. Indeed, it is interesting to note that in the early stages of capitalist development in the Southwest, a layer of upper strata emerged among the natives—the *patrones* in New Mexico and California, for example—who acted as a buffer between the dissimilar social orders of the native Mexicans and the invading Anglos. A few members of this layer eventually merged into the dominant Anglo social order—the Bandinis in California, the Oteros in New Mexico, and the Navarros in Texas, for example. These early elites served as prototypes for middle-class Mexican Americans who attained assimilation much later, beginning in the 1920s.

As a general rule, however, the triumph of capitalism in the Southwest ensures a relationship between Anglos and Mexicans in which the basic productive dichotomy, capitalist/proletarian, sets the pattern for and, throughout the nineteenth and the early twentieth century, lines up neatly with the social dichotomy, dominant/subordinate, and its racial-cultural articulation, Anglo/Mexican:

$$\frac{\text{capitalist}}{\text{proletarian}} = \frac{\text{dominant}}{\text{subordinate}} = \frac{\text{Anglo}}{\text{Mexican}}$$

The ideological derivatives—the set of cultural symbols that each group uses to categorize the other—correspond to these crude dichotomies, at least in principle. But as a result, first, of the actions and counteractions of the contending groups as they adjust to each other's presence; second, of built-in contradictions between American capitalism and the Utopian, liberal-democratic principles that both sustain and challenge it; and, perhaps most important, of shake-ups within the capitalist system itself, the neat correspondence between the basic dichotomies necessarily erodes, forcing Anglos and Mexicans to redefine the intercultural relationship and in the process move toward new, more progressive modes of interaction. It is this dynamic interplay between productive and ideological forces that constitutes the dialectic of conflict.

More empirically yet, the American victory in the Mexican War of 1846–1848 laid the framework for the Anglos' domination of the territory and all of its native inhabitants, whom the Anglos considered their inferiors. Furthermore, as American capitalism cemented itself as the dominant mode of production and created a corresponding demand for cheap labor in the face of expansion, the native Mexicans, as well as the tide of immigrants who eventually overwhelmed them, became in the eyes of the Anglos the logical source to satisfy that demand. In fact, the Mexicans came to be seen as suitable *by their very nature* only for cheap, menial labor (Barrera 1979; Foley 1988a; Reisler 1976; Sheridan 1986). This prevalent view was openly shared with the sociologist Ozzie Simmons by Anglo employers as late as the 1940s: "Unskilled labor is Mexican labor, not for a white man" ([1952] 1974: 204).

The Anglo perception of the Mexican as backward, unintelligent, lacking in ambition, and destined for menial labor crystallized very early on, and it persisted far into the twentieth century, as illustrated in the preceding quote. This perception was confirmed in the candid remarks of the superintendent of a rural school district who was interviewed in the early 1930s by the educational researcher Herschel T. Manuel. Note the irony in his statement between the implicit conviction that Mexicans are an inferior people and the need, just the same, to deny them an education:

Most of our Mexicans are of the lower class. They transplant onions, harvest them, etc. The less they know about everything else, the better contented they are. . . . So you see, it is up to the white population to keep the Mexican on his knees in an onion patch. . . . (Quoted in Weinburg 1977: 146)

Documenting the history of Mexicans in Tucson, Arizona, the historian Tom Sheridan put the matter of Anglo domination in blunt perspective: "Tucsonenses [Mexican Tucsonans], like Mexicans across the southwestern United States, encountered a society that institutionalized their political and economic subordination in countless subtle and not-so-subtle ways" (Sheridan 1986: 4). And, as Sheridan observes, as long as the economy demanded unskilled workers, the institutional machinery remained in place to keep the Mexicans as a subordinate labor force, in this fashion reinforcing divisions of race and class "in a number of profound and crosscutting ways" (ibid.; cf. Simmons [1952] 1974). The fate of the Tucsonenses was shared by their counterparts everywhere in the Southwest (see, e.g., Reisler 1976).

Of course, the Mexicans did not submit to Anglo domination without resistance (Acuña 1981; Rosenbaum 1972; San Miguel 1987). With resistance came animosity and a hardening of cultural attitudes on both sides. In the nineteenth century and a good part of the twentieth, interethnic conflict remained intense as cultural expression that defined one group against the other flourished (De León 1983; Paredes 1958, 1993; Simmons [1952] 1974). The point is, however, that the relationship between Anglo and Mexican was never static, never frozen in the unrelenting hostility of the initial conflict. Driven by the dialectic of conflict, the relationship of inequality between Anglo and Mexican was subjected to ideological manipulation almost from its beginnings, as various factors came into play to mitigate the cold reality of the Anglos' conquest of the Southwest and their exploitation of the Mexicans (Crisp 1976; Montejano 1987).[5] In the short term, however, crude economic interests prevailed over notions of "equaliberty," and these interests were reinforced by exclusionary racist policies that classified many Mexicans as "Indians," thereby depriving them of important constitutional rights from which the Native Americans were excluded (e.g., the right to own private property; see Menchaca 1993).

Despite such exclusionary practices, ideological sentiments rooted in class affinities and transcending the ethnic boundary played a role in mediating the harsh prejudice of the Anglos toward what they considered an inferior "Mexican" culture. That is, even as the Mexicans were being reduced generally to a state of peonage and proletarianization, a few native elites—those whom the Anglos were pleased to consider "Spanish" and whose way of life they had admired from the very first contacts early in the nineteenth century—prospered (Bell 1930; Crisp 1976: 23ff.).[6] These native elites buffered the Anglos' drive to eradicate Mexican culture and impose their own way of life throughout the region. The tradition-rich culture of the Hispanic elite ultimately helped to modify the Anglos' initial disdain toward the Spanish-Mexican heritage of the Southwest to a more complex response.

Thus did the presence of a few native elites amidst an otherwise despised population contribute to the dialectic of conflict, by giving rise to a romantic component in the ideology that emerged among Anglos vis-à-vis the Hispanic landscape of the Southwest. The contradiction between the ideology of Anglo superiority and the romantic vision of a "Spanish Arcadia" (Van de Grift Sánchez 1929) has been nicely captured by the historian William Goetzmann. Referring to the "Anglo-Texan myth"—a body of cultural ideas that define for Anglo-Texans the heroic origins of their "tribe"—Goetzmann proposed that the myth "necessarily involves, begins with, a relationship to Hispanic culture" (1985: 31). "The presence of a Spanish culture in Texas," added Goetzmann, "made it easier for the Texians [Anglo-Texans] to define themselves by contrast" (ibid.). But the myth was modified by the Texians' contradictory attitude toward their Mexican subordinates. Contemptuous of the Mexican but admiring of "Spanish" culture—that is, the lifestyle of the elites—they ultimately embraced many cultural elements of the people they had conquered.[7] Thus, as Goetzmann concluded:

In fact, a good many aspects of Hispanic culture actually appealed to the Texians. Thus, endemic to the Texian myth is a love-hate relationship with the Spanish [Mexican] people. For example, the Texian admired life on "the

Big Hacienda." . . . He also thrived on the food, the fandangos, vaquero-cowboying, the violent macho lifestyle, and especially the Spanish sense of pride. Love and hate made the Texian myth complex from the beginning. (1985: 31)

It is not belaboring the point to suggest that the "love-hate" relationship Goetzmann refers to is an integral part of the dialectic unfolding historically as Anglos and Mexicans adjust to each other's presence. In their long and tortuous history of face-to-face contact, the two groups have repeatedly attempted to cancel out the "Other," as it were, only to discover the existence of that Other is inevitably entwined with "mine." Thus, the unvarnished hostility attending the initial conquest and the subsequent relationship of inequality (dominant Anglo/subordinate Mexican) eventually gives way to subtle modifications that result in the intertwining of the two people's cultures. A complex set of responses evolved, which led to mediative impulses on the part of both—for example, acculturative aspects of the Texian myth (Goetzmann, above) and equivalent cultural expression among the Mexican Americans (the orquesta, for one). In the long run, the love-hate relationship between Anglo and Mexican ultimately yields a commonality of experience for both, as each absorbs from the other via a complex range of cultural practices.

Like Goetzmann, the literary historian Cecil Robinson was impressed by the Anglos' contradictory attitude toward the Mexicans. For Robinson, "the attraction which Americans felt [toward Mexican culture] is purely visual or sensual, the nostalgia of the northerner with his chilblains for the splendor and warmth of a lost Eden" (1977: 140). Elsewhere, Robinson has written of the many elements of Mexican culture that Anglos of the Southwest have borrowed. However, as he observed, "All too often the Americans will 'accept the best of everything in Mexico,' yet stupidly deny its attraction for them, repudiate their sympathy for it" (1992: 64).

Adding to the evidence of Anglo ambivalence toward the Hispanic people and their heritage, the journalist Carey McWilliams described the attraction/rejection paradox in acerbic but essentially accurate terms. In his landmark book *North From Mexico,* first published in 1948, McWilliams described the "fantasy heritage"—an attempt by Anglos to distinguish between a romanticized "Spanish" period and the contemporary presence of a despised Mexican population. For McWilliams, the Anglos' attempt to resurrect a glorious but imaginary Spanish past while denying the contemporary Mexican Americans their long-standing links to their homeland was as incoherent as it was reprehensible. Thus, with a tone of indignation, McWilliams wrote:

Throughout the Southwest today, the most striking aspect of Anglo-Hispanic relations consists in this amazing dichotomy between the Spanish and the Mexican-Indian heritage. There is scarcely a public building constructed since the turn of the century . . . without murals depicting scenes in which Cabrillo, Serra, De Oñate, and Coronado [Spanish explorers and settlers] played a part. . . . But there is scarcely a single community in the region in which the living side of this tradition [i.e., contemporary Mexican culture] has not been consciously repudiated. (Ibid.: 41)

CONFLICT AND MEDIATION:
The Mexican American Generation

The Anglos' attraction/repulsion toward Hispanic culture of the Southwest is not the only ingredient contributing to the dialectic of conflict that drives Anglo-Mexican relations historically. Far more so than the Anglos, the Mexican Americans have been deeply affected by this encounter between two antagonistic cultures. As the subordinate element in the interethnic equation, the Mexican Americans have had the most to lose (or gain) in this intercultural tug-of-war, and they have thus been the more reactive participant in the dialectic defining the historical struggle. In the domain of social relations, the latter have increasingly challenged the contradictions between lofty ideals and the harsh reality of everyday practice by insisting on equal opportunity for themselves and acceptance in American life.

The Mexican Americans' struggle for equal opportunity owes at least part of its success to major disturbances that have periodically visited the basic structure of capitalism itself. These disturbances work their way through the sociocultural chain, ultimately affecting the interethnic relationship and exposing the gap between economic practice and ideological consciousness. Included among the most important events that have shaken the capitalist system during the twentieth century must be the Great Depression, World War II and its impact on economic realignments on a global scale, and occupational shifts leading to the wholesale entry of women into the labor force. These events have had far-reaching consequences for the sphere of cultural/ideological activity, some of which were still unfolding in the late twentieth century, but the matu-

ration of a feminist consciousness and the emergence of a counterculture in the 1960s are, in my judgment, tangible examples of the complex
ways in which changes at the level of production (e.g., the absorption of
women into the labor force) can reverberate throughout the social and
ideological chain.[8]

For the Hispanic Southwest, these events take on a more localized
significance, as they foreground preexisting economic disparities and
magnify the intercultural schism—even as they hasten the dialectical
process. American participation in World War II stands out as a critical
event in that process. At least 400,000 Mexican Americans, many of whom
served with distinction, enlisted in the war effort (Romo 1983: 165). And,
as Joan Moore and Harry Pachón correctly point out, "Mexican Americans who served in the armed forces were exposed to social climates quite
different from those in the Southwest" (1985: 177)—that is, they experienced the world as full-fledged American soldiers, not as second-class
Mexican Americans. When they returned to civilian life, these proud
veterans expected respect and gratitude, and they were outraged when,
as often happened, they discovered the Anglos back home still considered them an inferior breed. Incidents of blatant discrimination against
returning soldiers abound (McWilliams [1948] 1968), as do those in
which an affronted Mexican served as a catalyst for the Mexican American community's political mobilization (Peña 1982).

For those Mexican Americans who did not serve in the military, the
shortage of workers in an expanding wartime economy created the first
substantial opportunity for employment in occupations other than menial stoop labor. Given a taste of nonsubordinate work, the Mexican
Americans did not readily accept reassignment to an oppressed status
after the United States returned to a peace economy. The booming
wartime economy also accelerated the urbanization of Mexican Americans, a factor with far-ranging implications for upward mobility, acculturation, and a whole new relationship to the Anglo political process. As
Fernando Peñalosa observed, "The World War II and post-war periods
promoted occupational and geographical mobility to such an extent that
rigid caste barriers against intermarriage and equality of employment
and housing opportunities have all but disappeared" (1973: 259).

Peñalosa may have been overly optimistic in his assessment, but the
years surrounding World War II—from the end of the depression to the
conclusion of the Korean War—do constitute a threshold in the history
of Mexican Americans and their evolving relationship with the Anglos.
These years witnessed the final urbanization of Mexican Americans; the
beginnings of a true differentiation of the society, with the emergence of

a middle class; and, most important, the ascendance of the historical bloc known as the Mexican American Generation. As Mario García has correctly observed, this was the first group of Mexican-descent people in the Southwest to stake out their future as American citizens (1989). All of these developments had repercussions, at both the inter- and intra-ethnic level.

At the level of interethnic relations, both Anglos and Mexicans were affected by the changes in the productive system that propelled Mexican American society onto a new level of development and initiated the re-composition of social classes. For example, despite a desire on the part of the Anglos to maintain their dominance over the Mexicans, the di-alectical process was irreversible. The war had ushered in a new era in Anglo-Mexican relations. The shake-up of the productive base by the wartime economy reverberated strongly throughout the whole society, and it had a particularly strong impact on ethnic relations in the South-west. Bolstered by their experiences as soldiers and laborers in the wartime economy, the Mexican Americans responded aggressively and initiated new demands for equal treatment from their Anglo counter-parts. These demands began to pay off, if slowly at first.

In all accuracy, however, the winds of change were in evidence as early as the 1920s, when the Mexican Americans, now fully transformed from peons to proletarians, began to redefine their relationship to the domi-nant Anglo majority. At this time they challenged the old dichotomies based on ethnic domination and, despite Anglo resistance, eventually won some concessions (Foley 1988a; M. García 1989; San Miguel 1987; Tay-lor [1934] 1971). But activism on the part of Mexican Americans reached new levels of intensity after World War II, and although prejudice and discrimination against them did not end, enough progress in interethnic relations was made to initiate more substantial change. Of particular im-portance were the host of everyday practices that appeared in the forties and fifties whose main purpose was to blunt the raw edges of intercul-tural conflict and to at least mask the relationship of inequality (Arnold 1928; Foley 1988a, 1990; Jordan 1972; Montejano 1987; Rubel 1966). Prob-ably the most significant happened in the schools, where the integration of Anglos and Mexicans first occurred (San Miguel 1987) and where nu-merous activities, such as band, football, and student government, were implemented to provide both groups the opportunity to participate in common gestures of citizenship (Arnold 1928; Foley 1988a, 1990).

Meanwhile, an increasing number of upwardly mobile Mexican Americans moved into what Mario Barrera (1979) has called the non-subordinate, "integrated" sector of the economy—occupations with middle-class status such as teacher, lawyer, business entrepreneur, and white-collar jobs in government. Concurrent with this upward mobility was the acceptance of at least a small number of Mexican Americans into such civic groups as the chamber of commerce, Kiwanis, Rotary, and other service clubs (Simmons 1952). Given the opportunity to participate in the mainstream of American economic and civic activity, the Mexican Americans responded vigorously. By the end of the twentieth century, after a long series of confrontations followed by concessions, a sizable proportion of Mexican Americans occupied positions with middle-class status (perhaps as much as a third of the population; see Peña 1985a). This group had substantially escaped the stigma attached to its Mexican ancestry and in the process had become considerably acculturated, even gaining some structural assimilation into the dominant society through close association with Anglos, including interethnic marriage.

Perhaps the most important barometer for progress was the increasing participation of Mexican Americans in mainstream political activity, particularly in the Democratic Party. Beginning in the 1920s, a number of politically oriented organizations sprang up throughout the Southwest, including such influential ones as the Mexican American Political Association (MAPA), Community Service Organization (CSO), and the GI Forum. But foremost among all political organizations was one of the earliest founded—the League of United Latin American Citizens (LULAC), which originated in San Antonio, Texas, in 1929 (M. García 1989). In a chapter aptly titled "In Search of America," Mario García describes the complex task LULAC set for itself, as well as the group it epitomized, the Mexican American Generation. According to García,

The search for America and their place in it shaped the consciousness and politics of the Mexican American Generation. . . . The [generation] aspired to move into the mainstream of American life. . . . They sought to synthesize their experience based on their relationship to their Mexican roots, their Mexican American reality, and their search for an American future. No Mexican American organization better exemplified this search for America than did LULAC. (1989: 25)

LULAC was an organization with a decidedly middle-class orientation, one that, as García points out, sought as its primary goal the integration of Mexican Americans into American society. The partial realization of this goal produced a citizenry with new ideas about its cultural loyalty and sense of participation in American life. Beginning in the late

1920s, the old antagonism between Anglos and Mexicans gradually yielded to the logic of dialectical progress, and it was at this juncture that the Mexican American Generation emerged (Alvarez 1973; M. García 1989). As Mario García informs us, this generation was eager to accelerate the process of social change, even if it meant abandoning the cultural strategies of its predecessor, the Migrant Generation, with its more "Mexicanist" outlook (M. García 1989; R. García 1983). Initially representing a tiny percentage of the total Mexican population in the Southwest, the new Mexican Americans had nonetheless attained enough upward mobility with its corollary attributes—a better education, economic security, and command of American political culture—to put a noticeable dent in the old ideological structures based on interethnic inequality.

The new group of upwardly mobile Mexican Americans constituted what Mario García defines as a "political generation" (not to be confused with a genealogical generation)—a group of individuals who share a sense that "their historical time or destiny has arrived" (1989: 4). Unquestionably a trailblazer in the history of the Hispanic Southwest, the Mexican American Generation spanned the period from about 1930 to the early sixties (see Foley 1988a). It was led by a small but growing nucleus of middle-class professionals, businessmen, and white-collar workers, although its political goals were also shared by selected members of the working class, unionists in particular (M. García 1989).

But most critical for the purposes of this study, the Mexican American Generation was the first bloc of middle-class Hispanics to link its fortunes to an American future (even if hyphenated, as in "Mexican-American") and to aspire toward equality with, and even assimilation into, the dominant Anglo-American majority. As the anthropologist Arthur Rubel wrote of middle-class Mexican Americans in Weslaco, Texas, in the late 1950s, "These chicanos aspire toward life goals which include equality with Anglos" (1966: 12). The push toward assimilation was accompanied by a corresponding effort by members of the generation to loosen their ties to traditional Mexican culture and to put some social distance between themselves and the poorer, less-acculturated common workers—especially the immigrants (Browning and De la Garza 1986; M. García 1985; Paredes 1966; Peña 1985b; Rubel 1966).

In sum, the Mexican American Generation yearned for a lifestyle that would reflect its relative affluence and newfound sense of American citizenship. Members of the generation translated this yearning into such cultural forms as the orquesta and other types of acculturative artistic expression. But the process of acculturation and its attendant distancing from traditional Mexican culture was not without its drawbacks. To begin with, although it represented a logical step in the dialectical movement of Anglo-Mexican relations, the generation's desire for Americanization was not particularly encouraged by the Anglos—especially if it meant accepting Mexicans into their midst. The latter were not yet ready to accept the Mexican as an equal, and prejudice against Mexicans was still the order of the day. In fact, the decade when the Mexican American Generation first made its mark, the 1930s, was beset by the calamities of the Great Depression and seems to have marked an especially bleak moment—a regression, really—in the evolving relationship between Anglos and Mexican Americans.

Yet, for a few fortunate Mexican Americans, the 1930s represented a window of opportunity, one during which the Mexican American Generation began to chart its own course. But here another difficulty arose: the upward mobility of the Mexican American Generation gave rise to a new phenomenon—an emergent intraethnic class cleavage characterized by a latent but occasionally visible rift between the nascent middle class and a less-acculturated working class. Class divisions were not new in the Hispanic Southwest; as noted earlier, they were as old as the original settlements (Downs 1971; Sheridan 1986), and the cultural vestiges of these divisions had no doubt survived among the native Mexicans (Madsen 1964: 5; Peña 1985a: 20ff.). But the harsh conditions of life in the hinterlands had exerted a mitigating effect on these divisions, and the conflict with Anglos had actually strengthened intraethnic solidarity (Sheridan 1986). Now, with the advent of the Mexican American Generation, class divisions resurfaced, and although seldom bursting into open dissension, they nevertheless served as the backdrop for cultural choices made on the basis of what Bauman (1972) has called "differential identity" (see Peña 1981).

The problems encountered by the Mexican American Generation in its efforts to negotiate the difficult transition from a Mexican to an American identity are complex and riddled with contradiction. (I will explore their complexity in Chapter 3.) In brief, as suggested by the quote from García above, the generation's dilemma revolved around and emanated from changes in the economic base (e.g., the shift toward urbanization and its industrial occupations) and new opportunities for upward mobility, the consequent differentiation of Mexican society in the Southwest, a subtle shift in interethnic relations, and, most important, ideological cleavages surfacing within the Mexican communities themselves. The core members of the Mexican American Generation—the small group of professionals, merchants, skilled laborers, and craftsmen—were in the vanguard of the transformative changes. They were particularly sensitive to those changes, grasping early on the essential dilemma they faced in negotiating the vast distance between two disparate cultural economies—that of their Mexican, subsistent folk heritage versus that of an American, urban, and capitalist future. The long-standing ethnic conflict between Anglos and Mexicans in the Southwest could only exacerbate matters.

The Mexican American Generation was caught in a double bind, an untenable position between two class and cultural worlds. This double bind ultimately impelled the upwardly mobile Mexican Americans to seek mechanisms that would mediate the inherent contradictions they faced in attempting to reconcile their Mexican past and their American future, their working-class roots and their middle-class aspirations. A pervasive biculturalism emerged as a "solution," expressed in bilingualism and such forms of expressive culture as the bimusical orquesta. This biculturalism, moreover, served at the conscious level to justify the Mexican American's desire for Americanization: by mastering "the best of both worlds" (Simmons [1952] 1974: 528) the Mexican American could compete in the commodity "materialism" of Anglo society and still retain the "spirituality" of Mexican culture (see Rodó [1900] 1988 on North American "materialism" vs. Latin American "spirituality"). Almost by definition, this biculturalism remained dynamic—indeed, unstable—as witnessed by the fate of both the orquesta and bilingualism in the Southwest (Sánchez 1977).

CONFLICT AND MEDIATION:
The Chicano Generation

Negotiating life on a bicultural border is not easy, of course, as the studies by García (1989) and others demonstrate. As long as the basic dichotomies outlined earlier persist, conflict reigns on the interethnic boundary, and periodic upheavals revisit the Anglo-Mexican relationship. These upheavals may be retrogressive, as in the case of the depression, or progressive, as in the case of World War II. If World War II represents a tremor that shakes and realigns Anglo-Mexican relations in the Southwest, then events of the 1960s—the era of Vietnam, the Hippie counterculture, and Lyndon Johnson's Great Society—create a powerful aftershock, felt in the Mexican American community in the form of a politico-cultural explosion that came to be known as "the Chicano movement." More important, that movement was launched by a group of

Mexican Americans who came of age in the 1960s, and who defined their cultural identity in terms sharply contrasted with those of the Mexican American Generation. I refer to the ideological bloc Rodolfo Alvarez (1973) and Mario García (1989) call the Chicano Generation.

The Chicano Generation self-consciously repudiated the assimilationist strategies of the Mexican American Generation; moreover, caught in the countercultural sweep of the sixties, it defined its own mission as an attempt to recapture the Mexican Americans' cultural past, which, "buried under the dust of conquest" (Valdez 1972: xiii), had ceased to provide the people with a sense of their historical purpose. The Chicano movement became the vehicle for recapturing that past, embodied in a "Myth of Aztlan" encompassing a vast history dating back to the Aztecs, who were seen as the putative ancestors of the Chicano(a).

Essentially an ethnic-revivalist effort propelled by a core of intellectuals centered at various universities in the Southwest (Muñoz 1989), the Chicano movement followed quite logically the series of countercultural reactions launched against the established order during the tumultuous 1960s—the antiwar, feminist, and Black Power movements. Furthermore, despite its romantic-nationalist, anti-American rhetoric, the Chicano movement, like similar upheavals of its time, served ultimately as another building block in American capitalism's drive to set its house in order, to seal the cracks between its economic foundation and an unwieldy cultural frame threatening periodically to collapse upon its base.

That the Chicano movement could have such an unintended effect— contributing to the equilibrium of American capitalism—would surely cause the most nationalist of the Chicanos to shudder, especially those who yearned to recapture the lost myth of Aztlán (M. García 1992). But the movement, shaped as it was by the ideological currents of the time, contained the seeds for its demise deep within its program. For its agenda, despite its call for a rejection of "neon *gabacho* [Anglo] culture" (Valdez 1972: xv) and the revitalization of the Mexican Americans' ethnic "roots," also contained a contradictory goal—to achieve a more successful integration of the Mexican American in the political economy of the United States.

In effect, the leaders of the Chicano movement wanted it both ways— cultural disassimilation from the Anglo-American mainstream, coupled with economic emancipation for the Mexican Americans. But whether the intellectuals acknowledged it or not, "emancipation" could only take place on terms set by the capitalist system itself, and, given the hegemony of its culture, calls for a spiritual-cultural "return to Aztlan" could only ring hollow. In retrospect, we can see that by the 1980s the message of the Chicano movement had devolved into a politico-cultural compromise differing little from the one the LULACers of the Mexican American Generation had advocated—maintaining "some functional balance between mainstream Anglo-American culture and the culture derived from their Mexican roots" (M. García 1989: 43). The only real difference lay in the movement's strident emphasis on an all-encompassing, anti-Anglo nationalism that would unite all "Chicanos."

Nonetheless, the cultural component of the movement's agenda, with its emphasis on a unifying nationalism based on an elusive concept of Chicanismo, cannot be dismissed. Promulgated extensively through Chicano studies programs sprouting up in many colleges and universities throughout the Southwest and beyond, the idea of Chicanismo, while meeting some resistance because of its strident anti-American tone, eventually led to a broad revival of ethnic consciousness. Ethnic revivalism was expressed in many ways: in the literary and artistic efflorescence known as the "Chicano Renaissance" (Ortego 1970), in a renewed acceptance of the Mexican Americans' Indo-Hispanic roots (with special emphasis on the "Indo-"), and, most important, in a legitimation of ethnic folk practices previously considered an impediment to assimilation.

But the most far-reaching impact of the Chicano movement was on the expression of class differences among the Mexican Americans. While no research exists to document this impact, the movement's insistent affirmation of ethnic solidarity based on the celebration of a folk, working-class culture increasingly discouraged overt displays of class hierarchies and their attendant cultural differences—of the kind so much in evidence in the forties, fifties, and early sixties (Madsen 1964; Peña 1985a, 1985b; Rubel 1966; Simmons [1952] 1974; Taylor 1934). Eventually, as more and more students were exposed to the ideology of Chicanismo, the gospel of ethnic power based on a unified cultural front rippled throughout the society, spreading transitory symbols of solidarity that masked fundamental class differences among Mexican Americans. The attempt to suppress social—especially class—differences was the movement's most lasting legacy, and was the one strategy setting it apart from previous efforts by Mexican Americans to upgrade their lot in American life.

The Chicano intellectuals' efforts to flatten social (especially class) differences is important, because it had significant consequences on the production of expressive culture. For example, the movement's legitimation of folk, working-class music via the proliferation of *grupos folklóricos* erased—or tended to erase—important class distinctions attached historically to the production of this music in its indigenous settings. *Norteña* music is a case in point. Historically, this music has been solidly associated with the working-class culture of northern Mexicans and Texas-Mexicans, even as it acquired a negative symbolic value among those who considered themselves above the "riffraff" (Peña 1985a, 1985b). Under the powerfully synthesizing influence of the Chicano movement, however, norteña music began to acquire a romantic tinge as a cultural form deeply embedded in what was considered the bedrock of a rich Chicano heritage, and it was eventually incorporated into the expanding pantheon of traditions to be cherished, not rejected. What had been a symbol of class difference became an emblem of ethnic unity.

Of course, class differences were not eradicated by the movement, only submerged. The movement's tough anti-middle-class rhetoric, couched as it was in language accusing the affluent Mexican Americans of "forgetting" their roots and selling out to the Anglo, did have some success in subduing the middle class's patronizing attitude toward working-class culture—especially as university-educated Chicanos, sensitized to the working-class roots of their culture, entered middle-class occupations in teaching, business, and government. Although no studies have been conducted on how a romantic-nationalist ideology shaped this younger Chicano Generation, it is safe to say that thousands—perhaps hundreds of thousands—of its members were influenced by their contact with Chicano studies programs across the Southwest and elsewhere, and that their class outlook was definitely subordinated to their sense of ethnicity and their desire to confront racism and discrimination.

In sum, in its insistent call for unity, the romantic-nationalist thrust of the Chicano movement did have a significant impact on Mexican American life. Besides its professed goal to reclaim the Chicanos' ethnic roots, it succeeded in momentarily synthesizing many disparate elements present in everyday culture, including the musical culture orquesta represents. As more and more Mexican Americans were exposed to the revisionist history espoused by faculty in Chicano studies, an appreciation for the Mexican experience in the United States intensified, and besides the all-important task of cultural reclamation, a stronger synthesis of folk and modern, rural and urban, and Mexican and American modalities ensued.

By way of concluding this thematic exposition, I turn once more to Mario García's thoughtful words for their applicability to the argument advanced here, namely, that the Chicano Generation and its accomplishments are an integral component of the dialectic unfolding historically between Anglos and Mexicans in the Southwest and that, as such, the Chicano movement is but one of the many upheavals linked to the broader march of American capitalism as it unfolds within its tangle of contradictions.

Like the Mexican American Generation, the Chicano Generation was a product of its historical time. Despite its rejection of the American experience, it was born out of that experience. . . . Instead of being marginal to U.S. history, it was part of the central forces shaping that history in the 1960s and early 1970s. (1989: 301)

And this is perhaps the strongest argument against the Chicano movement. For even as the movement posed as a radical alternative to the alienating influence of American life, it was very much a part of that life and indeed was but another step in the long dialectical journey traveled by the Anglos and Mexicans of the Southwest. As we shall demonstrate later, however, its presence did introduce important changes in the worldview of the Mexican Americans, changes that reverberated strongly in the cultural field we are examining here—the orquesta. For, true to its nature as a sensitive barometer of Mexican American cultural/ideological trends, the orquesta responded as vigorously to the ideological leanings of the Chicano Generation as it had to those of the Mexican American Generation.

PART ONE

Origins

CHAPTER I

Bailes *and* Fandangos

Music and Social Division in the Nineteenth Century

This study of the Mexican American orquesta is primarily concerned with its development during the twentieth century; however, since cultural continuities do exist between Mexican American society of the nineteenth and twentieth centuries, at least a sketch of the musical practices of the earlier century is warranted. Music-and-dance activity represents one of those cultural continuities. Numerous observers of life in the Hispanic Southwest during the nineteenth century noted the enthusiasm of the native residents toward musical activity, especially their frequent indulgence in the dance, or *fandango*.[1] Most of those observers were Anglo travelers who began arriving in the 1820s, many of whom stayed and married into the most prominent of the native families, especially in New Mexico and California. A few descriptions are included among the reports of Spanish officials, while some come from native chroniclers and municipal records; still other accounts are no doubt collecting dust in as-yet-unexamined archives.

In society, the fandango is not introduced; their dancing is called Bayle, or a ball.

WILLIAM BALLAERT
(1956: 218)

RACE, STATUS, AND MUSIC ON THE FRONTIER

Regrettably for students of Hispanic musical life in the Southwest, written descriptions of music and dance relating to earlier periods are sketchy —superficial and impressionistic for the nineteenth century, scarce for the first part of the twentieth. Moreover, the descriptions drawn by Anglo-

Americans of nineteenth-century musical life are highly ethnocentric. Imbued with the capitalistic ideology of success through self-motivation and thrift, the Americans appreciated neither the subsistence economy of native Mexican life nor its cultural rhythms. As noted in the Exposition, however, exceptions were made by the Americans in the case of the elite, giving rise to certain contradictions in the foreigners' evaluations of native Mexican life. Again and again, they tried to distinguish between the culture of the "better class of Spaniards," which they admired, and that of the "riffraff," which they scorned. On the whole, however, the newcomers from the United States considered the Mexicans of the Southwest a backward, idle people, who were "judged in the light of the Anglos' belief in enterprise and were found wanting" (Kenneson 1978: 79).[2]

A healthy dose of skepticism is therefore warranted in evaluating the eyewitness reports forming the basic data on which the present account relies, in particular those provided by Anglo chroniclers. Moreover, since these reports are not in any way the result of careful anthropological study of Mexican society, any conclusions drawn must be tentative. Helpful in this respect, however, is the moralistic and ascriptive tone of many of the accounts of the Anglo chroniclers. Their sketches of Hispanic celebration betray their strong biases against the "riffraff"—the impoverished common folk, mostly *mestizo* and Indian, who eked out an existence under both the Spanish-Mexican and American regimes. By contrast, Anglo narratives on the festivities connected with elite life are couched in much more favorable terms.

Thus, despite their inherent bias, the chroniclers' accounts alert us, at the very least, to the reality of bifurcation in Spanish-Mexican society, with two distinguishable classes emerging from their sketches—the elites and the common folk. This reported bifurcation allows us to make some generalizations about both the society and its music. We obtain a glimpse of a society isolated from the centers of civilization in New Spain (Mexico, after independence), one living in a geographical environment fraught with hardship and danger. In their relative isolation, as Anthony Shay observed of the *californios,* the Spanish-Mexicans of the Southwest "had to fall back on their own resources for entertainment and art" (1982: 99). Within such limits, the norteños took every opportunity to engage in various forms of play, ranging from horse racing and gambling at cards to music and dance.

Occasions for the latter were frequent, a fact noted repeatedly by American observers. For example, in addition to numerous public or official balls, seventy-two private dances were held in San Antonio during 1827, based on licenses issued by the *ayuntamiento* (De la Teja and

Wheat 1991: 16). Meanwhile, an American visitor to the city in 1837 claimed "there are seldom less than three or four [*fandangos*] during the night in different portions of the city" (Muir 1958: 104). This last statement was corroborated in a historical study by Fane Downs, who found that in 1847 the city of San Antonio collected a total of $560, at the rate of one dollar per dance (1971: 77). Much the same interest in the dance was observed in other areas of the Hispanic Southwest. The American Josiah Gregg, a celebrated naturalist, merchant, and physician, wrote of New Mexican society in Santa Fe that *fandangos* in that city were "very frequent" ([1844] 1954: 170). "For nothing is more general, with all classes, than dancing," continued Gregg:

From the gravest priest to the buffoon—from the richest nabob to the beggar—from the governor to the ranchero—from the soberest matron to the flippant belle—from the grandest *señora* to the *cocinera*—all partake of this exhilarating amusement. (Ibid.)

And, as if not to be outdone, the *californios* "would hardly pause in a dance for an earthquake, and would renew it before the vibrations ceased" (Van de Grift Sánchez 1929: 314). Nellie Van de Grift Sánchez's account of the *californios'* passion for dancing was buttressed by the historian Hubert Howe Bancroft, who wrote:

Dancing was a passion with the Californians . . . their houses were constructed with reference to this amusement, and most of the interior space was appropriated to the *sala*, a large, barnlike room. . . . If a few people got together at any hour of the day, the first thought was to send for a violin and guitar and should the violin and guitar be found together in appropriate hands, that of itself was sufficient reason to send for the dancers. (1888: 408)

Bancroft's report may be exaggerated, but, as can be gleaned from the accounts just cited, music making was a widespread form of amusement throughout the Hispanic Southwest. However, it was not a socially undifferentiated activity, at least not always and not everywhere in the region. As I indicated in the Exposition, early Hispanic society of the Southwest did experience some divisions—more social than economic, strictly speaking, but divisions nonetheless. In keeping with established custom throughout Spanish America, the norteños attempted from the beginning to enforce the system of *castas* imposed early on by the Spaniards. This "caste" system aimed basically to maintain intact the purity of the European strain, in order to draw a sharp distinction between those who ruled the new world, the white Europeans, and those who served them, native Americans and imported Africans.

As is well documented, however, the *casta* system soon became a morass of contradictions, as the Spaniards began immediately the process of miscegenation with both native and imported African slave women. In time, as increasingly futile efforts were made to sustain the system, *casta* types proliferated, and a colorful array of labels arose: *salta atrás, coyote, sambo, mulato, castizo*—to name but a few of the more than thirty "racial" distinctions that existed at one time or another (Cumberland 1968; MacLachlan and Rodríguez 1980; Morner 1970). As a result of the wild mixture of races and its inevitable confusion, strict adherence to the *casta* system became difficult, although general distinctions based on skin color remained strong. Whites continued their monopoly on power throughout Spanish America, a monopoly that persists to varying degrees in different parts of Latin America to this day (Burns 1980).

Nonetheless, as a result of the intensive miscegenation and the widening range of racial types, it became possible for those with less than pure European pedigree—the Euro-*mestizos*, for example—to buy their way into white society. In time, while power continued to reside in the hands of a Europeanized elite minority (Burns 1980), Spanish America evolved into one of the most racially blended societies in the world. And despite its stark racial and economic contrasts, this society developed a remarkably uniform set of traditions based on the three original racial-cultural strains—European, African, and native American (Burns 1980; MacLachlan and Rodríguez 1980; Morner 1970).

In the northern provinces, specifically those now located in the American Southwest, the *casta* system collapsed even more rapidly than it did in other parts of Spanish America, although this did not end efforts to divide the society along racial lines (De la Teja 1988; De la Teja and Wheat 1991). Thus, as Jesús De la Teja and John Wheat observed, "On the frontier, and in San Antonio, many passed as 'Spanish' despite their dark skin. The ethnically mixed were the rule rather than the exception" (1991: 32). Some socioeconomic distinctions persisted, nonetheless. Still predicated on the claim to Spanish ancestry, these distinctions were utilized to one extent or another in determining social hierarchies and their cultural practices. Among these sociocultural practices was the dance, which in time came to be distinguished between a *fandango* and a *baile*—the former "a public dance event of the lowest order" (Shay 1982: 101), or, as one newspaper decried it, "a moral pestilence that should be abolished" (*Daily Alta Californian,* November 11, 1857). The latter became an exclusive, invitation-only ball associated with the "higher class of Spaniards."

The distinction between *fandango* and *baile* appears to have been less pronounced in the earlier period of Hispanic settlement (before the 1830s) and seems to have reflected the egalitarian tendency of norteño society, as some have proposed (González 1969; León-Portilla 1972; Paredes 1958). This tendency was no doubt encouraged by the harsh and primitive conditions faced by the initial settlement of the northern provinces generally. In fact, throughout the provinces of the Southwest, the cultural label *fandango* glossed all forms of dancing events during the earliest period. Dmitry Zavalishin, a Russian officer who spent time in California in 1824, seems to strengthen the egalitarianist proposition in his description of the *fandango* as an event attended by all classes of people:

Social relations between different classes of society were very equable; since a sizable part of even the lowest class had claims to better origins . . . , from the outside the society did not exhibit that sharp cleavage between different classes that we see in other countries. . . . At parties given by the Russian officers or Spanish authorities everyone entered the dance hall without differences in rank and without a special invitation, except a general announcement that there would be a fandango. . . . (1973: 395)

Horace Bell, who arrived in Los Angeles in 1852, echoed Zavalishin's remarks. "A fandango of the olden times," he tells us, "was a curious conglomeration of all the elements of the population so promiscuously thrown together in this, at that time, curious, quaint old town" (1927: 198). Helen Elliott Bandini, a descendant of an old-line *californio* family, wrote in a similar vein. "In the early days there were many festivals," she wrote, "and after the church services there followed dancing, games and feasting in which all classes took part" (1908: 126). And Theodore H. Hittell, one of the early California historians, weighed in on the side of the "egalitarianists," offering this description of the 1832 wedding of Manuel Jiménez Casarin and María de la Guerra y Noriega:

In the evening the entire procession, invited and uninvited, gathered at a great booth prepared for the occasion, and there was dancing to the music of two violins and a guitar. All took part, and as the poorer classes exhibited their graceful performances, the two fathers threw silver dollars. (1898: 493)

Lingering on the California scene for one more narrative, we obtain this description of the shared participation of all citizens in the *fandango* from the author of *Two Years Before the Mast,* who described the 1836 marriage between Alfred Robinson, an early Anglo settler, and María de la Guerra y Carrillo, daughter of a prominent *californio* family:

39

After supper, the gig's crew were called, and we rowed ashore, dressed in our uniform . . . and went up to the fandango. The bride's father's house was the principal one in the place [Santa Barbara], with a large court in front, upon which a tent was built, capable of containing several hundred people. As we drew near, we heard the accustomed sound of violins and guitars, and saw a great motion of the people within. Going in, we found nearly all the people of the town—men, women and children—collected and crowded together, leaving barely room for the dancers; for on these occasions no invitations are given, but everyone is expected to come, though there is always a private entertainment within the house for particular friends. (Dana 1964: 236)

Finally, both J. C. Clopper (1929), who traveled in Texas during 1828, and Gretchen A. Schneider (1969), who researched the dances of California during the Gold Rush, agree with other observers that the *fandango* was originally a dancing event shared by all members of the society. Of the celebration in San Antonio on September 16, 1828, commemorating Mexico's recent independence from Spain, Clopper wrote, "the square was then lighted up with lamps and candles and everything cleared off for the enjoyment of the 'dearly beloved' fandango" (1929: 73). Meanwhile, in her survey of the dance in California life of the 1840s and '50s, Schneider recognized the existence of two periods in *californio* musical life—the first egalitarian, the second a more class-conscious one:

Because of the dichotomy of classes in Spanish society [during the Mexican period], the term fandango was reinterpreted during the Gold Rush. [Prior to this time] any major event on a Spanish rancho that featured an informal dancing party or general ball was called a fandango. The growth of towns and general population after 1840 had brought pastoral California into contact with less desirable elements. Through emerging social stratification, invitations had to be given for bailes (balls); the fandango became a lower-class entertainment. (1969: 23–24)

Thus, while the Anglo invasion of the Southwest affected each region in slightly different ways, the general tendency after the 1830s was toward a sharper bifurcation of Hispanic society based on class distinctions, at least until the 1850s, when the society began to suffer substantial disintegration due to loss of economic and political power. Hubert H. Bancroft noted this increasing bifurcation:

In earlier days, there was very little class distinction; the poor and rich associated on equal terms, and attended the same parties, "excluding only such persons—especially women—as were known as lewd, or of notoriously bad conduct in other respects." This state of things changed in later years, however, and class distinctions grew clearly defined—say from 1840 to 1850. (1888: 416)

Horace Bell seems to have had social difference in mind when he wrote that even in an earlier period (probably dating no further back than the 1830s) class distinctions were already in evidence. "Prior to and at that time [1853]," he reminisced, "the old wealthy and intelligent Spanish families had formed a strictly exclusive class," one whose *bailes*—not *fandangos*—were "select gatherings of invited guests for dancing and general jollification . . . even more exclusive than among Americans" (1927: 197). Bell's observations and those of others on the distinction between *fandango* and *baile* serve as a reminder that except during its earliest days, Spanish-Mexican society of the Southwest was not quite as egalitarian as some have suggested. The legacy of the Spanish conquest of indigenous America affected even this distant outpost of Spanish colonization.

FANDANGOS AND BAILES:
Music as Social Difference

Whether describing *bailes* or *fandangos*, the historical record is replete with reports of the bacchanalian bent of the people who inhabited the northern frontier of Spanish-Mexican culture. Additional examples of music-and-dance activities will help round out the picture. To focus, first, on the lower-class *fandango*, we turn to George W. Kendall's description of a "fandango of the lowest order" he observed in San Antonio. Like similar reports, it provides evidence for the Anglos' jaundiced view of the *fandangos* associated with the common folk:

As I entered the room, which was destitute of other floor than the hard earth, and lighted by two or three coarse tallow candles, a single couple were shuffling away, face to face, and keeping time to a cracked violin. . . . The woman was as destitute of beauty as an Egyptian mummy . . . her partner even more ugly. Some half dozen slovenly, badly dressed Mexican girls were sitting upon benches at either end of the room, while an old woman in one corner was selling paper cigars and vile whiskey. . . . (1935: 46)

Meanwhile, in recalling his arrival in Los Angeles in 1852, Bell described his first impression of a gambling-*fandango* house in the infamous "Nigger Alley" (*calle de los negros*) district: "the most perfect and full grown pandemonium this writer . . . has seen. . . . There were several bands of music of the primitive Mexican-Indian kind that sent forth the most discordant sound" (1927: 12). Later in his narrative, Bell informs us more explicitly of the difference between a *fandango* and a *baile:*

The *gringo* reader may not know the difference between a ball and a fandango, and the writer will inform him thereon. The ball, or, in Spanish, *baile*, means the same thing as in English, a select gathering of invited guests for dancing and general jollification and amusement, and in Spanish society is even more exclusive than among the Americans. On the other hand a fandango is open and free for all. Ladies of the higher ranks of society never go to a fandango, and Dons of the upper *ton* only go in a half-way clandestine manner. (Ibid.: 197–198)

Bell's recollection was echoed by Harris Newmark, another of the early Anglo travelers to settle in Los Angeles, who wrote of "Nigger Alley" as a place where, "in addition to the prodigality of feasting, there was no lack of music of the native sort—the harp and guitar predominating" (1930: 31). Still focusing on California, we find Bancroft describing *fandangos* as "very low class, the dances being the same (as the upper classes) but much exaggerated and unrestrained" (quoted in Shay 1982: 105). Unlike the *bailes*, where elegance and decorum prevailed, the former "generally ended with a fight, broken heads, filthy language, and insulting words" (Bancroft 1888: 415).

Anglo observers of music and dance in the Hispanic Southwest were much more generous in their assessment of what the *San Antonio Express* identified as the "respectable class" of Mexicans (August 20, 1881). Imbued with an instinctive respect for and a gut attraction to cultural expression that approximated their middle-class standards, the *Express* and other American chroniclers of Hispanic life in the Southwest were impressed with the elegant and refined celebrations of the Mexican elite—celebrations, however, that became less numerous as these elites lost their power and influence. Nonetheless, the ball as a cultural event never died out among the native Mexicans, and even in the latter part of the nineteenth century it was still in evidence, as the following story in the *San Antonio Express* indicates. By this time, however, the ball was no longer an event connected with old-line families; it seems to have been a cultural practice taken up by an emergent urban class of Mexican *co-*

merciantes, or entrepreneurs, and other middle-class types. Captioned by a glowing headline—"Mexican Social Club Ball: A Brilliant Fete Attended by a Galaxy of Beauty and Chivalry"—the report reads:

Last evening at the Casino occurred the inaugural ball of the Mexican Social Club, to which they had invited a great many lovely ladies and distinguished gentlemen. The ball was tastefully decorated, the American and Mexican colors being intertwined, symbolic of the amity between the two republics. The 8th cavalry brass band furnished a number of orchestral selections, of which the following is a list [13 are listed, including "Bay State March," by Keller; "Trovatore," from the opera *Misere,* by Verdi; and an aria, "Lucia de Lammermoor," by Donizetti]. A string band furnished the music for dancing. (February 24, 1884)

The *Express* concludes its report with a list of the most prominent in attendance and an assessment of the event as "an elegant evening."

The Mexican Social Club continued to attract the *Express*'s attention in later years, composed, as it was, of San Antonio's "fine class of Latin-Americans." For example, in 1891, the *Express* carried a story on the Club's latest ball:

The Mexican Social Club, composed of a very fine class of Latin-Americans, had an anniversary entertainment at Convention Hall last night, at which were present, on invitation, the active members of the French Day Association. Mr. Claudon made an address in behalf of the latter, and Messrs. Rivas, Cardenas and others spoke for the former, eulogizing the society which was celebrating its anniversary, and the president and other officers who had done so much to make it a success. Luncheon followed, and dancing to the music of Persio's orchestra was the order of the last half of the evening. (July 13, 1891)

As was the case with the reporters from the *San Antonio Express* and other newspapers, Anglo chroniclers like Kendall, Bell, Newmark, and others who wrote about the *fandango* qualified their descriptions of Mexican musical activities by reminding us that "the respectable class of Mexicans" did not attend these "low-class" functions. By contrast, all wrote enthusiastically about the *fandango*'s elite counterpart, the *baile,* or ball. Kendall, for example, having described the less-than-inviting *fandango* cited above, does admonish the reader not to "suppose that there is no better society among the Mexicans in San Antonio than this place" (1935: 46). Kendall's distinction is illustrated in the description by Mary A.

43

Maverick, a prominent resident of San Antonio, of a grand ball held in honor of President Lamar's visit to that city in 1841. Significantly, the ball was held not in an Anglo residence but at the home of one of the leading Hispanic families, the Yturris:

A grand ball was given him [Lamar] in Mrs. Yturri's long room—(all considerable houses had a long room for receptions). The room was decorated with flags and evergreens. . . . At the ball, General Lamar wore very wide white pants which at the same time were short enough to show the tops of his shoes. General Lamar and Mrs. Juan N. Seguin, wife of the Mayor, opened the ball with a waltz. ([1921] 1989: 49)

Meanwhile, in his journal of 1828, J. C. Clopper echoes the sentiments of other Anglo observers, stressing the difference between the "intelligent Gochapines" and the "ignorant" Mexicans. The former attended *bailes,* the latter *fandangos* (1929; see Introduction, n. 5). The observations of Kendall, Clopper, Maverick, and others make it clear that although the Texas-Mexicans apparently never developed the sharp class distinctions present among the *californios* in the 1830s, differences in class orientation were in fact evident in Texas as well. These differences registered strongly in the class-conscious sensibilities of the new Anglo settlers.

The *bailes* organized by the "better society" were lavish affairs. Bell provides us with a glowing description of a ball he attended at the home of don José Antonio Carrillo, "a first-class citizen":

The ball was the first of the season, and was attended by the *elite* of the country from San Diego to Monterrey. The dancing hall was large, with a floor as polished as a bowling saloon. The music was excellent—one splendid performer on an immense harp. The assembled company was not only elegant—it was surpassingly brilliant. The dresses of both ladies and gentlemen could not be surpassed in expensive elegance. . . . The dancing on that occasion was something more than elegant, it was wonderful, while the most dignified and staid decorum was observed to the end of the festivities, which broke up about two o'clock in the morning. (1927: 79–80)

William W. H. Davis, who spent two and a half years as U.S. Attorney in New Mexico, attended at least two *bailes* in the 1850s. Like other American chroniclers, he makes a distinction between a *fandango* and a *baile*:

In New Mexico the general name of all assemblies where dancing is the principal amusement is *fandango,* which is not, as many suppose, a particular dance. Those gatherings where the better classes "most do congregate" are called *baile,* or ball, which differs in no other particular from the fandango. ([1857] 1973: 315)

Davis was much more prejudicial in his evaluation of Mexicans than Bell and other observers, and although he offers us no descriptions of a lower-class *fandango,* his comments on the "upper crust" *bailes* leave no doubt not only that he was exceedingly class-conscious but that he held little admiration for the people he was supposed to be serving. His racist perception of New Mexicans is graphically illustrated in his description of the participants in a *baile* he attended in Taos. "We found a large number assembled in the *sala,*" he wrote, in a spiteful, ironic tone, "many of whom were pointed out as the genuine *upper crust* of Don Fernandez [Taos], being well baked for the upper crust, as a large majority of them were done very *brown*" (ibid.: 316 [italics in the original]).

Finally, Jovita González, probably the first professional woman folklorist of Mexican American extraction, offers us a more evenhanded portrait of both the upper-class *baile* and the *fandango* among the Mexicans of deep South Texas. In the nineteenth century, "the dances which were given by the owners of the ranches," she wrote in her master's thesis, "marked the social feature of the year":

To these functions were invited all the landed aristocracy from the surrounding country as well as from the towns. The ladies came in the family coach escorted by mounted cavaliers who rode by the side of the carriage. The dances gave occasion to the ladies to display their finery and their charm. An orchestra from town furnished the music, waltzes, polkas, schottisches. A midnight dinner was served, wine was drunk, and toasts were offered the ladies, and a convivial atmosphere prevailed throughout the evening. (1930: 62)

Besides providing a setting for conviviality and the reaffirmation of social ties, the *baile* (but not the *fandango*) seems to have been an important outlet for acting out gender roles. For women, in particular, the *baile* was, as González noted, "the only form of amusement which women shared with men"—a place, she reminds us, where normally sequestered young women could "display their finery and their charm" (ibid.). In a society that rigidly observed the norms of a patriarchal social order, women were expected to be chaste, demure, and yielding to the authority of men, at least in principle. A complicated set of social rules thus governed the conduct of men and women at a *baile*, rules that served to reaffirm gender hierarchies operating beyond the festive moment of the dance (González 1930; Van de Grift Sánchez 1929).

Along the same vein, Brígida Briones wrote, "the ladies of Monterey in 1828 were rarely seen in the street, except very early in the morning on their way to church" (1971: 43). For women, according to one of the *californio* "gallants," "dancing, music, religion, and amiability were the orthodox occupations" (ibid.: 44). The dance, in particular, marked a fleeting moment during which an otherwise repressive code of conduct was held in abeyance; women could, as González and others point out, openly display their feminine allure.[3] But operating just beneath the charm and conviviality of the dance was the reality of male control, especially with respect to what the historian Ramón Gutiérrez calls *igualdad de calidad*—the means by which the patriarchs ensured equality in social status between would-be marriage partners (1991). Not every dance partner was a potential mate. All the same, as a "ritual inversion" (ibid.), the dance in all its bacchanalian energy could only lead to the temporary breakdown of patriarchal rules, the weakening of normative constraints (Kenneson 1978). Gutiérrez assigns this inversive function to the dance:

> Unconstrained unison at festivals and dances had cathartic, as well as revolutionary, potential for resolving conflict; both possibilities had to be held in check by secular and religious authorities. Every bureaucrat thus hoped that when the lights went out, the music ended, and a new day began, life would continue as before—regimented and hierarchically structured. The fiesta should only be a temporary suspension and release, necessary to dispel internal community tensions. (1991: 240)

In short, after the *baile* the rules of patriarchy must reassert themselves, and women must resume their sequestered and repressed lives.

As can be concluded from the descriptions provided earlier, the conduct at *fandangos* was apparently far more unrestrained, perhaps because, as Gutiérrez argues, wage earners and peasants had little to gain from protecting their women from a loss of *igualdad de calidad* (ibid.: 231). In any case, more so than the *baile*, which dwindled as the elites declined, the *fandango* persisted as a cultural form, undergoing several transformations that guaranteed its continuity among working-class Mexican Americans well into the twentieth century. Meanwhile, the libidinous quality of the "low-class" *fandango* impressed itself (if negatively) upon

American chroniclers of the Southwest, and they devoted many unfavorable comments to its participants and its often unruly atmosphere. It is important to note that the Anglos' contempt for the *fandango* continued throughout the nineteenth century. Moreover, as the few Hispanic elites who survived the conquest became more and more acculturated, they too came to look with disfavor upon this principal form of celebration among their less fortunate peers.

Finally, despite the decline of the *baile,* the dichotomization of what had once been a universally shared celebration persisted, albeit in attenuated fashion, into the first part of the twentieth century, providing the Mexican American Generation a historical precedent on which to base its quest for an alternative type of music and dance to that of the working class. As the twentieth century wore on, the social and cultural distance between the working class and elite or upwardly mobile Mexican Americans came to coalesce around two types of dance, one associated with the lower-class *cantina,* the other with civic clubs around which the more affluent organized their social life. And in due course two rival styles, the conjunto and the orquesta, emerged to satisfy the aesthetic demands of each class (Peña 1985a, 1985b).

To sum up the discussion so far, in the Hispanic Southwest the dance celebration provides a clear cultural link between the nineteenth and twentieth centuries. Without a doubt, status distinctions between *baile* and *fandango* carried over into the latter century, and such distinctions laid the basis for the differential musical behavior of working and middle classes in twentieth-century Mexican American society. From the 1930s onward, especially, the attitudes of middle-class Mexican Americans do echo those attributed to Anglos of the earlier period. Like their Anglo counterparts, these affluent citizens viewed with disapproval the "licentious and unrestrained" atmosphere of working-class celebrations, in particular the *cantina* dance (Peña 1985a: Chapter 3).

EARLY MUSICAL PRACTICES:
A Descriptive Summary

Some of the social aspects of the dance have been described, particularly as embodied in the *baile* and *fandango.* I would like now to outline, insofar as the meager sources will allow, the nature of the music itself — the types of song and dance and instrumentation most common to the early orquesta in the Southwest, as well as the mode by which musical training might have been transmitted. Again, there is little in the way of documentary evidence that will allow us to make sound conclusions regarding performance practices and musical training generally. Nonetheless, the concept of the orchestra (or orquesta) did exist as a native musical category from early on, although it seems to have been applied loosely to almost any type of instrumental combination, much as the term "band" is applied today to various ensembles.

The ad hoc use by Anglo observers of the two labels "orchestra" and "band" is apparently related to the fact that although certain instrumental combinations were common—the violin and guitar, for example—dance-music ensembles of the Hispanic Southwest were of an improvisational nature. Any ensemble consisting of at least two instruments was often labeled an "orchestra" (or "band"). Standardized ensembles with fixed relationships between regularly combined instruments, of the type associated with formal traditions like that of the Western string quartet or chamber orchestra, were nonexistent. However, true orchestras—larger ensembles with more permanent instrumentation—did begin to make an appearance in urban areas by the late nineteenth century, as did military-style brass bands (Sheridan 1986: 195; see the comments in the *San Antonio Express,* above).

One major reason for the lack of stable ensembles was the nature of Spanish-Mexican society itself. Despite the social divisions prior to the American conquest, in cultural matters the society evinced a strong folk character, as was manifested in music and dance. This character was further cemented after the American invasion, when even elite Mexicans assumed a subordinate status in the new social order. As marginalized folk communities, the Hispanic settlements of the Southwest lacked the cultural institutions normally found in highly developed and stratified societies—institutions that provide the technical and formal training to transmit the cultural practices of the dominant classes, at least. Lacking a complex economy and the commensurate symbols that bestow prestige and power in such an economy—lavish dwellings and furnishings, immense liquid wealth, centers for the performance of elite art, and most important, educational institutions to transmit the high culture of a developed economy—the communities of the Hispanic Southwest remained minimally differentiated, with no vast sociocultural (or musical) gulf separating the elites from the impoverished masses.

Most important for our purposes here, the lack of a complex socioeconomic system in the northern provinces precluded the development of educational institutions to provide training in cultural matters such as art and music. Thus, as the historian William W. H. Davis wrote of *californios,* "The people had but limited opportunity for education . . . but they had abundant instinct and native talent . . . they talked well and intelligently" ([1857] 1973: 31). And despite the lack of formal institutions dedicated to the transmission of artistic culture, communities managed through oral means to pass on cultural knowledge. As Davis makes clear, the "wealthier classes," at least, taught their children not only how to read and write in the home but also how to make music (ibid.; see also Briones 1971). Moreover, according to Davis,

[young people] seemed to have a talent and taste for music. Many of the women played the guitar skillfully, and the young men the violin. In almost every family there were one or more musicians, and everywhere music was a familiar sound. Of course, they had no scientific and technical musical instruction. ([1857] 1973: 31–32)

Lacking the amenities associated with the urban life of a complex society, the Spanish-Mexicans of the Southwest practiced a hinterland culture—a kind of "inorganic democracy" in which orally transmitted cultural practices were the norm, and which only slowly, and in simplified form, assimilated the fashions emanating from the distant metropolitan centers of the mother country. In matters of musical practice, both the dance and instrumental styles were of a traditional character, although new musical forms were introduced from time to time, such as the waltz in the 1820s and salon music in the 1860s—the polka, redowa, schottische, and others. Performance practices did change, if gradually, after the 1830s, when contact with the more technologically advanced Americans made possible the introduction of hitherto scarce instruments such as the clarinet, flute, trumpet, and especially, the piano.[4] A frontier existence thus meant that formal musical training was virtually nonexistent except for that provided by the missionaries or an occasional immigrant with musical training. The former, however, concentrated their efforts on Indian neophytes, who in the early days often provided the music for both church and social events (Bancroft 1888; J. González 1930; Swan 1952; Vallejo 1890).

Of all the features of musical celebrations that Anglo chroniclers single out for mention, the specific dance types are the most thoroughly described. The Spanish-Mexicans of the Southwest were heirs to a rich tradition of dances, many of folk extraction but some of urban, elite origins. Most of the early dances, those introduced by the first settlers, were derived from Spain, but later ones came from other parts of Europe. With respect to the latter, European salon music was a particularly important source of music-and-dance innovation, as first the waltz, later the schottische, redowa, mazurka, *danza habanera,* and the polka made their impact on norteño dance practices. All of these dances, both ancient Spanish and more recent European, provided the repertoire for the frequent celebrations described by the chroniclers of life in the Hispanic Southwest during the nineteenth century.

Recalling the ball held in honor of Governor Pablo Vicente de Sola's visit to Alta California in 1815, Juan B. Alvarado wrote, "the program consisted of *contradanzas,* minuets, Aragonese *jotas,* and various other dances usual among the Spanish population" (quoted in Van de Grift Sánchez 1929: 313). The ancient *jota* and other folk dances—including, of course, the dance form known as *fandango*—were routinely performed in the first half of the nineteenth century. According to Van de Grift Sánchez and others, many of these were accompanied by sung or recited verses, which were often improvised. Besides the *jota* and *fandango,* the list of folk dances is long, and many had obviously acquired local characteristics—for example, the *zorrita* (little fox), *los camotes* (the sweet potatoes), *el borrego* (the lamb), *el caballo* (the horse), and *el burro* (the donkey). All of these are mentioned by Van de Grift Sánchez (1929) in connection with early California balls. Not mentioned by Van de Grift Sánchez but included in Alfred Robinson's early description of *californio* society (1829) is the *jarabe* and the recently introduced waltz.[5]

Meanwhile, traveling in New Mexico in 1828, James O. Pattie mentions an *ahavave*—by which he probably meant *jarabe,* popular by then throughout all of Mexico—as well as a waltz, which had recently been introduced into the Southwest provinces ([1831] 1930: 70).[6] However, like the *californios,* the New Mexicans also danced to their own local folk adaptations, which Aurora Lucero-White has dubbed "native Spanish-Colonial folk dances." These included *la indita* (the little Indian woman), *el vaquero* (the cowboy), and *el vals de la escoba* (the dance of the broom) (1940: 16–24; cf. Van de Grift Sánchez's description above).

The Texas-Mexicans were likewise heirs to the music-and-dance traditions prevailing more or less uniformly throughout the Southwest. According to William Ballaert, an early visitor, "originally, in the Fandango halls, the National, or *zapateos* [probably the *jarabe*] were danced, made up of a series of rather voluptuous movements," but by the 1830s "the waltz, quadrilles, and reels had been introduced" (1956: 218). After the middle of the century, schottisches, polkas, redowas, and other salon dances imported from Europe were the preferred types in Texas (J. González 1930: 62).

As mentioned previously, the instruments used in providing music for dancing were assembled in ad hoc fashion, although most reports mention the violin-guitar duo as the most prevalent throughout the Southwest, particularly during the first half of the nineteenth century. Sometimes a second violin was added, and most of the native folk dances, that is, those of Spanish origin, included vocalized verses as well. In California, the harp seems to have enjoyed some currency, particularly in elite balls, and the flute is mentioned occasionally (H. Bell 1930; Newmark 1930: 183). It is important to note in this respect that the instrumentation seems to have varied little between *fandango* and *baile* (with the exception of the harp and the flute), although the technical virtuosity of the musicians employed for *bailes* may well have been superior to that of the ones who played the *fandango,* if the reports of Anglo witnesses are to be believed.

In Texas, especially—although this may have been true of other regions where Mexicans managed to retain some measure of economic integrity (Tucson, for example)—ensembles connected with elite (or at least "respectable") functions did begin to coalesce into true orchestras in the latter part of the nineteenth century, while a new ensemble based on the diatonic accordion began to assert itself in the celebrations of the working class (Peña 1985a). Another ensemble also made its appearance among Mexicans of the Southwest in the latter part of the nineteenth century—the military-style brass band. This is an interesting development, since it bespeaks of a cultural renewal among Mexicans in the Southwest, at least in areas where they maintained some semblance of class cohesion.

Thus, to cite the example of Tucson, Arizona, we find the Banda de Música, a brass band, being organized among mostly Mexican machinists of the Southern Pacific Railroad in the early 1880s (Sheridan 1986: 195). According to Thomas Sheridan, the Banda was one of the most durable of Tucson's orquestas, and under various leaders it continued to provide concert and dance music until the 1920s (ibid.: 197). Another military-style brass band, the Banda Militar, was organized by Juan Balderas in 1893. Clearly, the appearance of the Banda de Música and the Banda Militar indicates that by this time there was a sufficient number of Mexicans proficient enough on the various brass instruments to make the creation of such a group an attainable task. Brass bands seem to have been quite common in the early part of the twentieth century, but the existence of the Banda de Música and the Banda Militar in Tucson, as well as others such as the "splendid" Mexican Brass Band that performed in the Brownsville-Matamoros area (Chatfield 1893: 13) and the 8th Cavalry Brass Band of San Antonio (composed mostly of Mexicans), indicates that the Mexicans of the Southwest were becoming accultur-

FIGURE 1. *Club Filarmónico, 1896.*
Courtesy of the Arizona Historical Society/Tucson, no. 29039.

ated to the modern trends developing in both Mexico and the United States by the latter part of the nineteenth century.

Modernizing also were the dance orquestas, most of them still of the string variety at this juncture, although some of a quasi–brass band type. Sheridan has provided us a well-documented sketch of the various dance orquestas springing up in the city of Tucson in the 1880s — orquestas that in time acquired the elements of permanent and stable organizations. Among these were Basilio Hernández's orquesta and one formed cooperatively between Lázaro Valencia, a music teacher, and Manuel Montijo, a lumberyard operator (1986: 195). But the best of these musical groups, products of a nascent middle class, was a quasi–brass band with the rather ambitious name of Club Filarmónico, organized in 1888 by a Mexicanized French entrepreneur, Federico Ronstadt. By 1896, the Club Filarmónico had grown to a sizable ensemble, consisting of twenty musicians (see Fig. 1). According to Sheridan:

The group consisted of a handful of young men who went on to become the leaders of Tucson's Mexican community, men like Lucas Estrella, Genaro

Manzo, Santos Aros, Carlos Jácome, Rufino Vélez, F. J. Villaexcusa, and a number of other local businessmen or politicians. (1986: 115)

Despite its ambitious goals and its subsequent success (the group eventually went on a successful tour throughout southern California), the Club's origins were not particularly auspicious, as its founder was later to observe. Of particular importance in the following quote by Federico Ronstadt is the ad hoc, self-taught manner in which the musicians learned their instruments:

We started with eight or ten members—some of them knew a little about music but the others didn't know a note. It was up to me to teach them what I could from my limited fund. Dick [Ricardo Ronstadt, Federico's younger brother] played the flute and I learned the fingering of the clarinet. The rest had to learn violin, viola, cello, bass, trombone and cornet. To encourage them we made special arrangements of a few well known pieces with most of the work for flute and clarinet and a few chords for the others with a note here and there for the trombone and cornet. We could have qualified for a circus burlesque, but in time we sounded better. (Federico Ronstadt, quoted in Sheridan 1986: 195–196)

The Club Filarmónico dissolved sometime at the turn of the century, but during its existence it "had given *Tucsonenses* a taste for good music," setting the pattern for the development of a new generation of talented musicians in the Tucson area who were to "serve as testimony to the vitality of Tucson's *barrios* and the artists they produced" (ibid.: 197).

The documentation Sheridan recovered on the musical activities of the Tucsonenses is unusually rich, thanks to the writings of one of the principal promoters, Federico Ronstadt.[7] Such documentation is not available for other areas of the Southwest, in particular those cities or regions where Mexicans maintained a strong presence. However, on the basis of fragmentary evidence, it is clear that the musical accomplishments of the Tucsonenses were repeated elsewhere, especially in Texas, where cities like San Antonio, Laredo, Brownsville, and El Paso contained sufficient numbers of Mexican entrepreneurs and other middle-class professionals to encourage musical activity appropriate to their middle-class tastes. New Mexico seems to have lagged behind, economically and culturally (Zeleny 1944), but it is not unreasonable to assume that at least in Albuquerque and Santa Fe there would have been some movement among the more affluent toward musical modernization as urbanized

Mexican Americans began to acquire the cultural practices of city life.

Newspaper accounts in Texas, for example, leave the distinct impression that among urban, middle-class Mexican Americans, a more cosmopolitan social and musical ambiance was evolving in the late nineteenth century. The *San Antonio Express*'s coverage of the Mexican Social Club hints at a higher level of sophistication in the musical resources available to affluent Mexicans in that city. The participation of the 8th Cavalry Brass Band in Mexican celebrations, as well as its eclectic repertoire, provides evidence of a fairly elaborate instrumentation, perhaps equivalent to that of Ronstadt's Club Filarmónico. Given the "brilliant atmosphere" of the Mexican Club's events, as described in the *Express,* it is unlikely the string orchestra hired for the dance would deviate from the otherwise genteel tone of the celebration (Pablo Persio's Orchestra is the name mentioned in later stories, e.g., the *Express,* January 3, 1891; July 13, 1891). Mixing a rustic, two-violin–one-guitar ensemble common in earlier years with the urbane atmosphere of this latter-day dance would seem to be inconsistent with the tone of the celebration as described by the *Express.*

Meanwhile, in El Paso, Mexican orchestras were playing band concerts in the plaza and park by 1893 (M. García 1981: 206). Trinidad Concha, who had once been an official in Mexican President Porfirio Díaz's administration, formed an orchestra in El Paso around 1896. This orchestra swelled eventually to forty musicians and performed for both Mexican and Anglo events, acquiring a level of sophistication that, according to García, was "intended to appeal to Mexican as well as American bourgeois tastes"—tastes clearly indicative of "cultural and class segmentation within El Paso's Mexican population" (ibid.: 207). As in San Antonio, El Paso's elites also organized such civic organizations as the Club Lerdo de Tejada (named after the famous Mexican composer) and the Club Progresista, both of which sponsored regular balls and parties at El Paso's most exclusive concert center, Liberty Hall. Although García does not specifically mention it, orchestras like that of Concha were probably employed for such functions.

Finally, folklorist Jovita González's description of dances in the Rio Grande Valley make an implicit distinction between the musical celebrations of middle- and upper-class elites and those of the peons and other working-class types. González's descriptions of the latter evince an undeniable folk character, while those of the former evoke a more refined atmosphere. Of working-class dances (apparently "respectable," and not of the rough-and-tumble variety described by the *Express*), González wrote that these were held in an open area, where dirt packed down to the consistency of brick served as the dance floor.[8] Crude benches provided seating, and kerosene lanterns provided light. Young and old attended the celebrations, while the music was furnished by an "orchestra" consisting of an accordion, violin, and guitar (J. González 1930: 53; cf. Dinger 1972).[9]

Elite celebrations, meanwhile, "marked the social feature of the year" for both urban and rural residents. Men and women dressed in their finest clothes, the halls were lavishly decorated, and "an orchestra from the town furnished the music, waltzes, polkas, schottisches" (J. González 1930: 62). The evidence we have for the development of orquestas in this part of the Southwest, scanty though it may be, suggests that the town orchestras González refers to could be quite fully equipped by the end of the nineteenth century. Both Octavio García (born in 1901 in the Mexican border town of Camargo) and my father, Francisco Peña (born September 16, 1895, in the Texas village of Salineño), recalled in conversations with this writer having seen *"orquestas grandes"* in their early childhood. Peña, who had an exceptionally clear memory, recalled the occasion of his fifth birthday in 1900, when he counted the fourteen musicians in Zeferino Garza's orquesta, which was playing for the Mexican Independence Day celebrations in the border city of Roma, Texas. Quite likely, orquestas like Zeferino Garza's provided the music for elite affairs of the type mentioned by González.

In summary, by the end of the nineteenth century Mexicans in at least a few strategic places, such as San Antonio, Tucson, El Paso, and the Lower Texas Border, where their power had never been fully eclipsed, had managed to recapture some of the social stability of the Hispanic period. This stability was evident wherever a small merchant and professional class, supported by a stable working class (e.g., men who worked for the Southern Pacific), was active enough to mediate the essential conflict still simmering between Anglos and Mexicans in the Southwest. It was among this population that a more modernized orquesta, still emerging as an identifiable ensemble with regularly combined instruments, first made its impact.

The orquesta's development was also cultivated among certain segments of the working class, in particular those affiliated with *mutualista* societies—fraternal insurance societies considered by Mario Barrera as "the most important social organizations among Chicanos from the late nineteenth century to the 1930s" (1988: 13). Responding partly to the need of newly urbanized Mexicans to organize themselves in a hostile society, but also to replace traditional, rural forms of social support (i.e., extended kinship and community ties), *mutualistas* emerged as strong practitioners of "rituals of intensification" (Chapple and Coon 1942; see Chapter 8)—social functions such as fiestas, dances, barbecues, and especially, patriotic celebrations that would create a sense of cultural continuity and community. Thus, for example, *mutualistas* were active in El Paso by the beginning of the twentieth century, sponsoring events like the Mexican Independence Day celebration, otherwise known as *el dieciséis de septiembre*. These celebratory events contributed to the development of the early Mexican American orquestas, since they, along with the balls of the more affluent Mexicans, provided the critical employment needed to maintain permanent and well-organized ensembles.

Finally, in considering the development of truly viable orquestas in the Southwest, and their hand-in-hand emergence with a slowly diversifying and more economically stable Mexican population (in particular the upwardly mobile sector), we must not lose sight of the presence of an occasionally accommodating but mostly hostile Anglo majority. The legacy of conflict—its dialectical movement between progress and retreat and its impact on a soon-to-emerge "Mexican American mind" (R. García 1983)—cast a long shadow over cultural developments within the Mexican community itself.

Nonetheless, while a more dynamic stage of interethnic conflict and its mediation was still at least a quarter century in the future, by the turn of the century Mexican American music and culture were already adumbrating the shape of things to come: Among the hard-core working-class folk (especially rural workers), musical practices and their attendant ensembles were building toward a proletarian aesthetic that eventually would constitute an antithetic pole in the dialectic of conflict. This would become especially evident in the formation of the accordion-based conjunto (see Peña 1985a). Meanwhile, among the upwardly mobile urbanites, a modernizing, better-equipped orquesta was emerging, an ensemble that would come to embody the most potent forces of accommodation and, ultimately, a more powerful synthesis of the contradictions inherent in the dialectic of conflict. Finally, as the reports of the *San Antonio Express* and other sources make clear, even at this early date, differences in the musical means available to the various sectors of the Mexican population bore witness to the social differentiation present among the Mexicans of the Southwest, a differentiation as old (or almost as old) as the earliest Hispanic settlements.

CHAPTER 2

The Dawning
of a New Age
Musical
Developments,
1910 to 1940

Charles Lummis, a musicologist, folk- *Phonographs and player-*
lorist, and devoted aficionado of His-
panic folk music of the Southwest, went *pianos are found in homes*
to California in 1904 to collect what he
thought were the remnants of a disap- *where they contrast sharply*
pearing "Spanish" folk-song tradition in
the Golden State. Many old songs from *with their other simpler*
the eighteenth and nineteenth century
were still being sung by *californio* sing- *furnishings.*
ers of the time (as they were by singers
in other regions of the Southwest), and JAMES K. HARRIS (1927)
Lummis wished to preserve what was
left of the tradition (Lummis 1905; Peña 1989). When he set up his Edison
Home Phonograph to record native vocalists like Manuela García and
the sister duet of Luisa and Rosa Villa, Lummis could not have imagined
that within twenty years Spanish-Mexican music would enter into an explosive stage of development—not only in California but also in the rest
of the Southwest. The massive influx of Mexican immigrants, accelerat-
ing changes within and without the Mexican community, especially in its
relationship with the Anglos, and the vigorous involvement of the recording industry in the music of the Southwest all contributed to a climate
of intense musical activity that would lead to the introduction of several
new musical traditions by the 1930s, including the modern orquesta.

IMMIGRATION:
The Catalyst for Continuity and Change

Mexican immigration looms as a large factor both in maintaining continuity and inducing change in the Hispanic Southwest. The steady, at

times floodlike, stream of Mexicans pouring into the Southwest during the twentieth century provides a constant reinforcement of Mexican culture, as those who brave the trek north bring with them ways of life that ensure a degree of cultural continuity on this side of the border. On the other hand, as the Mexican American population grows and experiences the process of upward mobility and cultural assimilation, changes overtake this population—changes that are magnified when contrasted with the culture Mexican immigrants bring with them into the United States. A cultural gap (as well as an economic one) develops between impoverished Mexican immigrants and upwardly mobile Mexican Americans, a gap that contributes to a sense of social distance, if not outright conflict, between the two groups (Browning and De la Garza 1986; Menchaca 1995). Moreover, this intraethnic gap is further complicated by the evolving relationship between Mexicans and Anglos, as the Mexican Americans are increasingly placed in a contradictory position between Anglos on the one hand and Mexican immigrants on the other.

Renewed migration of Mexicans to the Southwest began rather gradually in the latter part of the nineteenth century, and then it quickened in the first third of the twentieth. As American capitalism accelerated its expansion in the Southwest, the demand for unskilled workers in agriculture, mining, and the railroads increased accordingly. Coupled with Mexico's revolutionary turmoil and chronic economic stagnation, American capitalism's demand for workers provided the necessary "push-and-pull" climate that ensured a steady influx of Mexicans during the first three decades of the twentieth century (Reisler 1976). California and Texas became the principal destination points, although southern Arizona experienced its share of immigration, particularly from the adjacent Mexican state of Sonora (Sheridan 1986). The historian Ricardo Romo summarized the scale of Mexican immigration to the Southwest when he wrote that "Mexican migrants swept across the southwestern landscape in record proportions between 1910 and 1930, and this northward flow was responsible for many of the barrios in this region today" (1983: 7).

The immigrants' origins, however, varied from region to region, with Texas obtaining most of its new settlers from the adjacent Mexican states of Nuevo León, Coahuila, and Tamaulipas, thus ensuring the continuity of norteño culture (and music) in the Lone Star State (Taylor 1934). As mentioned, Tucson's immigrant population derived mostly from the border state of Sonora, strengthening old cultural ties there as well. California, however, whose Mexican population had been drastically depleted and which was farthest removed from the population centers of Mexico, experienced an overwhelmingly new repopulation. Its immigrants came principally from the distant states of Guanajuato, Michoacán, Jalisco, and Zacatecas, with additional ones from Durango. These newcomers naturally introduced a different strain of musical culture into California life, and that culture soon replaced the music Lummis wished to preserve.

As Albert Camarillo (1979), Mark Reisler (1976), Ricardo Romo (1983), and others have documented, the vast majority of the Mexican immigrants who were drawn to the Southwest were impoverished men and women, and they were absorbed into an expanding capitalist order as a subordinate, mainly unskilled labor force. The magnitude of the immigrants' economic misery, coupled with the long-standing Anglo perception of Mexicans as an inferior people devoid of economic enterprise, guaranteed a subordinate position for the latter in the economy of the Southwest. The old relationship of dominant Anglo/subordinate Mexican kept reconstituting itself throughout the first third of the twentieth century, as it reinforced the deep-seated racism and intercultural antagonism that the original conflict had spawned (Barrera 1979; M. García 1981).

Nonetheless, whatever discrimination and psychosocial dislocation the Mexicans may have faced when they settled in the United States (the presence of already established Mexicans helped), the situation on this side of the border was far better than the intolerable conditions in Mexico from which they had escaped. As the anthropologist Douglas Foley noted in connection with ethnic relations in a South Texas town, as long as the Mexicans accepted their inferior status in Anglo society, they could live relatively unmolested lives (Foley 1988a: Chap. 2). Life in this country might include prejudice, disempowerment, and confinement to second-class citizenship, but economic survival overrode all other considerations.

Not that the immigrants and their Mexican American peers remained forever passive in the face of exploitation and discrimination. In fact, it was through their active resistance that Mexicans in the Southwest accelerated the process of change in Anglo-Mexican relations. Numerous well-documented instances exist in which the Mexicans rose in protest against their mistreatment by employers and other agencies that affected their lives (see, for example, M. García 1989; Limón 1974; Rosenbaum 1972). In due time, Mexican resistance forced Anglo society to modify its stance toward ethnic relations, resulting in increasing accommodation and a shift in the dialectic of conflict toward more progressive modes of interaction between the two peoples. This resistance took many paths, from strikes and other direct forms of confrontation to symbolic and artistic production. Musical expression was one of the latter alternatives.

59

The corrido was certainly one of the most important musical genres for the expression of interethnic conflict and resistance. In fact, the corrido entered into an intense phase during the years surrounding the turn of the twentieth century, in both Mexico and the American Southwest. On this side of the border, a number of corridos came into existence, epic narratives that powerfully underscored the period in Anglo-Mexican relations Paredes has labeled the "open-hostility" phase—a time when conflict between Anglos and Mexicans was still strong and not yet modified by the process of cultural mediation connected with later stages in the dialectic of conflict. Probably the most important among these corridos of intercultural conflict were "Gregorio Cortez" in Texas and "Joaquín Murrieta" in California.[1] These and other corridos articulated the interethnic antagonism with exceptional clarity and power. They represented the undiluted conflict of two groups that still relied on sharply contrastive cultural symbols to define each other (Paredes 1993; Peña 1982, 1993).

But another song type emerged in the 1920s in the Southwest, and this one powerfully articulated the Mexican experience, particularly that of the immigrant. I call this new genre the *canción-corrido*—a hybrid that synthesized the distinct features of each genre, providing a dynamic artistic response to conditions in the Southwest and emerging as a potent expression in a world demanding change and adaptation. By combining the lyrical qualities of the *canción* with the narrative structure of the corrido, the *canción-corrido* captured the pathos of the everyday life of the common people while evincing a sense of the historical. In this way, it successfully documented a broad range of concerns, from the sense of uprootedness that immigration wrought to the hardships of daily life in the United States (Herrera-Sobek 1993).

It is therefore fitting, perhaps, that the *canción-corrido* would be one of the most recorded genres when the major record labels invaded the Southwest. The list of *canciones-corridos* recorded on wax disc is long, but fortunately for the modern student of musical culture in the Hispanic Southwest, it has been extensively reissued by Arhoolie Records through its Music of La Raza series (e.g., nos. 9003, 9004, 9005). Beginning with the first of dozens of *canciones-corridos* recorded by the major labels— "El lavaplatos," recorded in Los Angeles in 1926 by Los Hermanos Bañuelos—this new genre developed a widespread audience among the Mexicans of the Southwest. The cultural power of these lyrico-narrative songs derived from their graphic and often touching documentation of life for Mexicans in the United States. Sometimes bitterly, sometimes with a touch of irony and humor, *canciones-corridos* chronicled with perfect fidelity the hardships faced by Mexicans as they adjusted to life in the pits of American capitalism. The lyrics of two *canciones-corridos,* "El lavaplatos" and "El pensilvanio," are included here by way of providing examples of the poetically charged way in which these compositions voiced the everyday struggles of Mexican migrants.

EL LAVAPLATOS	THE DISHWASHER
Soñaba en mi juventud	I dreamed in my youth
ser una estrella de cine,	of being a movie star,
y un día de tantos me vine	and one of those days I came
a visitar Hollywood.	to visit Hollywood.
Un día muy desesperado	One day very desperate
por tanta revolución,	because of so much revolution,
me pasé para este lado	I came over to this side
sin pagar la inmigración.	without paying the immigration.
Qué vacilada,	What a fast one,
qué vacilada,	what a fast one,
me pasé sin pagar nada.	I crossed without paying anything.
Al llegar a la estación	On arriving at the station
me tropecé con un cuate,	I ran into a buddy,
que me hizo la invitación	who gave me an invitation
de trabajar en el "traque."	to work on the *traque.*
Yo el "traque" me suponía	I supposed the *traque*
que sería algún almacén.	to be some kind of warehouse.
Y era componer la vía	And it was to repair the track
por donde camina el tren.	where the train runs.
Ay, que mi cuate,	Oh, what a buddy,
ay, que mi cuate,	oh, what a buddy,
cómo me llevó pa'l traque.	how could he take me to the track?
Cuando me enfadé del traque,	When I grew tired of the track,
me volvió invitar aquel	he invited me again
a la pizca del tomate	to the tomato harvest
y a desahijar betabel.	and to thin beets.
Y allí me gané indulgencias	And there I earned indulgence
caminando de rodillas;	walking on my knees;
como cuatro o cinco millas	about four or five miles
me dieron de penitencia	they gave me as penance.[2]

Ay, qué trabajo,
tan mal pagado,
por andar arrodillado.

Es el trabajo decente
que lo hacen muchos chicanos,
aunque con l'agua caliente
se hinchan un poco las manos.

Pa' no hacérselas cansadas,
me enfadé de tanto plato,
y me alcanzé la puntada
de trabajar en el teatro.

Ay, qué bonito,
ay, qué bonito,
circo, maroma y teatrito.

Yo les pido su licencia
pa' darles estos consejos
a los jóvenes y viejos
que no tengan experiencia.

Aquel que no quiera creer
que lo que digo es verdad,
si se quiere convencer,
que se venga para acá.

Adiós sueños de mi vida,
adiós estrellas del cine;
vuelvo a mi patria querida
más pobre de lo que vine.

CORRIDO PENSILVANIO

El día 28 de abril
a las seis de la mañana,
salimos en un enganche
pa'l estado de Pensilvania

Mi chinita me decía,
"Yo me voy en esa agencia

Oh, what work,
so poorly paid,
for going on one's knees.
. . .

It [dishwashing] is decent work
that many Chicanos do,
although with the hot water
the hands swell a little.

To make a long story short,
I got tired of so many dishes,
and the thought came to me
of working in the theater.

Oh, how pretty,
oh, how pretty,
circus, somersaults and puppetry.

I ask your permission
to give this advice
to the young and old
who may be inexperienced.

He who doesn't believe
that what I say is true,
if he wants to be convinced,
let him come over here.
. . .

Goodby dreams of my life,
goodby movie stars;
I return to my beloved country
poorer than when I came.

PENNSYLVANIA CORRIDO

The 28th of April
at six o'clock in the morning,
we left under contract
for the state of Pennsylvania.

My curly one said to me,
"I'm going with that outfit

para lavarle su ropa,
para darle su asistencia."

El enganchista me dijo,
"No lleves a tu familia
para no pasar trabajos
en l'estado de West Virginia.

"Pa' que sepas que te quiero,
me dejas en Foro Wes;
cuando ya estés trabajando,
me escribes de donde estés."

Adiós estado de Texas,
con toda tu plantación.
Ya me voy pa' Pensilvania
por no pizcar algodón.

Adiós Foro Wes y Dallas,
pueblos de mucha importancia,
ya me voy pa' Pensilvania,
por no andar en la vagancia.

Cuando llegamos allá,
que del tren ya nos bajamos,
preguntan las italianas,
"¿De donde vienen, mejicanos?"

Responden los mejicanos,
los que ya sabían inglés,
"Venimos en un enganche
del pueblo de Foro Wes."

Estos versos son compuestos
cuando yo venía en camino;
son poesías de un mexicano,
nombradas por Concestino.

Ya con ésta me despido
con mi sombrero en la mano,
y mis fieles compañeros
son trescientos mexicanos.

to wash your clothes,
to prepare your meals."

The contractor told me,
"Don't take your family
so as not to have any problems
in the state of West Virginia."

"So that you'll know I love you,
you can leave me in Fort Worth;
when you're already working,
write me from wherever you are."
. . .

Good-by state of Texas,
with all your fields.
I'm leaving for Pennsylvania
to keep from picking cotton.

Good-by Fort Worth and Dallas,
cities of much importance,
I'm leaving for Pennsylvania,
to avoid becoming a vagrant.
. . .

When we got there,
and finally got off the train,
the Italian women asked,
"Where are you Mexicans from?"

The Mexicans responded,
those who already knew English,
"We came on a contract
from the city of Fort Worth."

These verses are composed
while I was on the road;
they are the poems of a Mexican,
given title by Concestino.

With this I take my leave
with my hat in my hand,
and my faithful companions
are three hundred Mexicans.

The Impact of Commercialization:
Music as Cultural Symbol, Music as Commodity

It is unlikely that the corrido, the *canción-corrido,* and the various in-strumental combinations emerging in the Southwest in the early part of the twentieth century would have flourished without the intervention of the recording industry—the major labels from 1924 to 1941, the local Mexican American companies after World War II. The introduction of recorded music changed the mode and pace of musical evolution by stimulating commercial activity through record and phonograph sales, radio programming, and especially, public dancing in ballrooms and *cantinas.* All of this commercial activity encouraged innovation, as both musicians and the Mexican American population at large responded with vigor to the novelty of the market.[3]

As I have suggested elsewhere (Peña 1985a: 39ff.), to Mexican musi-cians of the Southwest, the novelty of the recording experience was an enormous attraction, and most would have done it for nothing, simply to achieve whatever immortality the magical wax disc might confer on them. Indeed, despite the undeniable profits the major and local labels reaped, performers were actually paid very little—fifteen to twenty dollars per record, according to the "father" of the modern conjunto, Narciso Mar-tínez (personal interview). In any case, there is little doubt that under the sponsorship of the recording industry Mexican music of the Southwest was transformed from a collection of scattered traditions into a hotbed of musical production and stylistic breakthroughs—all of this activity homegrown and autonomously directed, since the agents from the big la-bels seem to have exerted little influence on musical selection, which was left entirely to local entrepreneurs and the musicians themselves.

Since the development of Mexican music in the Southwest is so inter-twined with the process of commercialization, it is critical that the role of the capitalist market be examined for the impact it exerts in the for-mation of the orquesta and other musical forms and styles. The question inevitably presents itself: What is the relationship between the mass market and local traditions? How does the intervention of that market affect those traditions? The ethnomusicologist Peter Manuel has posed a similar set of questions:

Does [commercially produced music] reflect and express [the people's] at-titudes, tastes, aspirations, and world view, or does it serve to indoctrinate them, however imperceptibly, to the ideology of the class and gender which control the media? Does popular music enrich or alienate? Can popular music challenge a social order? Do listeners exercise a genuine choice among musics, or can they only passively select preferences from the styles proffered by the media? (1988: 8)

These questions, especially the one on alienation, go to the heart of the debate regarding the production, control, and distribution not only of popular music but of popular culture generally (Mukerji and Schudson 1991). However, before we can address these questions, we need to advance one step further and grapple with an issue that bears on the very nature of cultural symbols and their relation to the basic processes of economic production. In the present context, we must determine whether Hispanic music of the Southwest is an integral part of cultural activity deriving its power from its use-value, that is, from the satisfaction of basic social imperatives, or whether commercialization transformed it into a commodity whose existence depends on its exchange-value (profit-making potential). A full explication of this distinction would take us well beyond my purposes here (see Israel 1979; Marx 1977; Taussig 1980; Willis 1991), but some discussion of the relationship between commodities and cultural symbols is critical, not only because it impinges on the questions posed by Manuel (such as that on the locus of production and control) but because, in the present case, an interrogation of this relationship can provide some insight into orquesta's capacity (as well as that of other musics of the Hispanic Southwest) to carry a symbolic load in the articulation of the dialectic of conflict as it operated both in inter- and intraethnic relations.

I have previously proposed (Peña 1993) that culturally powerful musical forms are organically linked to the communities that create them. These musics exist at, and draw their sustenance from, the very core of the culture, interwoven as they are into the fabric of everyday practice. The music-making processes in these communities emanate from within, as homegrown performers engage their audiences in an ongoing dialogue that determines the rate of change and continuity in musical performance. Especially when they are sacred in nature, such musical forms develop in response to a community's most basic epistemological and cosmogonic conceptions. They are, in short, governed strictly by their use-value and remain (for the most part, at least) beyond the pale of such superorganic influences as the commercial market. This is especially true of musics associated with preindustrial groups or those occupying marginal or subordinate positions within modern industrialized societies (e.g., the Quechuas of Peru).[4]

Contrastable to these organically situated musics are those produced in the industrial world, in particular those known collectively as pop, commercial, or mass music.[5] With notable exceptions, these musics may be termed "superorganic" commodities (rather than "organic" symbols), in that they are produced within and articulate the anonymity of an impersonal market whose main object is the creation of profit, or exchange-value. Lacking a strong use-value—for example, one through which specific groups ritually stake out their most basic social identity— commoditized musics generally reflect the anonymity of personal relations in modern capitalist societies, where the vast majority of people with whom we interact are faceless strangers. In such contexts of anonymity, the performance of pop music occurs more often than not in the atomized world of the isolated listener (e.g., the jogger with portable cassette player and earphones), rather than, say, as a communal ritual of intensification (Chapple and Coon 1942; Peña 1980; Chapter 8). In a real sense, the various forms of popular mass music are reified expressions long abstracted from communal contexts in which vital relationships are consummated, reaffirmed, or mediated. As received commodities destined for private consumption, mass musics lack the "grassroots" authority to stake out social territories.[6] Even mass performances (e.g., concerts) tend to evince the characteristics of spectacle, where performances assume the form of commodity exchange, rather than nonalienating celebrations of community (cf. Flores 1992).

In sum, musical forms circulating as commodities, as well as the performers who popularize them, ultimately depend on their exchange-value—the sheer volume of their unit sales (e.g., CDs and videos)—for their continuing existence. Their use-value—that is, their power to articulate fundamental social arrangements—assumes a distinctly secondary function, if it possesses any such function at all. Instead, a highly privatized relationship obtains between the consumer on the one hand, and the music and its performer on the other, a relationship, moreover, in which the latter are objects of pleasure, or, more accurately, fetishized objects. In short, music and performer represent an advanced stage of capitalist development in which the basic form of communication consists of impersonal relations among people, and personalized relations between people and marketable objects, or, in other words, commodity fetishism:

Relations determined by exchange-value are impersonal relations. They are objective relations, in the sense of relations between objects. They are reified relations. "In the exchange value the social relations of persons are

transformed into the social conduct of objects." (Israel 1979: 287; the quote is from Marx)

In his penetrating study of commodity fetishism in South America, Michael Taussig elaborates on the effects of commodity production on the process of reification. For Taussig, the capitalist mode of commodity production conceals the social nature of labor: "[E]ssential qualities of human beings and their products are converted into commodities, into things for buying and selling on the market" (1980: 4). A fundamental estrangement develops between humans and the products of their labor, and this estrangement distorts the nature of the social relations embedded in that labor. In fact, as a commodity itself, bought and sold for its exchange-value, labor activity contributes to the fetishizing process. There exists a vast army of workers who experience their labor-power as pure drudgery, an activity that dehumanizes them and "stresses them out"—an activity, in short, that exists as an alien force with great power to dictate the pace of one's life. In their turn, the products of capital-producing labor assume a life force of their own: they too become fetishized commodities with the power to communicate, not as symbols under the control of human agency, but as independent entities or "socialized abstractions" endowed with their own volition. Taussig summarizes the reifying process involved in the transformation of the products of labor into fetishized commodities:

On the one hand these abstractions are cherished as real objects akin to inert things, whereas on the other, they are thought of as animate entities with a life-force of their own akin to spirits or gods. Since these "things" have lost their original connection with social life, they appear, paradoxically, both as inert and as animated entities. (1980: 5)

Musics subjected to the process of commoditization so central to the commercial market—which is to say, most popular, mass music—inevitably respond to the logic of that market and its reifying effects. Driven by the principle of exchange-value, they become, like so many other commodities crowding cultural life in "late" capitalism, "socialized abstractions" that "speak" to a reified sense of the aesthetic. Disconnected from productive relations (other than their role as commodities), they are stripped of their power to articulate important intersections between economic and social activity (their use-value), though particular groups may "hijack" certain styles and reinvest them with socially symbolic power (e.g., punk rock; see Hebdige 1979). In most cases, however, musical commodities satisfy demands more or less artificially induced by the consumerist mentality that goes hand-in-glove with modern advertisement, wherein consumption is motivated not by basic "need structures" but by demand manipulated for the benefit of corporate interests (Willis 1991: Chap. 7).[7]

Finally, I would submit that in this era of "late capitalism" no music, regardless of its symbolic centrality in a people's culture, is totally immune to the process of reification once it comes into contact with the capitalist market and its function is transformed by the epistemology that makes commodity fetishism possible (Taussig 1980; cf. Todorov 1987).[8] Yet the outcome does not have to be reducible to an either/or alternative: popular music need not be either an organically situated symbol or a superorganic commodity, a la Muzak. As John Fiske (1989), Simon Frith (1981), Dick Hebdige (1979), and others have maintained, popular culture and music can in their enactment become sites for the struggle between use-value and exchange-value. People can reappropriate music. Commoditization can occur without the music losing its uniqueness as a situated cultural symbol, especially (in answer to Peter Manuel's question) when its constituents retain a large measure of control over its production and distribution, and when the music continues to play a vital role in defining key areas of articulation between culture and economy. That role is, in my estimation, the true function of cultural symbols, in particular those referred to as "summarizing symbols" (Ortner 1973) or "root metaphors" (Turner 1974).

When communities insist on stamping their own cultural signature on the process of commercial production (and consumption)—especially when they exercise substantial control over that process—a tension arises between reification and reappropriation, between the alienating tendencies of commodities circulating for exchange-value and the self-affirming power of artifacts produced mainly for use-value. A recording of a *canción-corrido* such as "El lavaplatos" may circulate as a commodity, but like the Kwakiutl gift in Mauss's famous study (1954; cf. Flores 1992), it retains much of the symbolic power wrapped up in its use-value. As a potent cultural symbol, it carries within it the spirit of a people's shared experience, and it therefore retains the capacity to speak for its constituents' most basic sense of group identity and, indeed, to offer resistance to outside threats to that identity.

MEXICAN AMERICAN MUSIC AND THE MARKET:
Autonomous Commercialization

Helping to maintain the cultural integrity of Hispanic music of the Southwest and, hence, its power to interpose itself in the dialectic of conflict is the commercial autonomy this music has historically exercised and the limited manner in which it has been absorbed into the large-scale American music market. In the early years, despite the intervention of large recording companies such as RCA Victor, Columbia, Brunswick, and Decca, none of the musical forms and styles then emerging in the Southwest were ever co-opted, in whole or in part, by the burgeoning market for popular music (as eventually happened, say, with country music; see Patterson 1975).[9] This is a critical point, because other similarly situated musics—country, the blues, and in Mexico, the mariachi—did undergo a wholesale transformation as they were absorbed into the mass market. This transformation stripped them of much of their original symbolic power, even as it was amalgamating them into a mass market with the labels "hit parade," "top forty," and a multiplicity of others, depending on the audience targeted (Patterson 1975).

In the specific case of Hispanic music of the Southwest, the major labels could not have been interested, obviously, in developing powerfully organic musical traditions that would promote ethnic or class solidarity and in the long run contribute to the cultural dialectic driving Anglo-Mexican relations in the Southwest. Rather, they were interested in exploiting existing musical practices for profit, just as they had done successfully with African American music since the early twenties. But their entry into the field of Hispanic music of the Southwest did just that: triggered the rapid evolution of several musical traditions reflective of change and continuity in Hispanic life of the Southwest.

Under the sponsorship of local agents like Felipe Valdez Leal in Los Angeles and *el señor* Acosta in San Antonio, vocal music flourished, as the corrido, the *canción-corrido*, and the *canción* itself became dominant. However, instrumental music experienced phenomenal growth and innovation as well, as the newly emerged norteño ensemble and old-fashioned string orquestas were swept into the commercial web. Thriving as part of vocal music and cementing itself as a dominant tradition was the duet, both male and female, as well as combinations of the two. The vocal-duet tradition preceded the advent of recorded music, but it exploded as a result of commercialization in the 1920s, becoming the principal vehicle for the performance of the corrido and *canción-corrido,* as well as the purely lyrical *canción* itself, with its dominant theme of romantic love. In combination, these three genres, usually performed by duets, constituted at least 70 percent of the music the major labels recorded between 1925 and 1941.

The prevalence of vocal music in the commercial arena is an obvious index of its popularity in the Southwest. As a tradition, it was as old as the original Hispanic settlements. What commercial development did was to certify its supremacy, particularly in the form of the duet. The twenties and thirties ushered in the golden age of the Mexican American troubadours—vocalists who sang about every imaginable subject affecting the lives of the public that so affectionately embraced them and their music. Thus, in California we discover Los Hermanos Areu, to whom evidently belongs the honor of the first vocal-music recording in the Hispanic Southwest, at least with the major labels. They cut a record for RCA on June 14, 1924, in Los Angeles (Spottswood 1990: 1643). Los Hermanos Areu, incidentally, were accompanied by a small—and, until the 1930s, not atypical—orchestral ensemble consisting of violin, clarinet, piano, and two guitars (ibid.).

Dozens of duets followed on the heels of Los Hermanos Areu, as the age of, first, the phonograph, and shortly, live radio performance dawned in the Hispanic Southwest. In California, Los Hermanos Bañuelos, Los Madrugadores, Los Morenos, Chicho y Chencha, the legendary Hermanas Padilla, and many others formed a parade of vocalists who could be heard on the Victrolas, so popular in the 1920s, and who, beginning in the 1930s, flooded the radio waves with live performances of *canciones,* corridos, and *canción-corrido* hybrids. Likewise in Texas, duets such as Los Hermanos Chavarría, Rocha y Martínez, Gaitán y Cantú, and others became household names. Among the women, probably the most influential was the legendary Lydia Mendoza, "*la cantante de los pobres*" (the poor people's songster), who for more than fifty years captivated the hearts of a vast audience throughout the Southwest and beyond. Both male and female duets crowded the commercial market during the twenties and thirties, until the major labels pulled their operations out of the Southwest at the onset of World War II.

Historically, much of the music of the Hispanic Southwest, both vocal and instrumental, belongs in the category of organic artistic expression, animated by the principle of use-value. This could not have been otherwise in the subsistence economy prevailing in the region throughout the nineteenth and even the early twentieth century. An organismic character is what lends the corrido, the *canción-corrido,* and the conjunto norteño their immense cultural power. The inevitable question arises, however: Did the capitalist market induce changes, that is, did it change the corrido and conjunto into fetishized commodities? Of course, like the blues, country, and mariachi, the music of the Southwest has also been subjected to the process of commercialization. Unlike the latter musics, however, none of the musical forms extant in the Southwest yielded fully to the massive commercialization and subsequent reification that overtook the blues, country music, and the mariachi.[10] In the first place, relative disinterest in the Hispanic music of the Southwest on the part of mass-market performers and producers, especially after 1941, insulated it from external influences. Second, local control of musical resources and haphazard distribution in an already circumscribed ethnic market necessarily placed limits on the scope of commercialization. The music of the Southwest thus remained marginal to developments in mainstream pop music and grounded to a specific cultural base.

To be sure, there have been isolated instances in which Mexican American performers have attained consistent exposure as major-market commodities—Vikki Carr, Andy Russell, and perhaps Freddie Fender come to mind here. In addition, there have been a number of Mexican American performers who have achieved momentary glory in the mass market: Ritchie Valens, Sunny Ozuna (and the Sunliners), Thee [sic] Midnighters, and Los Lobos are examples. But every one of these instances represents performers who were individually co-opted by the mass market and who stepped outside the boundaries of traditional music of the Southwest to gain fame. (Many, like Los Lobos and Sunny, returned to their musical roots after excursions into the pop field.) In the Southwest, none of the indigenous forms, or any of their performers, has ever experienced the glamorization or the massive marketing that transformed the blues and country into "rhythm-and-blues" and "country-western," respectively, and in their altered form absorbed them into the circulation of large-scale commodities.

As an example, conjunto music has been subjected to intensive commercialization since the 1920s, first through the efforts of the major labels, later through small local companies, and lately under the control, once again, of the major labels. Yet, with notable "crossover" exceptions (e.g., the Texas Tornados [sic]), the music has retained its regional, ethnic, and working-class identity. In short, it has never been stripped of its power as a "summarizing" symbol. Its organic connection with working-class Texas-Mexicans and other norteños remains intact to this day. Even in its slightly different form as *música norteña,* which has a much greater commercial reach than the Texas-Mexican conjunto, the accordion ensemble has resisted the reifying effects of commoditization—that process whereby music embedded in a community's deepest cultural folds is dislodged from its social base and recast as a superorganic form with little of its original symbolic substance left.[11]

The same can be said of other musical traditions extant in the Southwest when the commercial market invaded in full force. Despite the transforming power of that market, traditions like the *canción, canción-corrido,* duet-singing, the string orchestras, and the modern orquesta were never reduced to the status of commodities abstracted from their sociomaterial base. All remained circumscribed by their regional, ethnic, and class limitations, thereby retaining the very features that resist reification: close association with specific groups and a continuing function as flesh-and-blood symbols ineffably embodying the core identity of those groups. In what must be something of a paradox, the intervention of the major labels not only failed to reap a harvest of mass-marketable commodities in the fashion of rhythm-and-blues–based rock music, it hastened the crystallization of certain styles—duet-singing and the Texas-Mexican conjunto, for example—in this manner strengthening the capacity of these styles to carry out their function as emblems of ethnic, working-class identification and solidarity. The result—musics that strengthened the narrow aesthetic (and, in an unconscious way, the political) interests of a well-defined minority—was surely *not* what the major labels expected when they plowed their investments into the fertile soil of Hispanic music of the Southwest.

Of course, this is not to deny the major labels' benefits from the commercialization of Mexican music in the Southwest. On the contrary, beginning with the first recordings, they quickly turned a low-investment enterprise into a high-yield gold mine. To begin with, companies like Decca, Columbia, and RCA paid the most meager of wages to the performers. As noted earlier, recording artists were paid from $15 to $20 per record, a token investment for the companies, considering the thirty-five-cent price of records even as early as the 1930s. Narciso Martínez, singer Lydia Mendoza, and others verified in separate interviews that by the 1930s many Mexicans of the Southwest had Victrolas and that records were plentiful in many households—all of which attests to the drawing power of commercial music in the Southwest.

In any case, given the methods of the major labels in recording Mexican performers, the marketing costs seem to have been low indeed. For instance, recordings were not commonly done in studios but in local hotels in San Antonio, El Paso, Los Angeles, or other major cities. The company agents simply rented a room, soundproofed it, and set up the recording equipment. Nor was much time spent in trying to create the "perfect" recording, as modern pop-music studios do. On a typical recording date, a dozen or more groups were swiftly ushered in and out of the makeshift studios (Spottswood 1990; Strachwitz 1975: 30). According to accordionist Santiago Jimènez, his first recording session, in 1936, took less than an hour, because "the polkas I brought in were not too difficult, and the other musicians already had recording experience" (personal interview 1979).

The recording companies' venture into the field of Mexican music in the Southwest was helped by the network already in place among the Mexicans. This network expanded dramatically with the advent of commercialization. In the urban areas, especially, local Mexican entrepreneurs, particularly furniture dealers, branched out immediately into the music market, adding phonographs and records to their inventories. In this way they tacitly assumed the role of brokers between the major labels and the musicians: they identified musical talent for the former and may have been paid a small commission (Martínez, personal interview 1979). For the musicians themselves, the novelty of recording was a great incentive, and even if none of them ever attained the star quality of mainstream, mass-market performers, the thrill of becoming part of a special group singled out for commercial exposure was enough to motivate most of them to accept whatever "contract" the company agents had to offer. In sum, the large recording companies must have realized a lucrative profit from their venture into the Mexican music of the Southwest, and they continued to market the music until the beginning of World War II, when a lack of raw materials forced them to curtail their activities.

After the war, a strategic decision was apparently made by RCA and other companies to scuttle regional operations and concentrate their efforts on a far larger Latin American market. Other musics, with the potential for appeal within a wider Latin American audience and thus for greater profits, were targeted, and Mexico City became the center for Latin American operations. In cooperation with Mexican moguls like Emilio Azcárraga, RCA and Columbia, in particular, went on to exploit commercially a number of established and emerging styles (Saragoza n.d.). Principal among these was the mariachi, which was then surging in popularity in connection with the recently introduced *canción ranchera* and singing idols who specialized in the genre such as Jorge Negrete, Pedro Infante, and others (Jáuregui 1990). Other types of music exploited with great commercial success included romantic male trios with guitars (e.g., Trío Calavera, Trío Los Panchos), female duets, and a variety of sophisticated urban musics of middle-class extraction—orchestras like those of Pablo Beltrán Ruiz and Rafael de Paz, which were routinely used

73

to back up singers of the *canción romántica* genre, such as María Luisa Landín and Pedro Vargas.

Music produced in Mexico City by the major labels found a ready market in the Hispanic Southwest, which was hungry for any music that would strengthen its ties to the mother culture. To be sure, Mexican records had been imported into the Southwest since the 1930s, at least, but the postwar period witnessed a virtual explosion, what with the added financial power of the American companies and the increasing exposure of Mexican music over the radio and in movies, so popular with Mexicans in the Southwest. (All but the smallest of towns had at least one Mexican movie theater.)

Regional music of the Southwest, meanwhile, began to suffer a lack of exposure during the war, due to cessation of recording activity. When the war ended, however, the slack was picked up by local entrepreneurs, members of the nascent Mexican American middle class, and in the years immediately following, a number of record labels sprouted throughout the Southwest and beyond. These labels were for the most part shoe-string operations run by small-time entrepreneurs—men like Armando Marroquín and Arnaldo Ramírez, who, at least initially, had little capital to invest in the wholesale promotion of the music they recorded. They were consequently at a great competitive disadvantage in relation to the large companies, which vigorously pushed their internationally marketed music among local radio stations, augmenting the dominance of their products with frequent tours by Mexican stars into the Southwest. Mexican American labels could not compete with such high-powered promotion, and their efforts tended to be limited to locales such as Texas, California, or the Midwest.

Yet a few local labels, such as Ideal and Falcon in Texas and Taxco and Imperial in Los Angeles, managed to acquire sufficient economic clout to distribute their records on a larger scale, in this way contributing significantly toward the continuing development of Mexican music in the Southwest. Not that any of these labels achieved the stature of the major ones, of course, but they were sufficiently active, especially in Texas, to spur the final development of such styles as the conjunto and the Texas-Mexican variant of the orquesta. This recalls the point raised earlier: Major styles indigenous to the Southwest, such as the conjunto and orquesta, owe their existence not so much to distant market forces—though these do play a role, obviously—but to cultural and ideological impulses emanating from the music-culture communities themselves. Labels such as Ideal thus function historically as mediators in the process of musical development, responding, as the late Armando Marroquín of Ideal once put it, "to currents in the air."[12]

As mediators, Mexican American labels differed sharply from the large recording companies in that the latter have always been in a position to exert considerable influence on the kinds of music reaching the mass market—especially in the decades since World War II, when the recording industry became a monolithic power in the field of popular music. Practices that restrict competition, such as "payola" and other forms of pressure on local promoters, have been adopted by large labels in an effort to shape the market so as to favor the musical commodities they produce (Manuel 1988). In the United States at least, and to a great extent in Latin America as well, this effort has often been successful, enabling the powerful companies to maintain substantial control over the pace of musical innovation and change (Robinson et al. 1991: 42). Mexican American record producers have never enjoyed such a monopoly. To begin with, none of them ever achieved dominance in the market; instead, the Mexican American market has historically been dotted by dozens of small companies, some ephemeral in nature. Lacking the power to control the rate or the shape of musical evolution, Mexican American companies have traditionally allowed their artists much greater autonomy in determining what kind of music finds its way onto the vinyl disc.

The case of Ideal is instructive. Founded in 1946 by Armando Marroquín of Alice, Texas, and Paco Betancourt of San Benito, Ideal was one of the most successful of the Mexican American operations in the decade or so following World War II. When RCA Victor, Columbia, and the other American labels abandoned their operations in the Southwest, Marroquín became aware of the vacuum created, and he realized the potential existed for successfully marketing *tejano* music on a localized basis. Totally unfamiliar with the business of recording, he nonetheless "worked up the ability" (*me di abilidad*), as he put it, by making inquiries and initiating partnerships—with Betancourt, who had a music store, and with the Allen Company in Los Angeles, which helped distribute records there.

Beginning with his own wife's duet (Carmen y Laura), Marroquín went on to attract almost every important *tejano* performer to his label. He started with a $200 phonograph and used his living room as a studio, but eventually Marroquín turned Ideal into the most important producer of Mexican American music in the Southwest. Obviously familiar with the basic principles of capitalism, he recalled with some satisfaction that "since there was no competition, whatever you came out with was in demand." But Marroquín had other circumstances in his favor: he was deeply steeped in the musical traditions of the Southwest, having grown up, as he proudly admitted, on corridos and duets, and he was willing to let the artists determine what music would best compete in the *tejano* market.

Thus, for example, when the "father" of the modern *orquesta tejana*, Beto Villa, approached Marroquín and asked him to let Villa record a couple of tunes, Marroquín agreed. "The group at that time was not very good," he recalled, "not very professional, but it was a ranchero sound, and it seemed to me that it might give the accordion some competition." Over the objections of his partner Betancourt, who thought the group was "atrocious," Marroquín released Villa's first record. It was an enormous success, not only launching Villa's career but marking the birth of an orquesta tradition that was to define in a musical sense the very essence of Mexican American culture. But Villa's breakthrough was made possible because of Marroquín's instinctive feel for that culture's pulse.

Marroquín, then, was a mediator who facilitated the development of Mexican American music. He acted on his cultural instincts to promote music he believed would resonate in the public consciousness, and in this he was highly successful. In *The Texas-Mexican Conjunto,* I summarized Marroquín's role in the following manner:

We can suggest, then, that in Marroquín economic motives and cultural commitments intertwined; the former were mediated by the latter. He was an ambitious entrepreneur, but never a full-fledged capitalist, because his business horizon was limited by his cultural outlook. And both were subject to the narrow limits inherent in an ethnic, regional music market. Marroquín did make money (though hardly a fortune), but he remained rooted in a tejano cultural network, with all the contradictions and limitations that a culture forged in the crucible of interethnic conflict imposes. (Peña 1985a: 77–78)

In the next chapter I intend to discuss at greater length Marroquín's role in the emergence of the modern Mexican American orquesta. At this point I would contend that the intervention of the recording industry in the music of the Mexican Americans did not, in the end, transform the music into a full-fledged, reified commodity. Over the years, as the mass market threatened to appropriate their music, Mexican Americans consistently reappropriated it, refusing to give up the symbolic (use-) values they had invested in such indigenous creations as the orquesta. Thus, music and musicians remained tied to their cultural base, and for the most part, the music continued to function as an organic form of cultural communication in everyday life. As they continued to evolve, the various styles such as the conjunto and the orquesta came to articulate important aesthetic and ideological positions, in this manner being drawn into the ongoing dialectic unfolding historically between Anglos and Mexicans in the Southwest, as well as into the internal changes transforming the Mexican American community itself. In this the major labels and their Mexican American successors were important, albeit unwitting, contributors.

COMMERCIALIZATION AND INSTRUMENTAL MUSIC:
Emergence of the Conjunto and Orquesta

Vocal music may have been the most commercially exploited of the Hispanic musics of the Southwest during the heyday of the major labels, but instrumental music was far from neglected. In the midst of the musical ferment set in motion by the age of the phonograph (and, shortly afterward, the radio), the development of instrumental music was also energized, leading to the emergence of the two most important ensembles in the music of the Hispanic Southwest—the conjunto and the modern orquesta. Significantly, neither style achieved maturity during the period the major labels were active, between 1925 and 1941. The full flowering of both ensembles occurred after World War II, stimulated by local Mexican American–owned companies.

In any event, the powerful accordion-based ensemble, soon to be known in Texas as conjunto (known elsewhere as *música norteña*), was but an embryonic style groping for direction in the early twentieth century. Having been introduced into northern Mexico and South Texas from Europe sometime in the 1860s, the accordion had early on been appropriated by working-class norteños and subjected to some experimentation, as it was paired on an ad hoc basis with various other instruments, in particular the guitar and a folk drum known as *tambora de rancho* (ranch drum; Peña 1985a: 38). Very quickly after it was absorbed into the commercial market, the conjunto experienced an explosive rise to prominence as the ensemble coalesced into a standardized instrumentation and mode of performance that established it as one of the strongest musical symbols among Latin Americans anywhere (Peña 1985a).

Now anchored by the diatonic button accordion and a unique Mexican guitar known as the *bajo sexto,* the conjunto began in the late 1920s its ascent toward the pinnacle of popularity. Much more so than in its mature years, however, at this early juncture it was still the music of rural and generally impoverished folk on both sides of the Texas-Mexico border. Its humble origins notwithstanding, conjunto was swept into the commercial bustle then driving the music of the Southwest, and under the transformative power of the vinyl disc, it was launched on its way toward the powerful stage it would reach in the next thirty years. All of this was made possible by commercialization, as artists such as Narciso Martínez, Lolo Cavazos, Santiago "Flaco" Jiménez, and others became household names, especially in Texas. When the rural population began its massive migration into the cities, the ensemble took root in its new urban setting, and here it eventually eclipsed all other forms of music in popularity among working-class Mexicans, beginning in Texas and northeastern Mexico and later spreading to such distant places as California and Michoacán, Mexico.

The case of the conjunto conforms to the pattern of musical development in the Southwest during the twentieth century: The American recording companies introduced it to the commercial market, but ultimately they were not decisive in determining its stylistic or cultural development. That was left to the Mexican American labels entering the market after the war and, especially, to the performers who actually forged the style. Naturally, these performers were themselves members of the working-class folk who assigned to the music its charter and judged its progress according to their own sense of the proper aesthetic. In the end, the conjunto became a powerful symbol for working-class solidarity, enlisted in the ideological struggle that pitted working- against middle-class Mexican Americans, and Mexicans against Anglos (Peña 1985a). But ultimately the success of the conjunto, like that of the orquesta, is attributable to ideological, not commercial, forces. The commercial market strengthened rather than weakened the symbolic power of the conjunto.

Meanwhile, the dance orquesta—like the conjunto, originally a diffuse ensemble of variable instrumentation—began in the 1920s to shift from a string to a brass-and-reed orientation, although string orquestas continued to enjoy currency until the 1930s. As mentioned in Chapter 1, orquestas (as well as military brass bands) had been present in the Southwest since the nineteenth century, the evidence suggesting that the best organized were in the employ of elite or at least middle-class Mexicans. The brass bands appearing toward the final years of the nineteenth century may have been distant precursors of the modern orquesta, as it emerged in the 1930s. The string orquesta, meanwhile, had disappeared almost completely by the onset of World War II.

There is little documentation of an ethnographic nature to provide clues as to the social characteristics of the orquesta during the early twentieth century. In all probability, the trends of the late nineteenth century carried over into the twentieth—that is, the largest and better-organized orquestas were most likely urban in nature, and they were connected with the music and dancing activities of the more affluent Mexican Americans, small as their number might be. In the urban areas, especially, orquestas and brass bands played concerts open to the general public, as in Tucson, where the Banda de Música played open-air Sunday concerts in the 1920s, and in El Paso, where Rito Medina's band presented an outdoor concert in the summer of 1916 (M. García 1981: 206). Also in El Paso, the "most popular band" in 1917 was that of Raymundo S. González, who must have vied for supremacy with the "most respected musical group of the era," Concha's Band (ibid.).

Orquestas like those performing in El Paso and Tucson existed in almost all areas of the Southwest. With one or two exceptions (see Arhoolie Records, nos. 9007; 7017 [CD]), none of these was ever enlisted by the major recording companies, and they seem to have been restricted to local performances sponsored by the more affluent sectors of the Mexican communities. Thus, in the 1920s in Tucson, several well-placed orquestas and brass bands kept busy performing for different events:

> Among these groups were the *Quintero Popular Mexicano*, which performed at a *Liga Protectora Latina* dance in 1917, the *Orquesta Navarro*, which graced a series of summer dances at Armory Hall in 1922, the *Orquesta León*, which appeared in the Santa Rita Roof Garden in 1925, the *Orquesta Típica Mexicana*, which won an invitation to a "smoke" and private party held by the exclusive *Club Latino* in 1927, and the Gayo Jazz Orchestra, which held Saturday and Sunday dances at the Alianza Hall in 1930. (Sheridan 1986: 197)

The orquestas of El Paso, meanwhile, were kept solvent by the more affluent citizens of that city. As Mario García notes,

> Entertaining both Mexican and American audiences, bands such as Concha's played mainly European compositions that over the years had become Mexicanized. More sophisticated in their selection of classical tunes, which were apparently intended to appeal to Mexican as well as American bourgeois tastes, these local bands and their music stood in sharp contrast to the folksongs composed by Mexican workers themselves and indicated cultural and class segmentation within El Paso's Mexican community. (1981: 207)

Judging from the developments in Tucson and El Paso (other urban areas, e.g., San Antonio, also maintained similar musical groups), it is evident that even in the early twentieth century, musical distinctions based on class and degree of acculturation to American life were present. As García's quote indicates, these distinctions were already being articulated by the orchestral ensembles of the period.

Sheridan mentions one special type of orquesta worth dwelling on for a moment—La Orquesta Típica Mexicana. The *orquesta típica,* a variant of the string orquesta, experienced its heyday in the Hispanic Southwest during the 1920s and '30s. This ensemble also underwent some commercialization at the hands of the major labels; several recordings are to be found in the catalogue compiled by Richard Spottswood—for example, La Orquesta Típica Acosta, which recorded for Vocalion in San Francisco in July 1929; La Orquesta Típica Arias, for RCA Victor in San Antonio, July 1929; and La Orquesta Fronteriza (El Paso, 1930). Many other localized *típicas,* never approached by the major labels, existed throughout the Southwest during the first third of the twentieth century, as illustrated by Sheridan's example.

The *orquesta típica* had its origins in Mexico, where groups labeled as "*típicas*" actually date from the early nineteenth century, at least. These *típicas* were so designated because they were folk ensembles commonly associated with rural *mestizo* populations. They "typically" consisted of five to seven instruments organized around the violin, and they seem not to have been much different from the orquestas to be found in the Southwest throughout the nineteenth century. A common *típica* might consist of a violin or two, psaltery, contrabass, *bajo sexto* or guitar, and mandolin, with a clarinet or flute added on occasion (Baqueiro Foster 1964). Such was the makeup of a *típica* described by the writer Ignacio Altamirano on a trip to a rural area of Mexico sometime in the middle of the nineteenth century (Mayer-Serra 1941: 116).

The Mexican musicologist Gerónimo Baqueiro Foster has suggested that *orquestas típicas* may have been descendants of better-organized groups employed in conjunction with upper-class functions such as *zarzuelas, tonadillas escènicas, follas,* and even operettas. Through the process of *gesunkenes kulturgut,* or "the sinking of cultural goods," the instruments in these upper-class orquestas found their way into the rural, peasant communities, where they were organized into ad hoc ensembles commonly known as *orquestas típicas.* Of course, in their peasant context, as folk groups, *típicas* evinced a much simpler and far less polished sound than their elite counterparts. Finally, it is evident that folk *típicas* were quite variable in composition, their makeup being ultimately de-

FIGURE 2. *A working-class* orquesta típica, *South Texas, ca. 1915.*
Courtesy Houston Metropolitan Research Center, Houston Public Library.

pendent on whatever instruments and musicians might be at hand (see Fig. 2).

The "lifting" of the folk *típicas* to the level of the elites seems to have been a result of *gestigienes kulturgut,* the opposite process of *gesunkenes kulturgut.* In other words, the former is a function of the romantic nationalism that historically motivates elites to appropriate such folk forms for their own edification. As E. Bradford Burns (1980) has effectively argued, that spirit seems to have been endemic to Latin America generally and Mexico in particular throughout the nineteenth century and at least the early part of the twentieth (cf. Lafaye 1976). At various times during this period in their history, many Latin American elites were smitten by *costumbrismo,* or the desire to experience an invented "national" culture as attributed to the common folk. In their zeal to reconnect their lives with the roots of their national culture, these elites sought out expressions representative of the nation's popular (i.e., folk) culture, and they then transformed these into expressions of their own hegemonic power. However, these folk products had, first, to undergo a process of gentrification whereby their folk roughness was smoothed out before they could become acceptable to the more refined tastes of the elites.

This is precisely what happened to the Mexican folk orchestra known as *típica*. Evidently caught up in one of the romantic-nationalist surges that have periodically visited Mexico, the *típica* came to the attention of musicologists at the Conservatorio Nacional de Música (National Conservatory of Music), and under the direction of one Carlos Curti, the first elite, nationalist *orquesta típica* was founded in 1884—the fourteen-piece Orquesta Típica Mexicana (Baqueiro Foster 1964: 59). La Orquesta Típica Mexicana was a smashing success, and in short order other *típicas* were organized, including two whose popularity soon rivaled that of the Típica Mexicana—La Orquesta Típica Lerdo and Orquesta Típica de Juan Torre Blanca. These *típicas* attained tremendous popularity in Mexico and the Hispanic Southwest, and they toured extensively in the latter region during the late nineteenth century and the first three decades of the twentieth (Peña 1985a: 30).

The nationalist *típica* resembles the mariachi in many respects; indeed, it is quite possible the two were the same ensemble at one time. The attire worn by (elite) *típica* musicians was identical to that worn by the early mariachis; the violin was the anchor instrument in both groups; and, finally, their repertories were also similar if not identical. Both ensembles specialized in performing *aires nacionales,* such as "El jarabe tapatío" and other *jarabes; sones* of various sorts, such as the popular "Son de la negra"; and many folk songs with universal popularity throughout Mexico and the Southwest, such as "El sauz y la palma" and "Pajarillo barranqueño"—the latter recorded by the Orquesta [típica] del Norte in El Paso in 1930 (Spottswood 1990).

In the Southwest, the first nationalistic *típica* was probably organized in the early 1920s, though an earlier date is certainly plausible, since the Mexican *típicas* had been touring the region since the 1880s, and they may have inspired the formation of local *típicas* before the twenties. In any case, these symbols of Mexican nationalism were common throughout the Southwest by the 1920s, although *tejanos* seem to have been the most active in organizing such groups (see Figs. 3, 4).

The *típica* flourished at a time when *costumbrismo* and nationalism were particularly strong in Mexico. A romantic attitude toward folk life was very much a part of Mexican nationalism, especially following the Mexican Revolution of 1910–1917. This nationalism was shared by many Mexicans in the Southwest, as they still looked to Mexico for cultural affirmation. Not surprisingly, the ultimate symbol of nationalism, the *orquesta típica* (before the mariachi superseded it), found strong support among the Mexicans of the Southwest. In an Anglo society in which they were not yet accepted as full-fledged citizens, musical expressions like the *típica* gave these Americans of Mexican descent a feeling of "cultural

FIGURE 3. *Orquesta Típica Torres, Houston, 1930.*
Courtesy Houston Metropolitan Research Center, Houston Public Library.

citizenship," even if it was, to the displeasure of many Americans, that of a foreign country.

Meanwhile, the first orquestas recorded by the American companies were still of the string variety—the true *típicas* in existence in the Southwest since the nineteenth century. These orquestas were often used to provide accompaniment for the popular duets, although guitars, performed soli, still predominated in this task, as they had since the early days of settlement. In California, for example, numerous recordings featured various duets popular at the time—many of these accompanied by guitars. But a sizable number were backed by orchestral ensembles, and some of these were actually labeled as "mariachi." The appearance of these orchestras in commercial recordings—small as these were, usually—indicates that an orquesta tradition was thriving in the Golden State by the 1920s (as in other parts of the Southwest).

Richard K. Spottswood's highly useful discography of ethnic music recordings (1990) documents the variety of ensembles recorded in the Golden State. Interestingly, according to Spottswood, the first record

FIGURE 4. *Orquesta Típica Laredo, 1930.*
Courtesy of José Compeán.

made by the major labels was not of a vocal group but of a string orquesta—La Orquesta Rodríguez, cut on the RCA label on June 12, 1924, two days before the debut of the vocal duet Los Hermanos Areu. La Orquesta Rodríguez featured a cornet, flute, clarinet, trombone, two violins, cello, piano, and tuba (Spottswood 1990: 2263). La Orquesta Acosta-Rosete recorded ten selections for Columbia in September of 1927—a schottische, four polkas, two waltzes, a march, a one-step, and a *pasodoble.* The instrumentation consisted of two violins, trumpet, flute, trombone, piano, and contrabass (ibid.: 1614). Several other orquestas appeared on the big labels in California, including La Orquesta Josè Perales (RCA Victor, San Francisco, March 30–31, 1928), Orquesta Cervantes (Los Angeles, March 1928) and Orquesta del Castillo (Los Angeles, October 9, 1928). As noted previously, La Orquesta Típica Acosta had made recordings on several dates for the Vocalion label.

In the late thirties and early forties, the most prominent orquesta in California was that of Manuel S. Acuña, even though it was an ensemble organized strictly for recording purposes. (According to informants who knew him, his groups never performed in public.) Clearly a transitional group, Orquesta Acuña at first evinced many of the features of the earlier string orquestas, while in later recordings it pointed toward the reed-and-brass orquesta as it emerged during the years surrounding World War II.[13] Acuña was an accomplished musician who for several years was one of the leaders in the field of Mexican music in Los Angeles. Besides the numerous recordings his orchestra produced with the big labels (and later with local ones), Acuña's versatile group, sometimes featured as a "mariachi," other times as an "orquesta," provided the musical accompaniment for many a singer, while Acuña himself wrote the arrangements.

Acuña's orquesta varied in instrumentation—becoming more modernized as time passed—but in the 1930s a typical recording might consist of two violins, two clarinets, trumpet, piano, guitar, and string bass (Spottswood 1990: 1614). This was the composition, for example, of the ensemble he used to record twelve selections for Decca on April 4, 1938, in Los Angeles (ibid.). According to the legendary singer/composer Lalo Guerrero, who knew Acuña well, this violinist/arranger/composer, originally from the state of Sonora, Mexico, was a talented but "behind-the-scenes" man who contributed greatly to the development of Mexican music in Los Angeles (Guerrero, personal interview, Sept. 9, 1989).

Almost all of the music the big labels recorded in California (as well as Texas, the other center for recording activity) fits within the category popularly known as *música ranchera*—a rough equivalent to what in the United States is known as "country." Like American country music, *música ranchera* was originally a rural, folk, proletarian music (Peña 1985a; cf. Patterson 1975). Known originally as *música típica mexicana*, the label glossed both the popular folk songs, or *canciones típicas mexicanas* (most from the nineteenth century), and the "typical" ensembles used in their performance, among which should be included the folk mariachi from Michoacán and other west-central Mexican states (Jáuregui 1990). Beginning in the 1920s and '30s, and impelled by the cultural nationalism surging in Mexico after the Revolution, the mariachi and the *canción* were appropriated by the commercial market, which eventually stripped both of much of their folk identity, as rustic instruments and improvised melodies gave way to slick arrangements, prescribed instrumentation, and the typical *charro* attire of mariachi musicians.

Commercialization notwithstanding, *música ranchera* continued to maintain its association with the working class, since its mass-production was intended primarily for the consumption of that class, both in Mexico and the United States. In the United States, *música ranchera*, in its various manifestations from the mariachi to norteño to the *canciones* and dances typically associated with these ensembles, continued at least until the 1960s to be primarily a working-class expression. Even early

commercial orquestas, such as Manuel S. Acuña's, evinced a strong ranchero, working-class character. Later, the modern orquesta was to find
itself in a cultural dilemma as it struggled to reconcile the ranchero origins of its adherents with their aspirations toward more cosmopolitan
and middle-class forms of culture (see Chapters 4 and 5).

In Texas, meanwhile, the major labels made their first foray into *tejano*
music in 1926 (Spottswood 1990). As in California, the recording companies concentrated their attention on vocal music, and the corrido and
canción were the principal genres recorded. However, string orquestas
were quite prevalent among Texas-Mexicans, including the *típica* variety, and both types of orquesta found their way onto the vinyl disc (see
Arhoolie Records, no. 9007). The first two orquestas launched by the
major labels in Texas were both recorded in March of 1928; one was La
Orquesta Mexicana Francisco Maure, from El Paso, the other was La Orquesta Calvillo, from San Antonio. Many others followed, the total number actually exceeding that in California. And, as in California, much of
the vocal and instrumental music recorded by the major labels in Texas
was ranchera in character; however, a few more genteel orchestras were
featured—for example, La Orquesta Fronteriza from El Paso, a much
more refined group than most others then in the commercial market.
The presence of orquestas like the Fronteriza in the major-label listings
is an indicator of the greater social differentiation of Texas-Mexican society than that found among California Mexicans, a suggestion that is
supported by the data presented in Chapter 1.

SUMMARY AND CONCLUSION

The commercial success of Mexican American music of the 1920s and
'30s suggests several lines of interpretation. First, it is evident that by the
twenties a large pool of musical talent was available among the Mexicans
of the Southwest, a pool the major labels were able to exploit to great advantage. Second, the recordings from the period suggest a certain continuity of musical culture from the nineteenth to the twentieth century,
even in California, where most of the performers were recent Mexican
immigrants. That is, the vast majority of genres and ensembles recorded
were universal to all Mexicans and had their origins in the nineteenth
century or earlier, in some cases. Thus the *canción* and corrido, salon music, the guitar (as accompaniment), and the prototypical string orchestras—all of these had their origins in the nineteenth century. Finally,

commercialization strengthened the cultural position of such forms as the conjunto and the vocal duet.

Cultural continuities notwithstanding, new developments presaging the dramatic changes following World War II were in evidence by the 1920s, for example, the emergence of the *canción-corrido* hybrid. Such developments accompanied changes overtaking the Mexican and Mexican American communities throughout the Southwest by the twenties and thirties, especially with respect to their relationship with the dominant Anglo majority. Instructive in this respect is the classical corrido, which was itself undergoing a transformation during this period, in particular the corrido of intercultural conflict. Reaching a heightened level of consciousness vis-à-vis interethnic conflict in the late nineteenth and early twentieth century, the corrido experienced subtle changes in the twenties and thirties as a different political consciousness emerged in such corridos as "El deportado," "La muerte de Juan Reyna," and others.

A thorough analysis of the changes that overtook the corrido is impractical here (see Flores 1992; Peña 1982, 1993), but they have to do with a shift in emphasis. The earlier corridos featured a lone, larger-than-life Mexican hero who, pistol in hand, stood up for his rights (and, symbolically, for those of the oppressed Mexican community) against an army of cowardly, smaller-than-life Anglos (usually rangers or other lawmen) who persecuted him not because he had broken the law, but because he was a brave Mexican (e.g., "Gregorio Cortez," "Jacinto Treviño," "Joaquín Murrieta"). The new corridos, by contrast, portrayed everyday people who were caught up in an unjust economic system run for the benefit of Anglo oppressors. They were victims, rather than larger-than-life heroes, whose plight propelled an aroused Mexican American community into action against the dominant Anglos (Peña 1982).

In the field of instrumental music, the late twenties and thirties witnessed subtle changes in the composition of the ensembles that preceded the modern orquesta. Some of these changes may have been in evidence as early as the turn of the century, but in the thirties, especially, stylistic differences and new instrumental combinations definitely pointed toward the dawning of a new musical age when the modern orquesta would burst upon the scene and establish its own dominance over all other previous ensembles. Manuel S. Acuña's orquesta offers the best recorded evidence for the transformations of the orquesta taking place in California in the 1930s, while in Texas full-fledged, modern orquestas were in evidence as early as 1930 (see Chapter 3).

In summarizing the dramatic developments unfolding within the musical traditions of the Southwest in the 1920s and early '30s, we have noted, first, the impact of immigration, which replenished a Mexican culture under pressure from Anglos in all areas, especially in California. More so than in other regions of the Southwest, the tidal wave of immigrants reinvigorated local musical activity in the Golden State as transplanted traditions like the embryonic mariachi began to flourish in the new environment. The *canción-corrido,* as well as the corrido itself, blossomed and left an indelible record of the hardships faced by Mexican immigrants, even as it underscored the ethnic chasm that separated the Anglos and their capitalist culture on one side from the Mexicans and their pastoral culture on the other. Not surprisingly, these two genres served as the catalysts for the duet tradition of singing that was to become dominant in the Hispanic Southwest.

The other important center of commercial music, Texas, experienced a parallel development. There, too, the corrido, the *canción-corrido,* the *canción* itself, and the duet tradition thrived during the twenties and thirties, thanks to the recording industry. In fact, as a recorded genre the corrido is originally linked most closely with Texas, perhaps because its strongest development took place in the Lone Star State. As Amèrico Paredes has noted, a distinct possibility exists that the modern corrido originated along the Texas-Mexico border—a plausible hypothesis, since the Texas-Mexico border was a hotbed of ethnic conflict in the latter part of the nineteenth and early twentieth century (Paredes 1958). The corrido was simply one of several folk forms marshaled in the war of words that fired the conflict, and, quite logically, its popularity made it a prime target for commercial recording.

One notable distinction between the California and Texas experience was the conjunto, which was forged exclusively by *tejanos* and norteños and did not exert an impact in California until the 1960s. Like the Texas-Mexican corrido, the conjunto, though still in embryonic form in the 1920s, was extremely popular with *tejanos,* and it, too, was targeted early on for commercialization (in the person of accordionist Bruno Villarreal, who recorded the first conjunto tunes in 1928, in San Antonio). Both the Texas-Mexican corrido and the conjunto stand out historically for their strong ideological association with working-class people, an association strengthened, not diminished, by commercialization. But their specificity to the Texas-Mexican experience speaks forcefully to the intensity of the interethnic conflict between Anglos and Mexicans in the Lone Star State. In the dialectic that governs Anglo-Mexican relations throughout the Southwest, Texas functions as ground zero—the flash point of interethnic impact—and the corrido and conjunto found their function as absolute antitheses within the dialectic, twin expressions that drew sharp contrasts between their exponents: working-class Mexicans and their adversaries, the Anglos.

The Mexican American orquesta, meanwhile, began to change dramatically during the 1930s, with the modern ensemble, patterned after the dance orchestras popular in the United States at the time, making its first appearance. Interestingly, with one or two notable exceptions, the major labels apparently never tapped the potential of this vibrant new musical form—a puzzling omission, since the modern orquesta made a cultural impact from its first appearance. Clearly, the new orquestas were proliferating by the late 1930s, but neither RCA Victor nor any of the other major companies seems to have been paying attention to this new phenomenon, a musical style that began immediately to redefine for the Mexican American Generation its position in American life. As such, the orquesta was to emerge within the next decade as the major source of cultural synthesis for Mexican Americans in the evolving dialectic of conflict that marks Anglo-Mexican relations in the Southwest. In the process, the new orquestas were also to articulate an element hitherto dormant in Mexican American life—intraethnic class difference.

PART TWO

The Mexican American Era

Orquesta's
Social Base
The Mexican
American Generation

The emergence and development of the modern orquesta cannot be fully appreciated without taking into account the social context in which it flourished. Just as its rival style in the Southwest, the conjunto (Peña 1985a), is the product of a working-class aesthetic, the orquesta is at its core the expression of a middle-class aesthetic. Moreover, this aesthetic has its origins in the 1920s, when that historical bloc known as the Mexican American Generation made its first, albeit tentative, impact. And, as we shall see, the orquesta mirrored in a highly symbolic manner the conflicting cultural and political currents that shaped the social life of this the first significant group of Mexican Americans to stake its fortune on an American future. Since the early course of the orquesta is so intertwined with the fortunes of the Mexican American Generation, at least the salient developments of the generation's social life during the years of its ascendance, from 1930 to 1960, need to be profiled.

We have American ways

and think like Americans.

A LULACer, CIRCA 1929

THE RISE OF THE MEXICAN AMERICAN GENERATION

Anyone interested in historical aspects of the social life of Mexican Americans owes a debt to Paul Schuster Taylor, the economist who studied the Mexicans of Nueces County, Texas, in the late 1920s and early 1930s ([1934] 1971). Taylor was the first scholarly researcher to glimpse the problems encountered by the Mexican American Generation in its efforts to negotiate the difficult transition from a Mexican to an American identity. He not only documented the various domains of Mexican social

life—residential patterns, education, employment, and class forma-
tions—but he also provided us with landmark documentation of Anglo-
Mexican relations in that county. Although he made no claims on the
general application of his descriptions to other areas of the Southwest,
numerous later studies (e.g., Barrera 1979; Foley 1988a; M. García 1989;
Sheridan 1986; Simmons [1952] 1974; Zeleny 1944) have confirmed that
the clash of cultures Taylor described in Nueces County was but a mi-
crocosm of the larger drama unfolding on the stage of the dialectic of
conflict that choreographs ethnic relations throughout the American
Southwest. To his lasting credit, Taylor was the first to capture in a detailed and evenhanded manner one scene of that epic drama.

In Nueces County, Taylor's script unveils the churning waves of ethnic conflict as they rippled through the Mexican American community
itself, creating eddies in the form of a new phenomenon—intraethnic
class cleavage that swirls out of and is both mitigated and reinforced by
the ethnic conflict itself. In other words, what had been a two-sided rift—
Anglo versus Mexican—began in the twenties and thirties a complicated
process that would result in a three-sided struggle: Anglos pitted against
Mexicans generally, and upwardly mobile Mexican Americans increasingly distanced from the mass of proletarianized workers, both unaccul-
turated Mexican Americans and recent immigrants (R. García 1991: 42–
43, 88). Taylor's upwardly mobile informants recognized their changing
sense of cultural citizenship and the widening difference between them
and other, less-acculturated Mexicans. However, they were also acutely
aware of Anglo prejudice against them, which they sought to overcome
by demonstrating their loyalty to America and competence in its civic
practices. The following statement illustrates their impatience with the
less-acculturative Mexicans, just as it betrays their increasing faith in
Americanization:

We tell our people, "If you have not been treated like you should, or have
not the standard of living, it is your own fault. Before asking for your rights
under the constitution you must be prepared. It may be too late for you of
the present generation, but see that the same thing doesn't happen to your
children." (Taylor [1934] 1971: 247)

Despite their endorsement of an acculturative agenda for Mexicans,
the Mexican Americans were painfully aware of the historical conflict
between Mexicans and Anglos, just as they were resentful of the latter's
continuing resistance to the integration of Mexican Americans into the
Anglo mainstream of American life. The thorny dilemma they faced on

the question of their place in American society was summarized by one
of the professionals Taylor interviewed. "There were a number of men
who had served in the war," he said. "Then when they came home, they
found that they were not served drinks [at some fountains], and were told
that 'no Mexicans were allowed.' They raised the question then," concluded Taylor's informant bitterly, "'What are we, Mexicans or Americans?'" (Taylor [1934] 1971: 245).

That question, "What are we, Mexicans or Americans?" poignantly
expresses the dilemma facing Taylor's informants, but it also goes to the
root of the historical relationship between Anglos and Mexicans in the
Southwest. As presented in the Prelude, this relationship is never static.
It is continually evolving, reconstituting itself according to the principles
of the dialectic of conflict, in which the opposing forces interact dynamically to propel themselves onto new and more complex levels of development. Of course, in this relationship the Anglos represent the dominant member. In the classic Marxian-Hegelian equation, they are the
antithesis to their opposites, the Mexicans. They represent the "positive"
side of the class/ethnic equation, "compelled to maintain [themselves],
and thereby their opposite [the proletarianized Mexicans], in existence"
(Marx and Engels 1956: 51). As Marx and Engels would say of the bourgeoisie and private property, the Anglos are the "self-satisfied," "conservative side of the contradiction" (ibid.). The subordinate Mexicans, on
the other hand, are the "restless," "destructive" side; they are compelled
to "abolish" their existence as alienated laborers, and if they cannot
"abolish" their oppressors in the process, they aim at least to gain a more
equitable balance of power.

As the "conservative side" in the ethnic-class relationship, the Anglos
of Nueces County were representative of the dominant society in the
Southwest. They wished to maintain the status quo imposed following
victory in the Mexican-American War, which installed the Anglos as the
ruling class, the Mexicans as subordinate. Thus, as Taylor cogently put
it, "In Nueces County the past lives vividly in the present. [Anglo] American residents both old and new cherish its dominant Texan tradition, and
all become steeped in its lore to an extent which it is difficult for outsiders
to realize" ([1934] 1971: xii). On the other hand, as the restless element in
the unequal relationship, the Mexicans are understandably the initiators
of change, which, again, is propelled by movement at the systemic, or infrastructural, level of capitalism itself. Taylor was sensitive to the shifting currents at this systemic level, correctly attributing ethnic conflict to
"changing economic and political backgrounds [against which] the attitudes toward each other were generated and expressed" (ibid.: xi).

As an economist, Taylor was particularly interested in linking economic with social development, and he provides critical details on the transformation of the Nueces County economy from ranching/pastoral to capitalist during the 1880s. In many ways, however, the Mexicans continued life as before, although Taylor's description of wage labor leaves no doubt that in sheer physical output, Mexicans in the American capitalist system worked much harder than did their peon ancestors in the pastoral economy. But, especially for the immigrants arriving from Mexico, there was no other choice. As Douglas Foley wrote of Mexicans migrating in the early twentieth century to the nearby city of Pearsall, "Most of the immigrants emphasized the poverty and turmoil in Mexico and their hope that America would offer more opportunity" (1988a: 5).

Still, as Foley makes clear, despite their dreams and hopes the Mexicans found only hard labor and discrimination, and they adapted to the new order under the most arduous of conditions. However, at least in the early days of Pearsall (and Nueces County), a tolerable *patrón-peón* relationship developed between Anglo employers and Mexican laborers, one not far removed from the type of relationship present in the subsistence economy of the old Hispanic Southwest. Thus, in both Nueces County and Pearsall (as well as in other areas, e.g., New Mexico [N. González 1969]), a transitional period bridged the old economic system based on subsistence and the modern one based on capital and wage labor. The formal and impersonal relations between employer and wage earner, typical of the latter system, did not take full effect until the 1920s—at least in agriculture, where most Mexicans found employment after the 1880s.

Although oppressive enough to promote occasional revolts among the subordinate Mexicans, the early economic relations of *patrón-peón* between Anglo and Mexican were tolerable enough to sustain a semblance of interethnic tranquillity—as long as the Mexicans did not challenge their subordinate status (Foley 1988a: 13ff.). However, as Taylor demonstrates in the case of the Anglos and Mexicans of Nueces County (cf. R. García 1991; Sheridan 1986), by 1930 the political and economic conditions attached to the Mexicans' existence had changed enough to compel them to challenge the oppressiveness of a system that denied them access to so much of the good life in American society. The most important development was the emergence of a Mexican American middle class, as the economy of the Southwest had diversified enough by this time to bring forth a group of merchants, professionals, and white-collar workers who evinced a new middle-class mentality (Taylor [1934] 1971: Chaps. 22, 27), especially in the urban areas. This middle class was principally responsible for spearheading the drive to bring about equality in the relations between Anglo and Mexican.

In our terms, the dialectic of conflict had evolved sufficiently by the late 1920s to enable the Mexicans to mount the first real challenges to Anglo dominance and the grossly unbalanced ethnic relationship prevailing since the mid-nineteenth century. It is therefore not a coincidence that the first effective civic and political organizations were formed among the Mexican Americans at this time—the Order of the Sons of America (1921) and the League of United Latin American Citizens (1929).[1] Nor is it a coincidence that these organizations were created and sustained by the small but influential cadre of upwardly aspiring individuals who made their presence felt in the 1920s. These were the founders of the Mexican American Generation.

More so than their proletarian peers, the upwardly mobile Mexican Americans experienced the psychological pain inherent in the social contradiction—dominant Anglo/subordinate Mexican—that had for so long defined the interethnic equation. For these Mexican Americans, the contradiction was doubly difficult to endure, since their middle-class status logically impelled them toward interethnic cooperation with their middle-class Anglo counterparts (Simmons [1952] 1974: 375). The doubly contradictory position of the upwardly mobile Mexican Americans— generally rejected by the Anglos but increasingly alienated from their working-class peers—was strongly evident in Nueces County, as it was in San Antonio (R. García 1991) and other areas (cf. Howard 1952 and Simmons [1952] 1974 on the Rio Grande Valley; Sheridan 1986 on Tucson; Zeleny 1944 on New Mexico). Although tiny cracks were beginning to appear in the castelike ethnic barrier, most Anglos insisted on maintaining the separation of the two groups. As Taylor saw it, "a variety of social distinctions which penetrate even the realm of business make publicly manifest the desire of Americans to avoid social contacts with Mexicans" ([1934] 1971: 250). The Anglos' discrimination "pained Mexicans of all classes" (ibid.: 262), but the upwardly mobile were especially vulnerable.

Taylor's historic findings were confirmed in subsequent studies by Américo Paredes (1966, 1968) and others (Jordan 1981; Madsen 1964; Rubel 1966; Simmons [1952] 1974). These more recent studies have demonstrated that the basic question asked by Taylor's informants, "What are we, Mexicans or Americans?" has never been adequately resolved. In fact, the Mexican Americans since the generation have had to walk a narrow path between the assimilation of American culture on the one hand and the retention of a Mexican one on the other. Responding to the logic of their circumstances, the Mexican Americans have adopted an ideology of biculturalism—an ideology perfectly embodied in the LULAC code discussed in the Exposition (and below). This ideology aims to bridge the chasm between the Mexican Americans' folk, ethnic heritage based on a subsistence economy and the demands capitalism and its "Anglo-conformity" ideology (McLemore 1980) make of all marginal groups (ethnic minorities in particular) in exchange for admission into the dominant social order.

Historically, those Mexican Americans who have attained middle-class (or, at least, "middling") status, or who share the aspirations of that status, are the ones who most acutely experience the disparity between Anglo and Mexican cultures. In his post–World War II study of Anglo-Mexican relations in San Antonio and McAllen, Texas, Ozzie Simmons ([1952] 1974) recognized that the working class was much more insulated, spatially and ideologically, from the tensions and contradictions resulting from direct contact with and a desire to assimilate mainstream (middle-class) Anglo-American culture. This was especially true of the 1940s and '50s, when the Anglos were most emphatically not ready for wholesale admission of Mexican Americans into their social order (Simmons [1952] 1974: 367ff., 524ff.). The middle class, meanwhile, finds itself in an awkward situation historically—strongly drawn to the material goods and cultural magnet of mainstream Anglo America but (until recently) constrained by the "semi-caste" status imposed upon it by the Anglo majority (Simmons [1952] 1974: 468–469). The middle-class Mexican American's dilemma was perceptively summarized by Simmons:

[T]he desire to mitigate his subordinate status may be thought of as motivating the middle-class Mexican [American] in two directions, somewhat opposed to each other. One of these is toward the development of *interclass* solidarity across the semi-caste line, the other toward the development of *intragroup* solidarity across Mexican class lines. These opposing goals are a direct reflection of the ambivalence involved in the Anglo principle regarding all Mexicans as composing an undifferentiated group but at the same time recognizing differences in practice. (Ibid.: 373)

Meanwhile, in his research on ethnic relations in the Rio Grande Valley in the late 1940s, Raymond Howard (like Simmons) found that until World War II, a rigid castelike system denied Mexicans equal opportunity in the political economy of the Valley (1952). Middle-class Mexican Americans were highly resentful of this unequal arrangement, although the situation had reportedly improved since the end of the Second World

War. The Mexican Americans' resentment is poignantly illustrated in the remarks of a successful merchant:

You Anglo-American people reject us Spanish [Mexican Americans], but you take in the Japanese and Jews, and everybody else. Aren't we just as good? Back in 1943, one of my sons and my three daughters went to the local pool. When they were ready to pay, they were told NO MEXICANS ALLOWED. Say, that burned me, because at that very time two of my older sons were fighting the Japs and there in the pool were three local Japanese kids; yet my kids could not go in the pool. . . . If you ask me, I say it's an Anglo vs. Latin set-up. (Howard 1952: 94)

The merchant's accusations were reinforced by an Anglo teacher, who presented the Anglo perspective in blunt terms. However, as became increasingly typical of Anglos in the post–World War II era, the teacher put the interethnic hostility safely in the past, claiming (not entirely incorrectly) a more tolerant climate in the present (1949):

We teachers accepted the Mexican students back in the twenties just like you would arsenic. I must admit I actually failed some of them just because they were Mexicans. I hated to have them in any of my classes. . . . However, there certainly has been a change in conditions, particularly since 1945–46. Our students, Anglo and Latin, work side by side. . . . The few Anglo students who resent Latin students do so because they are influenced by the resentment of their parents. (Howard 1952: 103)

The teacher's assessment of interethnic relations was far too optimistic for the 1940s (see Allsup 1982; Barrera 1979; San Miguel 1987), but there can be no doubt relations between Anglos and Mexicans were undergoing substantial—if not as yet visible—change at the very moment that researchers like Howard, Simmons, and others (e.g., Rubel 1966) were in the field. Nevertheless, at this early stage the fruits of change were yet to be harvested, and the Mexican American Generation was destined to lead a life of bitter contradiction—a contradiction whose magnitude no other generation of Mexican Americans has had to endure. Faced with continuing conflict with the Anglos and increasing alienation from their working-class peers, the Mexican American Generation struggled doggedly to maintain its sense of purpose and direction. It did this by adopting the only logical alternative available to its contradiction-filled existence—a strongly bicultural identity.

The development of a bicultural orientation was powerfully molded by the dynamics of the dual struggle the Mexican American middle class faced. Indeed, in the case of the Mexican Americans, biculturalism is a function of that struggle—and ultimately of the dialectic underpinning ethnic relations in the Southwest. The external conflict with the Anglos was the primary driving force; it loomed over the internal struggle between middle and working classes, acting as a powerful deflector. That is, Anglo rejection constantly pulled the middle class back into the Mexican fold, both culturally and spatially. Reminded repeatedly of the need for intraethnic solidarity, the middle class's alienation from its working-class peers was tempered by the Anglos' rejection, and this in turn reinforced the ethnic bonds uniting all Mexicans against a common adversary. Intraethnic class disparity was thus expressed in the form of different lifestyles rather than outright antagonism, although this did not preclude the emergence of friction, expressed in the form of in-group epithets (discussed below).

For the upwardly mobile, a relatively comfortable, increasingly Americanized lifestyle—one quite different from that of the common workers—was facilitated by such obvious markers as employment and education. The anthropologist Arthur Rubel accurately summarized the situation in one city, Weslaco, Texas, in the 1950s: "Those who move south of the tracks [the more affluent part of town] and others who seriously contemplate the action share significant objective indicators of [middle-] class status" (1966: 18). In sum, these upwardly mobile Mexican Americans had typically attained higher levels of education, including college in some cases, and they were consequently "employed in 'clean' occupations, and boast[ed] dependable incomes" (ibid.). Along with dependable incomes came "substantial" homes with "well-padded furniture," as well as status markers such as "relatively new automobiles, indoor plumbing, refrigerators, television sets, and barbecue 'pits'" (ibid.: 12, 19). These modern conveniences (commodities, to be exact, but with strong use-value) and the lifestyle attached to them functioned as markers that culturally distinguished the middle class and its daily practical choices from the working class and its everyday lifestyle.

By the 1950s, the status-conscious Mexican American Generation's increased use of English (mostly in a bilingual combination with Spanish; see below), its adoption of the orquesta as its musical signature, and its general air of middle-class propriety and social grace (roce social) had enabled its members to place themselves at a considerable remove from the cultural practices of the working class. Along with a middle-class lifestyle came disapproval of working-class practices, such as drinking in cantinas and other allegedly profligate behavior, including "low-class" dancing and music of the type associated with the accordion conjuntos (Foley 1988a; Peña 1985a). Again, however, it would be erroneous to equate disapproval with outright rejection or some kind of "class warfare." Rather, possessed with a sense of mission (and caught in its class-ethnic contradiction), the middle class seemed to cultivate an attitude of impatience mixed with sympathy (and some patronization), as evidenced by the comments of a prominent San Antonio businessman: "There's a big job to be done to teach the [working-class] people how to behave," he lamented, "not only education, but—I don't know how to say it—but moral education, you know, better habits" (Simmons [1952] 1974: 383).

Ultimately, however, as the businessman quoted above makes quite clear, the middle class saw the common people, especially immigrants, as an impediment to the progress of the Mexican American in an Anglo-dominated society. The historian Richard García correctly identified the inevitable schism embodied in this view of the working-class-as-obstacle:

A middle-class gestalt formed, as people adopted an attitude of *gente de razón* or *gente decente* as opposed to the *gente corriente* (the high society of reason, manners and culture versus the mass society of emotions, ill manners and no culture). . . . The [middle] class was attempting to remove itself from the cultural world of the cantinas . . . and to distance itself from the neighboring world of the pecan shellers and the agricultural workers. (1991: 88)

In a similar vein, Thomas Sheridan described the reality of class cleavage in Tucson, and the obstacle this cleavage presented at times for Mexican Americans who wished to forge a unified community in the face of Anglo discrimination:

The generally conservative political ideology of these prominent individuals prevented them from becoming the leaders of any broad-based coalition of Mexicans in southern Arizona. Despite their political activism and their protests against discrimination, these business and professional men were unable to forge any lasting ties with miners, migrant workers, or other members of the Mexican working class. Bound by their own class interests, they ultimately remained committed to the same economic principles as their Anglo counterparts. (1986: 93)

Finally, sociologist Ozzie Simmons saw very clearly the thorny dilemma facing the middle class. He perceptively analyzed the "gulf" separating the middle class from the common workers, but he also understood the complications introduced by the conflictive relationship between Anglos and Mexicans:

The huddling of all Mexican Americans into the narrow confines of subordinate status and the Anglo American assumption of the homogeneity of the Mexican group has impelled middle-class Mexicans to distinguish themselves as much as possible from the lower class in order to demonstrate the Anglo error in identifying them with the latter group. ([1952] 1974: 356–357)

The central problem thus persisted for middle-class Mexican Americans: how to juggle their cultural citizenship so as to insulate themselves from Anglo discrimination, which they at times felt was due to a confusion on the part of the latter. Some of them, at least (see the statement of the middle-class professional below), seemed to have convinced themselves that if the Anglos could only recognize the difference between them as *gente de razón* and the common workers as *gente corriente,* then they might be more willing to accord the *gente de razón* better treatment, if not acceptance into the dominant group's social circles. In this they were not altogether mistaken, as a few voices were even then being raised in the Anglo community on the need to accept "high-type" Mexicans. As one Anglo told Taylor, "If a Mexican dresses well and is clean and wealthy, he gets by; but the old greasers, no way" ([1934] 1971: 251). Nonetheless, although comments like this represented a critical shift in the evolving dialectic of conflict, from the thirties to the sixties they were the views of only a small (though growing) Anglo minority, and middle-class Mexican Americans were forced to seek other avenues (in lieu of cooperation across the ethnic boundary) to mediate the stubborn conflict and its consequences.

Thus, as one member of the League of United Latin American Citizens (LULAC) put it, in reference to the contradictions inherent in the middle-class status of the acculturative Mexican American, "We have American ways and think like Americans. [But] we have not been able to convince some [American] people that there is a difference between us [and the old Mexicans]" (Taylor [1934] 1971: 245; brackets in the original). Or, as a prominent businessman explained to Simmons twenty years later, "I think a great deal could be accomplished right now if Anglos could only learn to distinguish between the deserving [Mexican American] and the undeserving" ([1952] 1974: 368). As the evidence indicates, this view of the middle class—the *gente de razón*—as "deserving" and the working class as obstacle was forthrightly expressed on a number of occasions by affluent Mexican Americans. One final comment from a frustrated middle-class professional may help stress their point:

> To the Anglos, a Mexican is a Mexican, regardless of how different he may be from the mass. . . . If we could find some way to prevent any more Mexicans from coming here, in twenty-five years you wouldn't be able to tell the difference between a Mexican and an American except by the name García or López, which wouldn't mean anything anymore because the Mexicans would be American in everything else. But the person who does strive to improve himself gets lost in the shuffle, since there are so many who are ignorant and primitive because of where they come from. (Simmons [1952] 1974: 381)

Of course, not all members of the Mexican American Generation felt as alienated from the working class as the individuals quoted above. Many, especially those involved with organizations such as LULAC, were possessed of a sense of mission that conceived of the Mexican community as an organic whole. But a distinct difference in ideology emerges from the historical record. Moreover, the middle class's presumptuous view of its privileged position vis-à-vis the working class did not go unchallenged. Indeed, the counterchallenge offered by the working class stands as a significant factor contributing to the rift between classes, as described by Simmons ([1952] 1974) and others. For in asserting its right to practice its own Mexicanized culture, the working class signaled its readiness not only to resist "Anglo conformity" and its assimilative pressures (McLemore 1980) but also to put the middle class in the uncomfortable position of defending a pointless course of action, given the Anglo's resistance to interethnic assimilation. By way of underscoring their disapproval of the middle class's approach, working-class people derided the *agringado* (Anglicized) practices of those they called *jaitones* (from "hightoned")—people who were seen as sellouts and dupes of empty Anglo ideals like "equality before the law."

This clash of goals between the middle and working classes generated considerable strain, resulting in cultural epithets that trenchantly captured the divergent ideologies motivating the two. From the former came such verbal arrows as *gente corriente* (common or vulgar people), *animal de uña* ("clawed" beasts, i.e., uncivilized savages), and *el peladaje* (the scum, mostly in reference to proletarian men). The latter returned the fire in the form of their own caustic epithets, such as *gringos fundillos prietos* (dark-assed gringos), *gente jaitona* (hightoned people), and *ay, sociégate* (a play on words between "high society" and "settle down").

The net effect of this verbal crossfire was to underscore the reality of class difference and, more important, to muddy the waters of interethnic conflict and its dialectical course.

CONFLICT AND MEDIATION:
LULAC as a Middle-Class Response

This, then, was the contradictory bind in which the Mexican American Generation was trapped: They desired to achieve parity with and perhaps become acceptable to a prejudiced Anglo society but were rejected by the latter; they tried to distance themselves from the affairs of their less fortunate proletarian peers but were compelled to defend their common ethnic interests. Nowhere are the contradictions inherent in the Mexican Americans' position more compellingly projected than in the League of United Latin American Citizens—the cornerstone to their political and cultural strategies. As powerfully evidenced by the LULAC code, the new Mexican Americans ardently wished to be recognized as true American citizens, a wish the first aim of LULAC clearly articulated: to "develop within the members of our race the best, purest and most perfect type of a true and loyal citizen of the United States of America." Yet, painfully aware of their stigmatized Mexican heritage and, especially, their rejection by the Anglos, the LULACers staunchly defended their right to practice a dual culture: "We solemnly declare once and for all to maintain a sincere and respectful reverence for our racial origin of which we are proud."

Caught on the horns of a class-ethnic dilemma, the members of the Mexican American Generation practiced a cultural balancing act: they continued to strive for Anglo acceptance by embracing the Americanization of Mexicans, but they were not willing, for the most part, to completely forsake their cultural heritage. That is why in the city of Tucson, despite their tacit approval of cultural assimilation, the Mexican elites "tempered their enthusiasm for capitalism [and its assimilative tendencies] with a deep reverence for an idealized vision of Mexican society and culture" (Sheridan 1986: 93). Or, as Simmons put it, "There are few middle-class Mexicans who do not express pride in their Mexican origins regardless of how preoccupied they may be with acculturation and assimilation to Anglo ways" ([1952] 1974: 401). In the face of interethnic conflict, the need for intraethnic solidarity transcended the reality of class cleavage.

The desire for solidarity—defined, of course, in terms of the Mexican

American Generation's integrationist strategies—and the prospect for an effective challenge to Anglo hegemony were crystallized in LULAC. Between 1930 and 1960 no other civic organization matched LULAC's record in uniting Mexican Americans, promoting Americanization within a middle-class ideal, and pressuring Anglos for change. In this protean task that LULAC set for all Mexicans in the United States, it came to epitomize the hopes, ideals, and contradictions of the Mexican American Generation itself. Justifiably, this organization has emerged in recent scholarship as a key to understanding the "Mexican American mind" (M. García 1989; R. García 1983; Márquez 1993; Orozco 1992). As Mario García wrote, "Bridging the past, present, and future, LULAC proposed a synthesis of Mexican, Mexican American, and U.S. experiences and traditions" (1989: 30). However, a stronger synthesis of experience (in the dialectical sense) was some years down the road—a task accomplished not by the Mexican American but by the Chicano Generation (see Chapter 6). In the shorter term, LULAC's code of conduct poignantly captured the contradictions inherent in the double bind in which the middle class found itself: Mexicans by heritage and ascription, Americans by ideology and birth.

Consider two of LULAC's central objectives:

1. Respect your citizenship, conserve it; honor your country [the United States], maintain its traditions in the minds of your children, incorporate yourself in the culture and civilization;
2. Love the men of your race, take pride in your origins and keep it immaculate; respect your glorious past and help to vindicate your people.

These two contradictory themes—the Mexican American Generation's desire to integrate itself into American life and its steadfast defense of its Mexican heritage—resonate throughout the studies that document this period in Mexican American society and its difficult integration into the "host" Anglo culture (e.g., Foley 1988a, 1988b; M. García 1989; R. García 1991; Madsen 1964; Rubel 1966; Sheridan 1986; Simmons [1952] 1974; Taylor [1934] 1971). Handicapped by the Anglos' unrelenting racism but determined to emancipate themselves from the working-class roots of their Mexican heritage, members of the Mexican American Generation mounted an at-times-heroic effort to negotiate the arduous transition from a Mexican to an American cultural orientation, from a rural to an urban lifestyle, and from working- to middle-class status.

In the sociocultural odyssey the Mexican American Generation embarked upon, LULAC functioned as both compass and barometer. It charted for its members (and for Mexican Americans generally—it was that ambitiously conceived) the lofty course of full integration into American culture; yet highly sensitive to the pressure of interethnic conflict and the vulnerable position of the Mexicans, it reserved for its members the right to practice a dual cultural citizenship. Sifting through the documents that LULAC has amassed during more than sixty years of existence, particularly the convention programs and the monthly newsletters, one is struck by the LULACers' balancing act. In one breath, LULAC could invoke the inspiring example of "our" founding fathers, Washington and Jefferson, only to defend and extol in the next the virtues of Mexican culture and its heroes. Over and over LULAC preached Americanization and the values of middle-class ideology, yet over and over it defended biculturalism and (in later years) such politically charged issues as bilingual education.[2]

But most important for our purposes, in the archival record accumulated during LULAC's years of ascendancy, we can glean the essence of the middle-class ethos that motivated its activities.[3] The stylish convention programs—themselves icons for a middle-class sense of organization—afford us an excellent glimpse into the kinds of social activities considered important by these relatively affluent Mexican Americans. For example, glancing through the program for the 1930 annual convention, held in Alice, Texas, we find a piano solo, "Rapsodia mexicana," performed by Z. M. Beattie, and another by Natalia Longoria, "El torbellino," included as part of the afternoon's activities for May 4. As with all LULAC conventions, a Grand Ball was held at 8:00 on the final day of the convention. (Although the program does not explicitly announce it, we may be reasonably sure that an orquesta provided music for the ball.) The 1937 program included a salute to "Professor Bañuelos for his wonderful achievement"—teaching the "boys in the Baytown Juvenile Band." Rounding out the 1930s, a Grand Ball was held at the 1939 convention in San Antonio, featuring the "most famous orchestra in the Alamo city" at the time, that of Eduardo Martínez. (Martínez and his "International Orchestra" also played for a dance at the LULAC convention held in Corpus Christi in 1952.)

The same middle-class gloss evident in the tastefully packaged convention programs of the 1930s is carried over into the forties, fifties, and sixties. A concerted attempt to imbue the conventions with a sense of order and a professional, middle-class luster is clearly present in all of the LULAC convention activities. In their organization and choice of cultural performances, as well as the careful preparation of the programs, the conventions are unmistakably American, and they stand as testimonials to the Mexican American Generation's efforts to stamp its middle-class seal on these annual congregations, so central to their ideology of Americanization. To offer one more example, at the 1947 convention in Santa Fe, New Mexico, the program included a performance by an old-fashioned *típica*, the Pablo Mares Típica Orchestra (shown on the program cover dressed as *charros*). On June 13, a cocktail reception was held at the Governor's Mansion from 5:30 to 7:30, and a dance followed at the Palomino Club ("formal dress optional"), featuring Freddie Valdez and his Orchestra. A floor show was included, featuring "Lupe and Lily" dancing the *rumba* and *tango*. As a grand finale a banquet and dance were held on Friday, June 14, at La Fonda Hotel, with music provided by La Fonda Orchestra.

The newsletters evince the same middle-class, American orientation as the programs, although these were also an active forum for the clash of cultures. On the one hand, the newsletters enthusiastically endorsed any activity that promoted the integration of Mexican Americans into the cultural fiber of American life—whether it be educational, political, or civic. The civic club—a central institution in the American culture of volunteerism—was highly prized by LULAC, and in the early years especially, several articles appeared in the newsletter in praise of the civic-mindedness of Mexican American clubs, multiplying by then in cities such as San Antonio. In the latter city, an article in the November 1931 issue speaks proudly of the proliferation of civic clubs—Círculo Social Chapultepec, Ideal Club, Club Loma Linda, Tuesday Night Club, Modern Maids Club, Lucky Star Club, Kollegiate Koeds Klub (*sic*), and the Club Femenil Orquídeas. All of these were reportedly involved in civic affairs, and many at one time or another sponsored dances for their activities. For example, an article appears in a 1931 newsletter announcing a dance to be given by the Kollegiate Koeds Klub, with music provided by "one of the finest orchestras in San Antonio."

Yet, the LULAC newsletter also emphasized the *Mexican* in Mexican American. Indeed, many of the newsletters were printed bilingually, in both English and Spanish. A number of articles written by well-known intellectuals of the time—George I. Sánchez, Jovita González, Herschel T. Manuel, and others—appeared in the newsletter during the thirties and forties. These were didactic articles intended to provide knowledge about Mexican contributions to the development of the American Southwest or information about issues important to Mexican Americans. For example, Jovita González contributed an article, "Historical Background of the Lower Rio Grande Valley," in which she documented the contributions of the old Hispanic settlers to the development of the territory.

On a more contemporary and assimilationist note, the Hon. B. C. Hernández, an ex-congressman from New Mexico, wrote an article in 1934 entitled "Americanism and What It Means," lauding the advantages of Americanization for Mexicans in the United States.

In sum, just as the orquesta may be considered a cultural metaphor for the contradictions besetting the Mexican American Generation, LULAC functioned at the level of civic and political activity as a "summarizing" symbol (Turner 1974) for this middle-class bloc in its attempts to synthesize the divergent cultural and ideological impulses that tugged at the generation from different directions. The principal result of those attempts was the emergence of a pervasive biculturalism, one that transcended the Mexican American Generation and persisted in various forms into the 1990s.

CONFLICT, CONTRADICTION, AND MEDIATION:
Biculturalism and the Struggle toward Synthesis

In its most fundamental aspects, the philosophical approach of LULAC reflects an effort to come to grips with life on the border between two cultures in conflict. Like the middle-class Mexican Americans studied by Paredes, who expressed their cultural ambivalence through the intercultural jest, LULACers were both attracted to and repelled by American culture, just as they both defended and demeaned their working-class, Mexican roots. Faced with such a contradiction, not only LULACers but middle-class Mexican Americans throughout the Southwest opted for the only logical solution available to them—a biculturalism whose ultimate aim and result was a synthesis of the two cultures, American and Mexican. Tentative and emergent among the Mexican American Generation, this biculturalism reaches full-blown proportions during the era of the Chicano Generation, when cultural synthesis permeates everyday life. Biculturalism as a form of synthesis occurs at multiple layers of social life and manifests itself in such everyday communicative practices as verbal art, folk medicine, culinary arts (though these have not been adequately researched), and the most dynamic of all bicultural practices— bilingualism and bimusicality.

In the domain of verbal art, interesting results were forged, which are well documented in the studies of Rosan Jordan (1972, 1981), José Limón (1978), Américo Paredes (1966, 1968), and José Reyna (1980). Jordan, for example, discovers in bilingual joking a desire to control the contradictions attached to the bicultural predicament. For Jordan, "the problem of split cultural loyalties is a recurrent one" (1972: 83), and, as she proposes, "much Mexican-American folklore may be seen as a creative response to the problems and tensions engendered by [the Mexican Americans'] conflicting cultural loyalties" (1981: 253). Jordan cites several examples of bilingual joking to illustrate the tensions attending the transition from a Mexican to an American cultural orientation. As Reyna has demonstrated, many of these revolve around the cultural misunderstandings that inevitably visit the new immigrant, which are parodied in the absurd antics of characters such as the following, a recent immigrant who attempts to "interpret" for another, even more recent arrival:

A man came from Mexico, and a *compadre* of his came by. He had been here for about six months, and he already felt superior to the other, and he said, "*Compadre*, I want to buy a pig," he said. "Will you please interpret for me?"

He said, "Of course. Let's go see that *gringo* over there."

And he said, "Say, mister, You *vende la marranana* ["You sell the pig" (pronounced in Anglicized fashion)]?"

"I don't understand," he said.

"He says he doesn't sell it, *compadre*." [The *compadre* hears "I don't understand" as *no la vendo* ("I'm not selling it"), pronounced, again, in Anglicized fashion.] (1980: 41)

Both Jordan (1972, 1981) and Reyna (1980) agree that bilingual humor is an important component in the Mexican American's verbal-art practices and that it represents a creative attempt to synthesize disparate cultural experiences. For Jordan, bilingual speech play, in particular, represents an artistic effort by Mexican Americans to validate their dual cultural identity. In the novel juxtaposition of the two languages, English and Spanish, the Mexican Americans are striving symbolically for a reconciliation of two incongruent cultural modalities. The following "knock-knock" jokes are illustrative examples of this linguistic-symbolic reconciliation:

A: Knock, knock!
B: Who's there?
A: Elsa.
B: Elsa who?
A: *Elsapato [el zapato] me aprieta.* [The shoe pinches me.]

A: Knock, knock!
B: Who's there?
A: *Güera.* [Blondie.]
B: *Güera* who?
A: Güera [where are] you hiding the cookies? (Jordan 1981: 257)

Besides the simple delight that verbal manipulation of such bilingual combinations provides, folkloric expressions such as the above also capture the "tensions created by biculturalism—the 'clash,' the being caught between [two cultures in conflict]," which "increases the need for certain kinds of control" (ibid.: 258). In short, "the power to play with both languages suggests the power to control both cultures and hence to deal effectively with one's biculturalism" (ibid.: 260).

José Limón (1978) has analyzed the tensions within the Mexican American community resulting from the disparate levels of acculturation experienced by different segments of that community. Such tensions are carried over into what Limón labels *agringado* joking, a form of verbal art, often bilingual in nature, in which "culturally conservative Mexicans" and *agringados,* or Anglicized Mexican Americans, constitute two opposing forces. Oddly enough, in Limón's study only one instance is cited in which upward mobility and acculturation coincide and are pitted against lack of mobility and cultural resistance. The other examples of "differential identity" (Mexicanized vs. *agringado*) cited by Limón pit people from the same middle-class background against each other—one group, the "conservative Mexicans," using folklore to ridicule another, which is perceived as Anglicized.

Thus, we find enacted one folkloric scene in which Limón and a fellow student at the University of Texas are invited to the home of a student from a less-prestigious university in South Texas (Texas A&I, dominated by Mexican Americans), where they quickly become the butts of a joke that symbolically pits "real" Mexicans against *agringado* ones. The joke revolves around two animals—the *tacuache* (possum), symbolically associated with Mexicans, and the *zorillo* (skunk), which is associated with Anglos (and *agringados*). Perceived as having been hopelessly Anglicized through their association with the Anglo-dominated University of Texas at Austin, Limón and his fellow student must endure being symbolically linked to the *zorillo*'s ridiculously *agringado* behavior, while the *tacuache* saves the day for those who proudly defend their Mexican culture (Limón 1978: 42–44).

Like Jordan's study, Limón's ethnography provides an excellent glimpse into the tensions and contradictions ever present in the bicultural predicament of Mexican American society—especially the middle class, which is historically the most likely to succumb to the acculturative pressures of the dominant Anglo society. (Historically, and especially during the Mexican American era, the working class has been less susceptible—though not immune—to the allure of American culture.) Even as late as the 1970s, when the Chicano movement was making substantial strides in glossing over the fundamental socioeconomic differences within Mexican American society, Limón's study demonstrates that interethnic conflict was still a potent force in fomenting divisive ideological positions internal to the Mexican community in the Southwest. Indeed, if we take Jordan and Limón's studies as cues, even in the early seventies bicultural practices still constituted the symbolic battleground for the tripartite expression of conflict: the antagonism between Mexican and Anglo spilling over and giving form to in-group friction in the form of bilingual and *agringado* joking.

But perhaps the most penetrating of the folkloric studies that focus on the inter- and intraethnic triangle of conflict and contradiction is one published by Paredes in 1968 on the folklore of middle-class Mexican American men in south Texas. Paredes's collaborators, a group of professional and business leaders who were ideal representatives of the Mexican American Generation, cultivated a type of verbal art Paredes labeled "intercultural jests." Through these jests the men poked fun at Mexican folk practices while they simultaneously vented their resentment at American society for condemning so many of their ethnic peers to an oppressed status as second-class citizens. In their bilingual/bicultural thrust, the jests perfectly embodied the Mexican American Generation's contradiction-riddled existence. Paredes summarized the cultural function of this type of verbal art by stressing its ambivalence:

This is not, then, a relatively simple case of second-generation Americans ridiculing the culture of their ancestors and thereby rejecting it. . . . There is an underlying conflict between [the jest tellers'] Spanish-Mexican heritage and an Anglo-American culture they have embraced intellectually without completely accepting it emotionally, in great part because Anglo-American culture rejects part of themselves. (1968: 114)

As Paredes reiterates, the men who collaborated with him in his study of the intercultural jest were solid members of the middle class—people "who play important roles in community life, not in the life of a 'Mexican colony' but in that of the city and the county as a whole" (1968: 111). In other words, these men were in total command of the cultural equipment required to function in an American city; yet, as Paredes notes, "it is quite obvious that they place a high value on many aspects of Mexican culture and are proud of the duality of their background" (ibid.). But they lived "double lives," and no matter how competent they may have been in the affairs of an American community, their ethnic duality inevitably introduced tension and contradiction into their life, and it was this tension that was symbolically articulated in the folkloric performances observed by Paredes.

That contradiction, displayed in the form of the cultural ambivalence surrounding Mexican versus American medical practices, revolved around the *caso* (belief tale)—one of the few surviving folk genres that harkens back to an earlier period in the Hispanic culture of the Southwest. In its modern adaptation, in which Mexican folk medicine (*curanderismo*) triumphs over American medical science, it represents a quixotic attempt to reverse time and restore confidence in a vanished culture. But the belief in *curanderismo* is an anomalous survival from a simpler form of political economy; by the 1960s (the period of Paredes's fieldwork) it was an anachronistic cultural form kept alive by Mexican proletarians living at the margins of American (and Mexican) capitalism. Thus, until very recently these proletarians took the *caso* quite seriously, precisely because they were under duress from a social system that condemned them to poverty and alienation, and from a Mexican American middle class unsympathetic to practices such as *curanderismo* (folk healing), which it considered an index of an impossibly backward people. Paredes's jest tellers were perfectly aware of the anomalous presence of the magical premises of *curanderismo* in the rationalistic system of capitalism, and this awareness, coupled with their sympathy, is what lends their folklore its poignancy.

By parodying the *caso*, the jests told by Paredes's consultants confirmed their subscription to the rationalist and empiricist side of Western capitalist culture and their rejection of the magical elements so much a part of the folk culture the *caso* represents. Nonetheless, in the resentment expressed toward the cold and impersonal treatment of Mexicans by the American medical establishment, the intercultural jest also demonstrated the men's sympathy toward their impoverished ethnic peers. Or, as Paredes himself writes in summarizing the impact of the jests, "In the satirizing of folk medicine and *curandero* belief tales they express a mocking rejection of Mexican folk culture; in their expression of resentment toward American culture they show a strong sense of identification with their Mexican folk" (ibid.).

In summary, biculturalism among Mexican Americans is historically a function of their existence on the border between two cultures in conflict. Moreover, as a system of communication that simultaneously taps two distinct cultural experiences, it represents an attempt to synthesize those experiences. Finally, the rapid evolution of this biculturalism into a complex synthesis of various communicative codes speaks powerfully to the dialectic of conflict operating in the American Southwest, which itself witnessed an accelerated rate of progress in the second half of the twentieth century.

CONTRADICTION AND ITS SYNTHESIS:
Bilingualism, Coordinate and Compound

If biculturalism generally, and its verbal art in particular, serves as a mechanism by which the Mexican Americans mediate their contradictory status in a dominant Anglo society, then bilingualism itself, as the primary vehicle for all communication, artistic and prosaic, plays an even more basic role in defining mediative cultural strategies. Beginning with the Mexican American Generation, this bilingualism assumes a major role in the Mexican Americans' efforts to resolve the contradictions that plague their bicultural existence.

Bilingual communication probably dates as far back as the nineteenth century (its historical development has never been adequately traced [see Sánchez 1978]), but until the 1930s it evidently remained at an elementary level, with the Mexicans of the Southwest confining their use of English to those situations in which communication with Anglos was essential. Indeed, it is likely that even the native-born were Spanish monolinguals, and the few bilinguals were almost certainly Spanish-dominant, with only limited proficiency in the English language. In any case, to the extent they spoke two languages, Mexican Americans were probably what some linguists refer to as "coordinate bilinguals" (Erving and Osgood 1954; Lambert 1978). As such, they would maintain a more or less rigid distinction between the two linguistic codes, English and Spanish, seldom mixing them in normal conversation. Some "loan words," however, were in evidence as early as the 1920s, to judge from the *canciones-corridos* of the day (e.g., the calque *"traque* [track]" found in the corrido "El lavaplatos"; see Chapter 2).

Beginning in the 1930s, however, as LULAC's basic strategy demonstrates, Mexican Americans began in earnest their quest for integration into American life. Linguistic assimilation followed, and coordinate bilingualism quickly gave way to a new, more complex form. This new form came to be marked by the constant interchange between English and Spanish, as the dominant language began to spill over from the public, Anglo-dominated arena into the private, everyday affairs of the Mexican Americans. Linguistic interchange of this type is known among some linguists as "compound bilingualism," a unique method of communication in which two languages are mixed freely even within the same utterance (Erving and Osgood 1954; Lambert 1978). Among Mexican Americans, it is aptly known as "Spanglish," and it came into its own in the 1960s and '70s, before it gave way to the English-dominant, "vestigial" bilingualism (Sánchez 1978) that characterizes the speech of many Mexican Americans born after 1960—members of a new historical bloc I have labeled the "post-Chicano Generation" (see the Coda).[4] In any case, in its most developed form, compound bilingualism, or Spanglish, is more properly associated with the late stages of the Mexican American Generation and the entire period dominated by the Chicano Generation.

Since compound bilingualism has important implications for the study of orquesta (it is homologously related to the "compound bimusicality" associated with the latter), and since it has its origins in the Mexican American Generation, a brief discussion of its formal features is warranted at this point. I leave for later (Chapter 7) a fuller discussion of the homology between Spanglish and the bimusicality of the orquesta. For the moment I wish only to emphasize that this form of bilingualism develops as a kind of linguistic counterpart to bimusicality, and that, as Jordan (1972, 1981) suggests with respect to bilingual verbal art, the two forms of expression represent the ultimate attempt to synthesize the contradictions surrounding life on a bicultural border between two antagonistic cultural systems. An interesting parallel thus obtains between bilingualism and bimusicality in the Southwest, as both types of expression would seem to make use of the universal cognitive principles underlying any interaction that simultaneously taps two distinct cultural systems of communication (Vaid 1986).

Before we examine specific examples of Spanglish, the difference between compound and coordinate bilingualism needs to be more firmly established. I submit the latter is a more "static" form, while the former represents the dialectical interplay between two cultures in contact—one dominant, the other subordinate. Like "dynamic" and "transitional" bilingualism in Rosaura Sánchez's typology, Spanglish illustrates "those contradictions within society itself which simultaneously promote language shift and reinforce language maintenance" (1978: 209). It is, in short, a sharp reflection of the dialectic of conflict charting the course of ethnic relations in the Southwest.

It must be understood from the outset that Spanglish is by its very nature an illegitimate mode of communication, first, because it deviates from (and violates) the standard practice of monolingualism and its rules of performance, but more important, because, like the orquesta, it forces a synthesis between two disparate cultural modalities existing historically in a state of tension and opposition. As the linguist Edna Acosta-Belén observed, "There is a widespread negative attitude toward its [Spanglish's] use, which creates feelings of inferiority and alienation among those who allegedly use it" (quoted in Jacobson 1978: 234). This has not, however, discouraged Mexican Americans from practicing this form of bilingualism, at least in situations conducive to an informal, relaxed, and intimate style of interaction. In sum, as John Gumperz and Eduardo Hernández-Chávez argue, "in spite of the fact that [compound bilingualism] is held in disrepute, it is very persistent, occurring whenever minority language groups come in close contact with majority language groups under conditions of rapid social change" (quoted in Jacobson 1978: 234). In our terms, compound bilingualism is critically linked to a particular stage in the dialectic of conflict in the Southwest—a stage in which relations between Anglos and Mexicans were undergoing rapid and profound change.

A conceptualization of the two types of bilingualism—coordinate versus compound—was first put forward by Susan Erving and Charles Osgood in 1954. After some initial confusion (Erving and Osgood did not adequately distinguish between the two terms), a sharper, more precise distinction between compound and coordinate bilingualism was finally advanced by Wallace Lambert. A seminal figure in the development of the compound-coordinate theory of bilingualism, Lambert wrote,

Early bilinguals seem to develop more pervasive, superordinate systems which subserve both languages [these are the compound bilinguals]. By way of contrast, late bilinguals seem to have relatively more compartmentalized semantic systems for each of their languages, and in general their two language systems seem to be more functionally independent [coordinate bilinguals]. (1978: 218)

The key word here is "superordinate," for it is the fusion of two semantic systems into a superordinate one that makes compound bilingualism such a unique phenomenon. Learned early in life and practiced in a setting where two languages compete on a more or less equal footing—in the home, for example, and other intimate settings—compound bilinguals present a special challenge to linguists, sociolinguists, and psycholinguists. Erving and Osgood were apparently the first to glimpse the cognitive and cultural dynamics involved, and over the next thirty years or so, utilizing increasingly refined research techniques, students of compound bilingualism were better able to identify the cognitive and symbolic mechanisms involved. The implicit syntactic and grammatical rules that govern the process of code-switching were also mapped out. Thus, by 1986 the psycholinguists François Grosjean and Carlos Soares could assert with some confidence that "a compound bilingual's knowledge of two languages makes up an integrated whole that cannot easily be decomposed into two separate parts" (1986: 179).

In the case of Mexicans of the Southwest, the ascendance of the Mexican American Generation marks the onset of compound bilingualism. As an everyday practice, this bilingualism transcends the mere knowledge and use of two discrete, separate languages, as is the case with coordinate bilingualism. Unlike coordinate bilinguals, Mexican Americans after the 1930s no longer maintained "compartmentalized semantic systems for each of their languages," nor did they maintain two separate and "functionally independent" language systems (Lambert 1978: 218). Instead, the new bilinguals, enmeshed as they were within a society undergoing rapid cultural change, quickly transformed everyday communication into a deeply structured diglossia—a unique synthesis of the Mexican American's bicultural experience.

By way of familiarizing ourselves with Spanglish and the principles underlying its practice, let us now consider two excerpts from interviews I recorded, one with Isidro López, an important transitional figure in the orquesta tradition,[5] the other with Moy and Delia Pineda, two veteran orquesta musicians. Both López's and the Pinedas' speech is perfectly typical of people raised during the latter stages of the Mexican American Generation, as it is of the Chicano Generation generally. My conversation with López and the Pinedas is characteristic of the interviews I conducted with at least two dozen orquesta musicians in Texas, California, and Arizona.

First, in reviewing the transcript from which the López excerpt was lifted, I noticed the first three pages (about thirty minutes of conversation) were conducted exclusively in Spanish. Then, suddenly, thirty minutes into the interview, López begins to mix the two languages freely:

. . . *Bueno, el sonido del mariachi tienes que criarte con él. El mariachi tiene su sonido, su estilo. Es como los saxofonistas que quieran tocar como Beto Villa o como yo; es muy diferente, no puede[n] hacerlo.* They don't have the feeling *como nosotros.* We don't play the music *como lo de ellos. . . .*[6]

Interestingly, at this point I too began to switch codes. In the very next question (unconsciously, I now realize), I began in Spanish and switched to English in the middle of the utterance:

Yo sé que usted dijo que las orquestas eran diferentes—Beto, Eugenio—pero, is there such a thing as *un estilo tejano, de orquesta tejana?*[7]

To which López responds:

There is, because we do have a different sound. We have a different style from any band from Mexico or from the U.S. *Cuando yo toco mi saxofón, todos saben que es Isidro López. Los músicos me conocen, por el* **feeling. We have a different style than any band** *de otro país.* **Why is it? I don't know.** *Puedo traer músicos del otro lado, pero aunque quieran,* **they can't blow like me.**[8]

The key to understanding the type of speech López and I engaged in is the switching that takes place within sentences as we move back and forth between English and Spanish. Called "intrasentential code-switching," it is considered the hallmark of compound bilingualism (Jacobson 1978; Nishimura 1986). Intrasentential code-switching is simply the linguistic exchange that takes place in the middle of an utterance, usually at some strategic juncture, as in the following examples:

1. "They don't have the feeling *como nosotros.*"
2. ". . . *pero,* is there such a thing as *un estilo tejano* . . . ?"
3. "*Puedo traer músicos del otro lado, pero aunque quieran,* they can't blow like me."

It is clear from the above utterances that a person who is a compound bilingual switches unconsciously between the two languages. But the switches are not random; they occur at logical grammatical junctures, such as between clauses or after conjunctions. In other words, just as in monolingual speech, there are rules operating in the linguistic universe of the compound bilingual, rules that dictate when and where codes may be exchanged. In (1), for example, the exchange takes place at the beginning of the dependent clause "*como nosotros [tenemos]*" (as we [have]). In (2), the first code-switch occurs after the conjunction "*pero*" (but); the second appears less grammatically "correct," since it seems not to follow the pattern of the previous switches: it follows the preposition "as." However, the integrity of the phrase "*un estilo tejano*" is preserved, and that is the critical consideration. The integrity of the switch itself would only have been compromised if I had said something like, "is there such a thing as an *estilo* Texan?" Finally, (3) falls squarely within the bounds of "correct" code-switching in that it does so at the beginning of the independent clause "they can't blow like me."

Let us now examine a strip of conversation from the interview with Moy and Delia Pineda. Unlike the Isidro López interview, this one had begun mostly in English, but as the conversation wears on, an increasing use of code-switching becomes evident from the transcript. At the time, I was trying to define the musical parameters of the Mexican American orquesta: to what extent was it a Mexican or an American expression, or a combination of both? Specifically, I asked about the influence of American big bands on orquestas like that of Eugenio Gutiérrez, with whom both Delia (Gutiérrez's daughter) and Moy had played:

MP: Tell me, did Beto Villa and Eugenio Gutiérrez play exactly like the American bands—was there a difference?

DP: There was a difference, *porque también tenían como los conjuntos* [because they also had like the conjuntos] and all that. You had to give people a little bit of both to keep them happy. If you would play *pura pieza americana* [nothing but American pieces] and all that, then something was missing. That's why you had to come up with *polcas* and *boleros*.

As in the case of Isidro López and others (e.g., Gibby Escobedo and Oscar Lawson; see Chapter 6), Moy and Delia Pineda rely on both languages to express their most introspective thoughts on the orquesta (described further in Chapter 6). At the level of grammar and syntax, meanwhile, the speech sample from Ms. Pineda conforms to the rules of code-switching enumerated above. In the sentence "There was a difference, *porque también tenían como los conjuntos* and all that," the first switch is introduced by the subordinate conjunction *porque* (a grammatically "correct" switch), while the second is introduced by the conjunction "and"—also an acceptable switch. The interjection of *polcas* and *boleros* should not be considered instances of code-switching, properly speaking (Jacobson 1978: 228), but rather of semi-code-switching, to emphasize ethnic aspects of the polka and *bolero*.

Much more can obviously be said about the process of "intrasentential code-switching," which, again, is considered the defining element in compound bilingualism (see Jacobson 1978). But since the object here is simply to demonstrate its most salient features and to remind ourselves that it is a critical mode of communication for people situated in a bicultural environment, I conclude this section by drawing out a few more implications inherent in the coordinate-compound difference.

The cognitive mechanisms involved in the development of a compound bilingual—not to mention the sociopsychological ones—are complex and have yet to be fully elucidated (Jacobson 1978; Vaid 1986). However, even if all the psycho- and sociolinguistic dynamics ultimately remain uncharted, the concept itself remains a powerful heuristic device for interpreting key aspects of the communicative behavior of bilinguals, especially individuals such as Isidro López and the Pinedas, who learned the two languages early in life and whose most natural speech style tends toward heavy use of intrasentential code-switching—at least in intimate, relaxed settings in which all the interlocutors are competent in both languages.

As sociolinguists have demonstrated, this type of speech is highly sensitive to social, cultural, and psychological cues, in that the occasion for such speech is usually informal and intimate, and the interactants must all demonstrate shared competence in this type of code-switching (Blom and Gumperz 1972). In short, they must all be members of a special kind of speech community, and all must share the norms that govern verbal performance as well as the more or less unconscious rules for the articulation of this kind of communication (Bauman and Sherzer 1974; Gumperz and Hymes 1972). Rodolfo Jacobson puts it well when he notes, "the bilingual is faced with a series of language-related decisions through which he reveals that he has examined the social situation, he has assessed it to the best of his knowledge, and has made the language choice that the situation demands of him" (1978: 236).

Beyond the specific principles involved in the production of compound bilingualism is the metaphorical relationship between it and bimusicality. In the case of Isidro López and other orquesta musicians, the unconscious choice to discuss the bimusical orquesta in bilingual speech is, in my estimation, key to illuminating the cultural meaning of orquesta, a meaning I shall explore later. But there is also a more homologous relationship that links the two types of expression—speech and music— namely, the formal manner in which the code-switching occurs at the level of the individual utterance in both domains (the sentence, usually, for speech; the phrase for music). We have seen how this code-switching operates in the realm of speech; in Chapter 7 I shall repeat the procedure for the realm of music, and then we shall be in a position to fully understand the homology.

Finally, aside from the fact that the conversations from which the exchanges cited above were extracted represent two ideal examples of intrasentential code-switching (the hallmark of compound bilingualism), the topic itself provides an astonishing example of how such an intensely bimusical phenomenon as the orquesta can most properly be addressed in a mode of speech that symbolically parallels the musical: bilingualism, or more precisely, compound bilingualism. And so time and again, as musician after musician discussed his or her deepest understanding of what orquesta signified for them and their public, the most proper way to describe it was through the use of this type of bilingual speech. Indeed, Isidro López's own discussion of the orquesta provides us with a linguistic condensation of much of what I have presented so far in this chapter.

CONCLUSION:
The Mexican Americans as "Compound Biculturals"

In discussing the prevalence of compound bilingualism and its relationship to biculturalism, we are confronted with another question: Is compound bilingualism a specific manifestation of a more global phenomenon—namely, compound biculturalism? This is an intriguing proposition, one raised by the sociolinguist Fernando Peñalosa:

> Perhaps the relationship of linguistic to sociocultural variables might be profitably explored by suggesting the concepts *compound biculturals* and *coordinate biculturals*. That is, a compound bicultural would have a single cultural system . . . whereas the coordinate bicultural would have *two* cultural systems which he keeps cognitively and affectively separate. (1980: 47)

To be sure, enormous complications arise when we try to sort out and map the specific psychological and social dynamics involved in the development of a compound bicultural. For if discovering the precise cognitive-affective mechanisms that come into play in compound bilingualism is difficult, then the task of identifying the factors involved in the total range of bicultural communication must be staggering. Nonetheless, Peñalosa's suggestion is provocative, although identifying even the formal features of compound biculturalism—as it might manifest itself in such domains as religion, kinship, culinary codes, mythology, and even everyday practice—is problematic. This is so because, unlike language, whose structure has been rather extensively mapped by linguists, sociolinguists, and other specialists, other codes involved in cultural communication lack the explicitly referential function and the more or less decipherable system of grammar and syntax that language possesses.[9] As we shall see, however, at least one domain is amenable to the formal analysis compound bilingualism has been subjected to, and that is the phenomenon of bimusicality.

Finally, the biculturalism of the Mexican American Generation, however conceived, is a function of the contradictory position this historical bloc occupied as a result of the co-occurrence of two factors—its middle-class position and its stigmatized ethnic heritage. Struggling to resolve its mammoth contradictions, it aimed, to recall Mario García's words, "to bridge the past, present and future" by more or less unconsciously recasting disparate elements—American/Mexican, ranchero/jaitón, working/middle class—into bimodal structures more consistent with their dualistic existence. In this effort they achieved only partial success. A richer synthesis of contradiction awaited the emergence of the next politically defined bloc, the Chicano Generation.

CHAPTER 4

The Formative
Years of Orquesta
The Texas-Mexican
Connection

THE MASTER TROPES:
Ranchero versus Jaitón

Any informed discussion of the Mexican American orquesta must address the one principle that organizes its role in the total experience of its constituents and installs the orquesta as the most synthesizing form of artistic expression devised by the Mexican Americans. This organizing principle is none other than the dialectic prevailing between the master tropes that figuratively circumscribe the breadth and depth of the modern orquesta: *ranchero* and *jaitón*. This dialectic eventually fuses the antithetical sociocultural polarities inscribed in the two terms. I thus begin the first of two chapters on the formative years of the orquesta with a discussion of this important discursive dyad and its dichotomous relationship.

Historically, two ensembles and their respective styles serve as symbolic contrasts between ranchero and jaitón in the Southwest—the conjunto and the orquesta. The contrast arises initially in Texas but follows the two ensembles as they collide elsewhere. Wherever it migrated, the conjunto represented not only *lo ranchero* but other compatible categories: a folk sensibility, a working-class aesthetic, a form of ethnic resistance, and the continuity of norteño culture on this side of the border. The orquesta represented the opposite: a middle-class lifestyle, the ideology of acculturation, a gap between the "modern" and the "traditional," and a general sense of "sophistication." Yet, despite the obvious contrasts, the two ensembles are best seen as tending to diverge at the

What helped Beto Villa

was that he could play

both ranchero and jaitón.

ARMANDO MARROQUÍN

level of class consciousness but to converge at the level of ethnic consciousness (Peña 1985b). This was particularly true during the period from the 1930s to the 1960s, when the conjunto and orquesta were the primary aesthetic correlatives of the ranchero-jaitón opposition. Indeed, the two pairs of opposition—ranchero-jaitón and orquesta-conjunto— may be seen as leitmotifs that illuminate the other polarities: country-city, rustic-cosmopolitan, Mexican-American, working–middle class, cultural resistance–assimilation, and a host of cultural practices defined by such oppositions.

By exploring the ranchero-jaitón opposition itself, I hope to untangle some of the complexities attending the sociomusical difference between orquesta and conjunto, as well as the range of dichotomies I have enumerated. To launch the argument, I offer a quote from the English critic Raymond Williams that captures much of what can be said about the ranchero-versus-jaitón cultural complex and, especially, its association with country versus city (or rural versus urban):

On the country has gathered the idea of a natural way of life: of peace, innocence and simple virtue. On the city has gathered the idea of an achieved center: of learning, communication, light. Powerful hostile associations have also developed: on the city as a place of noise, worldliness and ambition; on the country as a place of backwardness, ignorance, limitation. (1973: 1)

Such contradictory associations as Williams ascribes to the city-country opposition have historically attended the terms *ranchero* and *jaitón* among Mexican Americans. Of the two, however, *ranchero* carries by far the most cultural baggage—*jaitón* being far less ambiguous. Indeed, except for a certain connotation of envy that *jaitón* may convey— as when people complained of being slighted by someone considered more affluent—the term tended toward the pejorative, denoting plain snobbery.

Lo ranchero, on the other hand, is a highly ambivalent concept. As Williams notes with respect to the concept of "country," *lo ranchero* is associated in the minds of Mexican Americans with the rugged but pristine, unspoiled and virtuous life that *el rancho* promotes. This image of the *rancho* as wholesome and rugged has a long history in Latin America (as "country" does in the United States and Europe; cf. Burns 1980; Franco 1970; Williams 1973), but in the case of Mexicans and Mexican Americans such an association derives principally from the Mexican

Revolution of 1910–1917. The Revolution's exaltation of peasant life and its folk traditions was central to the spirit of romantic nationalism that underpinned its ideological thrust.

A romantic-nationalist ideology and its glorification of *lo ranchero* survived the Revolution; in fact, it was co-opted by Mexico's nascent mass-media capitalists, who took one of the Revolution's most enduring symbols—the armed *campesino*—and wedded it to the mounted *vaquero* (cowboy) to create the dashing *charro* figure of the enormously profitable films known as *comedias rancheras* (country musicals, e.g., *Allá en el rancho grande, Ay, Jalisco no te rajes;* see Saragoza n.d.). To complete the portrait of ranchero life exalted in the *comedia ranchera*, the hitherto improvisational folk mariachi was upgraded and standardized. The union of singing, pistol-packing *charro* and mariachi ensemble created a powerful national icon that came to embody the best of the Mexican male's self-ascribed qualities: manliness, valor, self-sufficiency, candor, simplicity, sincerity, and patriotism (*mexicanidad*).

Yet, as I argued elsewhere (Peña 1985a: 11–12), the sentimentalized image of *lo ranchero* confronts a negative opposite. *El rancho* may evoke an idyllic life undisturbed by the pressures of modernity, but this imagined life quickly evaporates in the Mexican American's struggle for acceptance in contemporary American life. Thus, the attitude toward *el rancho* can easily shift from nostalgia to disdain. Today, as in the past, an *arrancherado* (usually a *campesino,* not the dashing *charro*) is someone without *roce social*—a coarse, backward country bumpkin who is out of place in the contemporary world of urbanized, culturally assimilated Mexican Americans.

The negative side of *el rancho,* then, exists in a dialectical relationship with the romanticized image. *Música ranchera* itself, a symbolic complex that includes the mariachi, the conjunto, and, lately, the Mexican *banda,*[1] remains vulnerable to the contradictions inherent in the root concept. These contradictions notwithstanding, many Mexican Americans have leaned on the romantic aspects of *lo ranchero* to reclaim their Mexican heritage, their memories of the homeland awakened through the strains of *música ranchera.* In its undulating melodies, the music symbolically carries the Mexican American to the womb of the mother culture: it momentarily evokes a simple, idyllic folk heritage—an evocation tempered, nonetheless, by the Mexican American's realization that it is an ineffable heritage, "lost forever like the elusive lover of most ranchera song lyrics" (Peña 1985a: 11).

Once again, however, the negative side of *lo ranchero* has never been completely expunged from consciousness, notwithstanding the raw power of the mariachi, the simple charm of the conjunto, or, more overtly political, the cultural reconfigurations achieved by the Chicano "Renaissance" (see Chapter 6). For just beneath the figures of the daunt-less *charro* and the stoic *campesino*—indeed, the whole ennobling cul-ture of the pastoral evoked by *música ranchera*—is the reality of class *and* gender exploitation that the ranchero-jaitón dichotomy masks. Thus, short of exposing the full set of contradictions the dichotomy conceals, popular ideology pounces on the weak element of the ranchero com-plex—the *campesino*—and singles him out as the epitome of the short-comings that bar the Mexican from adjusting to modern life—especially on this side of the border, where the sleeping man with the wide-brimmed sombrero is cast as the stereotype for fatalism, ignorance, and laziness. In the Mexican Americans' efforts to conform to American modernity, the *campesino* assumes the role of spoiler. He hovers at the margins of the romanticized *rancho*—a "low-class," barely civilized Mex-ican incapable of adjusting to the refinements of contemporary culture.

Paradoxically, despite the contradictions (or perhaps because of them), *música ranchera* continues to enjoy an encompassing symbolism in the aesthetic domain of the Mexican Americans, even in the era of post-Chicanismo. Indeed, thanks to the revitalizing influence of the Chicano movement (see Chapter 6), *música ranchera* has maintained its sway over the collective musical consciousness, from the aging urban-ites of the Mexican American Generation to the "postmodernists" of the post-Chicano era, many of whom ground their ethnic allegiance on mu-sical personalities as diversely ranchero as Los Lobos, Dr. Loco and His Rockin' Jalapeño Band, Emilio Navaira, and Vicente Fernández.

The power of *lo ranchero* was not lost on Armando Marroquín, Beto Villa, or any but the most jaitón orquestas of the 1940s and '50s. Indeed, the Mexican Americans' attachment to *lo ranchero* prompted Marro-quín's *post facto* dictum: "Everybody had to play *polcas*" [rancheras] (per-sonal interview, January 31, 1980). The *rancho's* powerful association with "our ancestors," as Delia Gutiérrez Pineda put it, ensured its continuing popularity, even among orquesta supporters. As Ms. Gutiérrez Pineda summarized the matter, "I think we have always included rancheras be-cause it goes back to our ancestors and the type of music they liked and we listened to when we were little" (personal interview, July 9, 1979).

In its juxtaposition against *música jaitona*, *música ranchera* satisfied powerful but contradictory aesthetic and ideological impulses deeply embedded in the bicultural experience of the Mexican Americans. Not accidentally, Beto Villa's masterful juxtaposition of ranchero and jaitón installed him as the "father" of the modern orquesta. Juxtaposition is a far cry from synthesis, of course. Despite its contiguity to *lo jaitón*, the negative side of *lo ranchero* could not be lost on orquestas either, especially its association with backwardness and ignorance. Thus, even Isidro López, who alone among orquesta musicians staunchly defended working-class culture, equivocated on the issue of *lo ranchero*. Having himself climbed to the pinnacle of popularity on the strains of *música ranchera*, López nonetheless revealed his bias against *lo ranchero* when he equated ignorance with a preference for the conjunto. For López, as for other orquesta musicians, the only alternative to the demeaning influence of the conjunto was *lo moderno*: the urban, the sophisticated, the "high class," or jaitón—in short, the orquesta.

On closer examination, however, *lo moderno* turns out to be a code phrase for the assimilation of middle-class elements, as these had coalesced around the cosmopolitan sounds of the big bands, both in the United States and Mexico. In the context of practical musical knowledge shared among Mexican Americans, the polarities symbolized by *lo ranchero* and *lo moderno* came to be associated with two classes of people— the poor and "uncultured" on the one hand, the "upper-crust" or jaitón on the other. Conjunto was the property of the former, orquesta of the latter. Among all the musicians who collaborated in this study, perhaps Paulino Bernal, leader of the "greatest conjunto of all time" (Tony "Ham" Guerrero, personal interview, March 31, 1980), phrased the basic polarity between orquesta and conjunto in the most unambiguous terms:

Siempre había entre la raza, entre los Chicanos, lo que llamábamos nosotros, "N'hombre, te crees muy 'high society.'" O sea, había una clase entre los Chicanos de gente que era más "high" y quería vivir como el americano, y vivir mejor. Claro, ya habían alcanzado alguna posición más alta económicamente, y todavía había mucha raza que apenas estaba llegando, y con mucho—struggling all the way. Entonces sí había la división; y allí es donde se dividía no tan solo la posición social o la posición económica, sino que también se dividía la música—el de la orquesta y el del conjunto. (Personal interview, May 9, 1980)[2]

Assigned such symbolic roles, these rival ensembles, orquesta and conjunto, played a powerful role in articulating status distinctions and their attendant ideologies throughout the Hispanic Southwest (but most emphatically in Texas). As I mentioned earlier, World War II represents a powerful tremor that not only realigns Anglo-Mexican relations but also results in increased differentiation of Mexican American society. Culturally, the chief legacy of this differentiation was the emergence of a dualistic identity for Mexican Americans, in the form of bicultural practices. Socially, the principal result was a deepening distance between upwardly mobile, rapidly acculturating Mexican Americans and their working-class peers, both U.S.-born and immigrant. The ideological sum of these developments was the intensifying contradiction embedded within the Mexican American experience, and orquesta, in both its ranchero and jaitón guises, perfectly played out that contradiction.

This contradiction was articulated at the musical level via the ranchero-jaitón polarities materializing rapidly by the end of the Second World War. By 1946, while Texas-Mexicans were overwhelmingly supportive of ranchera music, many, especially the upwardly mobile, had turned against the conjunto (Peña 1985a). Yet—and this is surely a testimony to the contradiction-filled experience of the Mexican American Generation—the *tejanos* were in no position to transcend the ethnic power inscribed in the concept of *lo ranchero*. In the end, *lo ranchero* and *lo jaitón*, the country and the city, "culture" and lack of it, resistance and assimilation—in short, all the contradictions besetting the Mexican Americans—would be maintained in a state of tension until the Chicano Generation imposed its own synthesizing stamp on the order of things.

THE FIRST ORQUESTAS

Among Mexican Americans, the first modern-style orquestas were probably organized in the late 1920s, although they continued to compete with the older string ensembles and combinations of an ad hoc nature until the beginning of the Second World War. The newer orquestas, featuring trumpets and saxophones as the principal melodic instruments (clarinets and trombones were less frequently used), were first in evidence in the large urban areas, and in this respect, one of the first in the Southwest was an orquesta from Houston, known, oddly enough, as Los Rancheros (The Ranch People, or, more colloquially, The Country Folk; see Fig. 5). Los Rancheros was organized by Mónico García around 1928 or 1929; it was the successor to an earlier makeshift orquesta García had led during the 1920s—the Bacon Orchestra (see Fig. 6).

Notwithstanding the pastoral image attached to the name, Los Rancheros was inescapably urban in orientation, from the modern business suits the orquesta wore for performances to the almost exclusively American repertoire it had adopted (Eloy Pérez, personal interview, September 21, 1993). In short, Los Rancheros poignantly mirrored the con-

FIGURE 5. *Los Rancheros, Houston, ca. 1930.*
Courtesy Houston Metropolitan Research Center, Houston Public Library.

traditions discussed above—contradictions embodied in the sharp juxtaposition between the group's pastoral name and its thoroughly urban performance practices. In that juxtaposition, Los Rancheros betrayed not only the extent of musical assimilation taking place among certain urbanized segments of the Mexican American population, but also the persistent efforts to evoke a romanticized (though stigmatized) ethnic heritage.

As mentioned in the last chapter, the Mexican American Generation had begun to assert its assimilationist presence by the late 1920s, and it is not surprising that groups such as Los Rancheros should begin sprouting up all over the musical landscape of the Hispanic Southwest at this precise historical moment. And, although most of the musicians who participated in these early wind ensembles were well versed in the European music long Mexicanized in the Hispanic Southwest (*valses, redovas, danzas, polcas,* etc.), they were all apparently caught up in the excitement of the swing-band era. Thus, as old-time musicians such as Eloy Pérez in Houston, Don Tosti in Los Angeles, and Manuel Contreras in Fresno recalled, traditional Mexican music was overwhelmed by the American, and the Mexican Americans, responding to the modernity en-

gulfing the world around them, forsook tradition and began turning to
the big-band styles then sweeping the American mass market.

Interestingly, American record companies, which seem to have been
most eager to record almost every type of music present in the Southwest, cast a deaf ear on the new orquestas such as Los Rancheros. Columbia, Decca, and the other major companies seem not to have been
impressed by the imitative nature of these Mexican American orquestas,
perhaps because most of them were reduced versions of the large bands
forged by such big names as Tommy Dorsey and Duke Ellington. The recording companies—or, more accurately, their local Mexican American
intermediaries—may have also realized that Mexicans in the Southwest
were still preponderantly tied to their ethnic, working-class roots, and
that other musics such as the conjunto, the ad hoc string bands, and the
vocal duet were much more marketable than the new orquestas—these
yet-to-be-proven experiments of a fledgling middle class. In short, the
orquestas of the 1930s had not yet solidified their presence enough to attract the attention of the major labels, and so they remained largely un-
exploited, commercially, until the end of World War II.

World War II, then, marks an important turning point, not only for the
modern orquesta but, more fundamentally, for the society that spawned
this new musical phenomenon. As described in Chapter 3, participation
in the wartime economy brought about the final urbanization of Mexi-

FIGURE 6. *The Bacon Orchestra, Houston, 1926.*
Courtesy Houston Metropolitan Research Center, Houston Public Library.

can Americans, while it also offered them the first real opportunity to crack the American work force in occupations other than menial labor. Upon reentering the peacetime economy, the upwardly mobile members of the Mexican American Generation, in particular, which had barely begun to challenge the prevailing order in the 1930s, launched a vigorous campaign to upgrade the socioeconomic status of Mexican Americans and to promote their cultural, if not structural, assimilation into American society (M. García 1989; cf. Gordon 1964; McLemore 1980). More specifically, at this time the better-positioned Mexican Americans—the nucleus of the Mexican American Generation—began in earnest their own "search for America," as Mario García (1989) has characterized the long process of sociocultural transformation. Part of that search included the discovery of new sources of cultural expression, and the orquesta proved to be one critical source.

Originating as hand-me-down versions of the large American swing bands, the Mexican American orquestas naturally emulated the former in style and repertory, at least during the 1930s and early '40s. Don Eloy Pérez, "The Glenn Miller of Latin American hipsters," as a LULAC dance poster described him, recalled a group with which he played in the late 1930s, in the city of Houston. A partial transcript of our September 21, 1993, interview follows:

MP: What kind of music did you play with La Orquesta Montecarlo?

EP: At that time we played only American music. We did not play Mexican music.

MP: Why didn't you play Mexican music?

EP: I don't think there was any available.

MP: You didn't know Mexican music at the time?

EP: No, not at that time. We would hear songs that some people sang, but orquestas that would play Mexican music—recordings—there were none.

MP: And how did you obtain American music—to play it like—?

E: Well, we played, like the music of the big bands like Glenn Miller and Harry James and all those big bands.

MP: But did you play it by ear, did you write it?

EP: By ear.

MP: And your audience—was it Mexican?

EP: Mexicans.

MP: And they liked American music?

EP: Yes, that is all they heard.

MP: And then after World War II, tell me what happened—what kind of music did you play?

EP: All Mexican music.

MP: It wasn't American anymore?

EP: No, no more.

MP: When did the music change from American to Mexican, then?

EP: Sometime after the war. In my case, when I organized my own orquesta, I put in mostly Mexican music—a swing or fox-trot here and there. That was in 1949.

MP: You told me earlier you had played with the Razo and García orquestas during the war. Did you still play American music then?

EP: We mixed it up.

In Fresno, California, a city nearly two thousand miles from Houston, the same acculturative process seems to have occurred. Band leader Manuel Contreras remembered the early 1930s, when the Jesús Torres Orchestra used to play Saturday nights for one of the *mutualista* organizations in Fresno, La Sociedad Morelos. Interestingly, although the *mutualistas* are considered "traditional" Mexicans in many ways (Barrera 1988), the music featured by the Torres orchestra was not Mexican but American. As Contreras recalled, "Jesús Torres had a band—he had an orchestra—but they didn't play Mexican music; they played the popular music at the time—American music" (personal interview, September 15, 1982). Moreover, in a gesture pregnant with the symbolism of biculturation (not to mention cultural contradiction), during special Mexican holiday programs, such as *el dieciséis de septiembre,* Mexican and American musics shared billing. To become bimusical, Mr. Torres would team up with another orquesta of the older string variety, Francisco Reyes's, to perform traditional Mexican music:

MC: So when they had these *fiestas patrias* [Independence holidays] then somehow or other he [Torres] would get together with Francisco Reyes and get a big group together. And then they used to play Mexican songs like "Alejandra vals," "El zopilote," "El jarabe tapatío," and music like that.

MP: This was for the fiestas?

MC: For the fiestas, yeah, but during the dance, of course, they still played American music. That was in 1931, and I'll tell you, the reason I remember is, see, Carmen's first husband, he used to make moonshine—you know, whiskey. See, it was Prohibition at the time, so my grandmother would take a pint of whiskey to the dance in her purse, and my sister Carmen another pint; then my mother would take one, and I used to take a couple of them in my pocket, you know, and sell them there for fifty cents a pint. . . . It was pretty good money. And so, that's how we got to go to the dances, otherwise they would never have taken me, as a kid. (Ibid.)

But again, as was the case in Texas, California Mexicans began to re-claim *latino* music in the early forties. Contreras recalled that as late as 1937 Mexican music had not yet earned a place in the repertoire of the Fresno orquestas, except for special occasions such as the *fiestas patrias*. For example, another of Fresno's orquestas, the Frank Domínguez Or-chestra, also played for the Morelos lodge, and according to Contreras, "he had a pretty good group, but he also didn't play much Mexican mu-sic. They played a few, like 'Las gaviotas' and I don't know what else." But then, in 1941, "Latin music—*boleros* and *rumbas*—became popular, songs like 'Aquellos ojos verdes' and 'Frenesí.'" Thus, by 1946, when Con-treras organized his first orquesta, Latin American music had reclaimed its place among the Mexican Americans of Fresno, and Contreras began to specialize in *lo latino,* never abandoning, however, the always-popular swings and fox-trots of the time.

Judging from the narratives of Eloy Pérez and Manuel Contreras— and others who bear out their recollections—the Mexican Americans' love affair with the big swing-band sound had peaked by the end of the war, and as biculturalism asserted itself as the dominant cultural mode in the Hispanic Southwest, a desire to revive traditional folk music en-sued, most particularly in the form of the ethnic *polca*, especially in Texas. However, more sophisticated Afro-Hispanic forms such as the *bolero, rumba,* and *danzón,* recently popularized in the United States by musicians like Xavier Cugat, also assumed increasing importance in the orquesta repertoire. In other words, an exclusively American repertoire was inadequate to the cultural needs of the Mexican American Genera-tion; bimusicality was the only solution to the generation's search for a form of expression that would coincide with its existence at the margin between two cultural worlds.

In the Mexican Americans' inevitable search for musical expression compatible with their bicultural orientation, the Texas-Mexicans were in the vanguard, and it was in the Lone Star State that a new breed of musician and entrepreneur first emerged, of which two quintessential members were, respectively, the band leader Beto Villa, from Falfurrias, Texas, and the record-promoter Armando Marroquín, from nearby Al-ice. The latter was briefly introduced in Chapter 3 in connection with the commercialization of Mexican American music; a more detailed dis-cussion of his contributions follows.

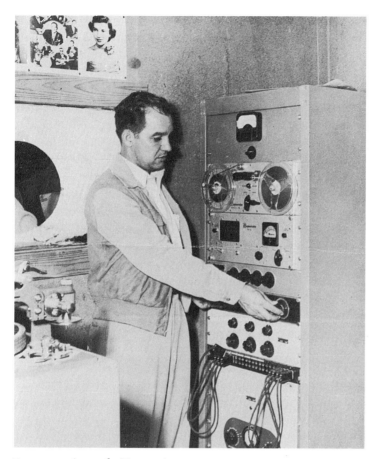

Figure 7. *Armando Marroquín, 1950.*
Courtesy of Armando Marroquín.

Ideal Records and the Resurgence
of Regional Commercial Music

In recognition of capitalism's total penetration into the cultural economy of the Mexican American community by the end of World War II,
a discussion of the birth of the modern orquesta must account, first, for
the entrepreneurs who helped launch the new ensemble—men like
Manuel Peláiz of Los Angeles and Armando Marroquín of Alice, Texas
(see Fig. 7). Marroquín's Ideal label was a central player, not only in the
marketing of the modern orquesta but in the commercial survival of
conjunto and other musical forms deeply embedded in Mexican Ameri-

can culture. It seems therefore appropriate at this point to sketch a brief profile of the man and his entrepreneurial life, and in this way illuminate the initial relationship of orquesta to the commercial market.

Armando Marroquín was born in 1912, in Alice, Texas, the city where he spent all of his life. His father died in 1918, and young Armando spent much of his youth with his maternal grandmother.[3] His grandmother's family was apparently of "respectable" origins, if not possessed of substantial wealth. In any case, unlike most Mexican Americans of his generation, Marroquín was able to complete high school, and he actually spent two years at Texas A&I College, in nearby Kingsville. His family and educational background lent Marroquín a decidedly middle-class outlook, although it would be a gross distortion to speak of him as elitist. Unlike the snobbish and influential Mexican expatriates who had fled to South Texas during the Mexican Revolution (with whom Marroquín was familiar), or the elites of Monterrey or Matamoros, Marroquín was steeped in the rustic lifestyle long associated with the genteel families native to South Texas (J. González 1930). As such, he had developed as much of a taste for the folk music entrenched among the common people of the region as he had for more genteel forms, such as the string orquesta.

Consequently, Marroquín was never averse to promoting the music of his working-class contemporaries—the conjunto, for example, or the traditional corrido—nor did he cater to those tastes in a condescending fashion, although he obviously kept a critical eye out for the profit potential of any music he considered for the commercial market. Indeed, as he himself admitted, from early childhood he had entertained a special bias toward corridos such as "Jacinto Treviño," "Gregorio Cortez," and others that were very much a part of the working-class masses but popular, apparently, among all segments of Texas-Mexican society (Paredes 1976). In sum, although Marroquín early on became acquainted with the rudiments of capitalist enterprise and learned to harness them for his financial benefit, he never lost touch with his "roots." He may have been driven by the profit motive, but ideologically his sense of identity was invested in the music most closely associated with his cultural core—corridos, *canciones,* the conjunto, and other musical forms more or less indigenous to the Hispanic Southwest. Thus, as I wrote elsewhere, "Beyond Marroquín's desire for profit was his obvious sense of artistry, shaped and cultivated within the confines of a strong ethnic environment" (Peña 1985a: 77).

At the beginning of the war, the major labels, which had played a key role in launching the commercial course of Hispanic music of the Southwest, ended their involvement in that regional enterprise. A vacuum was thus created, since the recorded music that Mexicans of the Southwest had come to embrace suddenly became scarce—the troubadours, the conjunto, the various kinds of instrumental ensembles. Armando Marroquín, a young entrepreneur in search of a profitable venture, was quick to recognize and exploit that vacuum. During the heyday of the major labels, Marroquín had acquired a number of jukeboxes and placed them in service in various *cantinas* and other public places, where the music produced by those labels was in great demand. As in other regions and among other populations, in the Hispanic Southwest these coin-operated jukeboxes were immensely popular, providing local entrepreneurs like Marroquín an easy source of income.

But during the war, as the big record companies ceased production, a crisis of sorts ensued for those dependent on the supply of records from those companies. Marroquín recalled his dilemma in an interview (the translation is mine):

I had my jukeboxes, and there were no records. I said, "What can I do?" I went around investigating, and at last I developed the ability to produce my own records. It cost me less than $200 for the recording machine—the type that records directly on the acetate. It wasn't the technology we have today. . . . And I saw that it was less expensive for me if I could find someone who could produce records in volume. I inquired in California, and I found someone. But, since there was no competition, whatever one came out with would hit. Right away they produced them—it cost me a dollar per record—Allen Recording of Los Angeles. I think they made 300 records for me [initially], and Paco Betancourt from San Benito found out about it. He knew how to distribute, I didn't know anything. . . . He became my partner.

This was in 1946. Before long Marroquín was recording all the performers who had gained popularity in the days of the big labels, especially Texas-Mexicans, and Ideal soon became the leading record producer in the Hispanic Southwest. The upstart company attracted well-known artists such as the troubadours Gaytán y Cantú and Pedro Rocha y Lupe Martínez, the accordionists Narciso Martínez and Santiago Jiménez, the celebrated Lydia Mendoza, and even the internationally famous Hermanas Padilla, headquartered in Los Angeles. Starting out under the most primitive of conditions—the first recordings were made in Marroquín's living room—Ideal expanded rapidly, and by the late 1940s it was arguably the most important regional label in the Hispanic Southwest.

As much by happenstance as by Marroquín's acumen, Ideal found it-

self at the strategic core of a growing seedling that was the regional Hispanic music market. That core was Texas. The major labels had sown the
field and fertilized the cultural soil. By the end of the war, the Mexican
Americans of the Southwest were hungry for the music whose germina-
tion had been arrested by the war effort. All Marroquín had to do, as he
quickly recognized, was provide a little fertilizer—money—and the field
was harvest-ripe for exploitation. The target population, the Mexican
American working class (but also the increasingly affluent members of
the Mexican American Generation), was primed for consumption. To recall Marroquín's own observation: "Since there was no competition,
whatever one came out with would hit." It was in this ideal sociocultural
setting that the modern commercial orquesta was packaged and sold. Deriving its strength from a formidable set of cultural, economic, and ideological impulses, it quickly established itself as a major artistic vehicle
for mediating the contradictions that ricocheted among those impulses.

BETO VILLA AND THE TEJANO ORIGINS
OF THE MODERN ORQUESTA

The Texas-Mexicans have always been major contributors to the evolution of a musical aesthetic in the Hispanic Southwest. In the development of the corrido, the *canción-corrido,* and the *canción,* they were in
the vanguard; in the birth of the conjunto, they were the principal procre-
ators; and in the emergence of the modern orquesta, they forged a powerful synthesis of Mexican and American elements to create a uniquely
bimusical ensemble and its style. Why the *tejanos* should play such a leading role in the musical developments of the Southwest may be related to
their unenviable position in the Anglo-Mexican encounter. They were the
first line of contact with and defense against the encroaching Americans,
but the life-line connection they maintained with the Mexican mother
culture emboldened them both to resist Anglo domination and to offer a
countercultural response to the ethnocentric attitude of the new invad-
ers. Caught at the fault line where the two cultures first clashed, the *tejanos* could not help but be active participants in the dialectic of conflict
unfolding in the aftermath of the Anglo invasion and the series of cultural and countercultural aftershocks it triggered.

That one finds the principal architect of the Mexican American orquesta to be a Texas-Mexican is therefore not at all surprising. That the
architect was, at the same time, the prototypical member of the Mexican American Generation comes as no surprise either. His name, Beto

FIGURE 8. *Beto Villa, ca. 1950.*
Courtesy of Beto Villa.

Villa, still evokes at the end of the twentieth century a mystical allegiance among surviving members of the generation, who look nostalgi-
cally to a past in which a great tradition-in-the-making and its most visible icon embodied their cultural aspirations and the prospects for a new
era among a people on the march (see Fig. 8).

Villa's rise to fame began in 1946, when, as an ambitious thirty-one-
year-old alto saxophone player, he visited Armando Marroquín, owner of
the newly established Ideal Records. Villa was convinced he had discovered a style of playing with the potential to reap great success for him
among the Mexican Americans in Texas, and he wanted his friend Marroquín to give him an opportunity to test his hunch. Villa's idea was to
blend the ranchero elements of the by-now-popular accordion conjunto

with the sound of the horns used in the modern big band—the trumpet and saxophone—to create a novel *tejano* style. Villa had been honing his musical skills since he was drafted into his first orquesta as a youngster of eleven or twelve, and in the intervening years he had played the gamut from Mexican to American music. In 1946, he sensed that he had found the winning combination for commercial success in the fledgling *tejano* market.

Marroquín, who was himself a mere novice in the recording business, listened with interest to Villa's proposition, and he even agreed to cut a "demo," or demonstration acetate disc, which was done in Marroquín's living room on an old-fashioned gramophone, for Ideal did not yet have access to more modern equipment or a recording studio (magnetic tape recording was not introduced until 1948). As primitive as the recording conditions and the finished product may have been, Marroquín was satisfied with the results, and he sent the demo to his partner, Paco Betancourt, who worked out of San Benito, seventy miles to the south. Betancourt, who was in charge of distribution for Ideal, was not impressed. He felt Villa's orquesta—such as it was—did not possess the necessary polish to make the commercial grade. "No," he told Marroquín, "not this junk" (*este mugrero no*). In Marroquín's words, here is what happened next:

"O.K.," said Beto, "tell him I'll pay [for the cost of making the record]." So then we came out with the record—it was a *polca*, "Las delicias," on one side and a *vals*, "¿Por qué te ríes?" on the other. Ooh! Within a month after Betancourt started distributing it, he called and said, "Say, tell him to record some more." They were asking for it in bunches. (Personal interview; translation mine)

In such less than auspicious circumstances was the commercial course of the modern Mexican American orquesta launched: on a primitive acetate recorder in the living room of a struggling entrepreneur; in the form of a group that was, in Marroquín's own words, "not even an orquesta yet"; and by a progenitor who had to pay for his own recording. Yet, as Villa's first record proved, the moment was ripe for the commercial birth of a uniquely Mexican American orquesta. While the accordion-based conjunto and its brand of *música ranchera* had by this time eclipsed all other ensembles and cemented itself as *the* commercial choice among the working-class masses (thanks, at least initially, to the intervention of the major labels), as late as 1946 no alternative style had emerged among the middle class to give musical expression to its newfound biculturalism and increasing affluence. At this critical juncture, enter Beto Villa, the "father" of the modern orquesta.

Of course, orquestas with modern instrumentation had been in evidence at least since 1930, as the popularity of Los Rancheros attests (see Fig. 5). But the string orquestas had held their own until the onset of World War II, and, in any case, the major labels had largely ignored the modern orquesta. And, as noted earlier, the imitative nature of the first ensembles, which were watered-down versions of the big American swing bands, did not help the cause of the modern orquestas. They possessed no particular characteristics identifying them as Mexican American. To recall Eloy Pérez's comments, the orquestas of the 1930s and early '40s played "only American music"—swings, fox-trots, pieces like "In the Mood" and "Stardust"—a repertoire that readily betrayed their imitative nature. In any case, the major labels seem not to have been sufficiently impressed to enlist any of these recently emerged orquestas into the commercial market.

But by 1946 the social and cultural conditions had ripened to the point of yielding the inevitable—a musical ensemble capable of expressing the complex cultural range of the Mexican American Generation, especially its rapidly developing sense of biculturalism. Beto Villa seems to have intuited the need for a new musical alternative, and although he overplayed his strategy initially—he tilted too far toward *lo ranchero*—it did not take him long to recognize that the future of the Mexican American orquesta lay with a bimusical repertoire, one robust enough to exploit what Marroquín saw as the ultimate secret of Villa's success: the ability to bring a set of musico-symbolic polarities together—ranchero and "high class," Mexican and American, country and urban. Thus, alone among the orquesta leaders of his time, Beto Villa redirected the course of the ensemble, then in its infancy among the Mexican Americans of the Southwest.

Predictably, perhaps, like many of his musical peers of the time—Eloy Pérez, Manuel Contreras, Eugenio Gutiérrez, Mike Ornelas, and countless others throughout the Southwest—the man who fathered the ensemble's modern, bimusical style embarked upon an orquesta career not in search of an aesthetic ideal that would mediate the contradictions of his generation, but with a desire to master American big-band music. The seeds of that desire had been planted when he entered junior high school and joined a student band that played "only American music" (I. García n.d.: 1). His early encounter with that music was to influence Villa for the rest of his career. He had come under the sway of American musical culture, and his attraction to it would last a lifetime.

To be sure, Villa did not break his ties with Mexican music. In the early years, he was not in a position to turn away from his ancestral music, since his father, who was a rather prosperous tailor, also moonlighted as a musician, and he seemed to have been strongly motivated to launch his son on a musical career of his own. Thus, in 1925, when the youngster was only ten, the elder Villa bought him a saxophone, and then, according to Ignacio García, "he pushed him along, promising him a suit if he finished his lessons and made good grades [in school]" (ibid.). Beto Villa's first lessons were with a *maestro* from Monterrey, Mexico, a Mr. Valenzuela who "had a small Mexican band that played at the local *placita*" during Mexican holidays (ibid.: 2). It was with this group that the young Villa began his musical career, and for many years he was obligated to participate in this and other *orquestitas* with which his father was involved.

But unlike the vast majority of his ethnic peers, Villa remained in school, thanks to his father's secure economic status and the encouragement he constantly offered his son to continue with his musical and academic studies. Villa was exposed in the latter to American musical culture, and here he began his life-long love affair with that culture. Villa was one of the fortunate. Like his friend Armando Marroquín, he was among the few Mexican Americans of that era to reach the lofty educational accomplishment that was a high school diploma. But his close contact with the middle-class culture promoted by American schools clearly affected his sense of cultural citizenship, and the musical sensibilities he cultivated were very much a part of that citizenship.

Thus, when he formed his first band in 1932, Villa, who was then a junior in high school, did the inevitable: he named his American-style band "The Sonny Boys," although it was composed exclusively of Mexican American students who, like Villa, had been captivated by American music. The band consisted of Villa, playing alto saxophone and clarinet, his brother Arturo on drums (he also played trumpet), Abel Rodríguez on tenor saxophone, Vidal Flores on trombone, Gilberto Guerra on alto saxophone, and Apolinar González on clarinet. By forming this youthful group, Villa himself was demonstrating his desire to "switch to American music" (ibid.), although for some time he continued playing with Mexican-styled orquestas.

A commitment to American music became a permanent feature of Villa's musical orientation, and even during his most ranchero (and most successful) phase, he always yearned for a "good" band—the kind that could execute the relatively more difficult arrangements associated with the big swing bands. Indeed, once his immensely successful first record-

FIGURE 9. *Beto Villa y su Orquesta, ca. 1947.*
Courtesy of Beto Villa.

ings had cemented his popularity, he began to reorganize his orquesta. Following an early period (1946–1949) during which he flirted with a conjunto-orquesta hybrid (although he utilized a piano-accordion, not the traditional button model),[4] Villa, as he later recalled, "changed for professional musicians and let go of the ones I had."[5]

But that "professional" band did not materialize until 1949. In the intervening years, Villa was rediscovering his ethnic roots—all the while reaping the profits a ranchero sound guaranteed. (At one dance in Phoenix, Villa collected so much cash they used a wheelbarrow to cart off the gate receipts [Fregoso interview, 1980].) The early Villa sound was generated by a rag-tag collection of musicians—folk performers, really—whom Villa had gathered around him. It included his brother Arturo, "El Tordo," on trumpet; another brother, Oscar, on drums; Ferro Flores on piano; Fidel García on contrabass; the blind Reynaldo Barrera on electric guitar; and Beto's long-time partner, Reymundo Treviño, on the piano-accordion (see Fig. 9). That was the group Marroquín had trouble convincing Betancourt to sponsor. It was also the group that took the Mexicans of the Southwest by storm.

The simple harmonies, the bouncing polka beat, Villa's wailing saxophone sound (*el sonido llorón* [the wailing sound], as it has been called), an unpolished delivery, and especially the piano-accordion-saxophone combination—all struck a responsive chord in the hearts of the Texas-Mexicans. It was the *orquesta tejana* version—the Villa-Marroquín version—of *música ranchera*. *Música ranchera* plus orquesta was the unorthodox union of two sets of musical polarities: the country and the city, the rustic and the sophisticated—in short, the folk-Mexican and the urban-American. The Mexican American Generation took the new style to heart.

Música ranchera plus orquesta: no other combination could have captured so poignantly the tangle of contradictions facing the Texas-Mexicans of the postwar period. Recall from the previous chapter that this was the moment when the Mexican American Generation was making the painful transition from working-class to middle-class existence, from rural to urban life, and from a Mexican to an American way of experiencing the world. Villa and Marroquín were themselves living testimonials to the web of cultural contradictions enmeshed in such a transition. One wants to say they were almost driven to invent this hybrid musical form. Had they not, someone else would have claimed the honor.

But the *música ranchera*–plus-orquesta format was culturally incomplete. It was too biased toward a conjunto aesthetic; it was unbalanced, weighing too heavily toward the ranchero side. A corrective maneuver was necessary if orquesta was to live up to its cultural expectations. In short, the jaitón element was missing. That element was added in 1949. By then Villa had had his fill of the purely ranchero—the orquesta-plus-accordion combination that Paco Betancourt had initially rejected. The father of the modern orquesta yearned for a denser sound, a purer orchestral style—in sum, a "more professional band," to borrow Villa's trope for the modern over the traditional, the city over the country, the jaitón over the ranchero. The ever-vigilant Marroquín may have nudged him in this direction. He recalled telling Villa, "Say, listen, why don't you fix up your [orquesta]? I know of some good musicians, arrangers—Pepe and Chuy Compeán." Villa needed little prodding. Don Reymundo Treviño, whose piano-accordion had been the orquesta's bridge to the ranchero ideal of the conjunto, recalled the inescapable next step:

Around 1949 Beto made the orquesta real big, and the trumpet, myself and Ferro—we were bounced out, because we couldn't read. Beto made a new arrangement, with new musicians, modern musicians. The Compeanes [renowned musicians from Laredo] came in and Fidel was kicked out too, because the Compeanes' father played the bass. So Beto made the band bigger, very modern—like Luis Arcaraz, like that. And the band didn't have the flavor it had before—the *rancherito* style. He lost some fans then. (Personal interview, March 14, 1980; translation mine)

With that fundamental shake-up—bouncing out the folk, musically nonliterate musicians and ushering in modern, literate professionals— Beto Villa and his orquesta had made the symbolic leap from a folk, monocultural style to the bimusical, multifaceted thrust of the modern orquesta. The gap between the old Villa and the new is nowhere more dramatically underscored than in the startling discrepancy between "Las delicias," Villa's very first commercial effort, and "Adiós muchachos," his 1950 rendition of a popular Argentinian tango, which he reinterpreted as a fox-trot. While it is difficult to convey the stylistic gulf between the two recordings through musical transcription, I offer two passages from the respective selections (see below), in order to provide at least a rough concept of the distance Villa had traveled in three years.[6] (For an aural demonstration, listen to the CD *Tejano Roots: Orquestas Tejanas*).

Despite his new, more jaitón strategy, Villa could never have dissociated himself completely from his basic staple, the *rancherito* sound. Thus, from 1950 on, the combination of ranchero and "high class" (to borrow Marroquín's terminology) became Villa's hallmark, a combination soon identified as "Tex-Mex." The juxtaposition of *polcas, valses,* and other genres of ranchero origin against a more sophisticated repertoire—fox-trots and swings from the United States, *boleros* and other Afro-Hispanic forms from Mexico and Latin America—ensured the continued success of the Villa orquesta. Altogether, Villa recorded over one hundred of the old 78 rpm records for Ideal (as well as a few for Ideal's rival, Falcon Records), in addition to a score of long-playing albums (LPs).

During his reign as the leading exponent not only of Tex-Mex but also of the Mexican American orquesta, Villa was the model for others to emulate. And, of course, wherever he went, he attracted legions of devoted fans. The versatile Armando Marroquín, who in the beginning also acted as Villa's promoter, recalled the fast pace Villa maintained once his music became popular: "We went to all the Western states—Colorado, New Mexico, Arizona. We went to all the barrios of the San Joaquin Valley [California], Los Angeles, Michigan, Detroit, Chicago, Nebraska. You name the place—we were there" (personal interview, January 30, 1980; translation mine).

Las Delicias

145

Adiós Muchachos

147

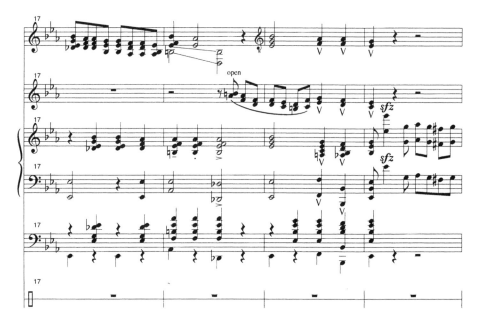

Other contemporaries have confirmed Villa's phenomenal impact, not only in his native Texas but in every state where a substantial Mexican American population was present, including unlikely ones like Kansas and Nebraska. Lalo Guerrero, the venerable California singer-composer who fronted his own orquesta for a time (see Chapter 5), recalled Beto Villa's days of triumph and the fallout of activity and excitement for orquesta music in general that Villa had set in motion:

We were all looking for the gold. I was in there with my band; there was Pedro Bugarín, from Phoenix; Mike Ornelas, from Texas. I used to travel all over the Southwest. Beto was around then, of course. We crisscrossed all over. Beto was going to Kansas, I was coming from there. I was on my way to Colorado, he had just been there. We met on the road all the time. . . . But Beto started it all. He was hot. Goddamn, he was hot. Anywhere in the Southwest—California, Arizona, Colorado—everywhere, the jukeboxes were full of his records. (Personal interview, September 9, 1989)

It is thus impossible to overestimate the enormous influence Beto Villa exerted on his peers and, of course, on the subsequent course of orquesta music. To a man and woman, Villa's surviving contemporaries agreed in interviews that he had started a new tradition and that his formula for success affected everyone who followed in his wake. Marroquín, again, put the matter of Villa's place, not only in the orquesta's development but in that of Mexican American music, in clear perspective (although he underestimated his peers' respect for Villa): "They talk about *música Chicana*—the truth is that Beto Villa was the one who invented it. He started it all, but they don't give him credit."

FROM RANCHERO TO JAITÓN:
Balde González

Once Villa had "invented" the Mexican American orquesta, the path was open, as Lalo Guerrero acknowledged, for others to follow. And they did, as epigones of Villa sprouted throughout the Southwest and beyond. Texas, as usual, led the way, with at least a dozen professional or semi-professional (i.e., commercially recording) orquestas making their appearance during the late forties and throughout the fifties. But Arizona produced at least one prominent orquesta whose style and repertoire imitated the hallmark ranchero style Villa had patented—that of Pedro Bugarín (see Chapter 5). And California's Lalo Guerrero also came under the *tejano* influence, while lesser California orquestas (such as that of Manuel Contreras in Fresno) also felt the impact and adjusted their style and repertoire accordingly.[7] But two immediate successors to Villa tower over all others, simply because in many respects they epitomized the two opposing horizons of the orquesta, ranchero and jaitón, and in this sense their respective location at the two poles of orquesta both accentuated and splintered what Villa had patched together. I refer to Balde González and Isidro López.

González stands out, first, because he succeeded early on in attracting his share of "modern" musicians, to use don Reymundo Treviño's apt term: performers whose professional skills quickly established González as the foremost representative of the jaitón wing of the orquesta. Second, González was a multitalented performer who, among other things, was considered an outstanding singer. Although he did not altogether banish the ranchero element from his repertoire ("everybody had to play polkas" was Marroquín's terse observation), he did attempt—and, in fact, was known for—a much heavier emphasis on the urban, "high class" and more Americanized side of the orquesta repertoire. This he accomplished by performing and recording more of the most sophisticated Latin American genre, the *bolero,* than anyone else, as well as his specialty, the fox-trot, which he sang in both Spanish and English.

Like Villa, or perhaps more so, Balde González presents an interesting portrait of the Mexican American artist who is educated in the public-school system and then is irrevocably captivated by the allure of American musical culture. González was born blind on May 30, 1928, in Beeville, Texas.[8] At the age of seven or eight, he was sent to a special school for the blind in the capital city of Austin. He remained there until he was in his teens, and according to his mother, María Delgado, he was in either the tenth or the eleventh grade when he returned to Beeville. He enrolled in school in the latter city, but he dropped out "*ya casi pa' acabar la escuela*"—just when he was about to finish high school (Delgado and Winton interview).

While in the Austin school for the blind, González took lessons on the violin, later switching to the instrument with which he was most associated during his heyday, the piano. He also learned to play the saxophone and clarinet, but as far as his mother could remember, he never took up singing while in Austin. That came later, when he organized his first orquesta, circa 1948. Meanwhile, at the school for the blind, Balde and a group of other students "formed a little group—they had a little band going" (Delgado and Winton interview), and they gained experience by playing at parties. When González returned to Beeville, he apparently began to approach his musical career more seriously, and the opportunity to lead a professional orquesta may have contributed to his decision to drop out of school. In any case, only a year or so after he returned to his native city of Beeville, the first photographs of Balde González the band leader appeared (see Fig. 10). And it was but a short time after this that he made his first recordings. He could not have been more than twenty-one years of age at the time.

González never attained Villa's fame, but he did have his share of followers. By the late forties and early fifties, many members of the Mexican American Generation—LULACers, especially—had developed a strong allegiance to González's type of orquesta. For their yearly conferences and, more important, for the dances organized by the locals scattered throughout the Southwest, the LULACers preferred orquestas with the jaitón sound Balde González so perfectly projected. By stressing musical forms conventionally identified as sophisticated—the Cuban-Mexican *bolero* on the one hand, the fox-trot on the other—González assured for himself (and for local orquestas that shared his repertoire) a core audience very much identified with the anti-ranchero, anti–working-class aesthetic wrapped up in the jaitón wing of the orquesta. Of course, like most band leaders of his musical persuasion, González always kept a small slice of his repertoire handy for the display of ethnic pride, so that as the occasion demanded, he did bring forth the *polca* and other forms of ranchera music, in this way keeping alive the nostalgia for a pastoral

FIGURE 10. *Balde González y su Orquesta, ca. 1950.*
Courtesy of Sylvia Winton.

heritage most middle-class Mexican Americans were otherwise content
to have left behind.

In this connection, the professional recording orquestas were only the
tip of the musical iceberg, not only in Texas but throughout the Southwest. Dozens, perhaps hundreds, of local, semiprofessional orquestas
plied their trade during the heyday of the modern orquesta: from the 1930s
to the 1980s. Like their commercial counterparts, some of these local orquestas emphasized *lo ranchero,* and some leaned on the jaitón, but most
tried to strike a balance between the two extremes. Since the jaitón style
best represented the aesthetic ideal of the Mexican American Generation, it is worth pointing out that in many cities, especially in Texas, the
growing number of local orquestas with a jaitón orientation (who were
just as likely to play for Anglos as they were for *mejicanos*) may be seen
as an index of the growing presence and influence of the Mexican American Generation. Well into the era of the Chicano Generation, highly active orquestas—for example, Oscar Guerra in the Rio Grande Valley,
Ricky Díaz in Houston (Fig. 11), Paul Elizondo in San Antonio, the Galván Brothers in Corpus Christi (Fig. 12), Eddie Cano in Los Angeles, and
Beto García in Fresno—all bore witness to the intense degree to which
affluent Mexican Americans celebrated through music and dance their
status as respectable members of the American middle class.

FIGURE 11. *Ricky Díaz and His Orchestra, ca. 1990.*
Courtesy of Ricky Díaz.

But the contradictions embedded in the ongoing dialectic of conflict between Anglos and Mexicans (as well as that between middle- and working-class Mexicans) always and everywhere interposed themselves in the celebrations of the Mexican Americans. These contradictions were perfectly encapsulated in the orquesta tradition as it evolved in the Southwest, with the ranchero-jaitón cleavage serving as its most visible emblem. The "schizophonic" nature of the ranchero-jaitón rift (to appropriate a term from the ethnomusicologist Steven Feld [1994]) is poignantly illustrated by the history of Alonzo y sus Rancheros, an orquesta from Houston (not to be confused with the original Los Rancheros, also from Houston).

TRANSFORMATIONS:
The Case of Alonzo y sus Rancheros

Alonzo y sus Rancheros was organized by the husband-and-wife team of Frank and Ventura Alonzo in the mid-1930s. It was an untypical group in that Ventura Alonzo was one of the few women instrumentalists in commercial orquestas—and possibly the only woman in a leadership position. While a few women associated with orquestas did achieve renown—Chelo Silva and Adelina García come to mind—they did so as singers. Moreover, like all singers, male and female alike, they were considered "outsiders"—soloists who were not full-fledged members of any orquesta. In fact, among local, "weekend" orquestas, singers were seen as "hangers-on" who often performed gratis, "for the fun of it," or else were paid a substandard wage.[9] In any case, many of the most commercially successful singers could and did cross ensemble boundaries, thereby further weakening their association with the orquesta tradition. For example, Chelo Silva, next to Lydia Mendoza the most popular of the Mexican American female soloists, recorded with several types of ensembles, including orquestas and Mexican-style trios. Ventura Alonzo thus stands virtually alone as a strong female leader in a musical landscape dominated by patriarchal figures.

When it was first organized, Alonzo y sus Rancheros was a makeshift ensemble, typical of the earlier orquestas, some of which, like Alonzo y sus Rancheros, were still active at this relatively late date. The group fea-

FIGURE 12. *Ralph Galván Orchestra, with the Mexican star Toña la Negra,* ca. 1950.
Courtesy of Bobby Galván.

FIGURE 13. *Alonzo y sus Rancheros, ca. 1939.*
Courtesy Houston Metropolitan Research Center, Houston Public Library.

tured Frank Alonzo on *bajo sexto;* his wife, Ventura, on piano-accordion; Irineo Calvillo on violin; and a bass player, whose name the Alonzos could not recall (personal interview, April 25, 1993; see Fig. 13). Unlike the modernized versions cropping up throughout the Southwest at the time, Alonzo y sus Rancheros "played nothing but *música ranchera,"* according to Mrs. Alonzo. In time, however, as they saw the modernized orquestas overrunning the Houston scene, the Alonzos began adding musicians to their group in an effort to keep up with the times. Over the years, Alonzo y sus Rancheros underwent a radical transformation, as the proud and energetic Mrs. Alonzo refused to cede the Rancheros' position to other orquestas.[10] "I wanted to enlarge the band," she recalled, "to expand the music, because I wanted us to achieve more, to be respected" (personal interview, April 25, 1993).

What Ventura Alonzo sought, in fact, was to upgrade the Rancheros, to move the band from its lowly ranchero groove to a more "respectable" stylistic terrain—in short, to acquire a more jaitón status. Mrs. Alonzo's desire for respectability is borne out by the conversation we held on April 25, 1993, some of which is transcribed below, but more important, it is graphically illustrated in a remarkable photographic chronicle (see Figures 13–15) of the transformation that Alonzo y sus Rancheros underwent between 1939 and 1950. From a small, rag-tag group of ill-dressed ranchero performers, they blossomed into a large, professional, and obviously much more jaitón orquesta. The Alonzos and I discussed their orquesta's radical change (the translations are mine):

MP: [Pointing to the photograph of the large orquesta] Here things had changed. Now you look very . . .

VA: The band was larger.

MP: Do you remember the word "jaitón"?

VA: Yes, of course.

FA: Hee, hee, hee, hee.

MP: Well, you look kind of jaitón here. Tell me, how did it happen? What brought about the change?

VA: Well, I guess we worked at it.

FIGURE 14. *Alonzo y sus Rancheros, ca. 1945.*
Courtesy Houston Metropolitan Research Center, Houston Public Library.

FIGURE 15. *Orquesta Alonzo, ca. 1950.*
Courtesy Houston Metropolitan Research Center, Houston Public Library.

MP: Well, tell me the difference between this old photograph and the other one.

VA: Well, there is a difference. We are all dressed alike, and we dressed well.

MP: You look like a society belle.

VA: Hee, hee, hee, hee! Well, yes, but that's how it was.

MP: There's something that interests me very much, and it's this: What motivated you to progress from the type of group—small, ranchero—to the type—what was the motive? Why didn't you keep . . . ?

FA: Because we were slighted.

VA: [We were slighted] because we were rancheros.

FA: We played all *música ranchera*—*polcas, valses,* and all that. And there were clubs here that didn't want that music. They wanted American. And so I said, "I'm going to bring in a saxophone." And I added a sax and then another. Later, I put in trumpets, until I had my orquesta: three saxophones, two trumpets, *bajo sexto,* and bass.

VA: And piano [accordion].

FA: And I dropped the ranchero label—we were then just Alonzo y su Orquesta. Then it was fine; the new musicians could read. For example, all
the new music that came out—*boleros,* cha-chas—I had my arranger.

Installed as a jaitón group, Alonzo y su Orquesta was able to compete
successfully in the Houston musical scene for many years, until the
couple's retirement from music in the 1960s. Of course, the Alonzos never
forsook ranchera music, but after World War II it was used only as a stylistic ballast against the weight of the jaitón. As both Mr. and Mrs. Alonzo
pointed out, no matter how "elegant" a dance, people always wanted to
dance their polkas. Such preference for musical code-switching was an
integral part of the bicultural experience of the Mexican Americans, just
as bilingualism was. Moreover, as with bilingualism, the Alonzos' bimusical repertoire mirrored the contradictions inherent in the Mexican Americans' position between several sets of disparate cultural realities—American versus Mexican, urban versus rural, middle versus working class, and
jaitón versus ranchero. Those contradictions are perfectly illustrated in
the following account, as recalled by a veteran orquesta musician, Moy
Pineda, from the Rio Grande Valley. Pineda referred to some of the
dances his orquesta played for elite clubs in the city of McAllen, Texas:

Every year I play for a club here. This is an elite club, the Alhambra Club.
Now, they hire me not because I'm Moy Pineda, but because I get up there
and I give them a big band for show. We don't even play what we play at "regular" dances. And now, look—I'm talking—these guys are all professional
people—doctors, lawyers—we're talking about the elite crop. I change my
whole book for them. We try to keep up with the times. We do a little disco,
salsa, los boleros, ballads, and some of the new fox-trots. But the reason they
hire a big band is they want something that according to them is the best....
They want that big band, and we got those fancy tuxedos, but the music—
if I started playing some of the stuff that we do elsewhere, they'd run me
off. So the first hour we do, man, special arrangements—and nobody's dancing. But [after] about an hour, I take off *con "Los laureles," "El abandon-
ado"* [ranchera tunes]. As soon as I start that, man—ching! Everybody gets
on the dance floor. When they start drinking, they go back to the roots. Like
I said, you can take the country out of—how does that go? You can take *la
raza* out of the country, but you can't take the *rancho* out of them. (Personal
interview, July 7, 1979)

In such ways, as described by Pineda and the Alonzos, does the dialectic between country and city, ranchero and high class, and the other

polarities discussed here operate. Until the 1970s, every orquesta had to negotiate the contradictions inherent in such a "schizy" environment. Some, like Ricky Díaz and Balde González, preferred the "high-class," or jaitón, which, however, limited the range of their audience. Others, such as saxophonist-singer Isidro López, the most celebrated orquesta-ranchera leader of the latter phase of the Mexican American era, chose the ranchero road to fame. Thus, if Balde González represented the jaitón horizon, then Isidro López spoke for its ranchero opposite.

FROM JAITÓN TO RANCHERO:
Isidro López

Isidro López, "el Indio," was born in Bishop, Texas, outside of Corpus Christi, in 1933.[11] Straddling the two generations, Mexican American and Chicano, López in many ways was a precursor, musically and ideologically, to the musicians of the Chicano Generation. Like Armando Marroquín and others similarly situated, López obtained a high school education and even spent one year at Texas A&I in nearby Kingsville. He learned to play guitar from an uncle when he was about twelve, but he did not learn the saxophone until he entered high school, where he joined the band. López also had the benefit of individual instruction from several *profesores* who were active in the music-rich city of Corpus Christi— orquesta musicians like Tony Ornelas and Mike Cuesta (whose son, clarinetist Henry Cuesta, was for many years a fixture on Lawrence Welk's television show).

In assessing Isidro López's musical ideology—his particular preference for and defense of *lo ranchero*—it may be enlightening to note that he did experience some of the hardships of working-class life in his youth, and this experience may have predisposed him toward a working-class aesthetic and sympathy for the downtrodden generally. In comparing the conjunto to the orquesta, López repeatedly expressed his conviction—one contrary to that of most orquesta musicians—that the former *es una música muy fuerte* (is a very strong music). "Among my musical friends," he said, "there are many who say, 'Accordion? that's trash.' But it is they whose minds are twisted. To me the conjunto is equal to the orquesta."

Yet, after we had discussed the orquesta-conjunto dichotomy for several hours, and despite his strong defense of the conjunto, López did yield some ground. Here is the heart of that segment of our conversation:

MP: Mrs. Ornelas [the wife of the late band leader/teacher Tony Ornelas] did tell me that her husband's orquesta catered to *gente decente,* and not *gente corriente,* like the conjunto did.

IL: Well, I saw that myself. It's just that for me, when it comes to classes of people—to me the *pachuco,* or the poorest or the richest—to me it's all the same. But, yes, the reason those people think of themselves [as superior] is because they act superior, and they cut themselves off from the other [poor] people. . . . And that's what I have always seen among ourselves—that there are people who, because they have better means— that we think that we are better than they are, but not as far as I'm concerned. It's true, though, that there are people who—I don't know how to put this—but among the conjunto there are people who are more ignorant, who go more to conjunto dances than those of the orquesta.

López's reluctance to condemn the conjunto may be related to his own life circumstances. Despite his enormous popularity in the late fifties and early sixties, he never seems to have prospered financially—another circumstantial factor linking him more strongly to a working-class experience than to that of his middle-class peers. His father was a mechanic, but López remembers living in a two-room house, and getting up at dawn to go pick cotton—an indication that hard times must have visited the Lópezes during Isidro's youth. Whatever the case may have been, López did, obviously, experience the acculturative effects of American schools, and this acculturation sets him apart from most of the exponents of the other *tejano* tradition, the conjunto—performers like Narciso Martínez and Santiago Jiménez who grew up in grinding poverty and had little contact with American schools and their acculturative influence (Peña 1985a).

In fact, "el Indio" did play saxophone with the "father" of the modern conjunto, Narciso Martínez; however, prior to organizing his first orquesta, most of López's professional experience was accumulated with the orquestas of Eugenio Gutiérrez, Juan Colorado, and, somewhat ironically, with Balde González, the epitome of the jaitón. His first professional experience came in the late forties when he joined Donato Garza's orquesta—a band that played "in the same style as Beto Villa." Surprisingly, given his tremendous popularity as a singer, López never tried vocalizing until one day, at a recording session with Juan Colorado, when the orquesta's regular singer failed to show. When no one else volunteered to sing the tune scheduled for recording, Armando Marroquín turned to López and said, "Isidro, tú cántala" (Isidro, you sing it). Summoning all his courage, López tried it, and Marroquín signaled his satisfaction by telling the newly made singer, "You know what, from here on you do the singing for the recordings."

Shortly after that, in 1955, López broke with Juan Colorado and started his own orquesta. From then on, the young saxophonist-turned-singer, mindful of the market potential among the working-class partisans of conjunto music, concentrated on developing a ranchero sound that would appeal to the mass of the people. His strategy was to emulate the well-tested ranchero sound of the mariachi as much as possible, while integrating it into the *orquesta tejana* style forged by Beto Villa. A disc jockey from Corpus Christi, Genaro Tamez, coined a fitting label for Isidro López's style—Texachi. And, as López pointed out,

But he didn't say "mariachi." Texachi is a *tejano* style mixed with mariachi. Because we tried a bit to sound like a mariachi, even though we could never say that it sounded exactly like a mariachi. That would have been impossible.

Furthermore, in differentiating the *orquesta tejana* style—or range of styles, actually—López offered his own description of its uniqueness:

MP: I know you said that your orquesta was different from Eugenio Gutié-rrez's and Beto Villa's, but is there such a thing as an *orquesta tejana* style?

IL: There is, because we do have a different sound, we do have a different style from any band from Mexico—or the U.S. . . .

MP: Is there, then, a common thread that links all of the *orquestas tejanas*?

IL: We have a different style than any bands from any other country. Why is it? I don't know. I can bring musicians from the other side; even if they try to blow like me, they can't. Our style—even our food—is very different from the other side.

MP: Do you think that *orquestas tejanas* in some way reflect our biculturalism?

IL: Well, it [*orquesta tejana* style] is not American. But then it's not Mexican either. (The strip was rendered in Spanglish; I have translated the Spanish phrases; see Chapter 3)

Armed with his new "neither-nor" Texachi style, López began to record song after popular song, and by 1960 he had overtaken all of the bands connected with the Mexican American era. His trademark was the *canción ranchera*, with which he made the *tejano* popularity charts regularly after 1956—hits like "Emoción pasajera," "Ando sufriendo y penando," and one of López's most remarkably innovative efforts, the ranchera-rock,

Mala Cara

"Mala cara." The last song strongly presages the bimusical synthesis that was to be the crowning achievement of the next generation of musicians. It begins as a straight late-fifties rock, then switches into a Texachi ranchero mode after the introductory riff, thus creating a dramatically novel effect, one that qualifies as an example of "intrasentential code-switching," as this is manifested musically. The transcription offered here attempts to capture the feel for the musical code-switching occurring at the phrase level.

Like Beto Villa and Balde González, Isidro López had been inevitably

me di

Americanized by his experience in the public-school bands, and although he seldom performed American music, he did make excursions into the Latin American versions of the "high-class"—the *bolero* and the *danzón*. His usual strategy was to record a ranchera he felt would "hit," and, on the flip side, to insert a sophisticated *bolero*, for example. In López's own words:

I knew that an Isidro López record was going to sell. So we would record one of my type of songs [ranchera], and on the other side I would fill in with a *bolero* or a *danzón*. People would listen to it because it was Isidro López.

By purposely including music with a higher social status, López attempted to "upgrade" the tastes of his (mostly) working-class public, while ensuring the support of the people "with better means." Such was the case, for example, with one of López's biggest hits, "Las bicicletas," which had on the flip side one of his most ambitious efforts at sophisticated arranging—the *danzón* "La hiedra," some of which is transcribed below by way of conveying a feel for its sophistication.

Ultimately, however, Isidro López justified his ambivalence toward the conjunto-orquesta nexus and its attendant social distinctions by insisting that the popularity of each depended on eras, or *épocas,* as he put it. He had recorded with orquestas in the beginning, he claimed, because that was the popular thing to do at the time. Later, he recorded with Narciso Martínez and Tony de la Rosa (conjuntos) because that was selling at the time. Still later, in the 1960s, he had a fifteen-piece orquesta, which he said, "*gustó mucho*"—was well liked. For Isidro López, then, the reality of a conjunto-orquesta dichotomy devolves into a question of eras, not social distinctions, although he maintained a basic, if inchoate, recognition that the social differences between the two musics cannot be denied, any more than the inherent contradictions:

IL: It's like I tell you—there are conjunto eras and orquesta eras. Although we as individuals, among our own people, do cut ourselves off from others. The poor people will go over to the conjunto rather than the orquesta. They spend more, too, and they are merrier, to my way of thinking. And the youth today—despite the fact that American music is very strong nowadays, a lot of them—I don't know if they are illiterate or not very well educated or what—but they're strong for the accordion.
MP: But Isidro López has always been comfortable with either style?
IL: Yes, any style. I have recorded—I think I was the first Chicano to do it, to record with mariachi. And I recorded with conjunto and of course with orquesta. But to me the conjunto and orquesta—they're equal.

La Hiedra

This last statement, on the equality between conjunto and orquesta, links Isidro López to the ideological sentiments of the musicians from the Chicano Generation. As López himself acknowledged, among his peers (i.e., musicians from the Mexican American Generation), *a los conjuntos los miran abajo*—they looked down on conjuntos. As I indicate in Chapter 7, this attitude of condescension declined sharply during the 1970s, when the romantic-nationalist ideology of the Chicano movement swept away status distinctions based on class and thereby enabled La Onda Chicana to freely synthesize musical differences based on such distinctions. The musical revolution La Onda Chicana embodied was still ten years in the future, however; in Isidro López's prime, such a sweeping synthesis was not yet possible.

CHAPTER 5

The Los Angeles Tradition
Triumph of the Anti-Ranchero

While *tejanos* were the principal innovators in the evolution of an aesthetics of the orquesta, the Mexicans of Los Angeles, in particular, were not idle bystanders. They, too, forged an orchestral music responsive in its own way to the same powerful cross-cultural currents that had fueled innovation in Texas.

I had a real distaste

for rancheras;

I couldn't stand them.

CHICO SESMA

Less obvious in California, perhaps, is the highly visible class difference of the orquesta-conjunto dialectic evolving in Texas. However, musically articulated status distinctions are not absent in the Golden State, by any means, as we shall soon see. It is simply more difficult to tease these distinctions out of the available ethnographic material—at least for the twentieth century (recall that status differences were sharply evident in the nineteenth-century *baile*-versus-*fandango* distinction; see Chapter 2). Still, one has only to recall don Lalo Guerrero's comments when asked what the late Eddie Cano, one of Los Angeles's most illustrious musicians, might have said about conjunto/norteño music:

Oh, are you kidding? It would turn him off completely! Knowing Eddie—and I knew him—he'd probably say, "Man, that's garbage, man. That's trash." (Personal interview, September 9, 1989)

Moreover, even as the modern orquesta was evolving in Los Angeles in the 1930s and '40s among the (generally) better educated Mexican Americans, a socioculturally distinct music was thriving underground, so to speak—a folk, ranchero music more appealing to the tastes of the working class, especially the immigrant sector. This music seems to have gone largely unnoticed, at least by the musicians who were busy forging their own orchestral styles.

I have already discussed Manuel S. Acuña's role in the early commercial development of the orquesta in Los Angeles. Indeed, he continued to be a major player in the post–World War II period, forming a bridge of sorts between the ranchero traditions of the working-class folk and the cosmopolitan tastes of an emergent middle class, particularly in Los Angeles. Very much in the mold of Armando Marroquín in Texas, Acuña possessed a keen sense of entrepreneurship, while his talents as composer, arranger, and musical connoisseur kept him in the forefront of musical developments in Los Angeles. In collaboration with Felipe Valdez Leal, who was himself an astute music entrepreneur, Acuña operated a successful recording company named Imperial.

As the principal musical arranger for Imperial, Acuña had a "house band" that accompanied many of the singers who recorded for the company, some of the most notable in the orquesta tradition being Lalo Guerrero, and singers Fernando Rosas and Adelina García. To accompany these singers, Acuña would assemble orchestral ensembles that could be quite sophisticated; on the other hand, for Carmen and Luis Moreno (Los Morenos) and other ranchero groups, Acuña would switch musical gears and bring forth a variety of folklike mariachi ensembles with names such as El Mariachi Coculense, El Mariachi Tapatío, and Los Costeños. As doña Carmen Moreno recalled in a personal interview, "They had different names, but it was the same group, Acuña's group." However, Acuña was never involved in the Los Angeles ballroom dance circuit, nor, apparently, did he ever go on tour.

Other orquesta standouts who came of age in the years surrounding the Second World War and who were more involved in the dance hall tradition as it evolved in Los Angeles include musicians such as Phil Carreón, Sammy Mendoza, Manny López, Lalo Guerrero, Don Tosti, Chico Sesma, and Eddie Cano. However, with the lone exception of Lalo Guerrero, orquesta exponents in Los Angeles followed a different trajectory than their *tejano* counterparts. They ignored—or rejected, in some instances—*lo ranchero,* and were, moreover, far more influenced by American swing-jazz music on the one hand and Afro-Hispanic on the other, especially what later came to be known as *salsa.* A ranchero style that would connect the orquestas of Los Angeles to the bedrock working-class public (again, heavily immigrant) mushrooming in the postwar years never emerged. Far more than in Texas, that public depended on imported Mexican music and musicians—including *conjuntos norteños* and even Beto Villa—for the satisfaction of its musical needs.

One might argue that the hyperurban Mexican Americans of Los Angeles may simply have outgrown ranchero music by the 1940s. Yet, as indicated in Chapter 4, the attraction to *lo ranchero,* particularly as expressed in music, was as strong among Mexican Americans of the 1940s as it is today, and evidence from urban areas—Houston, El Paso, and even Los Angeles itself—suggests that this attraction was a function of the Mexicans' real and romanticized links to an agrarian past. What the urbanization of Mexicans in the Southwest did was to complicate the symbolic link to *lo ranchero,* as the contradictions discussed earlier set in and as the urbanization process quickened the pace of acculturation.

In effect, urbanized Mexican Americans were coming under increasing pressure to adopt a wide range of American cultural practices, including some that clashed with the lifestyle transferred from the country to the city. This was especially true of upwardly mobile people, who, as in Texas, were much more susceptible to the niceties of middle-class American affluence. Big-band music was one American expression that appealed in particular to the upwardly mobile, (usually) better-educated Mexican Americans of Los Angeles, who, like their Texas-Mexican counterparts, seem in this respect to have been especially drawn to the enticements of American middle-class culture.

Again, however, even in Los Angeles of the late thirties, forties, and beyond, a stubborn working-class, ranchero subculture continued to undergird an otherwise rapidly Americanizing population of Mexican Los Angeles, a subculture many orquesta musicians did relate to, if only as an alternative to be rejected. As late as the war years, for example, Carmen Moreno, who with her husband, Luis, recorded folk ranchera music for both the major and Mexican American labels (Columbia, Imperial, Azteca), recalled that in her social circle of musicians and audiences, the modern orquesta was not a component of musico-cultural activity. In the late 1930s, when people she knew wanted to dance, they would go to "El Ranchito de don Daniel," where they danced to "accordion and guitar." When asked about orquestas in Los Angeles, doña Carmen replied, "I think there were orquestas, but they were in other places, such as the dance hall on Brooklyn and Bailey Streets. But I never went there" (personal interview, August 14, 1989; translation mine).

Yet, of course, modern orquestas were plentiful in Los Angeles by the 1930s. But we may better understand this cultural gap between the ranchero world of Carmen Moreno and the sophisticated one of orquesta musicians like Eddie Cano by briefly examining the musical careers of two such musicians, Don Tosti and Chico Sesma. By way of bridging the gulf that apparently existed between the music of a Carmen Moreno and

that of a Tosti, Cano, or Sesma, a profile of the more eclectic and synthesizing musical careers of two other orquesta musicians is offered—
one of Lalo Guerrero and the other of Pedro Bugarín. The latter's base
was actually in Phoenix, but he was influenced as much by the orquestas of Los Angeles as by those in Texas.

DON TOSTI:
The Chicano Zoot-Suiter as Musical "Snob"

Edmundo Martínez Tostado, whose stage name became the more Americanized "Don Tosti," was actually born in Texas, in El Paso, in 1923,
where he learned to play the violin and clarinet at an early age.[1] He was
born in the *barrio,* where "it was very rough":

> So, consequently, the people who adopted me, which was my mother's
> sister and my grandfather, gave me music lessons to keep me out of the
> streets, and out of the hands *de las gangas* [of the gangs]. So my grandfather
> forced me to study *solfeo;* solfège, it's called. I went through two books, and
> we were so poor, I had no instrument. Finally, my teacher says, "Hey, this
> kid knows more music than professional musicians now. He's got two books;
> there's four—he's got two more to go—what are we gonna do with him?"
> They got me a violin, and two years later I was playing with the symphony.

By the age of twelve, Tosti was playing violin with a hybrid group by
the name of La Orquesta Muro. In a variation of the ranchero-jaitón
paradox illustrated by Los Rancheros of Houston, La Orquesta Muro
dressed in *charro* outfits but played "nothing but American and some
tropical—no *mexicana ranchera* or mariachi" (see Fig. 16). In fact, Tosti
never cared much for ranchera music. Of Beto Villa, for example, he offered the following assessment:

> I thought he was, eh, ethnic. It was that type of thing. It was ethnic. It was,
> uh, you know—I would listen to a black vibraphonist named Milt Jackson.
> I would listen to Beto Villa. I mean, I could hear a black jazz musician play
> vibraphone so great, and I could sometimes—you understand? Maybe I'm
> a musical snob, [but] I'm not putting the music down. It is not, wasn't—it's
> like Chico Sesma told you.
> MP: "I hated Beto Villa and ranchera music," is the way he put it.
> DT: I didn't state it that way, but it's—that's the way it was.

FIGURE 16. *Don Tosti (left, kneeling) with La Orquesta Muro, ca. 1936.*
Courtesy of Don Tosti.

Thus, despite his association with La Orquesta Muro and, through it, his symbolic brush with *lo ranchero,* Tosti never developed an affinity for ranchera music. Indeed, he acquired a particular dislike of *música norteña,* which in his younger years he called "shit music." Later in life, however, he seems to have modified his stance toward *lo ranchero* somewhat. He acknowledged the importance of Beto Villa's "ethnic" music, as well as that of Little Joe y la Familia (see Chapter 7), although he dissociated his own career from that sort of musical performance. Instead, he went the way of American swing-jazz music associated with such big bands as the Dorsey brothers, Duke Ellington, and others.

Tosti moved to Los Angeles to be with his mother in 1938, and there he immediately distinguished himself as a first-rate music student. He was rewarded by being appointed concertmaster of both the orchestra at Roosevelt High School and the All-City Symphony. His long-time friend (Lionel) Chico Sesma recalled Tosti's impact upon his arrival: "He took the whole music department at Roosevelt High by storm." Once in Los Angeles, Tosti had plenty of opportunity to develop his skills, as big-band imitations were beginning to proliferate among the Mexican Americans of the "City of Angels." There were the Phil Carreón, Tilley López, Sal Cervantes, and the De la Torre orchestras, from which youngsters like Tosti could get their inspiration. In fact, Tosti got his first taste of Los

Angeles swing with Sal Cervantes's orquesta, but it wasn't long before he organized his own group.

By 1939, Tosti had established his reputation as a violinist, but he had also learned to play clarinet and saxophone. Smitten by a desire to play swing and jazz, he organized a high school band in which he played tenor saxophone and violin (see Fig. 17). The group was so impressive it soon came to the attention of a young entrepreneur and dance promoter, Joe García, who, after auditioning the band, hired it to play for his Club Juvenil Social, which held weekly dances at the Zenda Ballroom. In the early 1940s, the Don Tosti Orchestra, by then a semiprofessional group, also played at the Paramount Ballroom, the Diana Ballroom, and the Royal Palms Hotel. The latter, according to Chico Sesma, was the place to go for "big Saturday night dances for the Mexicans in Los Angeles" (personal interview, March 31, 1993).

Given Tosti's extraordinary musical talent (he also mastered the contrabass), it was not long before he was catapulted to the level of performance he had always yearned for—professional, top-flight, big-band swing and jazz. "I wanted to play jazz, you know," he said, and in 1943 his wish came true; he was picked up by Jack Teagarten's orchestra. Later, he also played with such notables as Bobby Sherwood, Les Brown, Jimmy

FIGURE 17. *Don Tosti's first orchestra, ca. 1942.*
Courtesy of Don Tosti.

Dorsey, and Charlie Barnett. During these years, Tosti shared the company of some of the greatest names in popular music, both in the United States and in Mexico. Having become one of the most accomplished bassists in the big-band market, he was never at a loss for employment.

But this employment took its toll on the Mexican "roots" for which he now displays a certain pride, just as it distanced him from his original constituency, the Mexican American community of Los Angeles. During the years 1943 to 1948, he moved in predominantly Anglo circles. More important, perhaps, is the imprint Tosti's experiences in Anglo social circles left on his personal history. He was irrevocably Americanized, to the point of claiming an Anglo wife after he divorced his first. His Americanization, however, was not one-dimensional; he was also impressed early on by African-American jazz, which in the 1940s was hardly the epitome of "mainstream" American musical culture. Thus, as he himself reflected:

I used to listen to jazz. That's why I went to a black teacher. I wanted to play jazz, you know. And the swing bands were the thing then. And this is the late thirties. And I'm a kid. And I got into it. And that's why, you see, I'm of Mexican descent, but I don't play mariachi or ranchera music, or anything like that. It's not that I don't like it—I love it. It's just that I was never interested in it—or exposed to it, let's say—a better word.

One detects a bit of hedging here, when compared to his unadulterated distaste for *lo ranchero* as a young man, especially *música norteña*, which he considered to be nothing more than *mierda* (shit). In fact, Tosti projects an unequivocal feeling of bicultural mastery when he says, "I may have been a jazz musician, but I'm very proud of my Mexican descendance [*sic*]." Moreover, as if the contradictions present in his early rush toward Americanization were not enough, vis-à-vis his retrospective pride in his Mexican descent (not to mention his love for swing music, as opposed to his distaste for the ranchera), Tosti further compounds the matter by pointing proudly to his participation in the rebellious culture of the proletarian *pachuco*. "I was a *pachuco*," he proclaimed:

I mean, I wasn't ashamed; I'm from El Paso [allegedly the birthplace of *pachuquismo*], I knew the language, I was brought up with the kids, I wore the pants. And the zoot suit. We all did in those years.

Tosti's engagement with *pachuquismo* through his music is an intriguing development—although one suspects this engagement was more vicarious than substantive. The subculture of the *pachuco* (and *pa-chuca*) is an enigma in the historical development of Mexican culture in the Southwest. Seen by some as linguistic heirs to an ancient gypsy tradition; by others as low-class scum; and by still others as "instinctive rebels," "cultural aberrations," and even an anticonformist vanguard to the ideology of Chicanismo (Mazón 1984: Chap. 6), the *pachucos* and their modern origins are best summarized by Mauricio Mazón:

The "birth" of the pachuco is linked to the movement of Mexicans from rural to urban centers, to a generational rebellion against both Mexican and American culture, to the influx of drugs, and to an enduring legacy of discrimination. (1984: 4)

Epitomizing in many ways the cycle of contradictions that defines the Mexican American experience in the Southwest, the *pachucos* were nonetheless scorned by the upwardly mobile, especially in Texas, where they were much more identified with the music of the working class, the conjunto. By contrast, in California, *pachucos* early on linked up with swing music, in particular the boogie, which Tosti identified as "a low-class type of piano playing invented by blacks." Ethnomusicologist Steve Loza noted this attraction of the *pachucos* toward the swing-boogie: "*Los pachucos,* or the zoot-suiters, were attracted to the swing sound in a way that seemed to reflect the phenomenon of their *caló* language, a slang form of Spanish that became their popular vernacular" (1993: 161). In an interesting development presaging the assimilation of black musical culture by Los Angeles Chicanos in the 1960s and '70s (as practiced by, e.g., Thee Midnighters or Cannibal and the Headhunters; see Loza [1993: 95ff.]), the young Angelenos of the postwar years seem to have been captivated by boogie culture, including the zoot suit. A number of Mexican American performers—Don Tosti included—adopted the zoot-suit culture, turning the fashion to commercial advantage by composing and recording several original and very successful boogie-inspired tunes.

The importance of the boogie style in the music of the Mexican Americans of Los Angeles lies not so much in the fact that the *pachuco/a* fashion became its principal icon (both music and icon were exploited in Luis Valdez's celebrated play and movie, *Zoot Suit*), but that in their most ambitious efforts, the Angelenos succeeded in forging a genuine musical alloy—if not yet a true synthesis—of three musical cultures: white, black, and Mexican/Latin. Although not on the scale of the ranchero style that Beto Villa invented in Texas, which evolved in a straight line toward the most important bimusical form created in the Southwest, La Onda Chicana (see Chapter 7), the efforts of Los Angeles Mexican Americans to develop the boogie hybrid represent a significant, if geographically limited, breakthrough toward a true bimusical synthesis of swing-jazz and Mexican/Latino.

In this breakthrough Don Tosti was a key contributor, and although both he and Lalo Guerrero have staked out claims as the first to introduce the Chicano-style boogie, each in fact played a role in creating an important substyle in the musical legacy of the Hispanics of the Southwest. To don Lalo apparently belongs the honor of introducing the linguistic aspects of *pachuquismo* to the commercial market, a feat accomplished as early as 1946, when he and El Trío Imperial recorded "La pachuquilla" and "El pachuco y el Tarzán" with Manuel Acuña's Imperial Records. These tunes were still strictly in a ranchero mode, although the heavy use of *caló*, the argot of the *pachuco*, set them apart from the more traditional ranchera. Guerrero later recorded several songs in which *caló* lyrics were embedded within a swing-boogie medium—"Marihuana Boogie," "Vamos a bailar," and "Chicas Patas Boogie," of which the latter's melody was borrowed from a Louie Prima song.

But it appears to have been Don Tosti who accomplished the ultimate mix in this small but significant development in the musico-cultural life of Mexican Americans. In 1948, Tosti and the Pachuco Boogie Boys recorded a tune, "Pachuco Boogie," that reportedly sold over a million records. The success of "Pachuco Boogie" no doubt prompted Lalo Guerrero to increase his output of *pachuco* boogie compositions, as it did others. Again, "Pachuco Boogie" fused *caló* lyrics to the boogie musical style, and in this it resembles Lalo Guerrero's own efforts. However, shortly thereafter, perhaps in 1949, Tosti recorded what is, in this writer's estimation, the closest to a synthesis of boogie, *caló*, and *tropical*—a tune titled, interestingly enough, "Chicano Boogie." Here we witness Tosti's decision to invoke a regional identity through the appropriation of the label "Chicano," as well as an effort to mold the three elements into a unified whole. This effort is underscored by a key spoken phrase inserted into the sung lyrics:

Ese Chicano Boogie está más loco, ese, porque guacha, tiene tiempo de rumba y tiene el del boogie, ese. Póngase locote, 'mano, y oiga este vatote, 'hora aquí viene el boogie y la rumba.[2]

By way of providing at least a visual representation of the "Chicano Boogie" and its bimusical shifts between Latino/*caló* and boogie, a partial transcription follows:

Chicano Boogie

ta mas lo - co   si lo han o - i - do man-no gua - cha   le   pue-de bai-lar el boo-gie

The Chicano boogie enjoyed a short but memorable history extend-
ing from the late forties to the early fifties. More important, it is perhaps
symptomatic of the way the Chicano Generation inverted old symbols
that at the end of the twentieth century, a formerly negative figure like
the *pachuco* was enthusiastically embraced by individuals as dissimilar,
ideologically, as Don Tosti and Luis Valdez. But embraced (and romanticized) it was, and, as is the case with the Texas-Mexican conjunto, the
pachuco-as-cultural-icon offers powerful testimony to the changes in attitude wrought by the Chicano movement. But that is part of the topic
for the next chapter; its appropriation by Tosti and others in the 1940s
attests to the contradictions inherent in the bicultural life of the Mexican Americans, as well as (we must admit) the power of the commercial
market—limited as this was in the Southwest—to induce artists to
make cultural compromises rife with ambiguity. Such was the case with
the Chicano boogie and its principal exponent, Don Tosti.

In Tosti's case, this ambiguity surfaces in his condemnation of *música
ranchera,* even as he embraced, at least in a commercial sense, the
lifestyle of the *pachuco*—a lifestyle even more stigmatized among "respectable" Mexican Americans than conjunto music. It was perhaps in
tacit recognition of the contradictions dogging him in his social life that

Tosti attempted to justify his equally contradictory musical life—his rejection of *lo ranchero* and his allegiance to swing-jazz and, most contradictory of all, his adoption of the stigmatized *pachuco* music-and-dress
fashion. Thus, in summing up his life, Tosti reaffirmed his dual (and ambiguous) cultural citizenship: "I am proud of my ancestry, but I'm Amer-
ican-born, so I speak well, don't I? I seem well educated, no?" But then,
reflecting further, he remembered with some bitterness the night when,
as a would-be patron, he was denied entry into an Anglo nightclub in
Hollywood—this despite the fact that he played there regularly with Anglo orchestras.

In 1948, after traveling for five years with Anglo swing bands, Tosti got
married and decided to settle down in Los Angeles. His musical talent
and reputation drew the immediate attention of local musicians and
promoters, who persuaded him to "come home musically," and this is
when he experimented with the Chicano boogie. This period—from
1948 to about 1960—also marked Tosti's emphasis on Latin-*tropical* (see
Fig. 18). At this time he recorded for RCA and with Taxco, a local label
that produced "Chicano Boogie." He also kept busy performing in numerous clubs local to the Los Angeles area. In the 1960s, he spent several years in Honolulu, where he performed a variety of popular musics
at some of the better-known hotels, such as the Shell Beach.

FIGURE 18. *Don Tosti and His Orchestra, ca. 1955.*
Courtesy of Don Tosti.

The years since Honolulu have been particularly disappointing for the still-active Tosti, in that the changing tide of popular music—or, at least, the popular music he has performed since the 1960s—forced him to adapt to new tastes and styles whose aesthetic standards he felt were beneath his dignity as a musical "snob." Rock music, as forged by Elvis Presley and others, destroyed for Tosti the integrity of American popular music. By 1993, performing once more for predominantly Anglo-club audiences, he had modified his musical repertoire to include Elvis and other pop-music favorites. "Now I have to play shit music from Elvis Presley," he complained, "'cause the people want it, and I have to play it"— a sour ending for a man who prided himself for the abundant native talent with which he was blessed and for the bimusical abilities that enabled him to move effortlessly between the musico-cultural domains of American swing-jazz, Latin American *tropical,* and the hybrid *pachuco* boogie he created.

CHICO SESMA:
A *"High-Class" Cosmopolitan*

Like his friend Don Tosti, Chico Sesma started his musical career early. In 1937, at the age of fourteen, he was playing trombone with the band of Tilley López. As a trombonist, his models early on were big-band virtuosos like Tommy Dorsey and Lawrence Brown, the latter a trombonist with the Duke Ellington Orchestra. Sesma's interest in music was so strong that when he finished high school, he attended Los Angeles City College for two years, where he majored in music. Don Tosti remembers him as "one of the most cultured young men I knew . . . a very educated, high-class gentleman." Unlike Tosti, who considered himself a product of the *barrio,* zoot-suit fashion and all, Sesma frowned on that subculture. Very much like Tosti, however, Sesma also developed a distaste for *música ranchera.* Sesma's feelings toward the cultural complex bound up in *lo ranchero* are summed up in a conversation we had on March 11, 1993, part of which is transcribed here:

MP: Did you consider yourself to be bicultural, or, I mean—or do you iden-
     tify more with American musical culture than you do with Mexican mu-
     sical culture, or Latino musical culture?
CS: Well, in my teen period, when I was just starting to work locally with
     bands—it was a good time for me because I had already developed a
     taste for big-band music. I had a real distaste for rancheras—I couldn't

stand them. This is all one heard out of Spanish-language radio as an adolescent, you know. I couldn't stand it.

MP: So, when you talk about alternatives, you mean that you were going to break away from that ranchero stuff and start playing a different kind of music?

CS: Yes—well, I wasn't a musician during the ranchera music that I heard as an adolescent [child]. But when I became a serious-minded musician, as a twelve-year-old, I immediately recognized the kind of music that I wanted to develop with. And it just so happened that all of East Los Angeles—the bands that existed at that time—were made up of, like 100 percent Hispanics . . . in the late thirties, yes. They were all big bands. Matter of fact, one of the first bands that I worked with—Sal Cervantes—had four trumpets and two trombones and five saxophones.

But, as Don Tosti verified, Chico Sesma acknowledged that even in Los Angeles the orquestas he played with did include *boleros* in their repertories "and a couple of rancheras"—this despite the heavy influence of the American big bands. Sesma recalled that he played the rancheras *a huevo*—grudgingly. Apparently, the Mexican Americans for whom Sesma performed, despite their urbanization and acculturation, still maintained a vestigial allegiance to their ethnic roots, as symbolically communicated in ranchera songs. But their real preference was big-band music. Sesma recalled the Angelenos' bicultural predicament:

Even then they were already English-speaking Mexicans. Such as myself. That was—it may have been our first language, but we were bilingual. But I think it would be fair to say that even then, we were more proficient in the English language than we were in Spanish. Not that we were ashamed of it—of being Mexican. It was just the way it was.

While he was a student at Los Angeles City College, Sesma was recruited by an American orchestra leader, Kenny Baker. He joined that band, and, as he recalled, "This was now an Anglo band. From that point forward I was the only Hispanic in all the other bands that I played with." Those "other bands" included that of the highly respected Johnny Richards (nee Cascález, the arranger for Stan Kenton's landmark album *Cuban Fire*) and also the one led by his brother, Shot Cascález, as well as Jimmy Zito's band and that of Russ Morgan. Sesma played with these from 1943 to 1949, when he was approached by an old friend and radio-station executive, George Barrón, to try a new enterprise—radio broadcasting.

Sesma, who in March of 1993 (at age sixty-nine) still possessed a marvelously deep, melodious voice, was intrigued, and he listened to Barrón's idea, which was to create a new kind of programming aimed exclusively at a Mexican American audience:

There was a lot of Mexican broadcasting already; this [was] the ranchera thing. Period. *Punto.* So they wanted something bilingual—in English and Spanish, with a Latin-music format, distinct from that which every other station had, you know.

Given an opportunity to experiment with a different kind of Latin-music format, one based on a bilingual concept, Sesma agreed to try it, sensing an opportunity to carve out a new and profitable niche. According to Sesma:

[Barrón] undertook to provide me with a concentrated course in radio broadcasting—two weeks, you know. So then I auditioned, and I was hired, and I started in February of 1949 with a half-hour program. And inside of six months, that little half-hour had increased to an hour, and by the end of the year was a three-hour program. It was so very well received.

The experiment had worked. Based on a strategy aimed at an unmet demand for bilingual programming with a Latin-music repertoire, Sesma's program lasted until 1957, when the station switched to the "top-forty" format overrunning radio at the time. Sesma attributes the program's success to his bilingual delivery (though "with a preponderance of English") and the type of music mix he played—*boleros, mambos, cha-cha-chas.* "It's what we call today *salsa.*" As well, Sesma featured the top artists of the time from Mexico—Los Panchos, Los Tres Ases, and Los Diamantes (vocal trios with guitar accompaniment), Fernando Fernández, María Victoria, Luis Arcaraz, Lucho Gatica. He also played the local orquestas—Eddie Cano, Don Tosti, Manny López. But Sesma refused to play *tejano* music—no Beto Villa. "No, no, I couldn't stand that," he said, emphatically. Later, however, when Sesma resumed bilingual programming on another station, KALI, where he worked for another ten years (until 1968), he did "develop a real taste—I must say my musical appreciation grew—when I became aware of Little Joe y la Familia, Sunny Ozuna and the Sunliners"—two of the top orquestas from the next stage in the development of *orquesta tejana.* "Great talents!" was Sesma's assessment of the new breed of *orquestas tejanas.*

Meanwhile, in 1954 his old friend George Barrón planted another idea in Sesma's head—to rent the popular Hollywood Palladium and organize Mexican dances there. The Palladium was an old establishment, controlled by Anglo interests, where big bands were featured six nights a week. But Sundays were available for rental to outside groups, and Barrón and Sesma booked a Sunday with the then-popular Pérez Prado, an Afro-Mexican orquesta, along with two *tropical* groups from the East Coast, Joe Loco and Tony Martínez, as well as the locally popular Manny López. Sesma paid $800 to rent the Palladium, while charging $2.50 per person at the gate. He called the affair "Latin Holiday," and four thousand people showed up. Sesma and Barrón "made a killing, so we staged another one the following year," recalled Sesma.

And then they became semiannual. And in the fourth year, I signed a new contract with the Palladium to stage them monthly. . . . And once again, it was very innovative, if only because most of these bands had never been here before: Tito Puente; Tito Rodríguez; Johnny Pacheco; La Orquesta Aragón, which I brought directly from Cuba before the sugar curtain went down . . . Benny Moré; Daniel Santos; El Gran Combo; from Mexico, La Santanera, Pablo Beltrán Ruiz, Carlos Campos. . . . Throughout all the fifties and sixties, and '73 was my last event. All the bands came here; I don't think you can name one band that I didn't have here.
MP: Beto Villa.
CS: Well, true, true.

Even without the enormously popular Beto Villa, Sesma was able to exploit the musical interests of the Mexican Americans of Los Angeles—young men and women who obviously shared Sesma's love of big-band Latin music, *tropical* music, and who were oblivious, we may assume, to the more dichotomous tastes of their Texas-Mexican counterparts, and the latter's vacillation between ranchero and "high class." Who were these fans of Sesma's music shows? I attempted to reconstruct the social scene:

MP: [Looking at a photo taken at one of the Palladium dances; see Fig. 19]
    Now, I'm looking at the people here, Mr. Sesma—
CS: Yeah, they're all of our own people.
MP: And they look pretty well dressed.
CS: Oh, yes! In those times we wore ties, we—ties at the dances. Oh, yeah! Nothing like back then.
MP: Is this a typical crowd at the Palladium?
CS: Oh, yeah, sure—very well dressed.

MP: No matter what the band, this is how they always dressed?

CS: Sure.

MP: Now, would that mean that these people—I know that this might be a hard question, but answer it as best as you can. Uh, would most of these people be like—sort of middle-class *mexicanos*? Or were they—

CS: Uhhh, well, I don't know. At that—in those years, there *was* a middle class, and because there was a middle class during that period, I would say yes—hm, hm.

MP: Well, they just don't have the looks of working-class people, the way they're dressed; they look pretty elegant.

CS: Well, you'd be surprised. Even the working-class people took a great deal of pride in their appearance, and spent a goodly amount of their salary on their wardrobe.

MP: I guess what I'm trying to say is that the typical day laborer, or farm-worker, probably wouldn't come to an affair like this.

CS: The farmworker would have no interest in an event like this.

MP: They liked ranchero music.

CS: Right, right. That's it.

MP: So these were probably urban people—

CS: Very cosmopolitan, very cosmopolitan.

Or very *jaitones,* as working-class Texas-Mexicans might have labeled them. Most of them, in fact, were young people like Don Tosti, Eddie Cano, and Chico Sesma—Mexican Americans with at least high school degrees who in the Los Angeles of the forties and fifties were distancing themselves from the people for whom Carmen and Luis Moreno performed. In this they were not unlike their upwardly mobile Texas-Mexican counterparts, who were also moving away from the working class through cultural practices such as music and dance. And, like the Texas-Mexicans, many of these Angelenos may in fact have belonged to the working class, but it was a relatively affluent segment of that class, one enjoying a measure of upward mobility and the kind of cultural assimilation Sesma and Tosti—indeed, Beto Villa—exemplified. Unlike the Texas-Mexicans, however, the California Mexicans lacked specific labels for class and cultural difference—no ranchero versus jaitón here, or *gente decente* versus *gente corriente.* Only musical taste and, perhaps, the rejection of certain styles such as the conjunto (but not the mariachi, a more romanticized version of *lo ranchero*) functioned as tacit indicators of the widening breach between class segments in the Golden State.

Yet there is a sense among many that Los Angeles, despite its demo-

FIGURE 19. *Dancers at the Palladium, Los Angeles, ca. 1955.*
Courtesy of Chico Sesma.

graphic importance as a magnet for the massive Mexican immigration during the latter third of the twentieth century, for a long time constituted a self-contained population unit as far as Mexican Americans are concerned—especially those in the area designated as East Los Angeles (cf. Loza 1993). To a remarkable degree, they did follow (and to an extent continue to follow: witness the localized explosion of *banda* in Los Angeles) their own cultural fashions and trends, as can be seen in the musical practices on display at the Palladium and other spots that Tosti and Sesma frequented. Outside of Los Angeles, however, the Mexican Americans of California displayed more commonalties with their *tejano* and Arizonan counterparts (see Chapter 6). The next two musical figures, Lalo Guerrero and Pedro Bugarín, catered to less-endogenous groups than the East Los Angeles Mexican Americans familiar to Tosti and Sesma, and they thus cultivated a different approach to musical performance.

FIGURE 20. *Lalo Guerrero, 1990.*
Courtesy of Lalo Guerrero.

LALO GUERRERO AND PEDRO BUGARÍN:
Bimusical Eclectics

Lalo Guerrero is without a doubt the most prolific musician-composer that Mexican America has ever produced (see Fig. 20). In his long and illustrious career, which spans from the 1930s to the 1990s, Guerrero experimented with almost every style and genre of any consequence in the Southwest.[3] Born in Tucson in 1916, Lalo Guerrero early on pursued a more eclectic approach to musical performance than did either Tosti or Sesma. He began his musical career as a singer in a Mexican-style vocal trio, a type of ensemble whose vernacular origin in the 1920s swerved toward a more cosmopolitan approach in the forties and fifties. The Mexican trio, epitomized by the internationally famous Trío los Panchos, was quite capable of shifting from ranchero to sophisticated, and this was the case with the various trios with which Guerrero was associated in the 1930s, his first years as a professional musician. When he moved to Los Angeles in late 1937, Guerrero was introduced to the glittering nightlife of the Anglo nightclubs—El Trocadero, the Mocambo, the Coconut Grove, and others. This was a period, according to Guerrero, when Latin music first invaded the United States, as the *conga, rumba,* and other Afro-Caribbean rhythms caught the fancy of American popular-music lovers.

Guerrero recalled that in Hollywood, especially, many nightclubs had adopted a Latin decor, complete with palm trees, coconuts, and flamingos. And to ensure "authenticity," Latin orchestras were brought in—some local, some from abroad. As a finishing touch, Mexican trios were hired to play during intermissions. It was in this capacity, as an intermission entertainer, that Guerrero was introduced to the Hollywood "big time":

When the band took a break, we would come on, with the three guitars, singing Mexican songs—from El Trío Calavera, Los Tariácuris, Los Murciélagos. That's how I got started, very young, about eighteen—in the big-time clubs of Hollywood.[4]

One can imagine the impression the glamorous settings of the swank Hollywood clubs made on the young Guerrero—a working-class Mexican lad from Tucson suddenly thrust into the limelight in places where Anglo patrons surely had little knowledge of Mexican culture beyond the strains of Lalo's trio. How does Guerrero view that time in his life? "I think we were like an exotic form of entertainment, but we loved it. At eighteen we felt like we were on top of the world." But that was only the beginning for don Lalo, the Hollywood nightlife being but one of the many disparate musical experiences to forge in him a thoroughly eclectic musical personality.

During the war, Guerrero moved to San Diego, where he held the only daytime job of his life, working in an airplane assembly line. While in San Diego, he sang solo with a USO orchestra that "used to travel all over California, entertaining the troops." His specialty was Mexican songs such as "Amapola," "Muñequita linda," "Cuando vuelva a tu lado," and others, some of which he used to sing bilingually. "I was the Latin star with the USO band," recalled Guerrero.

But then in 1946, the war now over, Guerrero returned to Los Angeles, where he found a changed musical environment. As in Texas, Mexican Americans were emerging from their isolation, and Mexican nightclubs and Latin music were now proliferating. He went to work at one of them, La Bamba, where "nothing but *raza* came." Guerrero had to switch cultural gears; he was no longer performing in front of Anglo crowds. Buoyed by the enthusiasm with which *la raza* received his music, he turned seriously to musical composition aimed at a Mexican market. During the next few years—now a budding star with Acuña's Imperial Records—he composed several songs that achieved universal popularity and became part of the greater Mexican repertoire—songs such as "Canción mexicana," a ranchera, and "Nunca jamás," a *bolero*. At this time, Guerrero committed himself to a dualistic mode of performance—both ranchero and cosmopolitan, of which "Canción mexicana" and "Nunca jamás" are respective examples. His popularity began to increase as he turned out hit after hit with Imperial, one of the most active labels on the West Coast and a rough counterpart to Marroquín's Ideal label in Texas. Guerrero would compose the songs, and Imperial's Acuña would write the arrangements—orchestral or mariachi, depending on the song.

In 1949, Guerrero decided to form his own orquesta and to begin touring. More important, of all the orquestas in Los Angeles, his was the only one committed to a touring itinerary aimed at a Mexican American audience. Guerrero was eminently successful, as mentioned earlier, but here is how he summarized his performance strategy, which was fundamentally based on a ranchero-cosmopolitan combination:

> What I played—I was a great admirer of Agustín Lara, Gonzalo Curiel, Luis Arcaraz [three of the most cosmopolitan composers-performers in Mexico]. I very much liked the *bolero*, and since I was a romantic singer, I used to do a lot of those. I also did *danzones;* I loved *danzones.* I always started my set with a *danzón.* And then I'd throw out a couple of *boleros.* And then I'd play music that might be popular at the moment, such as a *porro colombiano* like "María Cristina." When the *cha-cha-cha* hit, I would play that as well, and then the *mambo,* when that was in vogue. But since I played in that area where the people were very accustomed to Beto Villa's polkas— he had such an impact, you know, with the polkas—I incorporated into my repertoire several of his polkas and some from Mexico.

In short, like his Texas-Mexican counterparts, Guerrero was perfectly adept at "mixing it up," as he put it. He could play what *tejanos* would call jaitón music—the *bolero, danzón*—but he could also dip into the world of ranchera music. Our discussion regarding his musical versatility led us into an area of great interest to me—the socioeconomic context for these two broadly defined styles of music, ranchero and "high class." A transcription of the pertinent dialogue follows:

MP: In California, did you ever notice that there were some people who went for a more "high-class" music than others who were more, shall we say, poorer [*sic*]? Was there any sort of division like that here in California, in Los Angeles, that you were aware of?

LG: Yeah, there was, but only here in California [not in Nebraska or Colorado]. I noticed it, there were some groups, musicians, who played a lot of *tropical*. I'm talking about the late forties and fifties. And there was a certain crowd that followed those bands. And then there was another group that would follow bands like mine, that was more down to earth. See, I would play *danzones,* I would play *corridos*, and I would mix it up, you know, and I'd throw in some American music once in a while. And a certain crowd followed me.

According to Guerrero's analysis, the "*tropical* crowd" was a group of people who followed Tosti, Mendoza, Sesma, and the Los Angeles orquestas. Like their similarly situated jaitón counterparts in Texas (e.g., Balde González), Tosti and his contemporaries were the musical vanguard of a larger sociohistorical movement tied, precisely, to the emergence of the Mexican American Generation and its place in the unfolding dialectic of conflict. Guerrero, on the other hand, catered to a more ranchero crowd, perhaps in the mold of Isidro López fans in Texas, who were more strongly tied to their ethnic roots and less upwardly mobile than Sesma's followers. But none were completely immune from the contradictions embodied in the ranchero-jaitón dichotomy. Guerrero loved *boleros,* but he had to play *polcas;* Tosti hated ranchera music, but he flirted with a *pachuco*-inspired boogie, while spending years immersed in Anglo musical circles; Sesma flip-flopped in his attitude toward *tejano* music, even as he, too, inhaled deeply the ethereal air of the "high-society" music associated with luxury Anglo hotels. And all three at one time or another made the switch from an Anglo to a Mexican-Latino sociomusical ambience. In their totality, these oscillations between disparate social and cultural poles served to emphasize that as members of the Mexican Amer-

ican Generation, these musicians were not exempt from the contradictions plaguing that generation as it lurched forward on the long and tortuous path carved out by the dialectic of conflict.

To put it somewhat differently, in the contradiction-riddled movement
of the Mexican Americans toward a synthesis of two antithetic cultural
economies, the Balde González–Don Tosti constituency represented one
segment—the upwardly mobile, acculturationist—while Isidro López's
and Lalo Guerrero's more "down-to-earth" crowds represented another
segment in the churning mass of people that was continuously redefin-
ing its social, cultural, and ideological position vis-à-vis the forces pro-
pelling Anglos and Mexicans along the path of confluence. Only the contradictions generated by the massive polarities involved (Mexican versus
American, ranchero versus jaitón, working versus middle class) can explain the ambivalence of a Don Tosti when confronted with the challenge to reflect on the extreme duality of his musico-cultural past, or
Chico Sesma's aversion to Beto Villa contrasted with his enthusiastic support for Villa's principal heir, Little Joe Hernández. What we see in all
these cases—Guerrero, Tosti, Sesma, Villa, Balde González, and orquesta musicians generally—is the molding of musical personalities within
a context of intercultural antagonism, accommodation, contradiction—
in short, all the elements forged within a dialectic born of ethnic *and*
class conflict.

From the California perspective, nowhere is musical and cultural contradiction better expressed than in Lalo Guerrero's brilliant attempts at
synthesizing the disparate experiences that formed the raw material for
his musical genius. His emulation of Beto Villa is of course explained by
the fact that Guerrero, as he acknowledged, was anxious to please an audience whose tastes had been molded by the Villa example. But beyond
that, his own excursions into the *pachuco* fashion resulted in musical in-
novations of great synthetic power, as compositions like "Marihuana
Boogie" and "Vamos a bailar" juxtaposed stylistic formulas from swing
and Latin, as well as linguistic elements from *caló*, to deliver tightly wo-
ven, bimusical messages encoded and decoded within a uniquely bicultural Mexican American milieu. Once again, to provide a feel for the impact of such efforts, a fragment of "Vamos a bailar" is transcribed below
(note the use of *caló* and the switch from swing to *danzón*).

Although not an Angeleno but an Arizonan, Pedro Bugarín is best
considered within the purview of the California branch of the orquesta,
even though, more so than his long-time friend Lalo Guerrero, he was
strongly influenced by the *tejano* tradition. In fact, Bugarín contributed
several recordings to Marroquín's Ideal label, and in the 1950s he made

Vamos a Bailar

Swing tempo ♩=85

tempo di danzon (♩=125)

Tempo I

something of a name for himself in certain regions of Texas, where his orquesta played regularly on the ballroom circuit and for local LULAC councils. He may thus be considered a "bridge" between the *tejano* and Los Angeles traditions.

Bugarín was born in the vicinity of Phoenix, in 1917.[5] A solid member of the Mexican American Generation by virtue of birth date and socio-economic destiny, he graduated from high school in 1935, and he enrolled in college, majoring in accounting. Among his many occupations, Bugarín worked as a bookkeeper for a movie theater, and later for an army base in Phoenix. Eventually (in 1957), he obtained a master's degree in business education, and he went to work for a local school district as a teacher, rising through the ranks to become assistant business manager for the district. He retired from that position in 1981. As a teacher, Bugarín was able to maintain a dual occupation as a musician, and he toured extensively during the summer—indeed, his availability for touring was an important reason why he ultimately chose teaching over accounting.

But achievement in education was not enough for Bugarín. From an early age he displayed an unusual knack for capitalist enterprise; he was a mere eighteen, for example, when he invested his energy in the music business. In 1935 there were two radio stations in Phoenix, and he noticed there was no Spanish-language programming on either. He decided to approach the management and ask for some air time. He talked to Jack Williams, an executive at the station (later governor of Arizona), about buying some radio time. "I went in there and told him, 'We would like to put on a program; I'm going to have a live band and we're going to sell some spots.'" Williams was receptive to the idea, and within two weeks, having sold his first radio commercials, Bugarín was ready to premier his thirty minutes of Spanish radio:

He [Jack Williams] gave us a Tuesday from 7 to 7:30 [P.M.]. So I had a live band—I didn't play then, you know, so I hired Los Charritos Alegres. It was, like, a violin, trumpet, saxophone, guitar, and the bass. So I went to pick him up at 6:00, and the leader of the band was in a T-shirt. "Well, my brother couldn't make it—he's working, irrigating—so we can't make it." So I decided, "I got to pick up somebody." And we knew of a fellow named Larañaga, who loved to sing. He was a jeweler. And I said, "Do you want to sing?" He said, "Yeah." So, anyway, "Let's go." And then I picked two or three other musicians, and that's how I got started.

To make matters worse for Bugarín's debut as a radio producer, he had also hired an announcer (he didn't think he himself "was qualified") who also failed him. Undaunted, the young entrepreneur grabbed the microphone and took over as host of the program himself. About fifteen minutes later the announcer arrived, and Bugarín approached him, but he said, "You're doing fine, go ahead, you're doing fine." As Bugarín recalled:

He just pushed me back, and we went through the half hour. The following week, we came back on Tuesday. I had another band, you know, that played. And then we got a Tuesday and Thursday program and about three weeks later we had about 3,000 letters, you know, coming in, and they really loved it, because now we're getting a lot of letters, you know. So I was on the air for about two and a half years, and that helped me a lot later on to get into the music business.

Bugarín's radio audience at this early juncture was apparently very Mexicanized, just as it had been for similar radio programs in Los Angeles. Although the groups used by Bugarín were orchestral in nature (if somewhat rudimentary), they were nonetheless obliged to perform Mexican, not American, music. The program was evidently very successful, but the tenor of the repertory—traditional Mexican and ranchero—indicates that its primary audience was working class in nature. This did not deter the enterprising Bugarín, who throughout his career in the music business never hesitated to embrace both *lo ranchero* and the jaitón. In time he opened a highly successful ballroom, and he later branched out into the restaurant business, in the process becoming quite affluent ("wealthy," according to his friend Lalo Guerrero). But he never displayed the musical elitism of an Eddie Cano or a Chico Sesma. Indeed, he seems to have relished his association with such working-class groups as the historically important Conjunto Bernal, from Texas (see Peña 1985a), with which he had a long-lasting and friendly relation.

This sociomusical eclecticism led to Bugarín's eminent success in the business world of music, just as it did for his long-distance friend Armando Marroquín. And, as in the case of Marroquín, it is difficult to imagine that Bugarín was merely pandering to the tastes of his more proletarian public when he embraced ranchero musicians such as the brothers Bernal, or that he was using them as fodder for his own material gain. Of course, being the middle-class entrepreneur he became, Bugarín must have grasped early on the working-class, ranchero nature of the broader market in the Hispanic Southwest, and the need to reach out to that market. But this inclination toward interclass alliances seems to have come naturally to this sanguine man, described by Lalo Guerrero as "a type of guy with a great sense of humor—he'll keep you in stitches." In any case, like Marroquín, Bugarín's folk, Mexican roots enabled him to move easily between the workaday world of the (mainly) working-class public he entertained and the increasingly affluent world of his personal affairs.

In addition to his teaching and other business responsibilities—including a successful ballroom, the Riverside—Bugarín also formed his own orquesta, circa 1942. Unlike some of his California contemporaries, however, Bugarín did not begin his musical career early. He was already sixteen when he picked up his first instrument, the guitar. But his late entry into the world of musical performance did not deter him from cashing in on the field of activity he was barely getting to know. He learned to play the alto saxophone as well, and he "decided to get a group together—five or six people, you know." He began playing Sundays at the Riverside Ballroom, which was then under Anglo management. Sunday was "Mexican night" at the Riverside, Wednesdays and Saturdays were "Western nights," while Thursdays were "Blues nights" and Fridays and Mondays were "Big-Band nights." Bugarín recalled the socioethnic mix:

MP: Were there different crowds on different nights?

PB: Oh, yeah. Saturday was for western—people who liked to dance the western music. In those days you didn't intermix. I mean, you know, the blacks—"colored," we called them then—they went on Thursday for their dance.

MP: All blacks?

PB: That's right. That's it. And on Saturday, if a Mexican would go—maybe two, three Mexicans might go, you know—they kinda didn't want them there.

MP: And Sunday was Mexican night, *raza* night?

PB: Oh, yeah. An American or two might come by to watch us. They didn't last too long, because that's the way it was.

MP: What about on Monday, if a big band was here? Who went to listen to the band?

PB: Okay. Everybody went. Like when Harry James or Glenn Miller came in. But predominantly it would be white. Now Mexican big bands—Luis Arcaraz and all the big bands that were coming in . . . Pérez Prado—all those would come in on a Sunday.

MP: Right, so Sunday was mainly for the Hispanics.

PB: We used to have two or three thousand people there every Sunday. And that's when I [my band] started going up.

And up he went. Bugarín leased the Riverside Ballroom at this time (the late forties) and took over the scheduling of the various groups. For several years he kept a rather hectic schedule: he was an accountant by then, and he did this in addition to running the Riverside Ballroom (with his brother's help) and directing his own orquesta, which was the "house band" on Sundays. The latter was to take much more of his time in the fifties and sixties. In the late 1940s, Bugarín "got to know" Beto Villa ("he packed my ballroom when he came in here"), and the latter told him, "You have a good band; why don't you go out?" Bugarín reflected on that, and he said to himself, "I think I will go out."

The "pretty good band" Bugarín had at this time consisted of two trumpets, four saxophones, and a trombone, as well as a rhythm section of piano, bass, guitar, and drums. "I put in a trumpet[er] who was a real professional [an Anglo big-band musician who had come to Arizona for his health], and two saxophones who were real professionals, and we had a band," recalled Bugarín. With a competent orquesta in hand, Bugarín took his music on the road, following the "taco circuit," as one orquesta musician dubbed the Mexican American tour—California, New Mexico, Nebraska, Kansas, Colorado, and Texas. While touring Texas, Bugarín would stop in Alice and record for his friend Armando Marroquín, whom he had met on some of Beto Villa's first visits to the Riverside Ballroom.

As noted, Bugarín's style and repertory borrowed from both the California and Texas traditions. The Arizonan's orquesta tended to resemble Lalo Guerrero's, in particular. But Bugarín blazed his own little trail as part of the broad march of the Mexican American orquesta toward its pinnacle during the Onda Chicana era. Perhaps as a result of the equal doses of influence he received from the two traditions flanking his desert base, Bugarín occasionally transcended both by creating music that presaged the bimusical accomplishments of the next generation of orquesta musicians. For example, when we compare his relatively early mambo "Doña Chona" (1953) with any of the efforts of his *californio* and *tejano* contemporaries, we discover that his fusion of jazz and Latin has no exact parallel in either of the two traditions—although Don Tosti's "Chicano Boogie" comes close. In this sense, then, and like Isidro López in Texas, "Boogie" Bugarín should be considered a precursor of things to come in the Mexican American orquesta tradition. A few phrases from "Doña Chona" are transcribed here to convey a sense of Bugarín's hybrid style:

Doña Chona

CONCLUSION

When I asked him to compare the California and Texas orquestas of the 1940s and '50s—what I have here called the formative period—Chico Sesma exclaimed, "Oh, Manuel, you're talking—that's black and white! Los Angeles and Texas—black and white!" What Sesma was referring to, in particular, was the ranchero style forged by Beto Villa and his contemporaries, and its rejection by most of the Los Angeles orquestas (but not so by those in other parts of California, e.g., Fresno). Yet in other respects—and certainly to the extent Los Angeles orquestas played ranchero, if *a huevo*—the two subtraditions are clearly expressions of a more global musical phenomenon that emerged in the Hispanic Southwest during World War II and the subsequent decade. What the Texas and California orquestas of the forties and fifties had in common was the practice of combining, occasionally fusing, two broad musical horizons, embodied in American swing-jazz and *tropical* (that collection of genres and their rhythms evocative of a Latin American heritage), to create a bimusical experience.

In this respect, the California branch of the orquesta tradition can only be considered extremely active during its formative years, both in and outside Los Angeles (and we can include Pedro Bugarín's contributions here). Many of the musicians brought up in the California tradition were highly accomplished in both *tropical* and swing-jazz performance, as even a cursory listening of the recordings from the late forties and fifties reveals (see Discography). Except for the absence of ranchera music in their repertoires, performers like Don Tosti and Eddie Cano were every bit as accomplished as the best of their *tejano* counterparts. Chico Sesma confirmed as much when he observed that "the ranchero stuff aside, Texas and California had an equal share of great ones." Recognizing the dominance of the *tejanos* in the wider Mexican American market, however, Sesma suggested that "the Texans have achieved far greater commercial success and acceptance than any of the local Los Angeles musicians."

As Sesma recognized, in a retrospective assessment of the formative period, the California branch of the Mexican American orquesta cannot be positioned as an equal to its Texas-Mexican counterpart. Two factors help explain this inequality. The first is contained in Sesma's assessment that the *tejanos* quite simply developed a much wider market. They commanded a larger audience, one consisting of New Mexicans, Arizonans, Midwesterners, and many *californios* outside Los Angeles. A more important factor, however, is one related to a point raised earlier, namely, that owing to their strategic position in the unfolding dialectic of conflict, the Texas-Mexicans may be said to have been compelled, to a degree not imposed on the *californios,* to respond dynamically, first, to their harsh subordination in the Anglo social order and, second, to the increasing contradictions their successful challenge to that social order introduced. The symmetrical opposition between ranchero and jaitón (less detectable in California), and the Texas-Mexican orquesta's evolution toward the culturally dominant Onda Chicana, are the results of the *tejanos'* unique position in the interethnic conflict.

As I have maintained all along, the Mexican American orquesta generally—not just the Texas-Mexican branch—is particularly sensitive to the second factor enumerated above. The *tejanos* led the way in negotiating the tangle of contradictions that define the experience of all Mexican Americans. The California-Mexicans were themselves no strangers to the succession of events confronting the Texas-Mexicans: developments in the orquesta tradition in Los Angeles attest to their similar predicament. But they were not positioned at ground zero in the grand dialectical scheme. Thus, despite general similarities, the California experience differs from that in Texas. As more recent participants in the dialectic of conflict (recall that Mexicans repopulated the Golden State only after the Mexican Revolution of 1910–1917), they entered the spiral of contradiction at a later stage of development, and their cultural response was thus in some ways only an echo of that in Texas.

Events at the next level of development bear out this assessment, but that brings us to the period of the Chicano Generation, which is the topic of the next chapter. Here it is worth recalling that World War II represents a powerful tremor whose effects fundamentally realigned Anglo-Mexican relations. In the postwar period, the Mexican Americans posed strong challenges against Anglo domination, and these challenges triggered major movement along the dialectical fault line that propels those relations. In Chapter 3, I documented the rise of the Mexican American Generation and its key participation in charting new social and cultural directions for Mexicans in the American Southwest. Culturally, the first legacy of the generation's efforts was the emergence of a dual identity, expressed in the form of bicultural practices. Socially, the principal result was a deepening rift between upwardly mobile, rapidly acculturating Mexican Americans and their working-class peers, both native-born and immigrant. The ideological sum of these developments was the intensifying contradiction embedded within the Mexican American experience.

This contradiction was articulated at the musical level via the ranchero-jaitón poles, which were rapidly materializing by the end of the war. By 1946, then, while Mexican Americans (and, of course, Mexican immigrants) were overwhelmingly supportive of ranchera music, many, especially the upwardly mobile, had turned against that music generally, and its representative in the Southwest, the conjunto, specifically. Yet, as a testimony to their contradiction-filled experience, the Mexican Americans, whether in Los Angeles or Houston, were in no position to transcend the ethnic power inscribed in the concept of *lo ranchero*. Thus, orquestas in the Southwest were never fully able to extricate themselves from the burden of *lo ranchero* and the range of implications it carried. Caught between two sociocultural vectors, orquestas vacillated between the poles of *lo ranchero* and *lo jaitón*, or, as was the case in Los Angeles, between American and Mexican-Latino. Thus, one of the problems the ethnomusicologist faces in interpreting the significance of the orquesta is its stylistic extremes—its many faces, as it were.

In sum, the Mexican American orquesta emerges in the 1940s as an artistic solution to the range of adaptations initiated by the Mexican American Generation—their attempts to negotiate all the contradictions embodied in the master tropes, ranchero and jaitón. In rising to the challenge of socioeconomic diversity and the pressures to acculturate, the Mexican Americans embraced selected aspects of American culture while clinging at the same time to many of their symbolic antecedents. The orquesta became a central metaphor in the articulation of the biculturalism that resulted. In the betwixt-and-between position of the Mexican American Generation, orquesta found a niche, helping to negotiate the ideological contradiction between a frustrated assimilation on the one hand and a persistent allegiance to the mother culture on the other.

PART THREE

The Chicano Era

CHAPTER 6

The Chicano Generation
Conflict, Contradiction, and Synthesis

Just as the Mexican American Generation, in all its sociocultural contradictions, gave birth to the orquesta and nurtured it during its formative period, so did the succeeding Chicano Generation carry the tradition to its pinnacle under the banner of La Onda Chicana. Beginning in Texas in the mid-1960s, the ensemble style, especially in its ranchero guise, was subjected to an intense degree of experimentation. In the 1970s, again in the hands of the *tejanos*, it achieved a remarkable synthesis of all the disparate elements present since the inception of the orquesta—the ranchero, the jaitón, the Mexican/Latino, and the American. And, true to its or-

Without heroic dreams and cultural symbols of mythic proportion, the material aims of a nationalist movement may lack the spiritual center which sustains struggle.

GENARO M. PADILLA
(1989: 114)

ganic link to the innermost circuits of Mexican American culture, the orquesta faithfully reproduced at the musico-symbolic level the dramatic changes occurring at the level of social action. To understand the musico-symbolic changes, however, we need to probe the social and ideological impulses that energized the Chicano Generation in its drive to synthesize the disparate forces operating on the jagged edge of its existence between two antagonistic cultures.

THE BIRTH OF A GENERATION

Rodolfo Alvarez (1973), the first scholar to advocate a generational approach to the study of Mexican American society, proposed that the historical cohort he called the Chicano Generation reached an important threshold, or critical historical juncture, early in its tenure. Mexican Americans had reached the limits of acculturation and structural assimilation that the preceding generation and its integrationist strategies could attain. In the 1960s, further advancement in American society, achievable principally through upward mobility, had become problematic, despite the implementation of Lyndon Johnson's "Great Society" programs. These programs, which had promised to lift oppressed minorities out of their poverty and into the mainstream of American society and culture, had run into obstacles almost immediately (e.g., the resistance of Anglos to affirmative action).

In the Southwest itself, long-standing racial and cultural discrimination against Mexican Americans was reaping its costly harvest: The number of Mexican American youths dropping (or being pushed) out of school had reached such an alarming level that they had become a drag on further socioeconomic progress. The gains made by the Mexican American Generation were not enough to offset the growing army of unemployables who were rapidly becoming marginal to an increasingly technological workplace (Alvarez 1973: 939; cf. Barrera 1979: 150, on the reemergence of a marginal sector in Chicano society in the 1970s). The capacity of the Mexican Americans to make further inroads into what Barrera has called the "integrated sector" of the economy (1979: 130) was thus threatened by their "obsolescence at the bottom of the social structure" (Alvarez 1973: 939).

Paradoxically, the economic marginalization of Mexican Americans was occurring at a time when the "middle-class sector of the larger society [was] getting ready to acknowledge our capacities and our right to full participation" (ibid.)—at a time, that is, when the dialectic of conflict had evolved sufficiently to encourage more progressive (and productive) interethnic relations and better opportunities for Mexican Americans in the political economy of the Southwest. In sum, the prolonged dialectic between antagonism and accommodation was beginning to yield results, as the dominant society gradually acquiesced to the logic of liberal democracy and its principle of "equaliberty."

But the same acquiescence that moderated the dominant society's stance toward interethnic relations also begot a more universal challenge to the system as it had existed until the 1960s. Initiated by the blacks in the 1950s and fomented by disaffected youths and feminists, a countercultural surge erupted in the 1960s and shook the nation out of the cultural complacency that marked the two decades following World War II.

This surge, itself an outgrowth of critical shifts occurring within the political economy, engendered the Great Society programs and their attendant attitude that at last America had summoned the resolve to tackle its internal problems and fulfill the Utopian dream of a great and noble society. The countercultural rumblings began in the early 1960s and culminated in the fateful year of 1968, when a series of events (the deaths of Robert Kennedy and Martin Luther King, the disruption of the democratic convention in Chicago, the Poor People's March on Washington, the Tet offensive) signaled both the high-water mark and the beginning retreat of the Utopian liberalism of the 1960s.

For Mexican Americans, the Black Power movement, the opposition to the war in Vietnam, and the countercultural spirit prevailing after the mid-decade were the most influential in reinforcing the challenge that an emerging new generation (with some help from its predecessor) had begun to mount against the system that had for so long denied them the benefits of cultural citizenship. The militancy of the black civil rights movement, especially, and its increasingly separatist, nationalistic rhetoric, resonated in the deepening consciousness of the new generation as parallels between the two minorities' destinies inevitably surfaced. Ironically, as Juan Gómez-Quiñones points out (cf. Alvarez 1973), this separatist mentality was emerging at the very moment when the conscience of white America had been "aroused by the burgeoning Black civil rights movement" (1990: 66). It was this emerging conscience that facilitated enactment of such landmark legislation as the Civil Rights Act of 1965, whose chief purpose was to redress past injustices against African Americans and other oppressed minorities.

But such compensatory measures had come too late for an increasingly militant African America: the "Black Generation" could no longer be mollified by such reformist measures. An irreversible ideological transformation had occurred in the African American community; the threshold from integration to "self-determination" had been crossed, and black nationalism burst upon the scene, as evidenced by the increasingly militant voices heard within the African American community (Allen 1990; Carmichael and Hamilton 1968).

For the Mexican Americans, too, the threshold was crossed in the mid-sixties, and although civil rights legislation had actually begun to succeed in increasing minority participation in government-sponsored civic and economic activities (e.g., through the War on Poverty initiatives), this was not enough. In *Chicano Politics: Reality and Promise, 1940–1990,* Juan Gómez-Quiñones outlines the contradictory circumstances that compelled what we may now call the Chicano Generation to move from the previous generation's strategy of integration and accommodation to one of separatist nationalism and "self-determination." Triggering mechanisms included economic and civic gains in the midst of deepening poverty and marginalization, and increased participation in electoral politics as opposed to the continuing disenfranchisement of Mexican Americans (1990: 101). In short, "there was change as well as lack of change" (ibid.). Inspired by the growing militancy of the Black Power movement, younger Mexican Americans—the nucleus of the Chicano Generation— began in the mid-sixties to "reevaluate earlier ideological tenets" and to develop "a new style of politics" (ibid.: 102). The result was a "variegated burst of activity" (ibid.) that came to be known as the Chicano movement, or, in more nationalist terms, *el movimiento Xicano*.

THE CHICANO MOVEMENT

Gómez-Quiñones is hesitant to certify the "variegated burst of activity" that characterized the political and ideological ferment of the 1960s and early '70s as a true movement (he invariably encloses references to the constellation of movement-inspired activities in quotation marks, as in the "Chicano movement"). Others, however, have been less circumspect (e.g., Marin 1991; Muñoz 1989; Rosen 1975). In fact, despite the lack of a strong central leadership to direct and unify its programs, the Chicano movement was nothing short of a politico-cultural explosion that reverberated powerfully within Mexican society in the Southwest and beyond. While its activist core was relatively small, this "variegated burst of activity" had an impact far beyond the circles of militancy that made the mass-media headlines. Notwithstanding its manifold, even contradictory, program, the movement remained singularly focused, at least at the level of ideology, on a romantic (cultural) nationalist agenda upon which was inscribed the signature of a generation whose members shared a sense that "their historical time or destiny ha[d] arrived" (M. García 1989: 4).[1]

As mentioned in the Exposition, the political and cultural strategies of the Chicano Generation differed sharply from those of its predecessor, although in time these strategies necessarily shifted in the direction of the latter, as the Chicano movement (and the spirit of progressivism in American society, generally) ran its course and further progress was stymied by a reactionist political climate (M. García 1989; Gómez-Quiñones

1990). The differences are sharply articulated in the manifesto enunciating the goals of LULAC and in "El Plan Espiritual de Aztlán," two documents that epitomize the central ideological tenets of the Mexican American and Chicano Generations, respectively. As discussed previously, LULAC's goal was to integrate the Mexican Americans into the dominant Anglo society through acculturation and economic progress, though the former was tempered by the fall-back goal of biculturalism. On the other hand, "El Plan Espiritual de Aztlán" (discussed below) called for outright rejection of all things Anglo-American. Again, while the extreme position of the latter was not sustainable over the long run, some of its basic principles, such as ideas of "self-determination" and Chicanos' renewed pride in their heritage, outlived the movement itself and became basic identifying markers for the Chicano Generation and even its post-Chicano offspring.

The anthropologist Douglas Foley, who spent a number of years in a continuing study of "North Town" (the community of Pearsall, in South Texas; see Foley 1988a, 1990), summed up the general effects of the movement's nationalist ideology on later developments in North Town. It is clear, however (as Foley indicates), that these effects were felt in other communities throughout the Southwest:

What then was the impact of the Chicano movement? The Raza Unida Party [a separatist political party spawned by the movement] itself died quickly, but sometimes ideas live much longer than people and their organizations. In this case, the ideas of "self-determination/self-rule" and of ethnic pride live on in North Town. . . . No self-respecting Mexicano leader would downplay these ideas, even though they now express ethnic pride more moderately than in the Seventies. (1988b: 48)

Meanwhile, in the mid-1960s, as Richard Santillán pointed out, "several progressive Chicano groups [including MAPA and LULAC] had begun to criticize the legitimacy of cultural democracy as a strategy for concrete social change" (1979: 56). As other students of the Mexican American era have noted (Foley 1988a; M. García 1989; Gómez-Quiñones 1990; San Miguel 1987), the war effort (as well as the Korean experience) had raised expectations that Mexican Americans would now be treated as true "Sons of America."[2] However, dashed by the slow pace of progress, these expectations had given way to anger and disillusionment by the mid-1960s. Inspired, again, by the Black Power movement but also by liberation struggles in Africa (as publicized in particular by writers like Frantz Fanon and Albert Memmi), the Chicanos veered inexorably toward a more anti-assimilationist, militantly nationalist posture.

As it coalesced into the more or less coherent nationalism that defined its mission, the Chicano movement evinced many of the characteristics of its African counterparts, although it also shared some of the features of romantic nationalism as it came to be associated with the activities of the German archnationalist of the eighteenth century, Johann G. Herder (Bluestein 1972; Wilson 1973). From both Herder and the African nationalists came the romanticized notion of a glorious, unspoiled, and authentic ethnic-cultural past, somehow lost, repressed, or "buried under the dust of conquest," as Luis Valdez put it, and the need to reclaim the cultural roots in order to restore among the "colonized" a sense of pride in their unique history. More specifically from Herder came the notion that a "nation's" (read: ethnic group's) true heritage, no matter how distorted and fragmented by outside influences, can nonetheless be reclaimed by returning to the "roots"—that is, by turning to the "folk," who (at least to romantics) tend by their conservative nature to preserve intact the traditions of their forebears.

I shall have more to say about romantic nationalism and the Chicano movement shortly; meanwhile, the first stirrings of what can be characterized as a movement took place in 1965, in California, where César Chávez launched his drive to unionize farmworkers. Although never explicitly nationalist in character, the United Farm Workers of America (UFW) was nevertheless midwife to the birth of the first Chicano group to espouse a romantic-nationalist ideology—Luis Valdez's Teatro Campesino, or Farm Workers' Theater.[3] Again, while Chávez and the UFW never aligned themselves with the nationalist politics of the Chicano movement (one reason why Valdez parted company with Chávez), "[the UFW's] aura of moral crusade," as Mario Barrera noted, "and the self-conscious use of Mexican symbolism [e.g., the Virgin of Guadalupe] attracted many nonworker followers" (1988: 35). Furthermore, as the one group "with its heart in its hands and its hands in the soil,"[4] the union catalyzed the Chicano movement and served as a crucial source of inspiration for the Chicano Generation. As the primordial embodiment of the working-class Mexican's enduring ties to the land, the UFW inevitably emerged as the one symbol around which all Chicanos could unite (cf. Goldman and Ybarra-Frausto 1991: 85: "economic struggles in . . . the rural areas were the unifying symbol of the Chicano movement"). Most important, the union's mystical link to the Chicanos' agrarian heritage would provide a critical boost to the spirit of romantic nationalism generally, and more specifically, to the legitimacy of grass-roots expressions such as the corrido, conjunto, and La Onda Chicana.

In the latter years of the sixties, the nascent Chicano movement gathered both political and ideological momentum, as a series of events built one upon the other to coalesce into a full-blown movement. Besides the Teatro Campesino, among the most important building blocks toward a more or less cohesive ideology based on the principles of romantic nationalism were the founding of the Crusade for Justice in Denver by the archnationalist Rodolfo "Corky" Gonzales in 1966; the appearance in 1967 of several activist youth organizations, such as MAYO (Mexican American Youth Organization) in Texas and UMAS (United Mexican American Students) in California; and the inauguration of La Raza Unida Party in 1970. But perhaps most important, in terms of the advancement of a romantic-nationalist agenda, were two gatherings—the National Chicano Youth Liberation Conference, hosted by the Crusade for Justice in March 1969, and the Santa Barbara conference, organized the same year by the Chicano Coordinating Committee on Higher Education (CCHE). Both gatherings produced documents crucial in helping to define the dominant ideology emerging within the Chicano movement.

The Denver youth conference drafted "El Plan Espiritual de Aztlán," ideologically important because "it signaled the break at a national level from the assimilationist 'Mexican American' consciousness and politics of the previous decades" (Gómez-Quiñones 1990: 123). "El Plan" evinced a frankly romantic-nationalist posture in its call for the "liberation" of Chicanos through the politics of ethnic revivalism and self-determination—especially as articulated through the Myth of Aztlán. The Myth itself invoked the Aztec fatherland, popularly thought to be somewhere in what is now the American Southwest. The historian Ramón Gutiérrez (1989) has analyzed the appropriation of the Myth by Anglos as early as the 1890s. For the Chicanos, the Myth became a cornerstone for the ideology of Chicanismo, whose militant goal was the emancipation of Mexican Americans from an oppressive American culture. Of course, in appropriating the Myth and proclaiming themselves the true heirs of Aztlán, the Chicano nationalists never actually contemplated a liberation movement to recapture the land itself. Such an act would have been foolhardy. Rather, Aztlán remained an ideal, an inspiration, and a vehicle for cultural revitalization.

In the epic tone of its language, meanwhile, "El Plan Espiritual de Aztlán" articulated the budding movement's romantic-nationalist bent, as in the following passage:

In the spirit of a new people that is conscious not only of its proud historical heritage but also of the brutal "gringo" invasion of our territories, *we,*
the Chicano inhabitants and civilizers of the northern land of Aztlán from
whence came our forefathers, reclaiming the land of their birth and conse-
crating the determination of our people of the sun, *declare* that the call of
our blood is our power, our responsibility, and our inevitable destiny. . . .
With our heart in our hands and our hands in the soil, we declare the independence of our mestizo nation. . . . (Anaya and Lomelí 1989: 1)

"El Plan de Santa Barbara," drafted at the Santa Barbara conference,
followed on the heels of "El Plan de Aztlán," and the two documents
formed the twin pillars for the ideological master plan to implement a
nationalist agenda. Largely responsible for fueling the drive that created
Chicano studies programs in many colleges and universities across the
Southwest and beyond, "El Plan de Santa Barbara" called for such programs, but in a tone reminiscent of "El Plan Espiritual de Aztlán," the
call was couched in strongly nationalist language:

Commitment to the struggle for Chicano liberation is the operative definition of the ideology used here. Chicanismo involves a crucial distinction in
political consciousness between a Mexican American and a Chicano mentality. The Mexican American is a person who lacks respect for his cultural
and ethnic heritage. Unsure of himself, he seeks assimilation as a way out
of his "degraded" social status. . . . In contrast, Chicanismo reflects self-
respect and pride in one's ethnic and cultural background. (Muñoz 1989: 191)

Clearly, one of the Chicano movement's most enduring contributions
was its successful push to implement Chicano studies programs. By 1970,
due partly to pressure applied by activist students and a few vocal Chicano faculty but also to receptive college and university administrations,
Chicano studies programs (or at least curricula) had been implemented
at many institutions of higher learning in California, Arizona, Texas, and
elsewhere. Common to all the new programs were course offerings in
"Chicano" culture, history, literature, and politics—all of these packaged in what Alex Saragoza (1987) has called a "them-versus-us" approach to Anglo-Mexican relations.[5] Particularly in California, Chicano
studies programs and their nationalist, sometimes radical, approach to
scholarship long outlived the main thrust of the movement itself. As one
Anglo scholar wryly observed,

[Colleges and universities] have served as secure bases for Chicano activists pursuing their highly ideological brand of politics since the late 1960s and early 1970s, when these same institutions furnished the movement with scores of student cadres. . . . [I]n California, [the activists] have largely retreated into the state's far-flung system of higher education, especially to its many Chicano studies programs. (Skerry 1993: 260)

Skerry is right. Lacking a centrally positioned leadership, the Chicano movement came to depend heavily on a scattered but now institutional ized mouthpiece for its nationalist ideology—Chicano studies programs—to carry out much of its agenda. Chicano studies faculty and some of their students became the intellectual core of the movement, in this way complementing (but also often involved in) the work carried out in the trenches by organizations such as the Crusade for Justice. As mentioned in the Exposition, Chicano studies programs (most of which taught some mix of nationalism and democratic liberalism) influenced a multitude of Chicano Generation students, and in the late twentieth century they continued to reach (if in less zealous fashion) substantial numbers of what I call the "post-Chicano Generation." Their views molded by elements of Chicanismo that survived the movement itself (especially ideas of self-determination and ethnic pride), these students, in their turn, affected the communities in which they settled. Through such culturally sensitized individuals, the work of cultural retrieval, reparation, and synthesis continued much longer and in greater earnest than some analysts of the movement seem willing to concede (e.g., Gómez-Quiñones 1990; Skerry 1993).

THE "CHICANO RENAISSANCE"

One of the Chicano movement's most lasting monuments to the driving force of its romantic-nationalist ideology—indeed, the principal purveyor of the "romantic" half of the phrase—was the "Chicano Renaissance," a label coined by Philip Ortego (1970) to describe a broadly distributed efflorescence of artistic activity (heavily underwritten by Chicano studies programs), which put into aesthetic practice the basic tenets of a romanticized nationalism: exaggerated ethnic pride, self-determination, the exaltation of the Chicanos' indigenous heritage, and, above all, a rejection of what Luis Valdez called "neon *gabacho* culture" (*gabacho* is an

ethnic slur for Euro-Americans; see Valdez 1972: xv). The Renaissance
was spurred by the zeal to legitimize the cultural inheritance of the Chicanos, especially the (mythical) pre-Columbian, and in this it touched
many aspects of Chicano artistic culture, including musical practice.
However, it was most directly responsible for the flowering of a nativistic visual art, in particular the mural (Goldman and Ybarra-Frausto 1991),
and an avalanche of literature that flowed from the pens of *movimiento*
poets, novelists, and essayists.

As the artistic (and most explicitly ideological) component of the Chicano movement, the Renaissance complemented the movement's other
agenda, political action, although, as we shall see, in many respects the
two agendas—the artistic-cultural and the political-activist—were often (though unwittingly) at odds with each other. With respect to the
Renaissance itself, Genaro Padilla (1989) has ably demonstrated how the
romantic-nationalist ethos that imbued Chicano literature and other
artistic expressions at the height of the movement conforms to the general principles of a nationalist art of revitalization. According to Padilla,

... despite the relatively wide scholarship describing this Chicano appropriation of an indigenous past, rich in mythic power, little if anything has
been written which would place the Chicano revitalization movement within
a historical and comparative cultural context; that is, a context within which
Chicano nativism is considered alongside cultural revitalization projects in
other independence movements, many played out on a larger and much
more violent stage. (1989: 112)

Like nationalist ideologues in other times and places, Chicano poet-
activists such as Alurista and Corky Gonzales, as well as other intellectuals such as Luis Valdez, were engaged in a cultural reclamation project, one that would use myth to reinvigorate the battered collective image
of an economically subordinate and culturally "degraded" people. It was
out of these reclamation efforts that the Myth of Aztlán became such a
dominant force in literary production during the height of the movement's influence (the late sixties and early seventies). In the poetry of Alurista and others, the Myth of Aztlán "synchronized the mystical and the
political" (Padilla 1989:121), as it did in Luis Valdez's *actos* (short plays).
Alurista's "Poem in Lieu of Preface" (1972) provides us a perfect example
of this synchronization, which is not only mystical and political but actually temporal. Through the power of Alurista's pen, Aztec and Chicano
timelines merge:

it is said
that MOTECUHZOMA ILHUICAMINA

SENT

AN expedition
looking for the NortherN
mythical land
wherefrom the AZTECS CAME
la TIERRA
dE
aztlaN
mYthical land for those
who dream of roses and

swallow thorns

or for those who swallow

thorns

in powdered milk
feeling guilty about smelling flowers

about looking for AztlaN

The search for Aztlán and, indeed, the whole mythology of *indigenismo*—the body of ideas that restored for Chicanos their putative links to an indigenous past—was undertaken as well by the visual artists, particularly a new school of muralists. Most of the latter were anonymous *barrio* artists, but they included such well-known figures as Malaquías Montoya and Ernesto Palomino. Of course, the muralists' adoption of *indigenismo* for nationalist purposes was not new; the strategy dates from the postrevolutionary days in Mexico, when Diego Rivera appropriated indigenous themes "to offset the contempt with which the conquistadores had viewed the ancient Indian civilizations" (Goldman 1982: 113). Chicano muralists were thus engaged in a neoindigenist movement, one, however, at some remove from the source of Rivera's *indigenismo*. For, as Goldman points out, "mestizos and Indians were the majority" in Mexico, and Rivera's art necessarily addressed real and immediate *indígena* issues. Chicano art did not (ibid.: 129).

In any case, through the numerous efforts of muralists and other artists throughout the Southwest, the "proud-to-be-*indio*" message of *indigenismo* gradually gained circulation in popular culture as an ethnic referent that legitimized the Chicanos' link to the Southwest and to its mythically evoked first inhabitants, the Aztecs.[6] The cultural-political thrust of Chicano art has been explained by Malaquías Montoya: "It became an 'art of liberation,'" he wrote. "By the use of indigenous symbols of the Chicano heritage, artists began to explain the struggle and necessity to unite behind it" (1980: 4). Echoing the theme of romantic-nationalist rhetoric to be found in other contexts, Montoya offered this assessment of the Chicano art movement:

> The solidarity resulting from the Chicano Art Movement gave an understanding of an identity and a belonging. . . . It was felt that La Raza should be recognized by its uniqueness and that the differences should be separated from the dominant culture. Chicano pride, and the right to express it, became important. (Ibid.)

More directly pertinent to our discussion here is the fact that the Chicano movement not only attempted to recuperate the pre-Columbian past, but, in the manner of Herder, it also turned to contemporary folklife for inspiration. Unlike Herder, however, for whom the German peasant was synonymous with the folk, the Chicano nationalists looked to the common workers—the incarnation, for many, of the folk in advanced capitalist society—for inspiration. But again like Herder, the Chicano intellectuals saw the folk (i.e., the working class) as the repository of a rich and wholesome culture—one, moreover, that they claimed had preserved intact many of the traditions that formed a cultural lifeline to the Chicanos' indigenous ancestors. Thus, in his seminal article "La Plebe," Luis Valdez waxed lyrical about ancient cultural practices to be found in the modern *barrios*:

> The presence of the Indio in La Raza is as real as the barrio. Tortillas, tamales, chile, marijuana, la curandera, el empacho, el molcajete, atole, La Virgen de Guadalupe—these are hard-core realities for our people. These and thousands of other little human customs and traditions are interwoven into the fiber of our daily life. América Indígena is not ancient history. It exists today in the barrio, having survived even the subversive onslaught of the twentieth-century neon gabacho commercialism that passes for American culture. (1972: xv)

But in its ambitious task of recovering the folk heritage, the Chicano Renaissance went far beyond resurrecting distant myths, as these allegedly underpinned life in the *barrios*. In the works of poets and writers less antiquarian than Alurista or Luis Valdez, the more immediate and dynamic cultural adaptations of the working and even middle class were mined for their artistic yield. In this connection, the most creative of all adaptations, the Mexican Americans' supreme mastery of biculturalism, especially its bilingualism, became a central theme in a rapidly maturing biculturalist poetics. Thus, poets such as José Montoya, Inez Hernández, Ricardo Sánchez, and even Valdez (in his less *indigenista* moments) exploited the compound bilingualism so pervasive among the Chicano Generation. Montoya's work, in particular, symbolically celebrates the synthesis of two cultures toward which compound bilingualism drives, and in this he epitomizes much of the poetic effort to capture that synthesis in an artistic manner. The powerfully evocative poem "La jefita," (My mother) is illustrative of that effort; the following segment captures Montoya's sensitive nuancing of the bilingual mode of communication:

> When I remember the campos
> Y las noches and the sounds
> Of those nights en carpas o
> Bagones I remember my jefita's
>> Palote
>> Clik-clok; clik-clak-clok
>> Y su tocesita.
> . . .
>
> Y la jefita slapping tortillas.
>> Prieta! Help with the lonches!
>> Caliéntale agua a tu 'apá!
>
> (Me rayo, ese! My jefita never slept!)
>
> Y en el fil, pulling her cien
> Libras de algoda se sonreis
> Mi jefe y decía,
>> That woman—she only complains
>> in her sleep. (J. Montoya 1972: 266–268)

Here in poetic language is the compound bilingualism discussed in Chapter 3, now exploited by a poet thoroughly conversant with its underlying rules of grammatical application and its metaphorical power. Like many *movimiento* poets, Montoya used this bilingualism, the only form of speech that faithfully conveyed the bicultural life of the Chicano Generation, to evoke that life in its most intimate setting—the workaday rhythms of a farmworking family and its silently heroic (and exploited) mother. Through their choice of compound bilingualism, Montoya, Hernández, and other Chicano(a) poets were already signaling the high point of synthesis the Chicano Generation had wrung out of the Mexican Americans' contradictory existence.

And of course, bilingualism itself, as a daily communicative practice, reached its zenith during the era of the Chicano Generation. The phenomenon that is compound bilingualism has already been examined. Here it will suffice to say that this type of bilingualism achieved its widest distribution during the 1960s and '70s, as amply evidenced by previous research (Amastae and Elías-Olivares 1982; R. García 1983; Hernández-Chávez et al. 1975; Vaid 1986).[7] Although bilingualism preceded the Chicano movement itself, the climate of linguistic synthesis that the movement's poetry celebrated could only enhance the license to engage in what was, after all, a less-than-linguistically-legitimate form of communication. Compound bilingualism thus became the norm in everyday conversation among intimates and in certain kinds of verbal art.

In connection with the latter, an interesting development emerged in the 1960s—a form of joking based on the interplay of the two languages, English and Spanish. I mentioned previously Rosan Jordan's 1970s fieldwork on which she based her analysis of the unique verbal art that is the bilingual "knock-knock" joke-riddle. A well-known type in American folklore, the bilingual joke-riddle combines two incongruent cultural modalities to create arresting results. In juxtaposing two cultural worlds, this verbal art represents one of the best illustrations of the synthetic process at work, a rearticulation of compound bilingualism in the service of humor. Or, as Jordan emphasizes, "the power to play with both languages suggests the power to control both cultures and hence to deal effectively with one's biculturalism" (1981: 260). In terms more appropriate to our purposes here, the power to manipulate in a humorous manner the interplay of the two languages already signals the masterful synthesis of two cultures in opposition and the contradictions such opposition unleashes.

Complementing the strong and highly conscious manipulation of biculturalism as expressed in bilingual joking and poetry was the movement's renewed emphasis on cultural activities closer still to the subject of this book—the Mexican Americans' musical resources and traditions. Particularly apposite to our topic was the proliferation of folk-dance groups known as *grupos folklóricos*—dance ensembles organized by activist artists in an effort to foment romantic nationalism at the grassroots level. Patterned after the famous Ballet Folklórico de México, these folk-inspired ensembles sprang up at all levels of the educational establishment, from grammar school to the university. Through their picturesque costumes and dances, which were drawn from the diverse forms of folk-

mestizo and indigenous music and dance of Mexico's past (*jaliscience, jarocho, yaqui, azteca,* etc.), the *folklóricos* evoked a highly stylized and romanticized vision of Mexican folk aesthetics, in this way symbolically contesting the hegemony of Anglo culture while reconnecting the Chicanos with their imagined (and sometimes remote) cultural roots.

The romanticization of Mexican folk music and dance and, by extension, pastoral life in general, in turn forced a reevaluation of the concept of *lo ranchero* and, by implication, its relationship to the jaitón. In short, *lo ranchero* became respectable; its negative aspects were suppressed. Now seen as part of the heroic struggle of the working-class folk (especially the lowly farmworker) to attain dignity, *lo ranchero* and the complex of ideas and attitudes it embodied (see Chapter 4) were now thoroughly recontextualized and equated with ethnic pride, and they were accordingly assigned a special niche in the Chicanos' cultural inheritance. *Lo jaitón,* meanwhile, as a constituent element of middle-class, assimilationist culture, was unambiguously redefined as "degrading" and accorded an appropriate measure of derision. Encompassing a broad spectrum of cultural symbols reflecting middle-class status and acculturation (e.g., expensive cars, clothes, elegant homes, and other luxuries), *lo jaitón,* or the "bourgie," as any lifestyle deemed pretentiously Anglo was dubbed, was to be avoided by "culturally aware" Chicanos lest they be exposed as "tío tacos" or "sellouts."

In sum, as part of a generalized trend set in motion by the Chicano movement and its artistic renaissance, many Mexican Americans began to express both a tacit and an overt preoccupation with and, indeed, pride in their ethnic heritage. In addition to the changes in attitude toward *lo ranchero* and *lo jaitón,* the Chicano movement also generated a preoccupation with yet another symbolic dimension of language—its appellative function. Besides the self-conscious efforts at a bilingual poetry, the more ethnic aspects of language were foregrounded, as when parents chose to give their children indigenous names such as Moctezuma, Xochitl, and Cuauhtémoc. Highly significant, too, from a politico-cultural standpoint, was the decision by many Chicanos to stop pronouncing their names in an Anglicized fashion, opting instead for a Spanish pronunciation.

Last and most important, as the presumed repository of all the ancient traditions that acculturation was allegedly destroying, the working-class folk and all their expressions were installed as the cultural model to emulate. To reiterate, at least among the politicized nationalists, middle-class status became synonymous with selling out to the "gringo" establishment and succumbing to cultural genocide; henceforth it be-

came traitorous to *la causa*—the Chicano "cause"—to evince the acculturative airs of middle-class affluence. The middle class had been put
on notice.[8]

The zeal with which Chicano activists attacked middle-class Mexican
Americans and their culture has never been documented, but enough
anecdotal evidence exists to validate its effects. I personally witnessed several incidents in which someone dressed in "middle-class" garments—
dress shirt and tie, for example—was ridiculed as an Anglo imitator, or
"tío taco." In a few instances even the choice of car came in for ridicule, as
when a politically involved friend was chided when he bought a German-
made Audi, a car known as a symbol of middle-class status. One final vi-
gnette may help convey the disdain in which any object or activity suggesting middle-class status was held. Folklorist Américo Paredes, a man
retrospectively recognized as one of the movement's progenitors, recalled
in a personal conversation the comment by one of the apostles of Chicanismo, José Angel Gutiérrez, upon visiting don Américo's home at the
height of the movement, in the early seventies. Apparently displeased
with Paredes's living standard, Gutiérrez remarked in a disapproving
tone, "This is a middle-class home." Modest by any standards, the Paredes home and its occupants were nonetheless suspect in the intolerant,
anti-middle-class climate of that "who's-the-real-Chicano?" period. Ironically, in implicitly criticizing the Paredeses for their "lavish" surround-
ings, Gutiérrez was at the same time concealing his own middle-class background. His stepfather was a middle-class professional in Crystal City,
Texas.

That there are contradictions between Gutiérrez's public posture and
his private status is not particularly critical to our discussion here, other
than the fact that such contradictions cried out for some kind of resolution or synthesis. More important is the fact that at least some of the
leaders who formed the intellectual core of the Chicano movement were
initially drawn from either the middle class or the more privileged sectors of the working class. Their pronouncements against the evils of
middle-class status and the strategies of the Mexican American Generation thus take on an added poignancy. For what was occurring at the
height of the movement was the conversion of many middle-class Mexican Americans to born-again Chicanismo—the strident and often intolerant emphasis on self-determination within the confines of a nationalistic "sense of cultural rebirth" that "cut across class, regional, and
generational lines" (Navarro 1975: 72).[9] The willingness of middle-class
individuals to adopt the working-class culture of Chicanismo and thereby

repress their true socioeconomic status is important for our purposes, because it was this return-to-the-roots position of the middle class that legitimized such artistic forms as the conjunto, while intensifying the development of synthesizing forms such as bilingual joking and poetry as well as the Onda Chicana phase of the orquesta tradition.

It was this gross leveling of class-cultural differences—especially when coupled with the contempt for a middle-class lifestyle and its pre-sumed link to Anglo culture—that discouraged the display of class dif-ference and any discourse of the type presented in Chapter 3, in which affluent Mexican Americans openly bemoaned the backwardness they perceived within the working class, particularly the recent immigrants. While this leveling and its impact are not usually discussed in relation to the Chicano movement, a good case can be made for its efficacy in promoting ethnic unity at the expense of class difference. In the process, the synthesis of disparate cultural elements endemic to the Mexican American experience was accelerated, in this way providing a momen-tary resolution to the contradictions constantly being generated by the dialectic of conflict.

Not surprisingly, in the general cultural reevaluation carried out un-der the banner of the Chicano movement and its Renaissance, the con-junto (and *música norteña* generally) experienced an aesthetic reversal. This hitherto stigmatized style was suddenly upgraded to the status of a cultural treasure to be venerated, not rejected (see Peña 1985a for the conjunto's more traditional image). Gaining cultural respect through its incorporation into the repertoires of *grupos folklóricos, música norteña* began to receive its share of acceptance, and soon some of its creators (Narciso Martínez, Flaco Jiménez, Pedro Ayala) were being drafted into "halls of fame" (especially in Texas) and even awarded national medals, as institutions like the Smithsonian and the National Endowment for the Arts eagerly embraced the conjunto as a national ethnic treasure.[10]

To be sure, despite its newfound popularity beyond its traditional working-class context, the conjunto was not automatically embraced by all Mexican Americans. Even in Texas, its cradle and most entrenched base, many Chicanos outside its working-class constituency might pay lip service to its originality and its value as an "ethnic-roots" expression, but in their everyday musical practices they subscribed to other musical expression, such as the orquesta—albeit even that had by now "gone ranchero." To use an example from my own experience, I recall that as a graduate student at the University of Texas at Austin in the late sev-enties, I witnessed many regularly scheduled "Chicano Nights" at the

Student Union. "Chicano Night" was organized by the Chicano Culture Committee, and it featured a "DJ" (disc jockey) who was expected to play exclusively "Chicano" music. Interestingly, in selecting his repertory, the DJ always played the current hits of the orquestas popular at the time—Onda Chicana favorites like Little Joe y la Familia, Latin Breed, Sunny and the Sunliners, and others. Conjunto music was simply not part of the program.

Outside of Texas, conjunto's more generally recognized cousin, *música norteña*, which includes the Mexican accordion groups, was once again embraced as a valuable ethnic symbol, and it was regularly featured as part of the dance repertoire of the *grupos folklóricos*. But aside from special events, such as nationalistic "La Raza days" on college campuses, this music was confined to dance establishments primarily patronized by the norteño and *tejano* workers, who have traditionally been its core supporters. Particularly in California, even the most nationalist Chicanos subscribed to the mariachi for their ethnic affirmation, and in other matters of musical practice, such as dance events, they either followed their *tejano* counterparts in endorsing the by-now-powerful Onda Chicana or, in some instances, branched out toward pan-Latino styles like salsa, Latin rock, or even the black-influenced East L.A. sounds of Chicano rock groups (Thee Midnighters, Cannibal and the Headhunters, etc.).

Meanwhile, the orquesta tradition itself was at least indirectly affected by the Chicano Renaissance in that more or less consciously, it shifted noticeably toward the ranchero end of its repertoire—or, more accurately, it forged a stronger synthesis of *lo ranchero* and *lo jaitón* as it adjusted to the changing cultural climate (see Chapter 7). Indeed, both the cultural upgrading of the conjunto and the emergence of La Onda Chicana phase of the orquesta stand as forms apposite to a nationalism hungry for expressions indigenous to the Hispanic Southwest. I shall have much more to say about the newfound power of La Onda Chicana in the next chapter; for now, let me point out that as the most popularly grounded of the artistic forms caught up in the cultural upheaval unleashed by the movement and its artistic renaissance, orquesta and conjunto quite logically responded to that upheaval. Moreover, antedating the Renaissance—and being much more deeply embedded in everyday cultural practices than Chicano literature or art—the two musics were in a stronger position to mediate the radical changes taking place within Chicano society, especially when we locate those changes within the more global reach of an unfolding capitalist economy and the changes it wrought in the dialectic of conflict.

CONTRADICTION AND ITS SYNTHESIS:
Assessing the Chicano Movement

The Chicano movement stands as the central accomplishment of the
Chicano Generation—indeed, as its defining mission—and any assessment of that generation begins with the movement itself. I have maintained throughout that the Chicano Generation succeeded where the
Mexican American had failed in forging at least a surface cultural synthesis of the multiple contradictions attending life on the border between two antagonistic cultures and the dialectic of conflict that marks
their intersection. I must emphasize here that such a synthesis must
perforce be temporary, given the depth of the contradictions embedded
not only in the dialectic of conflict between Anglos and Mexicans in the
Southwest but also in the grand dialectic that drives the capitalist system toward some as yet undefined social order—of which the conflict
in the Southwest is but a local manifestation.

First, as several analysts have recognized (Gómez-Quiñones 1990;
Muñoz 1989; Navarro 1975), the Chicano movement was not without its
own contradictions, and so it never presented a unified front, despite the
pervasiveness of the romantic-nationalist ideology of Chicanismo. Although the movement was guided by an overarching (if uncritical) goal
of "self-determination" and economic independence, two clearly dis-
cernible and, in the end, mutually antagonistic agendas emerged to
achieve that goal. The first was driven by the romantic-nationalist spirit
and, through the Myth of Aztlán, aimed to raise the ethnic consciousness and pride of Chicanos. As such, it was essentially separatist and disassimilationist. "We reject efforts to make us disappear into the white
melting pot," proclaimed Luis Valdez. To the contrary:

**Our people are a colonized race, and the root of their uniqueness as Man
lies buried in the dust of conquest. In order to regain our corazon [heart],
our soul, we must reach deep into our people, into the tenderest memory
of their beginning. (1972: xiv)**

In short, for *movimiento* activists, we needed to reclaim our *Humani-
tät*, as Herder called the harmonious state of "one-unique-people, one-
unique-nation." But how were Chicanos to rediscover their "uniqueness
as Man" (let alone their uniqueness as Chicanas)?[11] This was the task
of the Chicano Renaissance, upon which literary production, in particular, set to work with zeal. Drawing inspiration from the colonization

theories emanating from Africa and black America, Chicano literature flirted with the notions of liberation and the creation of the nation of Aztlán. This was an illusion, of course, given the overwhelming dominance of the Anglo political system in the Southwest, but reality did not deter Chicano poets from evoking Aztlán as a state of mind—a mythological rudder for the romantic-nationalist ship. If Chicanos could not have a separate homeland, then they would somehow carve out their own cultural niche in the Southwest, autonomous and unspoiled by "neon gabacho commercialism that passes for American culture."

And this is where the full force of the contradiction struck. For, as Gómez-Quiñones correctly pointed out, there existed a yawning inconsistency "between the radical rhetoric preached by Chicano leaders and the modest reform programs they requested" (1990: 142). That is, preaching the separatist, anti-assimilationist gospel of romantic nationalism, Chicano activists were forced to bend to the capitalist system's rules when it came to the second agenda of the Chicano movement—the political and economic empowerment of the Mexicans of the Southwest. Here they were on terrain totally under the control of the capitalist establishment. Gómez-Quiñones put the dilemma in clear perspective:

Chicano leaders of the sixties were impeded by the contradictions between their assertive rhetoric and their conventional reformist demands and programs. . . . For instance, [Corky] Gonzales's demands for better housing, education, social services, and greater employment opportunities were addressed to the system. The demands for Chicano studies programs and college recruitment programs for Chicanos were addressed to the system. (1990: 142)

Every demand that formed part of the political agenda was in fact addressed to the system. But far more important from the standpoint of the overall goals of the Chicano movement, no matter how autonomously conceived, every political or economic demand addressed to the system would result, if successful, in the tighter integration of the Mexican Americans into the dominant social order. In effect, to the extent that it succeeded—and in many ways it did—the political-action agenda canceled the romantic-nationalist one. And it was this contradiction (aided, of course, by internal dissension and police repression) that eventually brought about the collapse of the movement. Material needs (and successes) triumphed over mythological ones.

By the late 1970s, the movement had devolved into a collection of scattered struggles on behalf of this or that issue, with older organizations such as LULAC and MAPA once more asserting control—though now in the hands of the Chicano Generation. Yet it would be a mistake to conclude that in matters political and ideological it was back to business as usual—the Chicanos fighting piecemeal to gain acceptance and empowerment in a hostile American society. Such a conclusion would be tantamount to writing off the movement as irrelevant to the course of Chicano (or American) history—a minor episode in the static struggle between a subordinate Mexican minority and a hostile Anglo majority. To the contrary, as Mario García has argued:

> . . . like the Mexican American Generation, the Chicano Generation was a product of its time. Despite its rejection of the American experience, it was born out of that experience. It marched in step with other Americans. Instead of being marginal to U.S. history, it was part of the central forces shaping that history in the 1960s and 1970s. . . . The Chicano Generation was part of a wider youth alienation and rebellion that sought alternative models of social change in post-industrialized America. (1989: 300)

Thus, by the time the occupations of public buildings and the mass demonstrations had died down, and poets began turning away from the Myth of Aztlán; by the time the word "Chicano" itself had lost its militant edge and the manifestos had been exhausted, the social and ideological landscape had been transformed. This is why, in arguing earlier that the Chicano movement (like the larger civil rights and feminist movements) contributed in a paradoxical way to the dialectical, self-correcting movement of American capitalism, I did not mean to imply that it had been a vain effort. On the contrary, I was implicitly assigning the movement a logically important role—first, as it contributed to the dialectical progress of Anglo-Mexican relations within the backdrop of the capitalist system, but also, and more important from the standpoint of our subject here, as it triggered a cultural ferment that resulted in an impressive push toward a synthesis of the contradictions that had long plagued Mexican American society.

In sum, for the Chicano movement, what began in contradiction ended in synthesis—if not at the level of the economic base, at least at the level of ideology. As diametrically opposed as the Renaissance's disassimilationist Myth of Aztlán and the movement's reformist demands might seem, they intertwined, and in dialectical exchange with other factors, they brought about the synthesis of disparate social and cultural elements that had previously coexisted in a state of tension. For example, although interethnic tensions increased at the onset of the movement, they quickly decreased once the myriad of scattered demands were met or mediated (e.g., the creation of Chicano studies, the appointment of additional minorities to this or that agency, the implementation of educational opportunity programs, etc.). The interethnic relationship was thus altered by the demand-and-accommodate pattern, and was propelled, in effect, to the next level of action and reaction.[12]

Second, and in inverse fashion, just as the level of interethnic tension was at first raised by the militancy of the movement, so was the level of intraethnic class distance correspondingly reduced, as middle-class Mexican Americans rallied to the cries for ethnic unity within the movement (as well as its condemnation of class elitism) and to the perceived need to fight Anglo "racism." (Eventually, however, class disparities inevitably crept back in, especially as a flood of impoverished illegal immigrants overran the Southwest.) Then, too, drama-filled events, such as the Chicano Moratorium of August 1970 in Los Angeles, strengthened intraethnic solidarity and the feeling among Chicanos across the class spectrum that they were an exploited and oppressed minority. As the historian Ed Escobar observed, "This increased sense of exploitation in turn led to a greater feeling of ethnic solidarity within the Mexican American community and a greater inclination to engage in collective ethnic politics"—politics that "cut across age, class and gender lines" (1993: 1508–1509).

To be sure, displays of intraethnic unity had always surfaced during moments of crisis, as when slain soldier Félix Longoria was denied funeral services (Peña 1982), but during the Mexican American era the divisive power of class difference and, especially, the middle class's desire to accommodate Anglo conditions for acceptance had driven a wedge between class and ethnic interests (see Chapter 3). Now, unified by the cumulative effects of denied opportunities, the apparent willingness of the dominant society to accommodate the needs of minorities, and the strident cries of Anglo "racism" and "Chicano power" coming from the militants, the middle class retreated from its assimilationist, anti-working-class position.

Thus challenged by the movement's insistent call for ethnic pride based on Chicanismo, the middle class moved toward greater acceptance of its stigmatized heritage, in this way aligning itself more and more with the working class in matters cultural. I would argue, however, that the legitimizing work of Anglo institutions like the Smithsonian on behalf of the "folk" helped in this respect. And both factors—pressure toward ethnic unity in the face of perceived injustice and legitimation of ethnic (mainly working-class) forms by mainstream institutions—help explain the ideological transformation of the middle class. It became "politically correct" for middle-class-oriented individuals such as Isidro López and Don Tosti, for example, to reclaim their working-class, ethnic roots. In the cultural climate fostered by the Chicano movement, in which at least a public display of ethnic unity was almost mandatory, the suppression of class-based aesthetic distinctions was bound to affect individual tastes. Given reinforcing praise not for his accomplishments as a performer of middle-class music but for his *pachuco* songs, Don Tosti could afford to display pride, as he now does, in the *barrio* roots that spawned such songs.[13]

A wholesale return to the cultural source was impossible, of course. Given the deeply historical structure of ethnic and class relations, as these were shaped by the still-evolving dialectic of conflict, a permanent reconciliation of the many competing—and often opposed—cultural elements that tugged at the Chicano Generation was not possible. However, cultural synthesis in the form of strongly hybrid expressions presented itself as a workable solution. And this is precisely what happened as cultural fragments from disparate realms—American, Mexican, indigenous, European, folk, sophisticated—were amalgamated in synthetic fashion to create hybrid Chicano forms. This process of synthesis had actually begun during the Mexican American Generation—as Don Tosti's "Pachuco Boogie" and Isidro López's "Mala cara" so graphically illustrate—but it expanded dramatically during the Chicano era.

Perhaps the most visible (and most consciously wrought) work of synthesis was accomplished in the field of literature, where the prevailing formal structure was a powerful biculturalism-bilingualism that transformed disunities into unities. José Montoya's work is paradigmatic here, but many others followed the pattern. In verbal art as well, a more unconscious but no less transformative process occurred, as witnessed by the proliferation of humor that depended for its effect on a tight union *and* juxtaposition of the two languages (Jordan 1972, 1981; Limón 1978; see Chapter 3 above). And, of course, in their daily speech the Chicanos proved to be at their most efficient as cultural synthesizers, the widespread practice of compound bilingualism—perhaps the ultimate form of synthesis—providing the final proof of the culturally transformative influence of the Chicano movement.

But bilingualism, whether in daily speech or as a special effect in verbal art, was not the only synthesizing force in the lives of Chicanos. Just as effective in mediating contradiction was the synthesizing power of music, specifically those styles that tapped the old ethnic and class dichotomies—jaitón versus ranchero, Mexican/Latino versus American—and transformed them into genuine bimusical forms. Among these, none was more emblematic of transformation than the orquesta, which all along had led the way in mediating the stark differences among the various cultural elements previously circulating atomistically in Mexican American popular culture. Now, with the impetus of the Chicano movement, the orquesta assumed a powerfully mediative role, and under the label La Onda Chicana, it entered into its last and most influential stage. The following chapter examines La Onda and the transformative power inscribed in its hybrid style.

CHAPTER 7

La Onda Chicana

The Tejano[1] Music Awards, a Grammy-type production that honors such categories as "male vocalist of the year" and "female vocalist of the year," has been held in San Antonio since 1981. It is a large-scale spectacle—a grand production in which this writer participated for the first time in 1994, as presenter for the "traditional conjunto of the year" honor. The Awards have grown larger and more lavish of late (over 30,000 fans of Tejano attended the 1994 event, held in the Alamodome), as more of the Tejano stars celebrated have begun to capture the international limelight, thanks to their promotion by the major labels for which most of them now record—Capitol/EMI, Sony, Arista, Fonovisa. But of special significance for our purposes is a historical footnote that attends the origins of the Awards: In 1980, when founders Gibby Escobedo and Rudy Treviño were planning the first event, they struggled with the name. Should they call it "Tejano Music Awards" or "Chicano Music Awards" (De la Torre 1993: 24)?

Little Joe is rancherón;

he's a farmer . . . and

Sunny was a big-city boy.

That's why I call Sunny

the city mouse and Joe

the country mouse.

TONY "HAM" GUERRERO,
TORTILLA FACTORY BAND

When the first awards ceremony was held, the *orquesta tejana,* not yet (though soon to be) displaced as the premier expression of a Chicano musical aesthetic, was still possessor of the label coined for it by a music promoter sometime in the late sixties: La Onda Chicana. Indeed, at that late juncture, when the Chicano Generation was about to mature into political and cultural complacence (or impotence, perhaps, in the increasingly reactionist climate of the 1980s), La Onda Chicana had been in ascendance for at least ten years. The decade of the seventies was a period in which the Texas-Mexican orquesta could justifiably claim to represent the musical spirit of the Chicano Generation throughout the Southwest. The very label attached to it presumed to transcend the *orquesta tejana*'s original borders and claim all of Mexican America as its domain. Escobedo and Treviño were thus tempted to adopt the more ambitious title, even if the awards were largely regional, conceived by and principally for *tejanos*.

To suggest that *tejanos* could monopolize the label "Chicano," insofar as La Onda Chicana presumed to do, is merely to ratify them as the leaders of the Chicano Generation in matters ethnomusicological, just as the *californios* may justifiably be declared leaders in matters politico-ideological. The leadership role throughout the Southwest of Chicano studies programs based in California supports the second assertion; the popularity of La Onda Chicana beyond its Texas borders provides ample evidence for the first.

This is not to say, of course, that La Onda enjoyed any kind of monopoly in the Southwest; to the contrary, it encountered plenty of competition, as the international Latino music market—not to mention the American—continued to flood the Southwest with highly commoditized sounds ranging from ranchero idols like Vicente Fernández to *música moderna* favorites like José José. Moreover—and this was especially true of California—the simplified version of *música tropical*, the *cumbia* (not to be confused with *salsa* or the *música tropical* of Don Tosti's day), exerted enormous impact in the 1960s and '70s, when Rigo Tovar, La Sonora Santanera, Mike Laure, and a host of other groups from Mexico and the Caribbean rim enjoyed a long spell of commercial success among recent immigrants and Chicanos alike. This success was attributable to the international Latino record market, but it was enhanced by the live appearances of groups such as Mike Laure's in the widespread network of dance halls that linked California and the rest of the Southwest.

The various types of Mexican-Latino music—ranchera (in the form of the mariachi and *música norteña*), *tropical, moderna*—saturated the Southwest through the power of radio and television. Moreover, all of these musical forms inevitably found local expression, as performers throughout the Southwest organized mariachis, *grupos tropicales, grupos modernos*, and other combinations to provide music for the principal form of live performance in the Southwest: the weekend dance. And, of course, American pop music, in all its manifestations from rock to "funk" to country western, enjoyed uninterrupted success among Mexican Americans. Many local groups imitated these styles as well, particularly in Los Angeles, where rock and funk groups were especially popular among the younger members of the Chicano Generation (Loza 1993). In sum, in matters musical, the Chicano Generation followed the path cleared by the Mexican American Generation, as imported styles, both Mexican/Latino and American, continued to play an important role in the everyday lives of the bicultural Chicanos.

But we must separate the chaff from the grain. The Mexican variety of *música tropical,* in the form of the *grupos cumbieros,* has a legitimate, organic connection to the Mexican working class in the Southwest, particularly the immigrant population, with whom it has been identified since the 1960s. Thus, despite its commercialization, *música tropical* remained an "organic symbol," a musical metaphor for immigrant culture (Peña 1989, 1993). But much of the other music saturating the commercial market was in the form of pure commodity, sold for profit and lacking the solid base of cultural identification that a "homegrown" music possesses. This was certainly true of the transnational form of *música moderna,* as purveyed by Julio Iglesias, José José, Camilo Sesto, and even the more "ranchera" Rocío Durcal. In the Southwest as elsewhere, major-label artists such as these were promoted as glamorous commodities of leisure, with all the hype that such promotion can bring to bear upon the market. Little Joe Hernández, the kingpin of La Onda Chicana, recognized the monopolistic power of the giant labels when he complained about the overwhelming competition La Onda faced:

You know, Julio Iglesias sells all over the world. . . . You can sell a product all over the world if you *sell* that product. You hear all kinds of music that are sold all over the world instantly, almost overnight. That's what a major, monster company can do, if that's what they want to do, [or] they choose to do. (Personal interview, November 23, 1991)

However, we should be alert to the possibility that the musical commodities marketed by the mass media (say, a Julio Iglesias song) could be given a "strong" symbolic charge (as opposed to the "weak" charge of commoditized music) if appropriated by homegrown groups such as an orquesta. In such a case, once the commoditized music was appropriated by local artists for performance in the "thick" context of localized cultural performances that I claim certain weekend dances to be (Peña

1980; see Chapter 8), a countermovement toward the music's (re)integration into what Edward Sapir (1949) termed "genuine culture" (as opposed to "spurious culture") might be expected. And this process indeed occurred, but the whole point of this line of reasoning is to advance the possibility that in the Southwest (as in other indigenous contexts) music as organic symbol and music as commodity can coexist and interpenetrate each other's domain.

In any case, as I argued in Chapter 2, musical styles and genres indigenous to the Southwest—the conjunto, the early troubadours, the string orquestas, the corrido and *canción-corrido*—have traditionally been far more resistant to commoditization than mass or pop music. Musics such as the former are much more intricately wired into the basic circuits of local "microcultures" (Slobin 1993); hence, they are less susceptible to the process of reification. Like other indigenous musics, the orquesta is historically an organic, symbolically charged musical form that also resists reification—especially since it remained rooted in the "rituals of intensification" that many Saturday-night dances in fact constituted (Peña 1980; see Chapter 8).

That La Onda Chicana should compete successfully with internationally driven musics and still maintain firm links to its core constituency speaks eloquently to its strong association with the Chicano Generation. For despite stiff competition from the various transnational forms, orquesta flourished in the sixties and seventies, balancing its existence between a (modestly) profitable commodity and a living, breathing music vital to the critically important enactment of a Chicano musical aesthetic—the public dance. I shall explore the public-dance-as-ritual later; for the remainder of this chapter I would like to trace in more detail the emergence and triumph of this final phase of the orquesta, La Onda Chicana.

BIRTH OF LA ONDA CHICANA

Isidro López's was the last of the Mexican American Generation orquestas, although he is a transitional figure who bridges the two generations and prefigures the next stage of development. Before considering the final, Onda Chicana stage, it may be worthwhile to review the earlier orquesta's relationship to the larger sociocultural context, by way of establishing a contrast to La Onda.

During its formative period, orquesta was riddled with contradictions that mirrored the transitional nature of the Mexican American Generation itself. Torn between their rural, working-class roots and their urban, middle-class aspirations, and between Mexican and American cultural modalities—in short, between ranchero and jaitón—the orquesta and its partisans could only equivocate. In many respects the polarities undergirding the ranchero-jaitón complex remained unmediated, affecting realms of social life as diverse as music and family. Both the orquesta and the family, for example, practiced rural and urban modalities simultaneously and often in conflictive patterns. At the level of the family, evolving gender relations provide a graphic illustration of this conflict—for instance, in the way parents might treat adult daughters. The long-standing rural (and patriarchal) custom of the cloistered, overprotected daughter clashed with urban practices in which young women were much freer to experience the outside world, often through employment beyond the home or prolonged education in the public schools (Foley 1988a; Madsen 1964; Rubel 1966; Taylor [1934] 1971).

A host of other customs practiced by rural, working-class families, and the conflicts that arose as these families made the transition to urban, upwardly mobile status, could be cited, especially in their intergenerational articulation—for example, attitudes toward education, commodity consumption (e.g., luxury items such as lipstick or perfume), employment opportunities, and, central to our topic here, leisure and play. As many Mexican Americans who grew up in the decades of the forties and fifties vividly remember (Foley 1988a; Saragoza 1980), and as I demonstrated in Chapter 3, the postwar period was marked by radical change, and much of this change not only exacerbated the interethnic conflict, it also heightened conflict within Mexican American communities. Rifts ensued between classes but also between men and women *and* between generations as differences in cultural orientation surfaced among husbands, wives, and their children (e.g., on the "correct" comportment of adult daughters).

Generational and gender conflicts were microcosmic expressions of the larger processes at work in Mexican American society, processes tied to the grinding wheels of a cultural economy driven by the vast dialectic with which I have been grappling throughout this work. Contradictions were inevitable in this process, and these contradictions echoed and re-echoed in the realm of expressive culture—from gender relations and grooming styles to linguistic practices and musical expression. Orquesta music responded, and in its multivocal stylization, it rearticulated those contradictions—especially those enmeshed in the master tropes, ranchero versus jaitón. Of particular interest to us is orquesta's metaphoric role in the double contradiction in which the middle class found itself—its attraction to, and repulsion by, middle-class American culture and its simultaneous rejection and defense of its ethnic culture. Responding sensitively to those contradictions, the Mexican American orquesta proved once again the old ethnomusicological maxim that music (or, anyway, music linked organically to its makers) is a key to understanding the complex process of change and adaptation (Blacking 1974).

Depending on the time and place and the social status of its clientele, orquesta could draw from a wide variety of Mexican-Latino and American styles to achieve intriguing combinations. Thus, in its most urbanized and cosmopolitan (jaitón) guise, crystallized in the romantic Mexican *bolero* and the American fox-trot, the orquesta spoke for the middle-class and assimilative yearnings of the Mexican Americans. Conversely, in its performance of folk-inspired music such as the *canción* and *polca ranchera*, which stood in symbolic opposition to *música jaitona,* the orquesta articulated the working-class, ethnic origins of the group. But I must emphasize that in the orquestas of the formative period all these disparate styles, while thrown together, remained unassimilated in a manner homologous to the mixing of languages in coordinate bilingualism (see Chapter 3). Amalgamated, then, as they were within one single orquesta tradition, these heterogeneous musical practices symbolized the conflicting currents swirling around the Mexican American Generation.

Events during the 1960s changed the political and ideological equation, and, again, orquesta responded with characteristic vigor. Indeed, as I have maintained all along, the decade of the 1970s should be considered the pinnacle of the orquesta tradition in the Southwest, as it interacted with the cultural ferment spawned by the Chicano movement to attain new levels of development. In the wake of the movement's sweeping changes, the orquesta entered its final stage of evolution, as a new generation of performers charted a freshly innovative musical course for the ensemble. Led again by the *tejanos,* the new orquestas synthesized once and for all the ranchero and jaitón, as well as the Latin and American, into a seamless, bimusical sound that came to be known during the seventies as La Onda Chicana.

That label, La Onda Chicana, is a pointed reminder of the undeniable link between orquesta's new phase and the coming of age of the Chicano Generation. More specifically, it attests to the power of the Chicano movement to shape musical expression. As outlined in Chapter 6, one of the movement's principal accomplishments was the coalescence of Mexican Americans under the ethnic banner of a Chicanismo rooted in folk, working-class traditions. The powerfully homogenizing romantic nationalism that swept through the Southwest in the late sixties and seventies succeeded in overriding class differences in particular, while it attained at least a moment of ethnic unity. This unity accelerated the process of cultural synthesis, and it was out of this moment of accelerated synthesis that La Onda Chicana was wrought. But the mechanisms involved in the birth of La Onda Chicana are best illuminated by turning to the human agents responsible for its genesis—the performers themselves.

LITTLE JOE:
The "Country Mouse" as "Big Cheese"

The "country mouse" (Little Joe Hernández) and the "city mouse" (Sunny Ozuna) are descriptive phrases coined during a playful moment by Tony "Ham" Guerrero, a trumpet player associated with orquesta leader Little Joe Hernández during the critical transitional years of the latter's career (1967–1973). A member of Hernández's orquesta when it metamorphosed from its original Latinaires phase into its influential stage as Little Joe y la Familia, Guerrero was intimately informed about La Onda Chicana's linchpin's most elementary sociomusical identity. For Guerrero, Little Joe was at heart a "country mouse"—musically, socially, and ideologically. The insight contained in Guerrero's description lies in his recognition that even under the strongly synthesizing influence of the Chicano movement, the outlines of the old ranchero-versus-jaitón distinctions could still be glimpsed in the public images projected by Little Joe y la Familia and by its chief rival in La Onda, Sunny and the Sunliners: ranchero for Little Joe, jaitón for Sunny.[2]

Little Joe's attraction to *lo ranchero* may be partly attributable to his socioeconomic origins.[3] Christened José María de León Hernández, the future king of La Onda Chicana was born into poverty in Temple, Texas, in 1940, the seventh of thirteen children in the Hernández family. He never graduated from high school, but instead went to work after he finished the seventh grade. "I grew up picking cotton and *desahijando* (thinning)," recalled Little Joe:

My mom was always there, pregnant, pulling the [cotton] sack with kids riding on it and kids under the trailer *del algodón* [cotton trailer]. In 1954 my

FIGURE 21. *Little Joe and the Latinaires, ca. 1965.*
Courtesy of Joe Hernández.

dad got busted for possession of a couple of joints . . . and in 1955 they sent him up. I was fifteen at the time he went in, and I was seventeen when he got out. And I assumed command of the family because my older brothers were in the service.

The grinding poverty he endured as a youth sets Little Joe apart from most orquesta musicians, as does his limited education and close association with a rural, working-class life. In this sense, he is indeed a "country mouse" whose ranchero roots have served as a leitmotif throughout his artistic life—even when he ventured into more jaitón dimensions of performance. But as a youngster in Temple, which in the 1940s was a semirural town whose *barrios* were well removed from the strong Mexican enclaves nearer to the border, Little Joe was enculturated within a matrix of Mexican and black cultures. He "hung out" with poor blacks, and this company helped shape his musical perspective; he developed a

lifelong taste for blues, rhythm-and-blues, jazz, and even country western. His taste for ranchera music surfaced later, when he came under
the influence of "aunts and uncles." Then there was the top-forty market, which attracted almost every would-be musician from the Chicano
Generation. In fact, Little Joe's first impulse upon embarking on a musical career was to crack that market.

Little Joe learned a few guitar basics in the early fifties, and he and David Coronado formed David Coronado and the Latinaires in 1954. It was
a minimal orquesta, of the type not uncommon in those days: the horn
section consisted of Coronado on alto saxophone and Tony Matamoros
on tenor. Little Joe played electric guitar and sang for the group, and a
Mexicanized Anglo, Mike Barber, played drums. In 1957, the group began booking out of town, in places such as Victoria, Texas, where a ballroom impresario liked the Latinaires and referred them to one of Corpus Christi's best-known Spanish-language disc jockeys, Genaro Tamez.
It was with the latter's Torero label that Little Joe, David Coronado, and
the Latinaires recorded their first selection—an instrumental rock tune
titled "Safari, Part I & II."

FIGURE 22. *Little Joe and the Latinaires, ca. 1967.*
Courtesy of Joe Hernández.

Coronado moved to the state of Washington in 1958, and Little Joe and one of his many brothers, Jesse, took over the group. It then became known as Little Joe and the Latinaires. The Latinaires expanded over the next few years, as both Johnny and Rocky, Little Joe's younger brothers, joined the ensemble as singers, and additional horns were added (see Figs. 21 and 22). During this period Little Joe continued his attempts to break into the top-forty market, although by the early sixties he had begun to establish a presence within the *música tejana* circuit and its more accessible market. In quest of the former, the Latinaires recorded with Corona Records of San Antonio two songs in the top-forty rock-and-roll format featuring Johnny as vocalist: "Ramona" and "Little Girl of My Dreams." For the *música tejana* market, the Latinaires recorded several tunes: "Qué chulos ojos," "El ciruelito," "Cartucho quemado," and others—all *canciones* and *polcas rancheras* with an *orquesta-tejana* flavor reminiscent of Isidro López.[4]

The Latinaires' stock within the *tejano* market took a major leap in the mid-1960s with the appearance of their first long-playing (LP) record album, *Por un amor,* which reportedly sold over 150,000 units ("Little Joe" [publicity flier] n.d.). Several modestly successful recordings followed, most of them in a ranchera mode, including "Borrachera," "El tejano enamorado," "Ojitos verdes," and others, many of which were recorded on an LP that established the Latinaires as one of the top groups in the *orquesta tejana* tradition: *Amor bonito* (reportedly a "gold" LP), which was released in 1966 under the Zarape label in San Antonio. Meanwhile, the group's status was also enhanced by the addition in 1967 of trumpeter Tony "Ham" Guerrero (aka Martínez), whose musical training brought a measure of sophistication to the Latinaires. By 1967, Little Joe and the Latinaires was the best-selling group in what was by then known as Tex-Mex (*orquesta tejana*), just as they were arguably the most musically polished.

In an interview on March 28, 1980, Guerrero recalled his experiences with Little Joe's orquesta. His is a lucid, articulate narrative of events affecting the evolution of the Latinaires, and I shall rely on it extensively. Guerrero, who is from San Angelo, Texas, first heard of Little Joe and the Latinaires in 1965 while playing with a jazz group in Oakland, California. He met a friend from his hometown, who informed him that there was in Texas "a new band *que se llama* (that is called) Little Joe and the Latinaires, *y otra que se llama* (and another that's called) Sunny and the Sunliners, and these guys are kicking Isidro López's ass all over the place." Eventually, Guerrero made his way back to San Angelo, where he met the Latinaires during one of their tours to that city. He "sat in" with the band, and Little Joe asked him to join. I quote a substantial portion of my conversation with Guerrero for the light it sheds on the state of *tejano* music in the late 1960s and, specifically, the vicissitudes that affected Little Joe and the Latinaires:

> TG: So I joined his band, and like I said, I changed a lot of things when I went in. None of the guys read music. As a matter of fact, I suggested that we read some good charts, and they all laughed at me. *Dijeron* [They said], "Reading music, man? That's old hat, that's old-fashioned." The original members, they used to play one style of music; they would all sit around for hours trying to figure out their part, rather than someone just writing the music.
>
> MP: Sunny told me something about that—that many times they just learned the parts by ear.
>
> TG: I call it "oreja de elefante" [elephant ears]. These guys *tienen oreja de elefante* [have elephant ears]. They hear harmonies and they put 'em together just by hearing. That's the way Little Joe used to do it. Of course, Sunny had a more sophisticated type group than Little Joe at the time.
>
> MP: Would Little Joe be considered more ranchero?
>
> TG: Yeah, Little Joe is *rancherón*—he's a farmer; he can relate to farmers. And Sunny was a big-city boy, San Antonio boy. That's why I call Sunny the city mouse and Joe the country mouse. Anyway, I dug Little Joe's group, 'cause it was the most *alegre* [lively] *tejano* group I had ever heard. On the other hand, Sunny had this sophisticated sound at the time. . . . The funny thing is that Little Joe's band, being country boys, they had some observance of dynamics. That blew my mind. "How can these guys, who don't know anything about music, play such soulful, *alegre* rancheras?" And then Little Joe would come down soft, express himself so beautifully.

So Guerrero joined the group, and its popularity continued to climb. But the Latinaires seem to have experienced a dip in the 1968–1969 period, depending on whose recollection we accept as accurate. For Little Joe, the Latinaires enjoyed more or less uninterrupted success right up until the moment the group changed its name, in 1970. Yet an examination of the group's discography reveals that *Amor bonito* (recorded in 1966) was the only original and substantive album until 1968, when the LP *Arriba* was released.[5] In any case, it is possible that even a lull in recording activity may have resulted in a loss of momentum, which would buttress "Ham" Guerrero's retrospective assessment, just as it makes more dramatic the final triumph of Little Joe y la Familia. According to Guerrero:

When I joined the group, we had a lot of changes and stuff. And Little Joe and the Latinaires, around 1968, had some good gigs and some bad gigs. I remember one time—that was when the Latinaires were the baddest band in Texas—we went to play in Midland, and I think we had about forty or fifty people on the dance floor on a Saturday night. That night Little Joe just blew his mind. He called a meeting after the dance, and he said, "Well, guys, we're doing something awfully wrong, 'cause nobody's coming out to see us. I think it's time to disband. . . ."

What Joe hadn't realized is that I had come into the band and the thing changed, the people weren't ready for the change. What he needed to do was give—show the people the change on an album. See, Joe had quit Zarape Records two years before I joined. And he didn't record anything for two years. The only thing that kept him going was his gigantic hit "Amor bonito," a monstrous hit. So we decided, "OK, let's record an album." So we put our heads together and started putting together another album— *todos los vatos de la banda* (all the dudes in the band). We decided we were proud of being Latinaires. *Hicimos un album que se llama Arriba* (We made an album called *Arriba*). We recorded it in the summer of 1968. . . . When we recorded that album, things started happening again for Joe. The album was so different, the cover. . . . And the size of the band went from six or seven to ten, and—the style of the band didn't change, *the sound* changed, became hipper, became a bigger sound. But *la alegría* was still there, and Little Joe was overriding everything . . . and the people accepted it right away; they loved it.

So after that we went on recording . . . we just kept on recording, and then in 1969 El Charro Negro [a Latinized African American singer] quit the band. See, Tony the Top [Joe's brother] had come in to work [supervising rehearsals]. None of us in the band liked him. He was a dumb ass. He was twenty years in the military, and he comes out of the military into a band of musicians—a bunch of *vatos locos, grifos* [crazy guys, dopeheads]— and he wants to run them like a platoon, and we're all telling him to go get fucked. . . .

The entrance of Tony the Top into the band's affairs was apparently an effort by Little Joe to regain control of an increasingly unruly group; he may have feared as well that the Latinaires might be slipping again. If so, Little Joe's fears were not unfounded. In Ham's own words:

So, Joe told me one day, "Hey, man, we're going nowhere real fast." Again, we approached a little stagnant period, after two years. He said, "Now it's really time to change: Santana's come in [a popular Latin-rock group from California], and all this bullshit, and we're still wearing this goddamn $250 . . ."

MP: Was this in 1970?

TG: No, this was in 1969, when we made the drastic change. "You know," he said, "like we're still called Little Joe and the Latinaires, and that sounds dated, and I don't like it anymore. And we're still wearing $250 suits, and we look like goddamn James Brown. That bullshit is out. Look at all those goddamn freaks going around [hippie-style rock groups]. And they're doing the thing; we're not doin' nothin'." Then he said, "I've decided we're gonna drop the Latinaire bullshit, and we're gonna go to la Familia, and we're gonna become hippies with long hair." So we did, we changed . . .

MP: But he didn't drop the name immediately—didn't he use both names for a while?

TG: No, he dropped it immediately, but a lot of people in the industry, they said, "No, Joe, don't do that, don't drop the name Latinaires, that's what makes you." "Naw," he said, "to hell with it." So we dropped it. And all of a sudden the guy says, "I'm gonna grow my hair long." And he became the first freak *en La Onda Chicana*—Little Joe with real long hair down to his ass. . . . *Y traía cadenas, y la chingada* [and he wore chains and all that shit]. He looked like a cross between a militant Chicano and a hippie.

Given his acute sense of chronology on other matters (and as generally corroborated by the official Latinaires discography), Guerrero is probably correct on most points of his assessment of events (except for the name change, which occurred in 1970, although discussion might have begun in 1969). However, the name change from Latinaires to la Familia needs to be examined more critically, for it represents an arresting metaphor for the transformation occurring at this precise moment on the sociopolitical level: from Mexican American to Chicano. For that matter, the label La Onda Chicana itself, as applied to *orquesta tejana* music, speaks powerfully to the link between orquesta's new phase and the emergence of the Chicano Generation. More specifically, both labels, la Familia and the broader La Onda Chicana, serve as testimonials to the Chicano movement's influence over musical culture. Thus, Little Joe's decision to adopt the evocative la Familia places him squarely at the point of intersection between the Chicano movement and developments in the field of music.

Little Joe's decision to "go hippie," incidentally, is also linked to the

Chicano movement, at least indirectly. Many young people in the movement were influenced by the antiestablishment stance of the hippies, which was consistent with their own rejection of "neon gabacho" culture. As a "cool," "hip" alternative to the rejected mainstream, a hippie lifestyle, particularly its unconventional dress (and its drug culture), was also compatible with certain *indígena* emblems associated with the movement, such as headbands, long hair, sandals, and turquoise necklaces and wristbands. A hybrid, *indígena*-hippie style of dress thus became almost normative for people involved in the movement. A shared lifestyle with the hippie counterculture also strengthens Mario García's assertion that the Chicano movement, far from being marginal to American history, is very much a component of that history, at least as it unfolded in the 1960s and '70s (1989: 294).

Meanwhile, the movement's role in Little Joe's decision to change the Latinaires' name to la Familia was revealed in an interview I held with Little Joe on May 6, 1993:

MP: Two things that I really wanted to touch bases with you on is how you came to choose the name of la Familia, and the other was your involvement in the Chicano movement and how this affected your approach to music. Can we start with—what brought about the change from Latinaires to la Familia?

LJ: Well, the fact that I was born and raised in Temple, where everything was pretty much—still is—black and white [i.e., in terms of racial segregation]. And then in the late sixties, hanging around the Bay Area, playing all around San Francisco, around there, and becoming aware of *latinismo*. That was during the days, late sixties, early seventies, when Santana was just taking off, when so many other groups from the Bay Area—I just became aware of, really, *latinismo*, *la cultura*, and our heritage, our music. . . . And I just became aware *que* [that] speaking Spanish was hip, you know; that was the thing happening. And I needed to make a change, from Latinaires to something closer to home, something closer to roots. And both my brother Johnny and I searched for a name and came up with all kinds, but la Familia just really stuck.

MP: What was it about la Familia that appealed to you?

LJ: One, the fact that I'd been working around with my family. My family had been involved in my business, and the music and the record business and all . . . but it went deeper than that. I recognized the fact that Latinos from all over the world were one big family. . . .

MP: So it's like a symbolic name.

LJ: It's that, plus anybody that comes around [and joins the band] becomes family, you know . . . so we thought that name was suitable.

MP: Was the fact that the Chicano movement was going strong at that time [1970]—did that have any influence on you?

LJ: Uh, the Chicano movement—la Raza Unida and all that—was not really at that time part of that [name change], but during that time, also, the early seventies, Luis Gazca and Jim Castle made me aware of César Chávez and the farmworkers' movement. And they got me involved in doing concerts, and I met César, and that was one part of it. Then la Raza Unida happened as well, you know.

MP: Did you become involved in that?

LJ: Very much so, *con* [with] José Angel Gutiérrez.

MP: Can you tell me some of the things—didn't you go to Mexico as some sort of musical ambassador once?

LJ: Yes, I did—with a delegation of representatives *de aquí de los Estados Unidos* [from here, from the United States], and I remember hearing the news in Mexico: "*Llegaron los líderes chicanos a México*" [The Chicano leaders have arrived in Mexico]. And we met *con el presidente López* [with President José López Portillo]. And, so, yeah, I was very much involved with the—you know—supporting *la causa* [the cause]. And it, again, you know, more so, I just reaffirmed my commitment to *música chicana*— that we have something of our own, you know. And I didn't wanna dilute it, and no matter what kinds of music I do play, I know we have our own, and that movement just made me reaffirm that.

In fact, of course, while the movement did help Little Joe reaffirm his commitment to *música chicana,* he and other Onda Chicana groups went far beyond "diluting our own" music. As we shall see, they forged a dramatic synthesis of Mexican and American musics, creating a bimusical style that defines La Onda as "our own." And, although Little Joe hedges on the direct influence the movement had on the highly symbolic name change, as he intimates, the powerful nativistic currents circulating in 1970 inevitably entered into that politically charged (if less than conscious) decision. Over the next ten years, that nativism would surface periodically in Little Joe's music, most overtly in an album he released in 1977 titled *La voz de Aztlán* (The voice of Aztlán)—a ringing testimony to Little Joe's preoccupation with the Chicano movement and the issue of romantic nationalism. No other Onda Chicana group was so directly affected by that movement.

Meanwhile, in 1970 "we were very busy," according to Tony Guerrero.

And despite his newly discovered "latinismo," Little Joe still had dreams of cracking the mainstream pop-music market. In fact, a major reason why la Familia "hung around the Bay Area" (as well as Los Angeles, where Little Joe had an office) was Little Joe's continuing desire to squeeze into the top-forty market. Thus, as he told "Ham":

I want to make my band the baddest, heaviest band that there's ever been, because we want to get into the rock market. I believe my brother Johnny has enough talent that we can get into the rock market, if we put the right band behind him. You know a lot of good musicians. Why don't you help me put a band together? (Guerrero interview, March 28, 1980)

And that they did, attracting such top-flight musicians as trombonist and arranger Joe Gallardo, an alumnus of the Del Mar School of Music in Corpus Christi, and Luis Gazca, a well-known and highly respected jazz trumpeter. A fine guitarist, Joe "Mad Dog" Velásquez, was brought in as well, as were the bassist Joe Medina and the keyboard specialist Gilbert Sedeño. Little Joe's ambitions to break into the top-forty rock market remained frustrated, but now in possession of the "baddest band" in La Onda Chicana, at least, the "country mouse" was ready to explore new fields in search of glory. Until this moment, he had matched Isidro López's ranchero style, but he had never been able to transcend the latter's more jaitón efforts—or those of Balde González and Beto Villa, for that matter. Quite simply, even with the addition of Tony Guerrero, he still lacked the talent to mount a successful challenge to the jaitón side of the orquesta. But now, with a more formidable crew on hand—especially the gifted Joe Gallardo—la Familia was poised for the final assault on the pinnacle of orquesta music.

That assault came swiftly. In 1972 the restructured la Familia recorded its first album for Buena Suerte Records, a label Little Joe had recently launched. Titled *Para la gente* (For the people), the album took Chicanos everywhere by storm, instantly becoming an emblem for a Chicano identity. Besides installing Little Joe as *the* icon of a Chicano musical sensibility, *Para la gente* became a landmark musical production, not only for its nationalistic title, but also for its artistic complexity. Quite simply, it represented the most elaborate arrangement of both ranchero and jaitón materials ever assembled within the orquesta tradition, one, moreover, never surpassed by la Familia or any other Chicano group since that day. As Guerrero has said of previous performances, in *Para la gente* "Little Joe was overriding everything," but the background arrangements and instrumental interludes—highly complex and bimusical—assert their presence on the listener, standing out in stark contrast to the folklike quality of the brothers Hernández singing solos and duets in ranchera fashion. In short, *Para la gente* represented the ultimate synthesis of the ranchero and jaitón horizons.

In speaking of a synthesis, I refer, first, to the virtual fusion of ranchero and jaitón that many of the selections on the album achieved—in particular those classified as *canciones rancheras,* performed in polka time, sometimes known as *canciones corridas* or simply as *corridas.* We may recall that the *polca* is, after all, the one genre that had lent the *orquesta tejana* its unique ranchero identity since the days of Beto Villa. After Isidro López grafted lyrics to the *polca,* the *corrida* quickly replaced the former as the mainstay of the *orquesta tejana,* and during the 1960s its *tejano* flavor was cemented through the development of certain stylistic conventions—for example, sharp staccato patterns in the horn section reminiscent of the mariachi trumpet style, as well as recurrent formulas utilized in the background obbligatos, such as the dotted-eighth–sixteenth-note pattern, which became a virtual signature of the *orquesta tejana* style.

Drawing from these formulas, and juxtaposing them against swing-jazz elements, Little Joe fashioned the new bimusical style, which was unique in that the juxtaposition of Mexican and American, or ranchero and jaitón, occurred *within the same musical piece.* A strong sense of musical code-switching thus emanated from these bimusical, jazzlike *corridas*—a code-switching that echoed its parallel expression in compound bilingualism.

Isidro López and Pedro Bugarín had both attempted a bimusical synthesis previously, but their efforts paled in comparison to the finely synthesized sounds emanating from *Para la gente,* in particular from such tunes as "Qué culpa tengo," "La traicionera," "El disco," and the most astonishing of all, "Las nubes." In all of these, the folk, ranchero quality of Little Joe's and Johnny's voices overrode everything else, but the background orchestration and instrumental interludes flowed effortlessly, from the brassy trumpet duets that lend *música ranchera* its distinctive *alegría* (what Little Joe described as "taking the mariachi feel and doing it with a band") to the dense harmonies and syncopations characteristic of modern swing-jazz—all of this musical code-switching taking place, again, within the same piece. The overall effect was markedly bimusical, as the orchestration repeatedly switched from one musical code to the other—ranchero/mexicano to sophisticated/American—to create a seamless web of bimusical synthesis, or what I am calling "compound bimusicality."

LA ONDA CHICANA:
Cultural Synthesis as Compound Bimusicality

It is this form of bimusicality—style-switching within the same musical piece—that I find homologous to compound bilingualism. More so than bilingualism, however, the code-switching in compound bimusicality is eminently aural, relying on recognizable stylistic codes, as it were—ranchero versus jazz, for example—to convey the interpenetration of two sound systems or styles not normally compatible with each other. But this interpenetration is not random; in the seemingly continuous flow of a song like "Qué culpa tengo," the transition from jazz to ranchero takes place at strategic junctures—between musical clauses, for example—and thus displays an equivalence to the transition from Spanish to English (and vice versa) at the level of the linguistic clause (see Chapter 3). Moreover, while this transition is consciously manipulated, it is my contention that the rules for musical code-switching (when is it proper to move from ranchero to jazz, when is it improper?) operate at the subconscious level, just as they do in compound bilingualism. Transferring the aural effect onto musical transcription is awkward at best, but an effort is made in the following examples to convey the sense of musical code-switching in two selections from the album, the *corridas* "Qué culpa tengo" and "Las nubes."

In "Qué culpa tengo," the band begins with a twelve-bar introduction, then Little Joe sings the tune's first seven-bar phrase. The overall style to this point is straightforward ranchero, but at measure seven, at the conclusion of the first vocalized phrase, the band switches abruptly into a jazz-mode obbligato, which lasts for four bars. The obbligato concluded, Little Joe then sings the song's second seven-bar phrase, again in his usual ranchero style. At the conclusion of the second phrase, the band once more switches musical codes, from ranchero to jazz, for another four measures. The entire two-phrase period, with horn obbligatos, is transcribed as follows:

Qué Culpa Tengo

Aaaaaaaaaaaaaaaaaaaaaay!

put it on!

The entire tune is marked by this constant back-and-forth switch between ranchero and jazz, with the conclusion following the by-now-predictable pattern. Little Joe finishes the song in a strongly ranchero style, while the horns end the piece with a little jazz flourish—a variation, Little Joe informed me, on the theme of Johnny Carson's "Tonight Show" (see below).

"Las nubes" represents one of the most remarkable efforts at code-switching, or compound bimusicality, to be found in La Onda Chicana—one reason, perhaps, for its phenomenal popularity during the seventies and even into the eighties.[6] The song features a duet by Little Joe and his brother Johnny singing in an *alegre* ranchero style, while the band, augmented by a string section borrowed from the Dallas Symphony, alternates between ranchero and highly sophisticated and dense backgrounds. But the most astonishing feature is a lush string interlude, consisting of quartal (open fourth) harmonies, followed abruptly by a solidly ranchero passage in the horn section, which itself is punctuated by an

Qué Culpa Tengo (ending)

extended *grito* by Little Joe, both *grito* and horn passage serving as a stark contrast to the just-concluded string interlude. The pertinent sections are transcribed below.

It is perhaps fitting at this juncture to introduce our last sample of compound bilingualism, since it pertains specifically to the musicians' attempts to explain the uniqueness of La Onda Chicana and its musical code-switching. Spanglish, the speech of our interlocutor in this case, Oscar Lawson, intrudes upon the moment as the only form of communication capable of conveying the metaphorical link between these two realms of biculturalism—bilingualism and bimusicality. Indeed, one of the most intriguing aspects of the interviews with orquesta musicians is this metaphorical relationship that obtains between code-switching as a form of speech and its use to denote what is essentially a homologous form of communication at the level of musical aesthetics—the orquesta (cf. Blom and Gumperz 1972). Over and over, the musicians would lapse into the type of code-switching employed by Lawson to express their deepest impressions of the artistic form they had created in La Onda Chicana. Thus Lawson, leader of an Onda Chicana group known as the

Las Nubes

..nar   pa - re - ce   que a - le - gran mi al - ma con   su a - gua   que

traen   del   mar

simile

very legato

simile   softly

softly

Ay!   Ay -   Ay Ay   ee hee hee hee!

a - li - via - ne - se ge - fe ci - to! o - ra - le co - to - rra

Royal Jesters, relied heavily on compound bilingualism as he articulated his understanding of the origins and cultural parameters of La Onda Chicana (personal interview, February 19, 1980):

[In the beginning] *todos nosotros* [all of us], including the Royal Jesters, *cantábamos puras piezas americanas* [sang nothing but American songs]. *No había nada de mexicano* [There was nothing Mexican]. *Mexicano* wasn't in, *hasta que Manny Guerra se metió con los* Sunglows [until Manny Guerra joined the Sunglows], *y tocaban en inglés y en español* [and they played in English and in Spanish]. Manny was influenced by Isidro López, so he integrated the Mexican sound into the English sound that was going on—the top forty. *Y* [And] I believe—I'm not an authority on this—*que* [that] that's where La Onda Chicana evolved from—*tratando de agarrar los instrumentos que estaban usando las bandas locales* [trying to take the instruments that the local bands were using] to interpret their English numbers and trying to—*con esos instrumentos tocar español* [with those instruments play Spanish]. And they couldn't play it too well, so *es lo que salió* [that's what came out]. It wasn't a Mexican Mexican—like Beto Villa. It was a Mexican *americanado* [Americanized].

"Mexican *americanado*" is in fact an apt description for the rather awkward style that Little Joe and the Latinaires, Sunny and the Sunliners, the Royal Jesters, and other orquestas cultivated until the late sixties. As Lawson implies, it was a rather unmediated mixture of Mexican and American styles—one in which neither had assimilated the other. But by the time *Para la gente* made its appearance, Little Joe y la Familia had thoroughly "synchronized" the two horizons; they had, in short, learned the art of compound bimusicality. Little Joe conceived of the "rules" behind this synchronization as follows:

You can't just put a round pad in a square; it doesn't work that way. Things have to follow a natural order, and they have to blend, and they have to connect. They have to synchronize. . . . If it's ranchera, then it should have the ranchera feeling. If it's jazz, it should feel like jazz. But when you go from the jazz feel to the ranchera, everything can blend if you ease it in. . . . So for me to blend all these things together *es una capirotada, una ensalada de música* [it's a capirotada,[7] a musical salad]. It's [possible] only because that's all in my head and in my heart—because I live it.

Having discovered the musical *capirotada*, Little Joe continued to experiment throughout the seventies with various bimusical combinations (as did other Onda Chicana groups), as well as with more conventional (monomusical) excursions into rock, Latin rock, Mexican (especially the *bolero*), and Afro-Latino. I should note here, however, that la Familia was influenced, as were many orquestas in La Onda Chicana, by brass-heavy rock bands such as that of soul singer James Brown and others popular during the late sixties and seventies: Chicago; Blood, Sweat and Tears; and a "funk" band from the Bay Area known as Tower of Power. The latter was especially influential, as Gibby Escobedo of the Latin Breed, another of the leading Onda Chicana orquestas, recalled:

We didn't plan to sound like Tower of Power; it's just that we listened to their songs a lot, and we realized after listening that our horns were exactly the same. And so we had the same reputation. If you listen to Latin Breed, the horns were always dominant—same basic horn section [as Tower of Power]. . . . And people were surprised that we sounded so much alike. And musicians started calling us the Tower of Power of La Onda Chicana. (Personal interview, February 19, 1980)

But despite surface similarities, the resulting sound was unique to the orquestas of La Onda Chicana; it was a true synthesis of American and Mexican musical horizons. Oscar Lawson remembered the sociomusical fusion taking place in La Onda Chicana in the 1970s:

Sure, we were influenced by *lo mexicano* [the Mexican]. But this music [Onda Chicana] is—*no es mexicana, no es americana, es mexico-americana* (it isn't Mexican, it isn't American, it is Mexican American), or Chicana, if you prefer. (Personal interview, February 19, 1980)

And, of course, Little Joe was perfectly aware of the hybrid, or synthetic, quality of La Onda Chicana. As he reminded me, "But again, *tejano* music is made up of two cultures, of two *lenguas* (languages), and that's why the music comes up on a different dimension" (personal interview, November 23, 1991). Indeed, it is worth transcribing this particular stretch of conversation for what it reveals about Little Joe's understanding of the processes at work in his pathbreaking arrangements:

MP: Would you consider yourself bicultural—in the sense that Mexican and American cultures are both part of you, and that's just the way you are?
LJ: Very much so. That's what the music is too—bilingual, bicultural music.
MP: Bimusical?

LJ: Yeah, very much so.

MP: Let's talk about "Las nubes," since that's such an important song. Was it Joe Gallardo who did the arrangement for that, or Tony?

LJ: Yeah, like I said, Joe did it for me. I gave him the directions to write, but I couldn't tell him what chords. I could hear those chords, but I can't play them, but I can hear them. And I would say, "no, no, no, wait till you hit the right one. That's the chord I want to play there." So I didn't know what effect it all was gonna have, but I knew that I was going to make a difference.

MP: Did you consciously think at that time about mixing a real heavy ranchero with jaitón? 'Cause you started off real ranchero. And then you get into that very smooth section with the violins, in quartal harmony. Were you consciously trying to mix ranchero with the more jaitón—a sort of synthesis?

LJ: I'm still doing it, and all bands did it; they're still doing it now. They do it with conjunto now, and then go into strings or orchestration with brass. But that was a whole new thing then—to take one song from scratch, where it feels real ranchero, and then go to jaitón. I like that word.[8]

MP: You did that many times after that; you did it in "Qué culpa tengo," where you said you borrowed from the *Johnny Carson Show*; you did— these are songs that come to mind right away—in "Juan charrasqueado," where you ended in a real jazzy mode, with violins.

LJ: Yeah, 'cause I'm aware; I think about these things before I do them. I really can't—nothing came accidentally, when it came to this [musical code-switching], and it's not like—I'm not the only one involved in these things, but I learn from others. Like I said, I get people, since I can't write the music, I find the right person to bring out what's in my head musically. And that's where good musicians like Ham and Joe Gallardo, Bob Gallarza are excellent.

"Good musicians like Ham and Joe Gallardo," however, sometimes outpace their audiences. A recurrent theme among orquesta musicians relates to the limits imposed upon them by a public that often did not appreciate what many musicians referred to as "good" music. Limits were placed, in short, on the degree of innovation—that is, on how far music could deviate from practices familiar to and accepted by that public. Beto Villa's strategy, built around a balance between ranchero and jaitón, was predicated on the constraining power of those limits, and every other orquesta had to contend with that reality. Little Joe was acutely aware of the delicate balance between tradition and innovation, but by 1972 he was willing to experiment, to gamble, especially on a reconceptualization of the ranchero-jaitón balance, and how this would resonate in the aesthetic consciousness of his generation:

MP: You know, there were people in California who thought Texas music was trash. But when they heard your music, they changed their minds. Some people in Fresno became big fans of yours . . . but anything else from Texas they thought was trash. So it's obvious to me that when you were recording that music [*Para la gente*], you were elevating it to a higher level. And I don't know whether you were aware of that.

LJ: Not as to where I am today, but I was aware enough to know that I wanted to use the symphony strings with my music.

MP: Why? Did you think it would give it more class, or was it just something you wanted to try?

LJ: I knew it would give it more class, because, like I said, as a kid I heard the big bands and I heard classical music. I like symphonies, I like all that good ol' jaitón. . . . When I did "Las nubes," I knew that's the project I wanted to do [add symphony strings]. . . . I knew that I wanted to do something different, and I wanted to put some class into the music. . . . I didn't know what effect it was gonna have, but I knew that I was going to make a difference. Some people told me, "Hey, *la raza no quiere eso*" [the Mexican people don't want that], and I said, "*la raza no sabe lo que quiere* [the people don't know what they want]; we have to give them something they can appreciate, even if they don't know about it."

MP: But did you ever feel—like when you had Gallardo and all those guys—did you ever feel that they were going too far, or did you go right along with it?

LJ: I let them go as far as I felt that I wanted it to go.

MP: Did you have your public in mind, or was it just your own feeling?

LJ: The public is always in mind, but more than that, I had the music in mind. I have to like it, whether the people are going to like it or not. Chances are that if I like it myself, people will too.

MP: And in a song like "Las nubes," you felt you could get away with mixing it the way you did [i.e., ranchero and jazz]?

LJ: Yes, because it's a beautiful, warm song, and I knew I could expand on it. We used all those beautiful chords—I like the sevenths, they give all those highs. I liked it, and I knew people would like it.

And like it they did. But aiding in the success of *Para la gente* was a felicitous convergence of factors that expanded the range of the acceptable and made possible the bold experiments of la Familia and other groups that followed. To begin with, rock music of the counterculture—the late Beatles, the Rolling Stones, and other groups, as well as the innovative soul music of James Brown and the "funk" of Tower of Power—broke down many of the practices associated with an older and more "conservative" pop music. The widespread spirit of experimentation opened the door for a surge of innovation and a liberation from older musical norms, just as it marked a juncture when rock music was reappropriated by the counterculture as an ideological vehicle.[9] This liberating musical impulse clearly spilled over and affected the local *tejano* and other markets of the Hispanic Southwest, as Escobedo's remarks regarding the influence of Tower of Power attest.

A second converging factor to influence music was the Chicano movement, which, despite its anti-Anglo rhetoric, looked with favor on the innovation taking place in the rock scene—especially the soul market, which appealed to many Chicanos. We may suggest that rock music's break with older practices appealed to Chicanos because, as part of the general direction of the counterculture, this break represented a rejection of the dominant order that had for so long oppressed minorities. Soul music, in particular, attracted many young Chicanos because in its decided difference from mainstream pop music, it represented a musical alternative to the rejected mainstream. In sum, the revolution in the world of rock music resonated sympathetically with the "revolution" unfolding within the Chicano community, and, reinforced by the Chicano movement's search for alternatives, an era of cultural confluence dawned. This confluence facilitated the intense process of synthesis that defines the Chicano Generation. Finally, more than any of the other musics extant in the Southwest, the orquesta became a nodal point of cultural confluence and synthesis, translated into the bimusical sounds of la Familia and other Onda Chicana groups that made their mark in the decade of the seventies.

SUNNY OZUNA:
The "City Mouse" That Soared

One of the most popular groups participating in the new spirit of experimentation and contributing significantly to the musical aesthetic unfolding in the 1970s was Sunny and the Sunliners. Actually, Sunny Ozuna, the "city mouse" from San Antonio, had crashed the top-forty market in 1963, soaring to the top of the *Billboard* charts and staying there for fourteen weeks. It was a one-time stroke of good fortune for this son of a westside *barrio*. Born in 1943 and raised in a working-class family of eleven children, Ildefonso Ozuna, later known as "Bunny" and then by his stage name of "Sunny," concluded his formal education upon graduation from Burbank High School, where he also began his career as a singer.

Sunny and his friend Rudy Guerra formed a group in the late fifties, while they were still in high school. It was a five-piece ensemble they called Sunny and the Sunglows, a group that grew out of the "record hop" phenomenon of that era. The record hop was contemporaneous with the advent of the top-forty market, and it often enlisted disc jockeys who took their shows to high school gyms and provided top-forty dance music for teenagers. At times these record hops also featured live entertainment, and it was in this context that Sunny and the Sunglows and many other groups came into being across the Hispanic Southwest.[10]

When the record-hop fashion died out, it was replaced by ballrooms, at least in the big cities, and these then became the sites for bigger, more commercialized shows and dances. This was the time when, as Gibby Escobedo of the Latin Breed put it, "we started taking things a little more serious, investing in clothes and equipment" (personal interview, February 19, 1980). Sunny and the Sunglows were coming into their own then as performers of top-forty music (although they also played an occasional ranchera), and mentored by Rudy's older brother, Manny Guerra, they traveled the local area working the ballroom circuit.

The propitious moment for the Sunglows came when they recorded a song arranged by Manny, "Talk to Me," in 1962. The song thrust Sunny into the national limelight, but before that happened, he came under the influence of an entrepreneur named Huey Meaux, who convinced him to leave the Sunglows and seek fortune and glory on his own. Hoping to further his career as a soloist in the top-forty market, Sunny broke with the Sunglows in 1963, and in August of the same year Meaux reissued "Talk to Me." The latter did decide, however, to build another group around his young singer, and it went by the name Sunny and the Sunliners. The song climbed *Billboard* magazine's top-forty charts steadily, until it reached number eleven in October of 1963.

Blurred by the mists of time, the events surrounding the success of "Talk to Me" and Sunny's departure from the Sunglows have lost their edge and acquired an air of inevitability. Here we had a group of teenagers who stumbled on a top-selling hit, a star-struck young singer seeking the best route to fortune, and big companies that offered glory and intimidating contracts—all contributing to the final break. Indeed, in an interview I held with Sunny on March 5, 1980, he dismissed his break with the Sunglows as a logical "next step." But Manny Guerra, who long since achieved success as a music entrepreneur in his own right, does betray a hint of bitterness when recalling those events. Of "Talk to Me" he reminisced:

I produced that, that was my arrangement; that was on my label. Just recently, I was telling my wife, "I can't understand. I chose the song, gave it to Sunny, I arranged it, I recorded it, it went on my label, and yet when people here talk about 'Talk to Me,' it's Sunny and the Sunliners." It's not Sunny and the Sunliners. Sunny just split our group when the thing was hitting. That's when they coaxed him to "come out from there, you don't need to carry that group. We'll get you to form your own group." . . . So he took off on his own, and he took advantage of the hit. (Personal interview, November 27, 1992)

Ever the pragmatic businessman, however, Guerra now looks at Sunny's actions for what they were—economic decisions induced by a capitalist market in which individualism and self-advantage are paramount to survival and a prerequisite for the maximization of personal success:

No, it was a thing that is always going to happen. I always tell people this: "If you sign a person to a contract for five years, and after five years that person goes to try with someone else, why should you be offended? The person gave you five years of his career." Nothing is forever. . . . That's the way it is. And I think that anybody that feels different shouldn't be in the business at all, because if you're gonna be upset because people leave you— sometimes they're leaving you because that's the only way they're gonna get any higher. (Personal interview, November 27, 1992)

As matters developed, "Talk to Me" was Sunny's only successful foray into the top-forty market, although much more so than Little Joe, he continued to produce for that market, and he did crack the top-100 chart at least twice more, with "Rags to Riches," and "Out of Sight, Out of Mind"—two rhythm-and-blues ballads cut from the same mold as "Talk to Me." Neither of these, however, approached the success of "Talk to Me," and eventually Sunny and the Sunliners faded from the top-forty scene. At that point Sunny began to rely more and more on the *tejano* market to stay in business. Thus, like his principal rival, Little Joe, Sunny did not have to depend on top-forty music to survive as a singer and band leader. The *tejano* market existed as an alternative shelter, and when he faltered in the dominant American market, he turned to that shelter for support. Sunny recalled the circumstances surrounding the

switch, and in his recollection he touched on the critical difference between a thoroughly commoditized ("white") mass market that creates
highly disposable stars, and one embedded within a stronger cultural
matrix—La Onda Chicana—where "stars" enjoy more permanence:

MP: Was there a reason for quitting the American market?
SO: There were several things. When I got to the stage which a lot of people
that are still in my—talking about Little Joe, Jimmy Edward—that would
still like to have . . . [with] a national hit like that—I lived in that jungle
for a while and I didn't like it. I'm not saying that I wouldn't like to have
another "Talk to Me," and make the money that comes off it, but it's a
jungle. You have friends and money only while you're there. The minute
the song dies—[it's] "Sunny who?" And in La Onda Chicana, what is nice
is that if you're cold for a while, they still come to see you. The white
market is not that way. Chicanos hold on more to their roots, and hold
on more to their stars. They back them better. (Personal interview,
March 5, 1980)

Sunny's response triggered another line of questioning on my part—
a line that relates to the earlier discussion on the Chicano movement
but also to Sunny's distinction between a market driven solely by profit
and one more encumbered by racial/cultural considerations:

MP: This might be way off, but do you remember the Chicano movement of
the 1960s—when Chicanos began to wake up, so to speak—and along
with this there was a back-to-the-roots movement? Did that affect you or
La Onda Chicana in any way?
SO: It brought us a lot more customers, because in the awakening, they
wanted to relate back to "OK, I'm Chicano," so a lot of people that were
lost in a white world at the time—when the awakening came, it made
them realize, "Hey, man, you do have black hair, and you do have brown
skin, and you are Chicano." So when they turned around to look for
roots, not only did they look into ancestry and all that, but they started
to look into "what music is gonna represent me? Where are my roots?"
If country western represents the cowboys, they [Chicanos] automatically turned to La Onda. So they related to Joe, Jimmy, and everyone else
[in La Onda Chicana].

Sunny may have cast his lot with La Onda in the mid-1960s, but his
strategy actually seems to have included the *tejano* alternative from the
outset of his professional career, apparently because of Manny Guerra's
influence. Guerra, who had played drums with the likes of Balde Gon-

zález and Isidro López, encouraged the Sunglows to include more Mexican music, especially polkas. He recalled his advice: "I told them, 'You guys should play a few polkas,' and Sunny said, 'I hate Spanish music; I don't want nothing to do with Spanish music.'" Despite his disdainful attitude (reminiscent of Chico Sesma), Sunny must have intuited the need to stay in contact with his "roots," for in 1959 he recorded a "Spanish" single (45 RPM) that was obviously aimed at the *tejano* market. The single's feature was "Pa' todo el año," a *canción ranchera* composed by the apotheosis of that genre, the Mexican José Alfredo Jiménez. In typical *tejano* fashion, the Sunglows performed the song as a *polca ranchera*.

In fact, when we examine Sunny's discography, we are struck by the balance he maintained throughout the 1960s between Mexican and American music. In what was an obvious attempt to corner two markets, he was no doubt inspired by the early admonitions of Manny Guerra, who, as a result of his own experience as a drummer with Isidro López, recognized the value of the *tejano* market. For example, even in 1963, when his stock was soaring in the top-forty field, the "city mouse" recorded Isidro López's popular ranchera "Emoción pasajera," and in the following year, besides "Rags to Riches" and "Out of Sight, Out of Mind," he also issued "Dime como le haces," a *bolero,* and "El taconazo," another *ranchera.*

Thus, despite his continuing excursions into top-forty music, by the mid-1960s Sunny had come to the realization that his future lay in *tejano* music, and with the appearance of his popular all-Spanish album *Cariño nuevo* in 1965, his commitment to—and success in—that market was assured. Thereafter, despite repeated efforts to duplicate the success of "Talk to Me," Sunny and the Sunliners were to make their mark exclusively in the regional market circumscribed by the Hispanic Southwest, where their principal rival was Little Joe y la Familia, from whose shadow Sunny was never quite able to emerge.[11] However, as noted by Tony Guerrero, the Sunliners did carve their own niche by consciously catering to a slightly more acculturated, more upwardly mobile, and more "citified" clientele than did Little Joe and other, more ranchero, orquestas of the time (e.g., Freddie Martínez and Agustín Ramírez).

THE QUEST FOR "SYNCHRONIZATION":
La Onda as Symbolic Sleight-of-Hand

The quest by Sunny, Little Joe, Oscar Lawson, and other Onda Chicana groups for a "synchronization" between ranchero and jaitón was, in effect, an unconscious effort to reconcile the asymmetries bound up in the ethnic and class dialectic of conflict. Class differences, in particular, no matter how suppressed by the Chicano movement, inevitably surfaced in this quest. Sunny's attempt to cater to a middle-class audience is a case in point. As he himself put it, "I wasn't born in the middle class, but I wanted to progress." His manager's statement on Sunny's attempts to cater to a more middle-class crowd has already been noted (see note 2 above). Here the comments of Marcelo Tafoya of KRGT, a radio station in the little town of Hutto, Texas, will confirm Sunny's middle-class strategy, even as these comments recall Chico Sesma's on the crowds that patronized the Hollywood Palladium (cf. Chapter 8 on the shifting strategies of Beto García y sus GGs). In an interview with Ramón Hernández, Tafoya recalled the atmosphere at Sunliner dances: "Besides being an innovator, Sunny put 'class' into La Onda Chicana. His dances were a gala affair. He offered quality, and people dressed up to go see him. Women wore gowns, and guys would at the least wear suits" (publicity bio, Manny Music, Inc.).

But, as often happened where orquestas and their public were concerned, the basic contradictions inherent in the ranchero-jaitón opposition intervened: What should be the proper repertoire, ranchero or jaitón? What, for that matter, was the target audience—upwardly mobile tejanos, the working class, or some kind of balance between the two? These contradictions came to light in Sunny's assessment of the Sunliners' most experimental efforts, which he attributed to his musicians' need to "progress forward," as opposed to the inclinations of his "average" patron, who preferred "simpler" music. In explaining the discrepancy between performer and public, Sunny revealed the class dynamic involved in the tension between ranchero and jaitón:

SO: [La Onda Chicana] fan is your everyday Joe walking on the street. He lives in the *barrio*. He does fix himself up and goes to discos, he does go to rock concerts, he does all this stuff, but mainly he stays within his own particular *barrio*, his own particular music.

MP: Let me interrupt you for a second. You're saying something different from what your manager told me—an interesting remark he made in talking about some of the differences between you and Little Joe. He said, "Little Joe is more ranchero; Sunny caters more to the middle class." How does that square with what you just said, about the "everyday Joe"?

SO: This is what it is: The reason why [Little] Joe sounded more ranchero is because Joe—again, we were talking earlier about how you can break Latin into four or five different things, when everybody thinks it's just

one basic thing. Same thing happens here between Joe and me. Joe records songs and flavors them more to where Roberto [Pulido, a hybrid
orquesta-conjunto group] is—taking what we call barroom songs, songs
that you're gonna hear in all your cantinas. . . . Now, what I try to do—our
type of thing has been more . . . this is gonna sound a little offensive—
Joe, Freddie, Agustín [the latter two were exclusively ranchera orques-
tas], they cater to what we call a lower class. By lower class we [mean]
migrants, real into-the-*barrio* people, people that have a tendency to
have more problems and be in the wrong place at the wrong time. What
we have tried to work for—Jimmy Edward, Latin Breed [two cosmopolitan orquestas], myself—is to go into what we call middle class. . . . Those
people know how to come into a place, and they know how to have a good
time and be cool. The lower class has a tendency a lot of times to cause
a lot of problems, maybe smoke things they ain't supposed to in the
building. It's OK, I'm not looking down on that, but I like my particular
audience.

On the surface, Sunny's statements about the "everyday Joe" and his
"particular [middle-class] audience" may seem contradictory, but by the
1970s that audience was, in fact, *both* ranchero and jaitón, just as it could
be both working and middle class. In short, Sunny's audience was the
Chicano Generation, whose ideology of Chicanismo was based on the
negation of class difference. As explained in Chapter 6, this generation
confronted its ethnic and class contradictions and struggled mightily to
resolve them, in the process achieving remarkable syntheses such as La
Onda Chicana and bilingualism. Moreover, as outlined earlier, events in
the larger society—the hippie counterculture, the Black Power movement, and their transformative power on rock music—resonated posi-
tively within the Chicano movement and aided, at least indirectly, the
process of cultural synthesis. Innovation in the field of rock, particularly
soul (e.g., James Brown and Tower of Power), influenced both Chicano
musicians and their audiences, encouraging the former to expand their
musical horizon, and redirecting the latter's aesthetic inclinations toward greater acceptance of the complex synthesis worked out by Onda
Chicana performers like Sunny and Little Joe.

The synthesis of contradiction, however, did not proceed without en-
cumbrance. In a modernist variation of the Caduveo of the Brazilian
Amazon, who "resolved" social-structural asymmetries through a symmetrical body art (Lévi-Strauss 1963), the Chicanos resolved the double
contradiction of ethnic and class inequality and conflict through an aesthetic movement (the Chicano Renaissance) that "synchronized" cul-

tural forms of unequal status. Moreover, just as for the Caduveo, aesthetic activity was for the Chicano Generation "an ideological act in its own right, with the function of inventing imaginary or formal 'solutions' to unresolvable social contradictions" (Jameson 1981: 79). Molded ideologically by the movement erupting within its midst, the Chicano Generation in fact resorted to cultural sleight-of-hand (as did the Caduveo) to resolve their social contradictions. As Gómez-Quiñones (1990) correctly observed, the Chicanos could make demands on the system that resulted in their tighter integration into American life, yet they advocated separatism and a return to their mythical Aztlán. The dialectically driven solution to this social-structural paradox was the synthesis of conflicting cultures, and this is where La Onda Chicana played its role.

Thus, along with Little Joe and others, Sunny was able to replicate at the level of musical creation the sleight-of-hand occurring at the level of political ideology: he could reconcile the ranchero and jaitón by "synchronizing" them, to use Little Joe's apt term, but he did so by compromising the purity of both, thus creating a hybrid music. But hybridity is what Chicanismo was ultimately about—if by hybridity we mean a fusion of forms that masks deep structural antagonisms, even as this fusion projects a surface unity. By fusing ranchero and jaitón (in the form of swing-jazz), the polka or *corrida,* in particular, resolved the range of antagonisms attached to these master tropes, thus giving an impression of cultural symmetry where asymmetry was the actual rule. The *corrida* lent itself to this sleight-of-hand maneuver because of its time-honored standing as an icon for ethnic identification. In sum, the *corrida* could be transformed by adding swing-jazz or other elements (the synthesizing process itself), as long as its ranchero core was not irrevocably violated. The final result, both at the musical and ideological levels, was the blurring of social distinctions that otherwise might serve as markers for middle- and working-class statuses. In music, as in society, the asymmetries bound up in lo ranchero and lo jaitón had been negated.

And so, in explaining innovation within the *polca-ranchera,* Sunny naturally drifted toward the concept of *lo ranchero* and thence to social distinctions. It was in this context that he attempted to explain both the difference and similarity between Little Joe's more ranchero approach and his own emphasis on the "middle class" (read: jaitón). However, in explaining their respective sociomusical positions, Sunny quickly realized that the link between his and Little Joe's styles was considerably more complex, stylistically and sociomusically, than he had originally suggested. The following question moved him to develop a rather elaborate response on the sociomusical nature of La Onda Chicana, one that reveals the depth of contradiction La Onda had to navigate in order to synthesize the asymmetries dividing ranchero and jaitón, working- and middle-class forms:

MP: Isn't Little Joe encroaching on conjunto music when he plays "bar-room" music?

SO: Very much so. Where a conjunto audience would not follow me, those people have a 75 percent chance that they're gonna follow Joe. Where really, they shouldn't be following Joe, 'cause Joe should be classified more to the middle class. . . . Now, don't get me wrong; there's a lot of people in the lower class who come see us, and wanna understand, and wanna come up. They don't want to stay there. They were born there, and they have been told all their life that they have to stay there, but there are a lot of them that don't want to stay there. And there's a lot of us— for example, I was from the *barrio* myself. I come from a family of eleven kids myself. And we had the john out in the backyard, and we used [the] Sears and Roebuck catalogue for toilet paper, you know? I came from there. I wasn't born in the middle class, but I wanted to progress, and I am what I would consider middle class, for now.

Like all orquesta musicians, then—and notwithstanding his initial disdain for "Spanish" music—Sunny had to negotiate the long symbolic distance between ranchero and jaitón, between Mexican and American, and between working and middle class. In relation to this essential con-tradiction, which surfaced early in Sunny's career, Manny Guerra elab-orated on his "play-polka" advice to the Sunglows:

I told Sunny, "If I'm gonna send you to the circuit where I play with Isidro, you need to play some polkas." And they learned two instrumental polkas. I left them on a Friday, and I got back from being on the road on Monday, and I met him. And the first thing Sunny said, he said, "You need to get us a whole bunch of Spanish music." I said, "Why?" He said, "They almost killed us over there," he says, "we played those two instrumentals, like, thirty times." So he didn't like Spanish music, but that's when he started [to play it]. (Personal interview, November 27, 1992)

In his own view—and in that of others, most notably Tony Guerrero— Sunny pulled himself out of the depths of the barroom ranchero by in-troducing a more complex, more cosmopolitan sound, one inspired by swing-jazz and other American models. It was this cosmopolitan sound that encouraged his public to wear gowns and suits. One notes these ex-traneous influences from early on, as in some of his music from the mid-

1960s, in which he adopts an odd amalgam of rock and ranchero—not as complex or highly synthesized as Little Joe y la Familia's later efforts, or those of the Sunliners, for that matter, but representative, nonetheless, of Sunny's awkward first attempt at compound bimusicality.

During the 1970s, however, prodded by Little Joe's pathbreaking bimusical experiments as well as by the impact of the Chicano movement, Sunny expanded his own group, and in some respects he outpaced even the king of La Onda Chicana in the sheer intensity of the quest for the ultimate bimusical synthesis. *Los enamorados*, for example, an album released in 1975, contains a wide variety of genres from mambos to cha-chas and, of course, *corridas*. As was typical for orquestas in La Onda Chicana, the practice of compound bimusicality emerged full-blown in the performance of the latter.

One number, in particular, stands out as perhaps *the* most thorough synthesis of ranchero and jaitón ever achieved in La Onda Chicana. In it, the practice of bimusicality is actually taken beyond what I have called "compound bimusicality"—so thoroughly intertwined are swing-jazz and ranchero as to be virtually inseparable. I refer to a piece that was originally a Mexican *bolero* titled "Y" (And), which Sunny and the Sunliners transformed into a *corrida* (but preserved, nonetheless, its relatively complex *bolero* harmony). Completely integrated into the piece, however, is a swing-jazz feel that pervades the arrangement. Unlike most *corridas*, in which the switch from ranchero to swing occurs at targeted junctures, in "Y" the musical code-switching occurs simultaneously and at different levels. Thus, while the singing itself may be characterized as ranchero throughout, the various instruments weave in and out of ranchero and swing—the bass, for example, switching from one mode to the other almost at will, with the drums and the horns following suit. All in all, the piece represents a complex tapestry of musical code-switching in which ranchero and swing-jazz become tightly interwoven.

"Y" set the mold for many similar efforts by Sunny and the Sunliners and others, particularly Jimmy Edward and the Latin Breed. The transcription below gives at least a hint of the complex process of synthesis as worked out in this one musical effort.

Conclusion:
Pinnacle and Decline of a Musical Tradition

Little Joe y la Familia, Sunny and the Sunliners, the Latin Breed, Tortilla Factory, and Jimmy Edward all represent the most bimusical wing

of La Onda Chicana, just as they represent the pinnacle of the orquesta tradition in the Southwest.[12] Right up until the end of the decade of the seventies, they continued to experiment with the ranchero-jaitón elements as first synthesized by la Familia. Some of the most innovative of these experiments include two LPs by la Familia (in addition to *Para la gente*), *Total* (1974) and *Sea la paz la fuerza* (1978); Sunny's *Grande, Grande, Grande* album (1978); Jimmy Edward's *My Special Album* (1978); the Latin Breed's *Power Drive* (1977); and Tony Guerrero and the Tortilla Factory's LP by the same name, *Tortilla Factory* (1974). In all of these productions, we witness the *orquesta tejana* in its most stylistically diverse suit, as the various groups traversed a broad range of styles and genres ranging from the ranchero to the most sophisticated jaitón. In all of these efforts, of course, the most arresting results are those that successfully synthesize the ranchero and the jaitón, a feat carried out, always, through the fusion of polka or its sung version, the *corrida*, and some variation of the swing-jazz idiom.

But all of this musical ferment came to an end in the 1980s. An album produced by Freddie Records in 1980 titled *Despedida de los años 70s—la mejor música de orquesta* [Farewell to the 1970s—the best of orquesta music] served as an ironic farewell not only to the 1970s but to the orquesta tradition itself. Within the next five years, La Onda Chicana and, with it, a fifty-year history of orquesta music in the Hispanic Southwest would suffer an irreversible decline, as several factors came into play that all but assured its demise as a viable expression by the 1990s. It is indeed an irony, moreover, that after fifty years of ascendance, and precisely at the moment when it achieved its pinnacle both as a strong style and as the emblem for a Chicano musical aesthetic, the orquesta would so precipitously lose its supremacy. What had happened?

Manny Guerra and I discussed that very issue in our interview of November 27, 1992. I transcribe the following strip of conversation for the light it sheds on the demise of the orquesta in the 1980s.

MP: As far as the old-fashioned orquesta—that's a thing of the past, as far as you're concerned. It's had its day. Can you summarize what brought about its demise?

MG: What did away with so many people working? Machines did. It's the same with the music. I get in the studio and I can take any part of any kind of music and put it any way that I want, electronically. I wouldn't be able to afford that, if I had to hire the people.

MP: So it's a matter of economics?

MG: That's what it is.

MP: So is Rubén Ramos [an Onda Chicana–type orquesta] kind of like a dinosaur that's survived from the older days?

MG: That's what it is.

MP: What about Latin Breed, do they have a chance?

MG: No.

MP: 'Cause I know they're playing in Houston this weekend.

MG: No, they're gone.

MP: What about Sunny?

MG: Sunny will, 'cause Sunny's electronic now.

MP: He has to adapt to the new system.

MG: He has adapted already, his new CD . . .

MP: How about Little Joe?

MG: Little Joe's better days are gone. Hey, we should do it gracefully. We should be proud. I am. At one point in my life, I accepted the change. I still deal with people *que están tan agarrados con* the tradition [who are so wound up in the tradition]. *Y les digo* [And I tell them], "but you are

a servant of the people. *No te puedes quedar maneado* [You cannot remain locked]—if a new generation wants something new, you give it to
them. That's the kind of business we're in."

Economics (in the form of downsized electronically synthesized
groups) and a new generation constitute, for Manny Guerra, the fatal
blows that wiped out the orquesta tradition. With respect to the former,
as I wrote in a previous article on the disappearing orquesta tradition in
my adopted city of Fresno, California, "In Fresno, the recession [of 1980–
1982] cast a pall over musical life . . . as people began to curtail non-
essential activities" (1987: 238; see Chapter 8). Indeed, that recession
had a devastating impact on Fresno orquestas, which saw their numbers
plummet from a high of a dozen active groups as late as 1975 to a mere
two by the end of the 1980s. But Fresno's fate was shared by other communities throughout the Southwest. In effect, the recession was the anvil
that crushed the proverbial camel's back. When the economy improved
in the mid-eighties, there was no corresponding musical renewal—at
least not as far as the orquesta tradition was concerned. While foreign
musics continued to bombard the Southwest, orquestas remained idle.

Even in Texas, where La Onda Chicana had only recently dominated
the commercial market, orquestas suffered a noticeable decline—at first
a stylistic and then an economic one. We notice a stylistic retrenchment
by 1980, when the dynamic duo of La Onda Chicana, Little Joe and
Sunny, began to streamline their operations and to pursue a less experimental course. Signs of stylistic decadence were in fact evident everywhere, and by 1985 Sunny had disappeared from sight (he was "rediscovered" in 1990 by Manny Guerra while working at Winn's, a variety
store in San Antonio), while Little Joe was rapidly becoming obsolete.[13]
By the late 1980s, only a handful of "dinosaurs" like Little Joe and Rubén
Ramos remained, as La Onda Chicana had by and large been superseded, on the one hand, by orquesta's old rival, the conjunto, and on the
other, by a new type of electronic group that was more attuned to the
economic and cultural trends emerging in the second half of the decade.
In other words, even as La Onda Chicana was expiring, its stylistic car-
cass was being scavenged and divided between the conjunto and the
new, electronic Tejano group. The latter was the creation of a younger
crop of musicians—members of what I call the post-Chicano Generation. These musicians responded to the new economic and cultural climate by turning to the use of synthesizers as substitutes for the mainstay of the old orquestas, the horns. Almost overnight, *música tejana* had
witnessed a radical change.

But the newer groups were still nourished with the old orquesta's lifeblood—the *polca* with lyrics, or *canción corrida,* which formed a link to the older tradition. Mostly missing from the newer Tejano groups, however, was the strong ranchero-jaitón synthesis so typical of La Onda Chicana groups. In essence they took the *style* but not the substance of La Onda. The result was a blander sound—a combination of the old ranchero style and the amorphous urban style that has sedimented around the synthesizer so much in use by the modern pop-music groups (*grupos modernos*) of Mexico and Latin America. Moreover, from a strictly musicological standpoint, in terms of harmonic complexity and the degree of bimusical experimentation, the electronic groups—Selena y los Dinos, Mazz, La Mafia, and others—represent both a retreat and a significant departure from the musical achievements of the orquesta, especially during its Onda Chicana period.

I shall have more to say about musical developments during the post-Chicano era in the Coda; for now it is sufficient to note, as Manny Guerra correctly observed, that the era of synthesized music—induced at least partly by economic restrictions and the advent of a new generation—marked the end of an orquesta tradition that had bridged two generations. The conjunto, meanwhile, which inherited much of the orquesta's mantle, had proven to be much more resilient than its rival, and it continued to thrive at the end of the twentieth century. Indeed, in the long and interesting dialectic that obtains between the two (see Peña 1985b), the conjunto had played the last note, so to speak. Always overshadowed by the higher social standing of the orquesta, the conjunto had "shrunk before the orquesta," as Narciso Martínez, the "father" of the modern conjunto, once admitted. Yet, as orquesta faded, the conjunto reclaimed for itself that which the former had wrested away and the Chicano Generation had elevated to mythical status—*lo ranchero.*

And here is an irony: The seeds for the demise of the orquesta were sown by the Chicano Generation itself. Bent on demolishing old status distinctions based on class and on forging a unified "Chicano" cultural front, that generation momentarily effaced such distinctions, along with their attendant contradictions—ranchero versus jaitón, working versus middle class, and rural versus urban. But by synthesizing the ranchero and the jaitón through compound bimusicality—and, by extension, managing to blur the class and cultural differences embodied in these concepts—the Chicanos had already begun to undermine the very foundation of the orquesta and its indexicality for distinction: middle-class respectability. The all-embracing ideology of romantic nationalism had forged a strong convergence between the working-class conjunto

273

and the middle-class orquesta, with the latter, quite logically, usurping many of the elements properly indigenous to the conjunto (see Peña 1985b for the stylistic "convergence" of the two styles in the 1970s). The reverse could never have occurred; the conjunto had nothing to take from orquesta—certainly not its sophistication or its jaitón identity, for it was the snobbish, middle-class quality of the jaitón that the Chicano movement most abhorred and wished to eradicate.

And so, in the convergence between the two styles that began in the 1960s and culminated by the end of the 1970s, in which previously sharp stylistic distinctions became blurred, the conjunto won out. It was the older of the two traditions, and it was more deeply embedded in the cultural fiber of the Mexicans of the Southwest. In the end, partly as a result of its economic portability, it survived the orquesta and reabsorbed the ranchero substance that orquesta had usurped. The partitioning of orquesta between the conjunto and the electronic Tejano groups would have important implications for the post-Chicano era, to which we will briefly return in the Coda. Meanwhile, the death of orquesta was pronounced by the great conjunto accordionist Oscar Hernández as early as 1980: "At one time, when orquesta played, one kind of people went. When conjunto played, another kind of people went. Today, when an orquesta plays—no people go" (personal interview, May 8, 1980).[14]

CHAPTER 8

Ethnography
The Orquesta
Tradition in Fresno

The lifeblood of orquesta music in the Southwest was the dance. In the early days, the dance was an adjunct to public and private celebrations—Mexican Independence Day (*dieciséis de septiembre*), for example, or a wedding. In the late 1800s, a new context emerged that was to assume increasing cultural importance for the next century: the public dances organized by civic organizations such as the *sociedades progresistas, clubs filarmónicos,* LULAC, and any

After Beto García we

stopped going to dances.

There's no place to go,

unless you want to dance

to that cantina *trash.*

GGs FAN, CIRCA 1987

number of volunteerist groups that proliferated in the Southwest during the twentieth century. Yet another type of dance sprang up in the 1940s—the ballroom dance, organized strictly for profit, at which modern commercial orquestas played before packed crowds. Beto Villa, Balde González, Pedro Bugarín, and Lalo Guerrero all played both local and on-tour engagements that cemented the popularity of the new ensemble in the ballroom circuit. Indeed, by the 1950s commercial orquestas came to depend heavily on a well-developed ballroom network for their financial survival.

Meanwhile, as organization-sponsored dancing increased, particularly after World War II, the demand for local, semiprofessional orquestas also increased, and many "weekend" groups emerged, ranging from the well-equipped and jaitón to the most elementary and ranchero, depending on the status of the constituency to which a given orquesta catered. In places like Corpus Christi and San Antonio, for example, or even Fresno, California, large jaitón orquestas such as those of Bobby Galván,

Paul Elizondo, and Manuel Contreras provided dance music for the most elite affairs of those cities—Mexican and Anglo alike. These fully outfitted ensembles of twelve or more musicians played both Mexican-Latino and American music, but they were what Manny Guerra called "copy-cat" bands: they played either type of music, usually from "stock" arrangements made for the original orchestras—Glenn Miller, Tommy Dorsey, and, in Mexico, Luis Arcaraz and others.

However, after Beto Villa introduced his mix of ranchero and jaitón, Villa imitations sprang up all over the Southwest, and these weekend imitations provided affordable dance music for local events, in particular for groups like LULAC and, in later years, veterans' associations, such as VFW Post 8900 in Fresno, California. In many locales, these dances became events organized on a regular basis—so regular, in fact, that weekend dances became focal points for celebrating a sense of community among the myriad organizations forming the backbone of social life for Mexicans in the Southwest. And, as the Beto Villa branch of the orquesta tradition evolved into its Onda Chicana phase, the local versions followed, introducing the new style to club-sponsored dances across the Southwest.

Among the many local orquestas active in the weekend civic-club dance circuit was that of Beto García y sus GGs, an orquesta based in Fresno, California, in which I participated regularly for thirteen years—from 1964 until 1977—and then sporadically from 1981 to 1985. I had occasion during the initial period, especially, to observe the dynamics of orquesta performance in its most organic context—the weekend dance. This chapter offers a retrospective assessment of the cultural significance of the orquesta tradition within a specific geographic setting—the city of Fresno—using my experiences as a performer to draw some conclusions on the nature of the orquesta in its ethnographic context (see Peña 1980, 1987).

Fresno is in many ways a prototypical site for the enactment of the intercultural drama that marks the progress of ethnic relations in the Southwest, although the city's Mexican-descent population is of much more recent vintage than that of, say, San Antonio or even Los Angeles. The first large waves of Mexican immigrants to descend on this agricultural city, located in the heart of the great San Joaquin Valley, did not roll in until the 1920s and '30s, when agriculture made its first large-scale impact on the regional economy (Saragoza 1980: 36). By the late 1960s, when the metropolitan population had reached approximately 200,000, at least 25 percent of its inhabitants were of Mexican descent (Bureau of the Census 1970: 1 [6:1]: 670). That ratio continued to increase over the years, approaching 40 percent of the population of 650,000 or so in the 1990s (Reddy 1993:149).[1]

Though made up initially of impoverished agricultural workers, the Mexican population had stabilized sufficiently by the 1960s to boast a core of working- and middle-class Mexican Americans. This core comprised perhaps 20 percent of the Hispanic population of the city (Bureau of the Census 1970: 1 [6:1]: 672).[2] Although late in coalescing, as compared to its counterparts in San Antonio or El Paso, this middle-class contingent solidified rapidly in the 1960s, and a few of its more politicized members formed the vanguard for a serious challenge against the entrenched Anglo power structure of the city of Fresno. Spearheaded by the Mexican American Political Association (MAPA), which was strongly aligned with César Chávez's United Farm Workers, the Mexican Americans of Fresno engaged in sporadic conflict with local government agencies, the various school districts, and, especially, agricultural interests throughout the late 1960s and most of the 1970s.[3]

Chávez's farmworker movement, born in Fresno's backyard (in Delano, seventy-five miles to the south), was an especially volatile flash point. Opposed by a sizable bloc of the Anglo population but supported by most Mexican Americans, that movement often galvanized public sentiment along the ethnic fault line, thus deepening the chronic state of antagonism between the two groups. Blatantly anti-UFW actions taken by authorities on a number of occasions were tacitly condoned by the Anglo majority, but to Mexican Americans such actions served as galling reminders that their full acceptance in American society was not yet at hand.

As discussed in Chapter 6, ethnic politics of the sixties and seventies were influenced everywhere in the Southwest by the civil rights movement generally, and the Chicano movement most immediately. Fresno was no exception. Like their counterparts elsewhere, local activists vacillated between the Chicano movement's two contradictory agendas—to push for the integration of Mexicans into the various levels of American civic life or to advocate Chicanismo and its goals of "self-determination" and cultural disassimilation. Given, as well, the ambivalence of the dominant society—its promises of affirmative action coupled with everyday discrimination—the political activity of the 1960s and '70s had mixed results, as far as its impact on interethnic relations in Fresno can be determined. It does represent, however, a microcosmic enactment of the larger dialectic of conflict at work. In other words, both progress and retreat marked the course of interethnic relations in Fresno, although the level of cultural and structural assimilation for the Mexican Americans increased, notwithstanding discrimination on one hand, the nationalist rhetoric of separatism on the other.

But the basic conflict, undergirded as it was by racially driven class disparities, was not eradicated, and as of the 1990s many of the inequities between the two groups remained unresolved. Even as the twentieth century waned, an undercurrent of ethnic animosity persisted, ever distilled in the image of César Chávez. His memory remained volatile enough to conjure up the ghosts of ethnic battles past—as when the city council voted to rename a street after the late labor leader, only to rescind its vote when a flood of protests rained upon it from outraged Anglo constituents. In sum, the history of ethnic relations in Fresno is consistent with developments elsewhere in the Southwest (see Foley 1988a, 1990; Menchaca 1995), as these relations are mediated by the dialectic of conflict. And, as in other locales, this dialectic forms a powerful catalyst for the symbolic expression of a political unconscious (see below)—particularly as mediated by the sort of celebrations that the dances I shall shortly turn to represent.[4]

Meanwhile, in the midst of their struggle with poverty and discrimination, Mexican immigrants in Fresno found time to make music. Orquestas, in particular, were in evidence from the late 1920s. As orquesta leader Manuel Contreras recalled, Jesús Torres and Francisco Reyes were providing music for one of the *mutualistas* in Fresno, la Sociedad Morelos, which hosted dances every Saturday night at the Ryan Auditorium. Like Mexican Americans elsewhere, Fresnans embraced the swing, and by 1937 the brothers Domínguez, from nearby Selma, "had a pretty good swing band" and "were very popular" among younger Mexican Americans (Contreras interview, September 15, 1982). In 1941, Latin music came into its own in Fresno—the *bolero,* rumba, and other Afro-Hispanic forms—the same year the Club Gaona was organized. This was the first club in Fresno to represent a nascent middle class made up of young people, "Chicanos who didn't speak any Spanish, just English, people like Frank Chávez, Emile Torres, Bernardo Cárdenas" (ibid.). Big swing bands like that of the brothers Domínguez and an Anglo, Mickey Mills, played for the club, which held its dances at the Palomar Ballroom.

The 1950s and '60s witnessed another upsurge in immigration, especially from Texas and northeastern Mexico, and it was at this time that norteña music and the Beto Villa brand of orquesta invaded the Fresno area. Thousands of *tejanos* and norteños, migrants who had long followed the cotton harvest in Texas but who were being displaced by cotton-picking machines, found their way to the Golden State. The San Joaquin Valley, with its intensive agriculture of grapes and fruit trees, was a natural magnet for these uprooted workers. By the early 1960s, then, when Beto García y sus GGs first introduced its music to the area, the orquesta tradition in all its varieties was well established in Fresno.

BETO GARCÍA Y SUS GGs:
The Evolution of a Weekend Orquesta

Beto García y sus GGs remained always a family orquesta. It was initially organized by the band's patriarch, don Octavio García, in Mercedes, Texas, in 1950. The group originally included García's brother, guitarist Chono, and his sons Alonso, Beto, and Eladio. The patriarch was born September 21, 1901, in Camargo, Tamaulipas, across the border from Rio Grande City, gateway to the "magic" Rio Grande Valley of South Texas, where Mercedes is located. A descendant of the earliest Spanish-Mexican settlers of the lower Texas-Mexico border—the area known as Nuevo Santander—García was brought to the Valley in 1909, and he spent most of his life there until he migrated to California in 1960. Don Octavio eventually became a naturalized American citizen, and he actually finished an eighth-grade education in American schools—a notable accomplishment for a Mexican American of his day.

Don Octavio's widowed mother, Florencia Sáenz de García, was a proud and educated woman, a teacher in Camargo, who edited a small Spanish-language newspaper when she moved across the border to Mercedes. Mrs. Sáenz de García had become a widow shortly after arriving in the Valley. Her husband, Bernabé, was a casualty of Texas Ranger justice (see Paredes 1958). A Ranger shot him in the head while he was sitting in a bar, unarmed, drinking with friends. As the family's sole breadwinner, Mrs. Sáenz de García struggled economically (in Mercedes, she subsisted on the income from a tiny grocery store), although she always considered herself to be *gente de razón*—someone whose background placed her a cut above most inhabitants of the *barrio* where she had settled.

Mrs. Sáenz de García's sense of cultural propriety, her self-identification as *gente de razón*, was inherited by don Octavio. Although he never rose above the rank of proletarian worker, in matters aesthetic he always subscribed to the genteel—that is to say, he embraced orquesta music as opposed to the lower-status culture represented by *música norteña* of the conjunto variety. He learned to play saxophone in the 1920s from a "maistro" in Brownsville, traveling the thirty-five-mile distance once a week for his lessons, which he paid for from the meager wages he earned

FIGURE 23. *Pete Peña's Orchestra, ca. 1937.*
Courtesy of Octavio García.

working in his uncle's dry-goods store. By the 1930s, García was performing in local dances with some of the first modern-styled orquestas to be
formed in the Rio Grande Valley. As was the case with other, similar orquestas throughout the Southwest, the groups with which the young
García associated—Pete Peña's Orchestra, for example (see Fig. 23)—
concentrated initially on American big-band music, such as swings, fox-
trots, and the like, with a few Latin pieces such as rumbas and tangos
added for the sake of variety. At this time in his musical career, García
did not play ranchera music.

On the other hand, as a member of the working class surrounded by
the strong ethnic ambiance of a *barrio,* don Octavio had become convinced by the 1940s that *música ranchera* was an indispensable part of
the musical life of Mexicans in South Texas. Thus, like most of his musical peers, he eventually yielded to the tastes of his public, which demanded its share of *música ranchera*—especially after World War II,
when Beto Villa legitimized *lo ranchero* as part of the orquesta repertoire.
In this respect, don Octavio developed as much competence playing ranchera music as he did more jaitón styles—whether Mexican or American. In short, like most orquesta musicians, García had acquired a dualistic musical orientation by the 1950s—ranchero and jaitón, Mexican
and American.

Octavio García's musical taste was his legacy to his children, a legacy that guided the GGs' orquesta from its inception in 1950 until its demise in 1985. As I wrote in an earlier article, "Like their father, the young Garcías learned to appreciate *música buena* ["good" music] and to depreciate *música arrabalera* ["low-class" music], although, given their class and ethnic limitations, they were forced to strike a balance between the two stylistic genres" (1987: 232). Beyond their dualistic musical outlook, however, the Garcías were somewhat conservative in their approach to repertoire. Perhaps because of don Octavio's influence, the GGs were cautious in adopting new styles. For example, it took some time, and a bit of prodding by the more progressive members, for the band to embrace La Onda Chicana—a style both Beto and Octavio initially thought was too radical for the tastes of their public. But the changes sweeping through the musical landscape during the late sixties and seventies inescapably caught up with the GGs, and eventually the group not only adapted to La Onda, it established itself as the premier Mexican American orquesta in Fresno, California.

In 1960, when the Garcías migrated to California in search of better employment opportunities, don Octavio was on the eve of his sixtieth birthday, and at this time he turned over the leadership of the GGs to his youngest son, Beto. The latter had begun his career playing trumpet as a youngster in his father's orquesta, but in 1956 he dropped out of school and joined the Air Force. While serving in England, he attached himself to an Air Force dance band, where he developed a taste for American big-band music. Like his Mexican American contemporaries, however, the young García could never have embraced American music as his permanent alternative. Thus, upon returning to his native Texas, he logically reverted to the bimusical repertoire common to most Mexican American orquestas, including that of his father. This repertoire consisted of Beto Villa–styled polkas, Mexican-Latino genres—*boleros, danzones,* cha-chas—and a few of the by then "standard" pieces from the big-band era, such as "In the Mood" and "Sentimental Journey."

Beto García's biography parallels that of many orquesta musicians in that it forms an interesting backdrop to the development of his musical ideology. Like many such biographies, it is marked by contradiction: he aspired toward the jaitón, but his ethnic predicament constantly veered him toward his working-class roots. He was born in Mercedes, Texas, in 1938, dropped out of school in the seventh grade, and soon thereafter joined the Air Force. When he moved to California, García worked at odd jobs, mainly as an upholsterer. He had no other vocational training. But his ancestral pride pushed him onward; he loathed the life of a proletarian worker, and he yearned for the independence and authority he exercised in his part-time occupation as a weekend orquesta leader. Finally, in 1969 he decided to take advantage of his "GI Bill" (an education underwritten by the federal government specifically for veterans), and he enrolled at Fresno City College. Eventually, and after considerable struggle, he earned a master's degree in social work, and he gained permanent employment in a middle-class occupation, as a student counselor in a local high school.

But the transition from upholsterer to counselor came relatively late and at some sacrifice for García. He had to overcome a lack of preparation for college study, and due to his late start, he was approaching forty when he began his career as a counselor. In the meantime, the band was undergoing its own transformation from a working-class-based group to the foremost middle-class orquesta in Fresno. Upon their arrival in Fresno, adverse circumstances had forced the GGs to begin at the bottom, so to speak, and to work their way up. Unfamiliar with the musical scene of their adopted city, the GGs necessarily started anew, as an unknown group. Under the young García's leadership, the band went through a period of reorganization, which lasted from 1960 to 1964. At this time the GGs was hardly an orquesta; it most often consisted of five musicians—Beto on trumpet (he was also the group's vocalist); Octavio on saxophone; an older brother, Alonso, on piano accordion; Carlos Almaraz, another Texas expatriate, on drums; and one or another local guitarist the GGs managed to enlist.

Since the GGs had no name recognition in Fresno during this early period, they were compelled to play wherever the opportunity arose—most often in hard-core, working-class *cantinas* on the "West Side," where the pay was low and the crowds unruly. But having weathered the rigors of proletarian life themselves, the Garcías were not ones to be intimidated by the rough-and-tumble of the *cantina* dance, where hardened men and women, many of them immigrants from Texas and northern Mexico, celebrated on weekend nights. However, having to perform in such déclassé conditions meant that the GGs had to forsake "good music," at least for the moment, and concentrate on *música ranchera*, the preference of the people who patronized such establishments. The small, improvisational ensemble they maintained at this time was more than adequate to the task.

I joined the GGs in 1964, at a time when the band was beginning to move out of the *cantina* circuit and into other kinds of dance engagements, such as weddings and activities connected with working-class groups like the Sociedad Progresista Mexicana, for which the GGs performed regularly in the mid-sixties. Meanwhile, the band was acquiring a reputation beyond the Fresno metropolis, and trips to outlying areas—for example, to the city of Modesto, ninety miles to the north—became common by 1965. The band's repertoire, however, was still heavily tilted toward *música ranchera* of the Tex-Mex variety Beto Villa had popularized; it even included tunes borrowed from the conjunto repertoire. Moreover, the music was still relatively simple and unpolished, learned and played "by ear" in improvised sessions. Written arrangements common to *música buena* were the exception rather than the rule. At this time the group consisted of six musicians—Beto on trumpet and vocals, Octavio on saxophone (tenor and alto), Alonso on organ (a cheap, portable Farfisa model) and piano accordion, Octavio's daughter, María, on electric bass, Pete García (no relation) on drums, and this writer on electric guitar.

A significant turning point for the GGs occurred in December of 1965 when the band was hired to play for a Christmas holiday dance at Fresno's most elegant dance hall, the Rainbow Ballroom. Since the 1950s, the Rainbow had been the preferred site for staging the most fashionable dance events in the Mexican community, from weddings to club socials. For-profit Sunday dances had been an established tradition since the 1950s, and they attracted large crowds of well-dressed and well-behaved Mexican Americans, generally from the middle and the more stable working class. For the GGs, entry into the Rainbow Ballroom, where they began to play with increasing frequency, meant a return to don Octavio's original status as a purveyor of *música buena*. It also meant a reevaluation of performance strategy: the unpolished ranchero repertoire suitable for a seedy *cantina* like El Tecolote was out of place in the plush environment of Fresno's finest ballroom.

A change in orientation was therefore in order—a change reinforced by another development in the sociomusical transformation upon which the GGs were now embarked. Not long after the GGs began to play at the Rainbow, they initiated a relationship with an organization that perfectly matched the band's basic musical ideology and that was to exert a lasting influence on its repertorial choices. I refer to the distinctly middle-class and strongly acculturative Veterans of Foreign Wars Post 8900—the VFWers—consisting almost exclusively of Mexican Americans. The relationship between the GGs and VFW Post 8900 was solid and long-lasting. Beginning with the New Year's Eve dance of 1967, the GGs were to participate on a regular basis in Post 8900 dances for the

FIGURE 24. *Beto García y sus GGs, 1970.*
Author's collection.

next seventeen years, ending, fittingly enough, with the orquesta's last performance on New Year's Eve, December 31, 1985.

The GGs' association with both the Rainbow and the VFW prompted a shift in the group's sociomusical emphasis, from a working-class to a middle-class modality—that is to say, from ranchero to jaitón. To begin with, the casual street clothes acceptable in the West Side *cantinas* were socially incorrect in a place with the Rainbow's reputation for jaitón affairs. A key symbolic change therefore ensued: the street clothes gave way to more formal attire. A haberdasher member of Post 8900 became the GGs' wardrobe consultant, and the group made periodic treks to the menswear store where he worked to be fitted for uniforms—usually suits in the latest fashion, embellished with eye-catching ties to give the band the "show-biz" touch (see Fig. 24).

More important was the change in musical style and repertoire. During their *cantina* days, the GGs had become accustomed to the simple, improvised arrangements of *música ranchera*. Now, however, in response to what the band members perceived as the more demanding expectations of both Rainbow and VFW supporters, the band began to experiment with written arrangements. I happened to be completing a degree in music in the late 1960s, and, eager to lift the group to a more complex level of performance, I wrote a number of arrangements for Mexican *boleros,* popular American tunes, and a few for rancheras—the latter aimed at raising that type of "country" music to a higher level of sophistication. Since the crowds at the Rainbow included younger people much attracted to rock bands such as Chicago, Tower of Power, and "soul" singers like James Brown, the GGs adopted some of their music as well.

With respect to the GGs' repertoire, we should recall that in matters of musical taste, GGs fans were no different from Mexican Americans elsewhere (with the exception of Rainbow regulars, who were more attuned to rock music). The VFWers, in particular, preferred a combination of ranchero and jaitón, Mexican and American, thus matching the tastes of orquesta enthusiasts in other locales across the Southwest. In their adherence to American music, they signaled their assimilative tendencies, while in their appreciation of complex *bolero* and *balada* arrangements (the latter a hybrid between the *bolero* and the American "slow piece"), they articulated their middle-class aspirations. Finally, like Mexican Americans everywhere, their sentimental attachment to *música ranchera* symbolized their not-yet-lost allegiance to their working-class Mexican roots.

Both the GGs' and their patrons' attitude toward *música ranchera* was powerfully affected by the ethnic revivalism within the Chicano movement (see Chapter 6), and its articulation within La Onda Chicana, in particular the ranchero-jaitón synthesis forged by Little Joe y la Familia in the early 1970s. Beto Villa had popularized the ranchero style since the 1940s, of course, and the GGs and older VFWers were no strangers to that style—indeed, Octavio consistently preferred Villa's music to La Onda Chicana. But the bimusical synthesis forged by la Familia presented a new challenge and an opportunity to experiment with bold new stylistic combinations. Thus the GGs quickly integrated songs like "Las nubes" and "Qué culpa tengo" into their repertoire. At the same time, they adapted other traditional rancheras to the bimusical synthesis pioneered by the *orquestas tejanas.*

As I demonstrated in Chapter 7, La Onda Chicana was a product of its historical moment—the musical signature of a Chicano Generation coming of age in the 1960s and '70s. It was perfectly natural, therefore, that this culturally powerful style should captivate the Chicanos of Fresno, and its bimusical experiments were thus enthusiastically received by GGs fans. VFWers, whether older members associated with the Mexican American Generation or younger ones belonging to the Chicano Generation, responded to La Onda with unbridled enthusiasm, as did

their peers elsewhere in the Southwest. "Las nubes," in particular, became a fixture at GGs dances, never failing to elicit its share of *gritos* (a
peculiarly Mexican yell expressing a deeply felt sense of Mexicanness).
As discussed further below, songs such as "Las nubes" and the *gritos* attached to them contributed to the ritualistic nature of the weekend
dances in which the GGs were key participants.

Meanwhile, in 1973 the GGs brought the first non-Mexican into the
group, saxophonist Bill Giddings. An accomplished musician and teacher
with a degree in music, Giddings had played Mexican-Latino music with
Manuel Contreras's orquesta for many years. His addition to the GGs
added considerable luster to the band's performance, while enhancing
its ability to play both ranchero and jaitón. In short, despite his Anglo
background, Giddings's expertise in Mexican-Latino music (including
ranchero) and his general musical training increased the GGs' stature.
He was much appreciated by both the band and its clientele, representing, perhaps, a token of interethnic cooperation in a society still plagued
by chronic interethnic conflict. Aiding in Giddings's integration into the
group was the strict observance of all interracial forms of etiquette: he
was never made to feel out of place anywhere the GGs played.

By 1975, Beto García y sus GGs was arguably the most versatile Mexican American orquesta in the Fresno area—with the exception, perhaps, of Ray Camacho and the Teardrops, a full-time professional recording orquesta that toured widely throughout the Southwest. Over the
years, the GGs had undertaken several measures to upgrade; besides its
fashionable wardrobe and more complex musical arrangements, the band
had purchased a new and more powerful sound system, as well as an electric piano and Hammond organ for Alonso, complete with Leslie speaker.
By this time I was playing both trumpet and trombone with the group,
and the added depth to the horn section allowed for yet more density in
the written arrangements. Thanks to its higher performance standards
(and snappy uniforms), the orquesta projected a more polished image,
and for the remainder of the 1970s, Beto García y sus GGs occupied a
prominent position in the musical affairs of the Mexican American community in Fresno. Besides their regular engagements at the Rainbow
and with Post 8900, the GGs kept busy throughout the year performing
for upscale weddings that could afford the band's escalating charges.

The Garcías always prided themselves on their adaptability. Although
somewhat conservative in its musical approach, the band's ability to play
a broad range of styles for diverse audiences increased its versatility and
appeal. But the one organization most congenial to the GGs' sociomusical ideology was the Veterans of Foreign Wars Post 8900. Its mixture

of middle-class professionals, petit-bourgeois entrepreneurs, and skilled working-class members coincided with that of the band, and their leanings in matters political, cultural, and musical meshed perfectly with those of the GGs. In short, like the GGs, VFW Post 8900 was the ideal blend of both the Chicano and Mexican American Generations. As well, the organization's intergenerational and socioeconomic makeup matched that of the GGs. As was the case with the GGs, the older members provided a sense of continuity with the past—hence the nostalgia for an older music, such as "El danzón Juárez" or the *bolero* "Solamente una vez" and American selections like "In the Mood" or "Stardust." Meanwhile, the younger members were more predisposed toward innovation, and they made possible the success of La Onda Chicana (though they appreciated the older music as well).

Oddly enough, while the political upheaval that gave birth to La Onda Chicana raged around these mainstream Mexican Americans, it went unrecognized among members of Post 8900, at least within the Saturday-night dance celebrations. On the rare occasion when someone tried to introduce politically charged discourse related to the Chicano movement, Post 8900 officials immediately took steps to stop the intrusion. The outward tone of these dances was thus distinctly antipolitical; indeed, they evinced a noticeable tilt toward the conservative, or at least a disinclination to challenge the basic order of American social life. Yet, as I argue below, in their ritualistic nature the dances were expressive of a "political unconscious" (Jameson 1981), whose repressed goal was a negation of the dominant culture that these conservative Mexican Americans otherwise endorsed publicly. But the means leading to that goal were laden with contradiction, in that the *conscious* content of the dance ritual—its value as a form of entertainment—was in important ways at odds with its subversive *unconscious*. Among most VFWers (there were exceptions), the gains in civil rights won by the Chicano movement and, in particular, the cultural synthesis forged by the Chicano Renaissance went largely unrecognized—canceled by their consciously held politics of acquiescence.

RITUAL AND THE POLITICAL UNCONSCIOUS:
The Structure of a Post 8900 Dance

In his central argument that class conflict in capitalist society is inexorably "driven underground" through a process of mystification and repression, Fredric Jameson (1981) coined the phrase that also serves as the title of his influential book, "the political unconscious."[5] Building on Marx and Freud, he develops a powerful theory on the operation of this process and its protean effects on ideological formation. Put simply, Jameson argues that since class exploitation cannot be reconciled with Utopian strivings for equality, systemic class conflict must therefore be "relentlessly driven underground by accumulated reification" (Jameson 1981: 280). Jameson's concept of the political unconscious can be fruitfully applied to the analysis of the VFW Post 8900 dances as forms of expressive culture that mediated the "return" of a repressed reality of ethnic-class oppression to which these middle-class Mexican Americans were heirs.

I have argued consistently in this work that certain aspects of Anglo domination—specifically, those related to Anglo notions of their own racial and cultural superiority—have, in fact, been challenged in the Southwest, both overtly and covertly (see Foley 1988a; M. García 1989; Menchaca 1995). Overt challenge begins early on and is expressed in the politics of racial-cultural (in)equality. Mexican Americans have constantly demanded that the dominant group abide by its own constitution and its mandate for equal opportunity for all citizens. This principle of a color- (and gender-) blind equality serves as the touchstone for all civil rights initiatives since the 1960s, and, like other minorities and women, the Mexican Americans have not hesitated to invoke the principle of civil rights to advance their cause. The problem of class inequality has never received such scrutiny, however, and among Mexican Americans, class issues seep into the social consciousness indirectly and only because they underpin ethnic relations: Mexicans cannot help but be aware that the Anglos historically enrich themselves at the expense of exploited Mexican labor.

Against ethnic and class disparities dividing the two groups, the Utopian, egalitarian impulses inherent in a liberal democracy invariably generate mediative actions that at least mask the worst inequalities. But these actions address ethnic, not class, inequality (as, for example, the Civil Rights Act). Following Jameson (and Habermas), we may suggest that class conflict remains repressed and unconscious—its effects "ideologically displaced" (Williams 1981) onto *individual* differences irrespective of the life opportunities that class position affords. Economic opportunity—the "rags-to-riches" myth—is thus held by most Mexican Americans to be a function of individual initiative, not class status, although awareness of ethnic discrimination tempers their position. Neal Gabler's observation that "the whole idea of class [has been] made to seem un-American and socialistic" (1994: B9) applies as much to Mexican Americans as it does to other Americans. In short, the reality of class inequality has been banished from social consciousness, replaced by the notion of "classless inequality" (see Habermas 1970; Miliband 1969; Williams 1981).[6]

Consciously held beliefs, then, based on liberal-democratic principles such as "equal opportunity," surround and contain both ethnic and class conflict in the Southwest, in this way contributing to a surface ethnic protocol that is nonetheless periodically shaken by a political *conscious-ness* deriving from the Mexicans' subordinate position in the ethnic equation. Meanwhile, at the symbolic level other mechanisms intervene to mediate the contradictions between Utopian principles and everyday *class* exploitation, and this is where the political *unconscious* bursts through, albeit under heavily censored poses. However censored and subterranean its workings may be, the political unconscious rises to the surface in various aspects of popular culture—in the status reversal in the "hero" corrido I discussed earlier, for example (see Peña 1982), or in ambiguous forms of verbal art like the intercultural jest (Paredes 1968). It also emerges in the ritualized structure of the Saturday-night dance, investing it with the power to speak to the contradictions facing the VFW-ers—their adherence to liberal-democratic ideology, for example, in the face of an oppressive ethnic-class conflict and its relentless dialectic.

I want to argue, in other words, that these ritualized dances were but a microscape on the larger canvas of expressive culture, whose overriding theme is ethnic and class struggle. That struggle has inscribed upon this canvas all the repressed narratives circulating atomistically in the collective unconscious and threatening to blurt out their hidden secret—the routine use of violence that has guaranteed to the dominant group both its ethnic and class superiority. It is in this jostling for a symbolic place on the canvas of intercultural narrative that musical activity, generally, and the Saturday-night VFW dances, specifically, assume their significance. For in the highly purposeful arrangement of symbolic action, these weekend gatherings were transformed into genuine rituals that must be read as efforts to restore to the "text" of the intercultural story the repressed consciousness of a fundamental reality—the intertwined presence of ethnic *and* class oppression in the Southwest.

Viewed from this perspective, the VFW dances evinced a dialogic-dialectical structure; they constituted a kind of discourse that addressed in highly symbolic fashion the antagonism, not between classes in this instance, but between ethnic groups—though class hovered at the edge of the action as an "absent cause" (Jameson 1981), an unarticulated reality that lent to these dances their dynamic quality.[7] In their *dialogic* function, the dances brought forth a "voice for the most part stifled and reduced to silence, marginalized, its own utterances scattered to the winds, or reappropriated in their turn by the hegemonic culture" (Jameson 1981: 85). In their *dialectical* function, they conflated real class differences present in the Mexican American community by encompassing the master tropes, ranchero and jaitón, within one single celebration. In either case, the surface merriment attending the dances must be rewritten as a "polemic and subversive strateg[y]" that in a paradoxical way sought "to contest and to undermine the dominant 'value system'" (Jameson 1981: 84; cf. Bakhtin 1986 on the dialogic principle in communication). Seeing the dances as subversive activity restores these seemingly innocuous celebrations to their proper place in the long-running dialectic of conflict that organizes ethnic-class relations in the Southwest.

Let us examine, then, the particular components of these Saturday-night dances—these exercises in symbolic inversion in which a sense of Mexican community replaced the reality of an Anglo-controlled social order these relatively conservative Mexican Americans otherwise endorsed as the most natural way to organize social life. It is worth noting that the GGs' crowd had counterparts in numerous other dance halls in the Fresno area. There were at least ten orquestas during this period, all of them sharing the GGs' style and repertoire and each enjoying its own following. On any given weekend there might be as many as a dozen dances, some sponsored by other Mexican American organizations, others in the form of weddings. Each of these dances drew from two to four hundred people, so that on any given weekend, as many as four thousand people might engage in this form of celebration.

VFW dances evinced a ritual structure, first, in the repetitive nature of the actions. Their "redundancy factor [was] very high," as Leach would say of ritual (1972: 334). Moreover, the "language" of these dances-as-ritual was effectively "condensed" (ibid.: 337) into a form of symbolic discourse loaded with "esoteric" information whose very redundancy served to encode the group's sense of comradeship and difference from the "exoteric" society that ruled beyond the boundaries of these marked areas of intense play (Jansen 1965; cf. Bateson 1972). The notion of play enters into the discussion for obvious reasons, as does that of "framing." Both of these have been elaborated by Gregory Bateson (1972) in his theory of play. They dovetail nicely into a theory of ritual in that many of the elements present in play—especially deeply intense play—conform to the norms that govern ritual (cf. Huizinga 1950).[8]

In the case of the VFW dances, the sequence of events was governed by a metacommunicative understanding among participants that the set of all messages or meaningful actions exchanged by them within the framework of the dance were delimited by this physically and psychologically defined moment of play. The people understood that as a form of play, the dance preempted the daily grind of life. Bateson's statement "Attend what is within and do not attend to what is outside" was in operation here. But at a tacit, metacommunicative level of understanding the dances were elevated to the status of ritualized play.

And so, at least a dozen Saturdays a year, the VFWers would gather for their communal celebrations—these "adventures into reality," as John Blacking wrote of the African Venda's music and dance (1974: 28). Within these specially marked spaces reserved for "deep" ethnic play (Geertz 1973), these Mexican Americans engaged in experiences that "made them more aware of themselves and their responsibilities toward one another" (Blacking 1974: 28). Moreover, in the earnestness with which they were celebrated, these hyperethnic gatherings became "rituals of intensification" (Chapple and Coon 1942), wherein a sense of empowerment and a negation of the dominant Anglo order was momentarily achieved. As we shall see, such a subversive effect was made possible by the deliberate emphasis on an alternative set of symbols, grounded in the participants' sense of their own separate historical reality—compromised as that reality might be by the VFWers' assimilative tendencies. Twelve times or more a year, these men and women congregated to reaffirm and "intensify" that reality.

Central to the ritual structure of the dance were two sets of ritual elements—one set consisting of "diachronic," or temporal, phases, the other consisting of "synchronic," highly condensed symbols. The diachronic elements were similar to critical phases of ritual action that Victor Turner (following Van Gennep) has labeled "structure" and "anti-structure," or *communitas* (1969; cf. Van Gennep 1960). These were clearly in evidence in the Post 8900 dances, marking out discrete stages as the evening progressed. Meanwhile, with respect to the symbolic (synchronic) elements present, both the "ideological" and the "orectic" poles of meaning were evident—the former clustering around ethnopolitical symbols that represented a "condensed statement of the structural and communal importance" of ethnic identity for the participants, the latter providing a sense of "security" deriving from the deeply communal nature of the celebration (Turner 1977: 184–185).

One final point needs to be addressed regarding the interpretation offered here, a point related to the earlier discussion (Chapter 2) on the critical difference between music as an organic activity closely linked to use, or symbolic, value, and music manufactured for, or coming under the influence of, exchange-value. As a commodity, the latter music is far more susceptible to the process of reification and its desymbolizing effects than "organic" music, which remains embedded in the cultural fabric of its makers, and—I would argue—is therefore more deeply implicated in the workings of the political unconscious. As organic activities, VFW dances were a symbolic mimesis of that political unconscious. Moreover, they must be distinguished from superficially similar celebrations going on in other parts of Fresno and, indeed, all over the country in nightclubs, discotheques, ballrooms, and other places where Americans engaged in dancing for more or less casual purposes. Of course, the VFWers saw their dances primarily as entertainment, but the purposive quality of their actions was suspiciously ritualistic: too many features of the dance betrayed the deeper forces operating here. In other words, a casual observer would have mistaken the VFW dances for a form of desultory entertainment that is common enough in American popular culture. Unless she were sensitized to the historical context in which these dances were enacted, the observer would overlook the ritual import of such symbolic elements as the *menudo* (a food with strong cultural overtones), the strategic placement of *gritos* (shouts), the style of dancing, the choice of powerfully evocative Mexican songs, and numerous other cues that clearly identified the events as ritualistic ethnic play.

To obtain a more rounded portrait of the dance-as-ritual, let us travel back to the one on Saturday, July 16, 1977, a date late in the series when the dances had already attained maximum elaboration, insofar as all of the ritual elements had evolved into a coherent bundle. This one was held at the most frequented site, the cafeteria located within the Fresno Fairgrounds. The cafeteria was a large, rectangular building lined with windows; it could accommodate up to five hundred people. For VFW dances, large tables were set up in close rows perpendicular to the wall, two end-to-end tables per row, so that approximately ten to twelve people could be seated on each side, with just enough space left to walk to and from the dance area. The table arrangement created a degree of crowding, ostensibly to maximize the space available, but I believe it was also conducive to close interaction among the throng in attendance. The tables were usually covered with white paper and decorations of one sort or another (such as flower arrangements) placed on top. A large area in the middle of the floor was left clear for the dancers. The band was usually set up at the long end of the hall, on a platform raised about eighteen inches above the dance floor.

Dances invariably began at 9:00 and lasted until 1:00. A few people arrived even before the appointed hour, to socialize in the relative quiet that preceded the moment of noisy merriment. Entry into the dance was gained by paying an admission fee at a small table set up at the main entrance. Participants, most of them married couples, usually arrived in groups of two or more, paid their admission, and began filling up the rows of tables. The hour between 9:00 and 10:00 was the busiest for the door, and it was not unusual for a line to form outside the building, as people waited to pay and join in the celebration. The cafeteria was surrounded by parking spaces, and by 10:00 a solid chain of cars encircled the building, providing a symbolic border for the activities going on inside.

As had long been common for orquesta dances throughout the Southwest, those of VFW Post 8900 required, at least tacitly, semiformal dress. Most of the men wore suits or sport coats with ties, although a few opted for an open shirt collar. The women dressed even more lavishly, some decked out in gowns adorned with stylish jewelry and salon-combed hairdos. In effect, the Saturday-night celebration was considered a time to "dress up for the occasion"—a special moment of dignified play marked by well-defined diacritics that included proper attire. The band observed the dress code in its own special way by wearing uniforms that distinguished the members as unique contributors to the celebration. But beyond their "show-biz" function, the uniforms evoked the power of the performers' special talent (often referred to, fittingly enough, as a *don de Dios* [gift from God]), which invested in them the responsibility for the bacchanalian deliverance of the festive throng. Furthermore, as well-paid specialists, the musicians accepted their role with appropriate seriousness, arriving well in advance of the public to set up their cumbersome equipment.

As noted, the area reserved for the band was a platform raised above the dance floor—a practical gesture, since it helped to project the sound, but a symbolic one as well, since it lent the bandstand a commanding presence. One might say that if it was not considered "sacred space," then it was at least off-limits, except by permission of the performers. The technological array of amplifiers, speakers, microphones, wiring, and other paraphernalia certainly lent the stage an imposing aura. At least in the first stages of the dance, most people thus shunned the stage, except to approach Beto and ask for musical requests. A real and a symbolic distance was thus maintained between performers and dancers; however, as the evening wore on, this distance increasingly broke down, as decorum became more and more lax.

As in countless previous dances, on the night of July 16, 1977, Beto stepped up to the bandstand shortly before 9:00 and began a tuning routine all of us had heard many times before—an arpeggio in D minor that signaled to the other musicians the hour of celebration was at hand. Alonso rushed to the bar to get another drink, his final "tune-up" for the long night ahead, as he often said. Bill Giddings, who had set up his saxophones earlier, climbed onto the stage and, as was his habit, shared the latest joke with the other band members. María and I tuned the bass and guitar off Alonso's organ, while Reggie Peña, the GGs' drummer since 1973, tuned and adjusted his trap set, all the while exchanging jokes with Giddings. Octavio was, as always, the last to climb on the bandstand, not being one to warm up before a performance. ("I can warm up with the first tune," he would say.)

The musicians' seemingly routine pre-performance habits may seem trivial enough, and indeed these habits were an economical way for the musicians to gear up to the demands of the performance. But these preliminaries were so stylized we should consider them symbolic categories in the ritual scheme—a contribution on the part of the musicians to the order of things that characterized the first phase of the dance. That order—what we may call Phase I—was an extension of the social structure governing the world beyond the walls of the cafeteria. Besides the musicians' routines, other elements foregrounded during this phase evoked a sense of organization not unlike that which regulated the lives of the VFWers in the workaday world—the decoration of the hall, the encirclement of the cafeteria by automobiles, the orderly entrance of the couples, and the measured quality of the celebration during the first musical set.

In sum, during the first hour the dance evinced all the characteristics of ritual *structure* as formalized by Van Gennep and Turner. The moment of *communitas,* or *anti-structure,* when order would give way to chaos, was not yet at hand. From 9:00 until 10:30, when the band took its first intermission, the participants were still building up to the moment of anti-structure. At this early hour they were still sober, the atmosphere was one of restrained celebration, of men and women not yet primed for the full-blown hour of merriment.

Reinforcing the order of Phase I was the sequence of selections the band played. Beto always called out the polka "Las alteñitas" as the first number, followed by the Mexican *bolero* "Sin ti," and the *cumbia* "El cable." He rarely changed this starting sequence, at least not during the last five years of the period I am discussing here (1967–1977), when the dance gradually evolved into a tightly organized temporal order. The initial sequence was also significant in that it introduced a thematic exposition of the three genres that would dominate the musical selection for the remainder of the evening—polka (or *canción ranchera, corrida*), *bolero*, and *cumbia*.

Listening to a recording of the July 16 dance (Beto was in the habit of recording GGs performances) and comparing the level of noise between the beginning of the dance and the band's intermission at 10:30, one is struck by the increase in sound decibels. This increase was reflected in the changing nature of the celebration. An hour and a half into the dance, the restrained politeness and measured dancing that had governed the first hour were gradually giving way to the rising din of voices competing to be heard and the quickening movement of people plunging into the moment of deepening play. The dance floor was filled by 10:30, and the dancers were attempting ever fancier maneuvers. I described the unfolding (dis)order in the following manner:

Faces began to glow with liquor and jollity, the mass of humanity going round and round in a counterclockwise circle, moving along in synchronous rhythm to the beat of Beto García's music. Mellowed by the beer, margaritas, screwdrivers, and other customary alcoholic drinks, the couples who had made such an orderly, even staid entrance, could now be seen to interact freely and noisily across tables, on the dance floor, at the bar, and in the long, impatient lines in front of the restrooms. Everywhere people socialized, the throng of voices rising in pitch, loudness, and incoherence until music and voices fused in a continuous din. The celebration was in full swing. (Peña 1980: 60)

By 11:00, Phase II of the dance had ensued; the critical transition from structure to *communitas* was at hand. The musicians were naturally responsible for transporting the merrymakers through this transitional phase and into the most intense level of play. They thus responded to the heightened excitement by jacking up the amplifiers, even as their musical technique was being compromised by the liquor they, too, consumed. The band's spirits rose in tandem with those of the crowd, and as the second set unraveled, Beto increasingly catered to his patrons' whims by inviting special requests. The level of drunkenness approaching its peak, rancheras like "Las nubes" and the ever-popular "Volver, volver" unleashed a chorus of *gritos* and cascades of applause at their conclusion, as did popular *cumbias* like "El dale y dale" and the pastorally evocative "Estos guaraches" (These sandals). Nostalgia set in at this time as well, and older tunes that evoked the past were increasingly requested, such as "El danzón Juárez," the *bolero* "Solamente una vez," and the only corrido popular at VFW dances, "Gabino Barrera," about the exploits of a tough Mexican bandit.

Canciones rancheras were particularly critical to the ritual process. Like Mexicans everywhere, VFWers responded enthusiastically to the *canción ranchera*. Deeply nationalistic sentiments were awakened by standard rancheras like "Ojitos verdes," "Llegó borracho el borracho," and others with the unique "country" flavor of the ranchera. These songs invariably provoked lusty *gritos* that approached virtuosity in the throats of the most enthusiastic fans. In short, more than any other symbolic element of the dance, the ranchera mediated the "structure of feeling" (Williams 1977) generated by the contradictions facing these Mexican Americans, momentarily transposing the Saturday-night dance from a regimenting Anglo mode to the liberating register of a *mejicano* celebration.

The intensity of the celebration reached its climax—Phase III—during the final hour of the dance, between the midnight hour and 1:00. By this time the river of liquor, the brimming spirit of camaraderie, and the flood of song and dance had swept away the normal structure of relations, suspended the passage of time, and dissolved many everyday inhibitions. Social taboos—some particular to Mexicans—were held in abeyance during this moment of *communitas,* or what Geertz referred to in another context as "deep play" (1973). For example, restrictions on the interaction between a man's male friends and his wife, which are typically characterized by formality and mutual respect, were loosened during this moment of play. Thus, while a man's wife would not ordinarily dance a romantic *bolero* with another man, in the atmosphere of *communitas* that pervaded this final hour of merriment, dance-partner swapping was common enough, although the proper decorum was still observed.

In sum, during the climactic hour a good deal of behavior normal to the structure of social life outside the hall was suspended. Public intoxication, for example, which would be emphatically condemned by most of the VFWers, was quite in evidence here, especially among the men—though some women indulged to excess as well. Not once, however, did the effects of liquor result in the breakdown of order to the point of violence, or even unruly behavior. Nor was the VFWers' restraint attributable to watchful "bouncers," as seems to have been the case in public dances described by Limón (1994: 158). Security at VFW dances was provided by a single "bouncer"—Joe ("Wyatt Burp") Bañuelos, a *compadre* of Beto García. As entered into by these Mexican American revelers, then, *communitas* was *not* synonymous with violent disorder.

Still other behavior, uncommon outside the present celebration, was much in evidence—embracing, back-slapping, boisterous laughter, exaggerated dance maneuvers, and a general tendency to loud expression. Moreover, any song that was particularly popular at the moment (e.g., "Las nubes") was greeted with rousing displays of enthusiasm—the foot stomping, cheering, and clapping continuing well after the song was completed. In sum, "the scene at this time can best be described as festive and chaotic, the atmosphere charged with an air of intense play, in which feelings of general camaraderie and mutual solidarity were given full expression" (Peña 1980: 62).

Phase IV, the short transition that signaled the impending end of the dance, arrived abruptly. On July 16, 1977, at approximately 12:55, immediately after a rousing *huapango*, "El chilito piquín" [The hot pepper], Beto announced the conclusion of the dance in a quick speech that he had been practicing for the last ten years:

Damas y caballeros, con la siguiente selección se da por terminado el baile de esta noche. Se despide de Uds. la orquesta de Beto García y sus GGs. Esperamos que nuestra música haya sido de su completo agrado, y hasta la próxima vez, que Dios los bendiga y manejen con cuidado. No se les olvide que todavía hay muy buen menudo; no se vayan con hambre. Good night everyone, and we'll see you next time. [Singing] *Echale un cinco al piano y que siga el vacilón . . .*[9]

"Echale un cinco al piano," a *canción ranchera* in polka tempo (*corrida*), was part of a medley the GGs always played at the end of the dance; its companion piece was a *cumbia*, "La bala." The combination was an odd mix in that the transition from a polka to a *cumbia* was awkward at best. The choice of such a final medley requires explanation.

Both the ambiance of VFW dances and the GGs' repertoire had undergone subtle changes between 1967 and 1977. In a dynamic process that was evolving toward the ideal form of celebration, the band discarded old songs and styles while adding new ones. Striving for the most effective way to end the dance, Beto eventually settled on the polka-*cumbia despedida* (farewell) as the ideal way to put an end to the climactic revelry of the final hour. In complementary fashion to the introductory set, the "Echale un cinco"/"La bala" medley became a fixed part of the musical order that characterized both the beginning and the end of the dance. In sum, coupled with the strict order at the beginning of the dance, the *despedida* helped round out the total structure of the ritual experience. In this totality, the music-dance ritual "condense[d] a range of patterns of culture in a more concentrated fashion than daily intercourse" (Blacking 1974: 75), thus creating the "perfect" ritual whole. And, in the ritual whole—structure, *communitas,* and restructure—the group found an aesthetically satisfying way to reaffirm its most basic sense of ethnic identification.

The *despedida* was such an important factor in the ritual nature of the dance—especially as it paved the way for the reintroduction of structure after such an intense state of *communitas*—that a few further comments are necessary. It is important to note that the hour of *communitas* extended to the very limits of the celebration. Phase IV, taken up by the *despedida,* had five minutes or so to effect the transition from flux to order—hardly enough time for a smooth passage back to the structure of everyday life. It might seem that Beto's farewell speech should be enough to bring the dance to closure, and, indeed, that would have been sufficient in "normal" time. But in the symbolic time ticking within the dance something more was required—something strong enough to jolt the revelers out of their state of deep play.

The polka-*cumbia* medley emerged as the ideal trigger for the abrupt transition. In juxtaposing the disparate rhythms associated with the two genres—the band literally stopped for a fraction of a second at every switch—the music replicated the bumpy transition from *communitas* to structure. In experiencing the braking effects that the stop-and-go change from *cumbia* to polka produced, the dancers were literally jarred out of their festive flow and into the sober realization that the party was over and normal time was now ticking. All of this end-of-the-dance activity had evolved through trial and error, of course, and the dancers (and musicians) would probably have had difficulty verbalizing its effects. Yet, they would have agreed that the polka-*cumbia* combination was an aesthetically satisfying (if ritually protested) conclusion to the dance—a way to end the celebration and step back into "cold reality."

The final medley contained one more element that clinched its efficacy. It was a gimmick Beto had repeated countless times, and everyone was anticipating it; yet it always elicited the same response. After playing the *cumbia*-polka combination a couple of times, the band would "end" the music with the horn introduction to "La bala." Beto would then ask the question, "¿*Ya se cansaron?*" (Are you tired yet?), whereupon the crowd would respond with a thunderous "No!" After a few seconds of silence, the band would strike up the refrain to "La bala": "*A bailar la bala, a bailar la bala . . .*" (Let's all dance "the bullet," let's all dance "the bullet"). This stop-question-and-go sequence would be repeated two or three times, and then Beto would cry out one last time, "¿*Ya se cansaron?*" After another resounding "No!" he would reply in a resigned and falling voice, "*Los músicos sí*" (The musicians are [tired]). After a loud collective groan of protest, the lights in the hall were turned on once more (they were dimmed at the beginning), signaling the end of the dance.

At this point, Phase V, the reestablishment of order, quickly ensued. A wave of quiet settled over the hall, as people began to reach for their personal effects and head for the exit. Within fifteen minutes most of the crowd had filed out, except for the few who remained to partake of the ritual *menudo*—which, as everyone knew, was the ideal antidote for the next morning's hangover. The din that had moments earlier dominated the scene was now receding into history, replaced by the deadening silence of people ready to go forth into the night. On the bandstand the tired musicians performed their last chores—dismantling the electronic equipment and preparing it for loading. After about twenty minutes or so, only Beto and VFW officials remained, settling accounts over a last drink, while the other band members finished loading and waited to be paid.

As portrayed here, the dance should be considered a form of ritual or, at least, ritualized play. Key to the concept of dance as ritual are the synchronic and diachronic elements I have described. None of these elements occurred randomly. On the contrary, their faithful repetition, time after time, generated a cumulative effect whose totality defined the dances as structural wholes with their own symbolic import. Thus, in terms of diachrony, or the temporal order of the dance, we find the celebration divided into five discrete phases, as described above.

Phase I served as a bridge between the structure that governed relations in the outer world and the state of *communitas*, or anti-structure, that would ultimately unfold within the dance. Phase II marked the irreversible transition from structure to anti-structure, the final moments of which blended into the hour of full-blown merriment. Phase III bounded the deepest level of play, the breakdown of everyday order and the consummation of the rite of intensification. The semifinal—and shortest of the phases—*la despedida* signaled the end of the celebration and the entrance once more into the structured world of everyday reality. The last phase, reentry into everyday reality, concluded the celebration. To reiterate, these five phases evolved into a more or less immutable whole during the period being witnessed here; they are critical to any consideration of the Saturday-night dance as a form of ritualization.

As to the synchronic elements, there were a number of features that lent the dance a strong redundancy, particularly since, like the diachronically ordered phases, these were activated time and again. Not all of the symbolic (synchronic) elements possessed the same strength, of course. On a scale of symbolic value, such items as the *menudo*, the *gri-*

tos, the *canciones rancheras,* and the bandstand itself (including the musicians) were more prominently significant than the chain of cars or the entrance fee (a symbolic token of initiation). It can be argued, however, that both the chain of cars and the entrance fee constituted a ritual threshold through which the revelers were transported from the everyday world dominated by Anglos into a hyperethnic encounter. Here, in the highly condensed symbolic structure of the ritual, ethnic and class contradictions were mediated.

In their totality, then, both synchronic and diachronic features contributed to the semantic loading of the dance event, such that it became, in effect, a rite of intensification whose ultimate aim was to give aesthetic embodiment to a powerful but repressed political unconscious. In returning again and again to the dance, the participants demonstrated their wish to engage in a communal experience, a cultural reality whose ethnic *difference* stood in opposition to the homogenizing power of the dominant society. Significantly, this experience—the dance—was rooted in an ancestral practice trailing back into the mists of the nineteenth century. Moreover, the dance can only be seen as symbolically motivated—marked as it was by highly focused and redundant actions. How else can we interpret the specificity of the experience—its choice of music and dance, for example, both of which evoked (and invoked) strong ethnic bonds? Or the choice of *menudo,* a food with powerful associations vis-à-vis *lo mexicano?*

In summary, caught on the horns of a class-ethnic dilemma, VFWers, like so many of their Mexican American peers, found it necessary to celebrate their distinct sense of ethnic heritage, not because of some desire for "multiculturalism," but because the workaday world they consciously endorsed as natural (if not inevitable) threw up constant reminders that a fundamental schism existed between them and the dominant society. But that world also fabricated countless ways to repress the reality of class-ethnic conflict, thus reinforcing the VFWers' sense that American society rewarded them for their hard work by granting them middle-class status, and that those who failed to gain such status had only their own shortcomings to blame.[10] While the Chicano movement was succeeding in awakening an ethnic consciousness in the face of intercultural conflict, even among these conservative Mexican Americans, the VFWers' faith in the ideology of "equaliberty" suppressed any full-blown sense of ethnopolitical solidarity. Thus, only in isolated islands of ritual—the Saturday-night dance, for one—could their political unconscious, their repressed desire for a "realm of freedom," find an effective outlet to sublimate unresolved class and ethnic antagonism. The VFWers would return to the dance again and again.

CONCLUSION:
The Decline and Fall of a Family Orquesta

In August of 1977, I left Fresno and the GGs to enroll in the graduate program in anthropology at the University of Texas at Austin. The GGs were at their peak in popularity. Yet, when I returned to Fresno in the fall of 1981 to teach at California State University, Fresno, the band was struggling to survive. Engagements had fallen off sharply, particularly since the Rainbow had dropped the Sunday-night dances and had begun booking Mexican groups that catered to the burgeoning population of legal and illegal immigrants in the Fresno area. The frequency of VFW celebrations had declined as well, and weddings increasingly hired one-person operations known by then as "DJs"—disc jockeys who carried a well-stocked collection of the latest "hits," Mexican and American, which they played on recording equipment amplified through sound systems similar to those used by orquestas.

In short, hard times had fallen on orquestas in Fresno. By 1985 the field had shrunk to two or three active groups—a far cry from the dozen or so active in the mid-1970s. The question we asked earlier arises again: What had happened? The fate of Fresno orquestas was the same as that which had befallen orquestas in other areas of the Southwest: economics struck the *coup de grace,* as Manny Guerra had observed. But equally important was the changing of the musical guard, so to speak—the emergence of a new generation of music lovers with a distinctively different taste. In Fresno, as elsewhere, those born after 1960—members of what I call the post-Chicano Generation—had turned their backs on La Onda Chicana and embraced other kinds of music, especially the MTV phenomenon. René Sandoval, a Chicano saxophonist with a long and distinguished career as an orquesta musician, summarized the impact of MTV music culture on the young Chicanos in graphic terms:

MTV is your biggest corrupter when it comes to musical changes, because the main contributor to what's happening today is MTV. The young generation is coming up, and they've got MTV twenty-four hours a day. And you've got these performers, you know, with smoke and bombs and so, the young generation is beginning to lose the musical aspects of it. . . . *Ahora* [nowa-

days] it's visual. If you don't have the smoke and bombs, and guys throwing the guitars around, it won't sell. So consequently, La Onda Chicana—the Mexican groups—they're gonna go into that. Because of the young generation out there. (Personal interview, April 5, 1993)

Thus, in Fresno as elsewhere, the strong recession that rocked the economy in the late 1970s and early '80s changed the cultural economy of Mexican American music, as did a younger generation. The recession, combined with the impact of the DJ, MTV, and the acceptance by both performers and audiences of sophisticated synthesizers capable of duplicating almost any horn sound, forced orquestas to downsize and to all but disappear. The newer and smaller synthesized groups—now equipped with "smoke and bombs"—were clearly more attuned to developments in both the American and Latin American mass-music markets, and after the mid-1980s these were the groups that provided music for (post-)Chicano celebrations. Orquestas like the GGs were quickly fading into history, and on December 31, 1985, the GGs finally succumbed to the new forces operating in the musical economy of Fresno: They played the final dance of their long career for the Veterans of Foreign Wars Post 8900.

The GGs' legacy actually lived on for the remainder of the 1980s, as Beto's children, Debbie and Bert, Jr., reincarnated the band under a new name, TAVO (a nickname for Octavio, the band patriarch's name). Still featuring a saxophone and trumpet, as well as a modified bimusical style that included much more top-forty material and heavier use of the synthesizer, TAVO held its own for a few years, but eventually it too succumbed to the scarcity of jobs for groups other than DJs and the most economical of synthesized groups. Even an orquesta such as TAVO, whose repertoire catered heavily to a more culturally assimilated audience, was unable to resist the inevitable.

As of the mid-1990s, only one group with any pretense toward the status of an orquesta existed in Fresno—Martin Uresti's Horizon—but even that group encountered difficulty filling its calendar. Meanwhile, except for a handful of tunes associated with the old orquestas—"Qué culpa tengo," "Las nubes," the *bolero* "Sabor a mí"—which have acquired the status of nostalgic icons harking to an older period, a new repertoire was the rule for the latest synthesized groups. Like other Mexican Americans of the Southwest, Fresnans of the post-Chicano era were drifting into new regions of musical culture.

Music in the
Post-Chicano Era

The cultural power of orquesta music ultimately derived from its organic connection with the Mexican American middle class. Moreover, as it evolved from the era of Beto Villa to that of Little Joe y la Familia, the orquesta faithfully reproduced the continuities and discontinuities that marked the progress of Mexican society in the Southwest: from a Mexican American to a Chicano orientation. But always it resisted the reifying effects of commercialization, while it symbolically embodied the deepest politico-aesthetic yearnings of its constituents. For the better part of fifty years, it maintained a prominent position in the ongoing dialectic of conflict that drives class and ethnic relations in the Southwest. And then, in the 1980s, it went into steep decline.

You want to know what changed La Onda Chicana? The bottom line, MTV . . . people started listening with their eyes.

Tony "Ham" Guerrero

What is most remarkable about the demise of orquesta music is its suddenness. As noted earlier, innovation in La Onda Chicana proceeded apace right up until the late 1970s, but with the release of such LPs as Sunny's *Amor de mis amores* and Little Joe's *De colores,* we are confronted with a noticeable stylistic retrenchment. Gone were the adventurous forays into musical code-switching, complex harmonic progressions, and stylistic syntheses, replaced by relatively simple two- and three-part background obbligatos and, in *Amor de mis amores,* a harbinger of things to come—greater use of the synthesizer. (Experiments using the synthesizer were tried in the 1970s, but they were minimal.) It can be argued that La Onda had reached its limits, very much as the conjunto had in the

1960s (Peña 1985a), and that it was experiencing an inevitable period of decline. The conjunto, however, remained a viable expression of working-class culture, despite its stylistic retreat after the 1960s. The orquesta was destined for near oblivion.

Not coincidentally, 1980 saw the emergence of the first of the Tejano groups that would dethrone La Onda Chicana—the soon-to-be-dominant La Mafia. Tony "Ham" Guerrero recalled his impression of this, the first of the Tejano ensembles built around the synthesizer:

I saw a little group called La Mafia in 1980, '81. *Apenas estaban empezando* [They were just beginning], and I saw these two young kids with long hair, singing, and a bunch of little girls out there in front of the band. And they're swinging their butts for the girls—these pretty boys. But, musically, they couldn't play their way out of a paper bag. They were horrible, and I said, "If this is any indication of where *tejano* music is going, I don't want any part of it."
MP: Was it an indication?
TG: Well, it was prophetic, because they happened to be the biggest act in the next five, six years.
MP: They were big, weren't they?
TG: They were very big, and now they've matured and their music still sucks. But they do their *cumbias,* and they're big stars now. (Personal interview, November 14, 1992)

Guerrero feels that modern Tejano groups have lost their musical "honesty," in that they rely too much on the synthesizer, but also on what René Sandoval called "lights and smoke," or the "MTV effect" (Sandoval interview, May 3, 1993). For Guerrero—and Sandoval as well—lights that dazzle, smoke that blurs the senses, and synthesizers that require little musical training have replaced real musicianship as the *sine qua non* of Tejano musical practice, just as they have, they would argue, for so much of American and Latin American pop music. For both musicians, traditionalists that they are, MTV, with its emphasis on the visual effect, "changed it all—that's why La Mafia *salían vestidos allí* [came out there dressed] with their tight pants and long hair. And people started listening with their eyes" (Guerrero interview, November 14, 1992).

As two of the premier musicians in La Onda Chicana—both steeped, moreover, in older traditions such as the orquesta and jazz—Sandoval and Guerrero may be forgiven for their harsh judgment of the modern Tejano groups. Other connoisseurs, such as record producer Manny Guerra, are far less critical, defending the new music as not just a departure from La Onda Chicana, but as an innovation in its own right. Guerra attributes this to the capabilities of the synthesizer:

In terms of innovation, today we have what I feel is the capability with the synthesizer of doing things that we never dreamed we could do. For example, with the drum machine you can just plug it in direct and you can program the thing, and it's the most beautiful sound you've ever heard. As a recording engineer, I remember how difficult it was to get a good drum sound. . . . That's why I welcomed the electronic age. . . . Once you have the feel [for the synthesizer], the feel for the trumpet [for example]—how it should sound, what it can play, or what it shouldn't, then you can lay it down, and it's a tremendous sound. (Personal interview, November 27, 1992)

Guerra is right. The potential of the synthesizer is virtually unlimited, but Guerrero and Sandoval would counter that it is not being exploited within the new Tejano tradition, which seems committed to a pan-Latino sound best described as a blend of violin and the old-fashioned Hammond organ with Leslie speaker. In this respect, one is struck by the contrast between the orquesta and its electronic successor, especially the latter's relative harmonic and rhythmic simplicity and, Guerrero and Sandoval would argue, monotonous repetition. René Ornelas, of René y René fame, and a former orquesta musician himself, does not consider the new music "horrible," as Guerrero does—indeed, he considers some of it "pretty." But, as he put it:

Es como comer pecan pie, pecan pie: te gusta pero después, "Ya, quítamelo." La misma tontería. A punto de que ya está aburriendo. . . . Pero, lo que está pasando es que la juventud is taking over.[1] (Personal interview, September 30, 1992)

It is the younger generation, then—the post-Chicano cohort—that in Texas has spawned such post–Onda Chicana groups as La Mafia, Selena y los Dinos, El Grupo Mazz, La Sombra, and others. These groups may share minimal stylistic markers with the older orquestas, most notably the polka or canción ranchera in polka tempo (the corrida). But in an effort to expand their marketability—and at the prodding of the major labels, which now hold contracts with the most popular Tejano acts—these newer ensembles are concentrating more and more not only on visual effects but on a synthesized sound universal to Latin America. And they are also concentrating on its predominant genre, the cumbia, although the balada in a slow rock tempo is also prevalent. In "going international," the Tejano groups have moved outside the parameters of the orquestas they displaced and wandered into the terrain of an international Latino market driven not by the principle of use-value, and all the symbolic activity involved in its utilitarian application, but rather by the market forces of exchange-value. In short, the Tejano groups are being transformed from organic symbols of *tejano* identity into market commodities with pan-Latino appeal.

The power and influence of the big labels—Capitol/EMI, Arista, Sony—cannot be overemphasized in the internationalization of Tejano music, although, as Little Joe complained, those industry giants have not yet committed themselves wholeheartedly to the total exploitation of this music. The substance of Little Joe's complaint is echoed in an article written by Don McLeese in an "Onward" supplement to the *Austin American-Statesman* (May 4, 1994: 6): "For all the growth that Tejano has experienced in recent years, there is widespread belief within the music industry that it hasn't come close to reaching its potential." McLeese buttresses his observation with a quote from Cameron Randle, vice-president of Arista/Texas:

Professional management has been sorely lacking in the Tejano world. Booking, the whole presentation at retail and radio, leaves a lot of room for improvement. . . . With Sony and EMI it has really been an embarrassment of riches. They open their back door in San Antonio, see who's out there, sign them, and know that the acts they have, for a really minimal investment, are worth X amount of dollars, a guaranteed return that is enough to make everybody happy in L.A. or New York. (1994: 6)

Such has been the cavalier attitude of the major labels toward Tejano music, much as their intervention has inevitably distorted the natural course of its development in recent years. For it is the subtle pressure of producers, and the prospect of success they hold out if *tejanos* will diversify their style, that has ultimately driven this regional music toward internationalization in the mid-1980s to mid-1990s. Carlos Villegas, a singer with Latin Image, a young Tejano band from Houston under contract with Sony, commented on the pressure new groups face in adjusting to the market, and the dependence on the producer that this pressure induces:

In our case, we're working for [producer] Bob Gallarza. And he is responsible to the record company, to Sony, for producing an album that's gonna be acceptable, an album that's gonna sell. Of course. So we do have to . . .

we have to let him go as far as telling us, "Do it this way, do it that way." Of course, big groups like La Mafia, they produce themselves. (Personal interview, April 14, 1993)

Villegas's comments are probably accurate. The biggest Tejano acts—La Mafia, El Grupo Mazz, and, until Selena's untimely death, Selena y los Dinos—are all established enough to dictate the terms of their musical productions, which, nonetheless, inevitably adhere to the prevailing dictates of the international market. More important, the burgeoning popularity of these groups in Mexico promises to perk up the attention of the corporate suites in New York and Los Angeles. Indeed, until the sultry Selena was murdered in March of 1995 (by the president of her fan club), there was talk of her becoming another Gloria Estefan or even the Madonna of Latin America (J. García 1994: 5). Endowed with a charismatic stage presence and a good voice, Selena was on the verge of international stardom. Had she realized her ambitions, however—had she become a pop goddess—it would have been on terms dictated by the capitalist market and its circulation of international commodities, and her links to the *tejano* orquestas and the cultural milieu that launched her music would have been effectively dissolved. And that is precisely the kind of distortion visited upon *tejano* musical culture by the intervention of the major recording labels.

Lingering for another moment on the always active *tejano* musical scene, we discover the emergence since the 1980s of groups closer to the conjunto but also dependent on the synthesizer. They rely as well on a "crossover" sound, one that introduces elements from country western into the traditional conjunto. The best known of these "progressive conjuntos" is Emilio Navaira and his Rio Band. Headlined by a photogenic and virile Navaira (dressed always in tight-fitting western attire), the Rio Band has achieved wide fame in Texas and elsewhere in the Hispanic Southwest. Thanks to his connection with Capitol/EMI, in the midnineties Navaira was being repackaged as a country-western singer and promoted in that American market as well. The Texas Tornados, meanwhile—Flaco Jiménez, Freddie Fender, Augie Myers, and Doug Sahm—exploited for a time (until the group broke up) this conjunto–country-western fusion, as has another popular *tejano* and his group, Ram Herrera. In other respects, however, and notwithstanding their broad popularity, these progressive conjuntos lack the ambitious sense of experimentation of "the greatest conjunto of all time," El Conjunto Bernal, during its heyday in the 1960s (see Peña 1985a).

One innovation with pathbreaking potential deserves mention in this brief summary of post–Onda Chicana music. I refer to an experiment tried successfully by the group Tierra Tejana in the late 1980s, in which the African American genre rap was combined in synthetic fashion with the popular *cumbia* to create a new hybrid. Particularly successful in this innovative effort was a song that gained immense popularity throughout the Southwest, the *cumbia*-rap, "Las hijas de don Simón." Here was a successful synthesis of two culturally powerful genres, both with strong ties to working-class cultures, despite their intense commercialization. Exploited further, this new hybrid could have rivaled the boldest experiments in La Onda Chicana. Yet, despite the huge success of "Las hijas," subsequent imitations aroused only mild interest, and this innovative path quickly reached a dead end. Most Tejano groups have since preferred to follow the "safe" path to success, continuing to rework the *cumbia* in its long standardized form.

Meanwhile, in California, the other state with a dynamic and growing Mexican-descent population, the demise of the orquesta witnessed no further indigenous developments.[2] Much of the post-Chicano Generation there seems to have been co-opted by the various manifestations of American pop music, such as rap, top-forty, and even country western. Much more so than in Texas, DJs have become a part of the live musical scene, and they can be found at weddings, nightclubs, and other musical events.[3] However, a much larger Mexican immigrant presence than is evident in Texas, especially in the populous Los Angeles metropolis, has invited innovation in a different and, surprisingly, more traditional (i.e., ranchero) direction. I refer to the explosion, since about 1990, of the so-called *banda*, which has taken Angelenos by storm (see Birnbaum 1994; Burr 1994). A semisynthesized version of an old and very traditional variant of the early orquesta, the *banda* is a technological reincarnation of the *banda sinaloense*—a type of brass band from the Mexican state of Sinaloa.

The *banda sinaloense* was not unlike the groups organized by Tucsonenses like Fred Ronstadt or others dating from the mid- to late nineteenth century. Featuring trumpets, trombones, euphoniums, and tuba (and often augmented by saxophones and clarinets), its distinguishing characteristic was the cacophonous, dissonant, and shrill sound produced by the generally small mouthpieces preferred by the folk, musically untrained *sinaloense* musicians. Introduced from Europe in the nineteenth century, brass bands of that type were universal to Latin America and may still be found in remote areas, such as the Andes mountains. Like their counterparts in the Southwest and elsewhere, *bandas sinaloenses* and other such Mexican ensembles (e.g., *el tamborazo zacatecano*, from the state of Zacatecas) relied on the popular European genres for their repertoires—the polka, redowa, waltz, etc.

The modern *banda* phenomenon, which sprouted in the Los Angeles area and has been spreading rapidly to other locales with heavy Mexican (especially immigrant) populations, uses trumpets and other instruments, but in what is known as a "techno-*banda*," it is also heavily reinforced by synthesizers that can duplicate the sound of any of the missing instruments, such as the tuba. Given its explosive rise, the modern *banda* seems to have struck a deep, responsive chord, especially among working-class Mexican immigrants, although it has gained popularity among Chicanas and Chicanos as well—even among some members of the middle class. It certainly has the potential to acquire the broad and deeply rooted ethnic power of the orquesta, particularly since it descends from a grassroots ensemble, the *banda sinaloense,* which was (is) similar to one of the modern orquesta's distant predecessors, the brass band (see Chapter 1). In other words, despite the commercial frenzy surrounding its (re)discovery and explosive popularity, the modern *banda* descends from a pedigree shared by the orquesta, and in this it would seem to fulfill all the requisites for an organically situated music.

But the potential locked up in *banda* remains unrealized. Although it packs a solid ethnic (and perhaps class) wallop, its market potential is not lost on the recording-industry giants, which have rapidly converted this newly rediscovered cultural treasure into a slickly packaged commodity. Like so many forms of expressive culture in what Jameson (after Mandel) calls "late capitalism," or "postmodernism," the whole culture of *banda* is always under commercial pressure to "deform" into a surface phenomenon, a simulacrum for "Mexicanness," much as the bells, rickshaws, and opium dens stood as tokens for "China-ness" among the French petite bourgeois of another time (Barthes 1972: 121). It thus remains to be seen just how long *banda* can maintain its cultural integrity. All the same, it represents a unique new cultural phenomenon that displays some of the characteristics of an organic expression: its vehement appropriation by both Mexican and Chicano youth as an emblem of *their* culture, its acknowledged links to the deeper roots of Mexican music, and its strong Mexican identification in the midst of a dominant American culture. However, at present it appears to tilt toward a working-class identity, where, presumably, it will have to compete with the ever-present *conjunto norteño,* and it would have to acquire a stronger middle-class orientation and much wider distribution before it could hope to replace the spot vacated by the orquesta.

Notwithstanding the immense success of *banda,* as well as that of

Tejano groups like Selena and Mazz, no musical expression exists in the Southwest today that can claim the universality of the orquesta, especially in its Onda Chicana phase, when it transcended its class roots to achieve near-hegemonic status in the Southwest. The lack of an ensemble with the overarching ideological reach and cohesive power of the orquesta raises an interesting point. I noted above that orquesta's demise occurred at the precise moment when the stylistic pinnacle had been scaled and the ensemble was at its peak in popularity. There seems to be no completely satisfactory answer, then, for its sudden demise. The statements of Manny Guerra and others on the effects of a dragging economy in the early 1980s go only so far, as does the more compelling factor of a new generation coming into its own, with new ideas about musical practice.

In point of fact, an explanation based on a dialectic of conflict offers the most compelling reason of all. As we have seen, the to-and-fro movement of this dialectic has been one of progress and retreat, synthesis and antithesis, and, for the Mexicans, empowerment and disfranchisement. At particular historical moments, the positive force of this dialectic has coalesced enough to create particularly opportune moments for great material progress for the Mexican Americans—World War II and the era of Vietnam and the Great Society are two auspicious moments. The latter was particularly conducive to a great leap forward, a period that also happened to coincide with the Chicano movement and its great synthesizing momentum. The Onda Chicana phase of the orquesta meshed with that momentum, and, propelled forward by the revitalizing power of the Chicano Renaissance, it was thus carried on the crest of the movement to its moment of climactic triumph in the 1970s. In other words, La Onda was the most successful attempt, at the musical level of cultural communication, to synthesize the historical contradictions unique to the Mexican American experience in the Southwest. In sum, in the larger context of intercultural history, the activist era of the 1960s and '70s, along with the Chicano movement and La Onda Chicana, represents the most progressive stage to date for the dialectic of conflict.

The problem is, of course, that in a dialectical conception of history, synthesis is inevitably short-lived: contradictions will resurface as new poles of antagonism develop. Thus, in what is surely a paradox, the moment both political and musical culture attain the point of coalescence and synthesis in the Southwest, they are shattered into a multiplicity of heterogeneous impulses that characterize the post-Chicano era. On the political front, new tensions have surfaced along the broad interethnic fault line, ranging from the backlash of Anglo reactionism toward affirmative action to a frightfully regressive, neonativist sentiment against Mexican immigration. A now-exhausted Chicano movement and its renaissance are powerless to respond decisively to these retrogressive developments.[4] Its momentum having run its course, the movement has been replaced by political fragmentation and localized responses lacking the ideological focus (and effectiveness) that fired the movement.[5]

At the level of musical practice, a myriad of styles have replaced La Onda Chicana. None of them possesses its dynamic or synthetic power, and none commands anything approaching the ideological consensus that empowered La Onda. From the modern Tejano groups to "progressive conjuntos" to *banda,* the key principle is difference and fragmentation. No one musical style can claim to represent the *élan vital* of Mexican American culture; no ensemble has attained iconic status. In short, no single music with the omnibus politico-cultural charter of La Onda is anywhere in evidence in the Southwest.

Finally, La Onda Chicana's pinnacle occurred at the very moment when the orquesta tradition was about to be superseded by the next stage of sociomusical development. That stage belongs to the post-Chicano cohort, which finds itself at a historical "conjuncture" (Gramsci 1971) substantially different from that of its predecessors, the Mexican American and Chicano Generations. Those generations mounted highly focused attempts to carve a realm of opportunity for Mexican Americans in an otherwise hostile Anglo environment. Lacking a conducive political climate or the ideological focus of its predecessors, the post-Chicano Generation has been drifting, politically and culturally, since the 1980s. In many ways their music reflects this drift, as today no powerfully unifying musical impulse exists among Mexican Americans, at least not of the magnitude of La Onda Chicana.

Whether a politico-cultural upheaval that launches another round of cultural and musical synthesis is anywhere on the horizon remains an open question. I am thinking of an upheaval that might surge from a forward lurch in the dialectic of conflict. The cultural renewal and synthesis accompanying such an upheaval may well challenge the Chicano Renaissance in scope, although the timing of such a scenario is impossible to predict. What we can predict at this juncture is that the dialectic of conflict will sooner or later trigger deep and systemic movement along the ethnic fault line, and that this movement will lead to turmoil and further adjustments in the balance governing interethnic relations in the Southwest. Retrogressive events, such as the passage in California of the anti-immigrant Proposition 187 and the anti–affirmative action Proposition 209, may well be the triggers needed to set off an intense new round of dialectical activity. As part of that activity, we may witness new forms of musical culture emerging within the Mexican American community. What character those forms will assume presents a challenging question, but its answer cannot at present be fathomed.

Notes

PRELUDE

1. The words *orquesta, conjunto, corrido, norteño(a), ranchero(a), and jaitón(a)*, which are used repeatedly, will only be italicized the first time they appear in the text.

2. "The realm of freedom actually begins only where labor which is in fact determined by necessity and mundane considerations ceases" (Marx 1977: 820).

3. The notion that capitalism represents a totalizing stage involving the whole of humanity may raise some postmodernist hackles, but in the late twentieth century, capitalism is increasingly the only real game in the global village.

4. The terms "Anglo" and "Anglo-American" are used interchangeably throughout the text. Strictly speaking, they are inaccurate labels, but in common usage they refer to all European-origin citizens of the United States, not just to people from the British Isles.

5. Cf. Vilar (1994: 21): "It was Marx's demonstration that 'rotations' and 'cycles' . . . never lead back to their point of departure, but create new situations not only in the economy but in the social whole."

6. Grossberg borrows these two terms from Foucault (1980) and Deleuze and Guattari (1977).

7. In an appraisal of the "encounter" between feminism and postmodernism vis-à-vis the problem of male domination in society after society, Nancy Fraser and Linda Nicholson (1988: 101) waver between postmodernism's disdain for metanarratives and feminism's need for theories robust enough to account for "sexism in its 'endless variety and monotonous similarity.'" Their solution, to "forswear neither large historical narratives nor analyses of societal macrostructures" but to remain, nonetheless, "nonuniversalist," evinces considerable ambivalence, if not a certain "paralysis of criticism" (Marcuse 1964: xli).

8. The contemporary notion of "freedom" is itself an ideological construct of capitalism, of course. But, like its parent system, it is the only reality we have to imagine a Utopia that transcends "blind necessity" and suffering.

9. In a graphic illustration of the unhappy union of Marxism and post-modernism in anthropology, José Limón wavers between a strong Marxist-Bakhtinesque reading of the subversive, carnivalesque folklore of his oppressed *carnales* (brothers) and his much weaker, postmodernist reading of the fragmented, politically numb bodies that dance at the Cielo Azul bar. Like some postmodernist feminists, Limón thus betrays a paralysis of interpretation in his inconsistent portrayal of Mexican American expressive culture (1994; compare, especially, Chaps. 6 and 7).

10. The practice of periodization is another casualty of postmodernist (anti)theory. Still, I wholeheartedly agree with Jameson when he suggests that "all isolated or discrete cultural analysis involves a buried or repressed theory of historical periodization" (1984: 55).

11. Cf. LaCappra (1983: 68–69): "Those working within the 'experimental' tendency will thus stress the importance of what is marginal in text or life as seen from the conventional view—what is uncanny or disorienting in terms of its assumptions. But the danger in this tendency [as opposed to the 'totalizing' tendency] is that it will remain fixated at the phase of simple reversal of dominant conventional assumptions and replace unity with disunity, order with chaos, center with absence of center, determinacy with uncontrolled plurality."

Exposition

1. My conception of class derives from Marxist theory. See Peña 1985a for its elaboration.

2. As we shall see, the modern orquesta, particularly in Texas, assumes a much more mediative function in this dialectic—this dynamic interplay between contending cultures.

3. Cf. Israel (1979: 306): "In societies which are economically underdeveloped, as the countries in Latin America, the transformation of man into a means of creating surplus value is not concealed as it is concealed in the highly industrialized countries."

4. As Néstor García Canclini contends, the basic antinomies of capitalism are more exposed in peripheral economies, where conflict between capitalism and indigenous practices yields contradictory results: "In societies as complex as those under periphery capitalism with a strong Indian element, sociocultural processes are the product of conflict among many forces of diverse origin" (1993:45). As examples, García Canclini mentions reciprocal forms of economic and cultural organization, which enter into conflictive interplay with the exploitive nature of the dominant capitalist system (cf. Taussig 1980; Nájera-Ramírez 1996). Until World War II, the Southwest retained some of the elements of a "periphery," at least insofar as a "residual" Mexican cultural economy survived (see Williams 1977).

5. Cf. Crisp (1976: 36) on the "dilemma" facing the Texans after indepen-

dence from Mexico: "[T]he desire to exclude Mexicans from participation in public affairs conflicted with a reluctance to violate the rights guaranteed Anglos and Hispanics alike under the Constitution" (cf. Montejano 1987: 38 on the debate on whether to allow the Mexicans to vote).

6. When the first Anglo frontiersmen arrived in the Southwest, they quickly began marrying the daughters of the elite. Horace Bell, who settled in Los Angeles in 1852, decried the shameless efforts by Anglo fortune seekers to gain economic advantage by marrying into Mexican elite families (Bell 1930: Chap. 23; cf. Crisp 1976: 156; Sheridan 1986).

7. A classic example of this schizoid attitude is that of J. C. Clopper, an American who spent time in San Antonio in 1828. Clopper characterized the "Mexicans" as "extremely ignorant in all the advanced arts of civilization . . . Popish and superstitious." But of the elites he had this to say: "The Gochapines [*gachupines*] or European Spaniards who dwell among them [the Mexicans] are exceptions to these remarks. These are mostly intelligent and wealthy" (1929:72).

8. I shall have more to say about the impact of infrastructural changes on Anglo-Mexican relations in Chapters 3 and 6.

1. BAILES AND FANDANGOS

1. The *fandango* was originally a single-couple dance. According to Bancroft, "After a *jaleo* with castanets, with changes and motions of arms, several walks were taken, while the music played and the singer finished the *verso* and *estribillo*" (1888: 411). At the end of the piece, the singer cried out, "*bomba!*" and the man was supposed to recite a verse, "generally of an amorous character" (ibid.). In time, however, the *fandango* came to be pejoratively applied to any low-status dancing event, to be distinguished from the *baile,* a genteel event (Gregg [1844] 1954: 170; see below).

2. For a litany of the Mexicans' alleged "vices," ranging from superstitiousness, immorality, cruelty, and cunning to extreme docility, see W. W. H. Davis's *El Gringo* ([1857] 1973: 214–231).

3. There were objectors, however, to this momentary "liberation" of women. According to the historian Ramón Gutiérrez: "One priest exhorted women in an 1800 sermon on penance to refrain from dance because of the occasion to sin that a swiveling hip or bouncing breasts might create. These enticements were the work of the devil and tempted men to indulge in the transitory pleasures of the flesh" (1991: 239).

4. Howard Swan describes the first piano to arrive in California, which was purchased in 1846 by don Eulogio de Celis and shipped from the East Coast via the Cape of Horn. "What did it matter," asks Swan rhetorically, "if no one in Los Angeles knew how to play the piano? The instrument looked well in the house, and all of his friends admired its walnut case and brass pedals" (1952: 106).

5. Van de Grift Sánchez wrote that Juan Bandini "introduced [the waltz] in

California in 1830" (1929: 317), but Robinson mentions its performance at two separate events in 1829—after a mass at Mission San Gabriel and at a house-blessing ball held at the same Juan Bandini's home (1925: 51, 72).

6. The *jarabe* dates from the eighteenth century. However, prior to the period of Independence (1810–1821), "every allusion to it . . . was clearly a disparaging allusion" (Stevenson 1952: 183). After about 1813, it was "adopted as the song and dance of the revolution" (ibid.: 185), surviving into the twentieth century as a symbol of Mexican folklife.

7. Much of the information Sheridan obtained for his description of musical life in Tucson during the late nineteenth century comes from an unpublished manuscript by Ronstadt, "Music in Tucson, 1880s."

8. González's description is consistent with those provided in personal interviews by older conjunto musicians like Narciso Martínez, who recalled that the dust generated by dancers inspired him to compose a *polca,* "La polvadera" (The dust cloud).

9. González is referring here to a variant of the norteño ensemble then emerging as the preferred music for working-class celebrations in northern Mexico and South Texas. See Peña 1985a for a discussion of yet another type of working-class dance, the disreputable *baile de negocio,* or "taxi dance," which had its origins in the *fandango* of the nineteenth century (cf. Curtis 1955: 10–11).

2. THE DAWNING OF A NEW AGE

1. "El corrido de Joaquín Murrieta" is something of an enigma. While it documents the exploits of a famous *californio* outlaw of the 1840s and '50s, it appears not to have been composed until the late nineteenth or early twentieth century (Herrera-Sobek 1993). In any case, it follows the classic formula of the corrido of intercultural conflict, featuring one heroic, larger-than-life Mexican fighting and terrorizing a large force of cowardly, smaller-than-life Anglo lawmen. It was popular by the 1920s—so popular it eventually found its way onto the wax disc (recorded in 1934, in Los Angeles, by a group known as Los Madrugadores).

2. This is an allusion to the penance associated with Catholic confession.

3. The legendary folksinger Lydia Mendoza once told me that by the late 1920s and early 1930s many *tejanos* owned records and phonographs, and the Mexican anthropologist Manuel Gamio wrote in 1930 that both records and phonographs were favorite purchases for immigrants returning to Mexico from the United States: "The musical and artistic tendencies of the immigrants are indicated by the figure as to phonographs, which is 21.82, and as to records, which is 118.00 [per every 100 immigrants surveyed]" (1971: 70; also see the epigraph above).

4. The advent of "world music" and "world beat," available on a commercial basis, has changed this principle somewhat. However, except in instances of cross-cultural borrowing—where some of the elements of indigenous musics

are incorporated into the repertoires of contemporary Western artists—these musics of the world (usually the Third World) retain much of their primal symbolic power among their "roots" adherents (Breen 1992; Feld 1988).

5. Much of this music is in fact derived from preindustrial forms, such as country and blues in the United States and the mariachi in Mexico, but as in these three examples, earlier musics were largely absorbed by the mass recording media after World War II, and they have since circulated very much as commodities, with only vestigial links to their original, organic constituencies.

6. See, however, Frith (1988: 469–470), who assigns a redemptive value to pop music, which for him, "takes up certain spaces in popular memory . . . that work to make a particular sort of unity out of the listening public." See also Hebdige 1979 for a perspective on pop styles as counterhegemonic.

7. Peter Manuel stresses the power to shape demand acquired by the "corporate bourgeoisie": "One socioeconomic class—the corporate bourgeoisie— established an unprecedented degree of financial control over world music . . ." (1988: 4). This control can come in the form of pressure exerted on the principal transmission media—radio and television—and includes such practices as "payola or rigging of polls" (ibid.: 5).

8. Speaking of money as the universal fetish, and of its nascent power in the days of the Spanish conquistadors as part of an emerging worldview and its epistemology, Todorov writes: "Certainly the desire for riches is nothing new, the passion for gold has nothing specifically modern about it. What is new is the subordination of all other values to this one. . . . Money is not only the universal equivalent of all material values, but also the possibility of acquiring all spiritual values. . . . This homogenization of values by money is a new phenomenon and it heralds the modern mentality, egalitarian and economic" (1987: 142–143).

9. The relative autonomy allowed to the music of the Southwest had to do with the major labels' strategies prior to World War II. According to Bruno Nettl, "the aim of the record industry was to provide each culture and subculture its own, local music" (1985: 62). A hegemonic approach to co-optation did not occur until the postwar years (Robinson et al. 1991, Chap. 2).

10. To be sure, in its pure form the blues continued as an organic folk expression for some time after its initial commercialization, in the early 1920s. But after World War II, much of its substance was absorbed into its highly commoditized cousin, rhythm and blues, as well as other forms of rock-and-roll. At that point the organic link with the black community was interrupted.

11. However, in the 1990s, once more under the influence of the major labels (e.g., Capitol/EMI), "progressive conjuntos," especially, have attempted to expand their market beyond Texas and to become large-scale musical commodities. Their efforts have been largely unsuccessful.

12. All statements attributed to Armando Marroquín were obtained during a personal interview, January 31, 1980.

13. This assessment is made on the basis of the rich collection of early recordings in the possession of Chris Strachwitz, of Arhoolie Records, to whom I ex-

tend many thanks for sharing them with me (see Arhoolie/Folyric CD/C no. 368, Tejano Roots: Orquestas Tejanas).

3. ORQUESTA'S SOCIAL BASE

1. *Mutualistas*—fraternal organizations formed for the purpose of providing death benefits but also serving as social clubs—had been in evidence since the nineteenth century, but these seldom functioned as explicitly political agencies (Barrera 1988: 18).

2. Mario García has suggested that biculturalism may be as much a function of pluralism as it is of contradiction (pers. com.). In a dialectical interpretation of history, however, pluralism is an alibi for contradiction.

3. I am indebted to Cynthia Orozco for granting me full access to her copious files on LULAC. All the following references come from Orozco's archive.

4. In a survey of bilingualism among Mexican Americans, Sánchez (1978) uses a four-term typology, taken from Lewis (1972), to characterize the development of bilingualism in the Southwest—"stable," "dynamic," "transitional," and "vestigial." The first is found in situations (especially along the border) where individuals "resort indifferently to either language in most situations"; the second and third stages refer to those situations in which considerable overlap occurs between the two languages—with one language, in this case English, gradually gaining ascendancy over the other. The last stage is one in which only a few symbolic terms of the mother language remain in the individual's vocabulary. Compound bilingualism represents a different typology from that of Sánchez and Lewis, but it is probably most typical of the "transitional" stage, during which "both languages overlap in informal or intimate functions" (Sánchez 1978: 218). Although elements of stable bilingualism are also present—many speakers do "resort indifferently to either language"—this happens only in *intimate* situations, where the speakers all share the rules for code-switching.

5. López and his contributions to the orquesta tradition are discussed in the next chapter.

6. "Well, the mariachi sound—you have to grow up with it. The mariachi has its sound, its style. It's like the saxophonists who might want to play like Beto Villa or like me. It's too different, they can't do it. They don't have the feeling like us. We don't play the music like theirs."

7. "I know you said that the orquestas were different—Beto's, Eugenio's— but is there such a thing as a *tejano* style, as *orquesta tejana*?"

8. "There is, because we do have a different sound. We have a different style from any band from Mexico or from the U.S. When I play my saxophone, everybody knows it's Isidro López. The musicians recognize me, by the feeling. We have a different style than any band from another country. Why is it? I don't know. I can bring musicians from the other side, but even if they want to, they can't blow like me."

9. Nonetheless, attempts have been mounted. The anthropologist Claude Lévi-Strauss has, in the special manner of French Structuralism, mapped the hidden "grammar" and "syntax" of myth (1963, 1974), culinary codes (1983), and primitive kinship systems (1969), while Roland Barthes has "decoded" the "fashion system" (1983).

4. The Formative Years of Orquesta

1. The so-called *banda*, which in the 1990s took Mexicans by storm (especially in Los Angeles), is often an electronic, digitalized version of an old brass ensemble of folk origins, the *banda sinaloense*, from Sinaloa. See the Coda.

2. "There was always among *la raza*, among Chicanos, what we used to call, 'No, man, you think you're really high society.' That is, there was one class of people among Chicanos that was higher, and they wanted to live like the American, and live better. Of course, they had already attained a higher position economically, and there was still a lot of *raza* that was just arriving, and with a lot of—struggling all the way. So there *was* a division; and that is where not only the social or economic position was divided, but the music was divided as well—that of orquesta and that of conjunto."

3. Most of the information on Armando Marroquín comes from a day-long visit I paid him on January 31, 1980. He died in 1990.

4. Actually, in what is the ultimate irony in the then-deepening rift between conjunto and orquesta, Villa did record very early on (in 1947) with a button accordion, played by none other than the "father" of the modern conjunto, Narciso Martínez. At Marroquín's prodding, Villa and Martínez recorded the most successful regional recording of the time, "Rosita vals"—a testimonial to the strongly symbiotic relationship between these two styles "in the form of a pair" (Peña 1985b).

5. Quotes from Villa come from an interview Rosa Linda Fregoso conducted with him in 1980. My sincere thanks to Rosa Linda for sharing this information. Except for a valuable hour we spent talking in 1980, I was unable to interview Villa before his death in 1986.

6. The names of the instruments in this and all other transcriptions are abbreviated. Following is a list of abbreviations and the instruments to which they refer:

acc. = accordion	a. sx. = alto saxophone
b. = bass	b.d. = bass drum
bon. = bongo drums	cb. = cowbell
gui. = guitar	h.h. = high hat
mar. = maracas	org. = organ
p. = piano	sn. = snare drum
sx. = saxophone	t.d. = trap drum set

tpt. = trumpet	t.t. = tom tom
vln. = violin	voi. = human voice

7. Other well-known names in California, particularly in the Los Angeles area, were less affected by the *tejano* tide unleashed by Villa. These are discussed in Chapter 5.

8. Biographical information on Balde González comes principally from an interview with his mother, María Delgado, and one of his daughters, Sylvia Winton, carried out in Beeville on April 8, 1993. He died in 1974.

9. Balde González and Isidro López achieved fame as singers, but they were also instrumentalists who led their respective orquestas.

10. A thoroughly delightful and sprightly woman of eighty-eight at the time of our interview, Mrs. Alonzo still displayed the fire that made her the de facto leader of Alonzo y sus Rancheros.

11. Information on López comes principally from two interviews—one on May 31, 1979; the other on November 29, 1979.

5. The Los Angeles Tradition

1. Information on Tosti comes primarily from an interview I held with him on March 31, 1993.

2. "That Chicano Boogie is really crazy, man, 'cause look, it's got a rumba rhythm and boogie [rhythm], man. Get crazy, bro', listen to this heavy dude, here he comes with the boogie and the rumba."

3. In 1992 the National Endowment for the Arts awarded Guerrero the National Heritage Award, in recognition of his contributions to the field of Mexican American music.

4. Information on Lalo Guerrero comes from two interviews I had with him, November 12, 1992, and May 27, 1993.

5. Information on Pedro Bugarín comes primarily from an interview I held with him on September 5, 1992.

6. The Chicano Generation

1. Marxian and feminist alternatives actually emerged early on within the leftist and feminist sectors of the movement to challenge the idealist and male-chauvinist tenets of romantic nationalism, respectively. But despite vigorous critiques from those sectors, the nationalist view prevailed and eventually seeped into the political consciousness that defines the Chicano Generation (see Gómez-Quiñones 1990; Muñoz 1989; Chabram-Dernersesian 1992).

2. The Order of the Sons of America, LULAC's immediate precursor, was organized in 1921, in San Antonio, Texas, by a group of Mexican American profes-

sionals and white-collar workers. According to Mario Barrera, "By stressing citizenship and the mastery of English—and indeed in its very title—the Sons of America sought to reassure Texas Anglos that they could be trusted to be loyal and upstanding citizens" (1988: 23).

3. Of Luis Valdez's importance as a seminal thinker in the Chicano movement, Carlos Muñoz had this to say: "Many of the ideas behind the conceptualization of the Chicano identity and the development of the Chicano Generation of the late 1960s emanated from the ideas of Luis Valdez and the cultural work of his Teatro Campesino" (1989: 53).

4. The quote comes from "El Plan Espiritual de Aztlán" (see further below), the manifesto issued by the First Chicano National Conference, held in Denver, Colorado, in 1969. It stands as one of the defining testaments of the Chicano movement "because of its emphasis on nationalism and the goal of self-determination" (Anaya and Lomelí 1989: 5).

5. In his rejection of the simplistic "them-versus-us" approach, Saragoza evinces a tacit appreciation for the dialectical nature of Anglo-Mexican relations in the Southwest.

6. Padilla discusses at some length the doubts regarding the efficacy of the mythologizing process that romantic nationalism—in particular indigenismo—so vigorously promotes. The danger exists that "the material aims of the group may indeed be led astray by idle dreams and empty symbols" (1989: 114). Such doubts, while highly pertinent, are not critical to our discussion; suffice it to say that on balance such mythologizing did help to contrast the ideological outlook of the Chicano Generation from that of its immediate predecessor.

7. The rise of bilingual radio stations in Texas and even in California during the eighties and nineties attests to the continuing power of bilingualism. However, based on my own observations, this bilingualism approaches the "vestigial" among the post-Chicano population, and accordingly, at least 80 percent of the discourse on bilingual stations is in English.

8. Of course, this anti–middle-class stance was not necessarily justified. Just as their predecessors did during the Mexican American era, many middle-class individuals remained committed to the civil rights of all Mexicans in the Southwest. They were active participants in such organizations as LULAC, MAPA, and even the UFW.

9. Cf. Goldman and Ybarra-Frausto: "The mystiques of nationalism and indigenism contained within the concept of chicanismo unified a heterogeneous movement" (1991: 86).

10. The transformation of the conjunto's status from "trash" to cultural treasure was cleverly exploited by the man I called the "forgotten genius of conjunto music" (Peña 1985a), Valerio Longoria. Ever since he was rediscovered and eventually awarded the National Endowment for the Arts National Heritage Fellowship, he carries business cards that read "Valerio Longoria—a National Treasure."

11. Again, the Mexican American woman's position in the Anglo-Mexican con-

flict was not immediately addressed by the ideology of Chicanismo, and women had to initiate their own corrective to such a gross oversight. In short, the gender issue complicates the race-culture dichotomy, and Chicana scholars, in particular, have been working since the early days of the movement to isolate gender relations from the more global ethnic struggle (see, for example, Chabram-Dernersesian 1992; Melville 1980).

12. This pattern—very much a part of the dialectic of conflict—was in effect at least since the 1930s (see Chapter 3), but in the late sixties and seventies it accelerated as a result of precedents like the Civil Rights Act of 1965.

13. In this respect, it is worth pointing out that Tosti was perfectly delighted with the Smithsonian Institution's efforts to add his "Pachuco Boogie" and "Chicano Boogie" to its archives. In the same breath that he proclaimed his pride in Chicanismo, he triumphantly displayed the Smithsonian's letter of intent.

7. LA ONDA CHICANA

1. "Tejano" is the generic label in current use to categorize the various types of groups originating in Texas since the 1980s. Groups as disparate as Emilio Navaira (a "progressive" conjunto), La Mafia (a *grupo tropical*), Mazz (a *grupo moderno*), and Selena y los Dinos (a hybrid) are all lumped under the rubric "Tejano." The label is capitalized in order to distinguish these groups from other referents of the word *tejano*.

2. This difference was corroborated by Sunny's own manager, Johnny Zaragoza, who put it this way: "Sunny tries to cater more to the middle-class people than Little Joe does" (personal interview).

3. Information on Little Joe's life and musical career comes from several conversations and interviews I held with him over the years, but principally from two—one on November 23, 1991, and another on May 6, 1993.

4. Information on Little Joe's discography comes from interviews and from the official Latinaires and la Familia discography prepared by Ramón Hernández. I wish to thank Ramón for sharing this information with me.

5. Several LPs were actually released during this period, including two original efforts aimed at the top-forty market, *Incredible* and *Unbeatable*. According to Ramón Hernández, Little Joe's personal biographer, some of these "went gold," but it is difficult to verify what "going gold" actually signified in the *tejano* market of those days. In any case, some LPs were reissues of materials recorded earlier.

6. The song became the anthem of the Texas branch of the United Farm Workers.

7. Among Mexican Americans, a *capirotada* is a dish made with bread, cinnamon, cheese, raisins, egg—all blended in such a way as to create a distinctive taste that combines all the ingredients.

8. Now in disuse, the word *jaitón* had disappeared from Little Joe's lexicon.

When I brought it up earlier in the interview, it took him a moment to remember the word, and then, chuckling in recognition, he acknowledged hearing it in his youth: "Yeah, *la raza decía, 'Qué jaitón,'* heh, heh" (people would say, "How hightoned!").

9. To my mind, two major changes—one rhythmic, the other harmonic—mark the break between post-1960s rock music and its older counterpart. The Africanization of the rhythm—shifting from a monorhythmic (often with a 12/8 meter) to a polyrhythmic feel (built around a 4/4 meter)—constitutes a major rhythmic change (the difference between Bill Haley and Little Richard on the one hand, and James Brown and Tower of Power on the other). Freeing the harmonies from the constraints of the I-IV-I-V-IV-I progression (and its blues-like variations) and opening them up to modal and chromatic experimentation constitutes the major harmonic change.

10. I was a member of one of those groups—the Matadors, formed in Weslaco, Texas, in 1958. Some of our first "gigs" were at record hops sponsored by radio station KRGV and disc jockey Bob Dixon, who eventually became our manager. In 1959, the Matadors signed a recording contract with Backbeat Records out of Houston, and a couple of tunes were actually on the top-forty hit parade in places like Baltimore and New Orleans. The Matadors dissolved in 1961.

11. Sunny, of course, is convinced that to him belongs the mantle of La Onda Chicana after Isidro López. For him, success in the top-forty market opened the door to La Onda: "Being that we were getting all this attention from 'Talk to Me,' that was the reason La Onda got a chance for someone to pay attention to it. Now, Little Joe had recorded a few things by then. But he was not really getting the attention. So coming out of 'Talk to Me,' and already people wanted to know, 'Ah, there's this Spanish boy that did this.' First time Spanish boy gets into the top forty with a national hit, and they looked into what we were doing—*Cariño nuevo* was there. And the Chicanos paid attention to it" (personal interview, March 5, 1980).

12. The other, more purely ranchero, wing of La Onda is represented by Freddie Martínez, Agustín Ramírez, and Joe Bravo. These orquestas seldom engaged in the musical code-switching typical of Little Joe or Sunny, and they seldom ventured into the jaitón range of the orquesta. Weekend orquestas across the Southwest were more heavily influenced by Little Joe than anyone else.

13. Little Joe weathered the economic winds that battered La Onda Chicana, however. Despite Manny Guerra's obituary, the king of La Onda survived into the 1990s as an icon of the past. Like the late Beto Villa, he is seen as a nostalgic relic of a disappeared but golden period in Chicano musical history.

14. *Más antes cuando tocaba una orquesta, iba una clase de gente. Cuando tocaba un conjunto, iba otra clase de gente. Ahora, cuando toca una orquesta—no va la gente.*

8. ETHNOGRAPHY

1. Marlita Reddy's statistics designate the percentage as "Hispanic," but given the region's immigration history, we may infer that the vast majority of that population is of Mexican descent.

2. I am including professionals, managers, salespeople, and skilled craftspersons in the "middle-class" category, which in the 1970 census numbered approximately 7,000 members of a total Mexican population of about 37,000. See Peña 1985a for a more comprehensive elaboration of the concept of class.

3. I was secretary for the Fresno chapter of MAPA during the mid-1970s, and I had occasion to participate in some of the protests waged on behalf of farmworkers and other disfranchised Mexicans in the area.

4. The dialectic of conflict is poetically and politically illustrated by recent events. At the same historical moment when the street-name–change fiasco was unfolding, *The Fresno Bee* carried a special story in its Fourth of July edition, 1994, datelined Chiapas, Mexico, on a celebration there (complete with a color photograph on the front page). According to the managing editor, the story was in recognition of the region's "changing demographics"—a sort of tribute to the still-growing Mexican presence in Fresno. But the story seems to have provoked resentment among some Anglo readers, who wrote to complain that *The Bee* was being unpatriotic for allowing foreign news to dominate the front page on *this* the most patriotic of days. On *The Bee's* alleged failure to pay adequate homage to the holiday, *The Bee* ombudsman wrote, "Reactions ranged from surprise . . . to passionate nationalistic statements . . . [to] harsh statements about Mexicans, Mexican Americans and immigrants" (*The Fresno Bee*, July 10, 1994: B9).

5. On the political unconscious, compare Habermas's position on class conflict in late capitalism: "State-regulated capitalism, which emerged from a reaction against the dangers to the system produced by open class antagonism, suspends class conflict" (1970: 107–108). Further on, Habermas argues that "the power structure, aimed as it is at avoiding dangers to the system, precisely excludes 'domination' . . . exercised in such a manner that one class subject *confronts* another as an identifiable group. This means not that class antagonisms have been abolished but that they have become *latent*" (ibid.: 109).

6. The instinctive fear of class antagonism and its potential revelation is so powerful that its very acknowledgment, even in the most innocuous of circumstances, is instantly attacked as subversive. The Republican Party is particularly vigilant against anything remotely suggestive of class as a dividing force in American life, accusing the Democrats of instigating "class warfare" (as George Bush accused Bill Clinton of doing during the presidential election campaign of 1992) any time the latter party brings up the idea of "taxing the rich."

7. Compare Jameson: ". . . the normal form of the dialogical is essentially an *antagonistic* one. . . . The dialogue of class struggle is one in which two opposing discourses fight it out within the general unity of a shared code" (1981: 84; italics in the original).

8. "Would it therefore be overbold," Huizinga (1950: 141) wrote, "to suggest that the theriomorphic factor in ritual, mythology and religion can best be understood in terms of the play attitude?"

9. "Ladies and gentlemen, the following song marks the end of tonight's dance. Always at your service, the band of Beto García and His GGs bids you farewell. We hope our music met with your complete approval, and until next time may God bless you and drive carefully. Don't forget that there's still some good *menudo* left. Don't go away hungry. [Singing] Put a nickel in the piano and let the fun roll on . . ."

10. Compare the comments in Chapter 3 by one of Taylor's middle-class informants on this "blame-the-individual" ideology.

CODA

1. "It's like eating pecan pie, pecan pie. You like it, but after a while—'Enough, take it away.' The same silly stuff [over and over]. To the point that it has become boring. . . . But what is happening is that youth is taking over."

2. But see Loza 1993 on the music of such groups as The Brat, Los Illegals, The Plugz, and others—all from East Lost Angeles. Although undeniably innovative, these groups fall under the broad rubric of American rock, and their music is far removed from the kind of bimusical syntheses worked out by Onda Chicana orquestas. Los Lobos, however, another band from East L.A., has accomplished some modest syntheses. In any case, none of these groups have had the protean impact that La Onda exerted in the 1970s.

3. It is worth observing that nightclubs catering consciously to young Chicanos and Chicanas, members of the post-Chicano cohort, are far less visible in California than in Texas. Whereas such nightclubs abound in the Lone Star State (some of them quite large, such as the Yellow Rose in San Antonio) and are major sources of commercial exposure for Tejano groups, in the Golden State many young Chicanos are drawn to top-forty and other pop-music clubs where Anglos predominate.

4. In October of 1994, however, 70,000 Mexicans took to the streets in Los Angeles, marching in protest against a very popular Proposition 187. Later approved by the voters of California, the new law excluded illegal immigrants from all public social services, including schooling for children, health care, and other essential services.

5. An alternative interpretation would no doubt attribute the denouement of a synthesizing Chicano aesthetic to the fragmenting effects of postmodernism and its depoliticization of the masses. The surging power in the 1980s and '90s of the reactionist right, and its devolutionary impact on American political culture, demonstrates, to my mind, both the continuing play of contradictory forces in American capitalism and the failure of postmodernist (anti)theory to account for the real consequences of mass agency. The dialectical motion of capitalism continues.

Selected Discography

Agustín Ramírez y su Orquesta. *El barco chiquito*. El Zarape ZLP 1013 (LP).

Balde González. "Cuéntame tu vida." Mission A-181 (78 RPM).

———. "No te preocupes por mí"/"Si no te amara tanto." Ideal 695-A (78 RPM).

———. "Qué me puede ya importar"/"Oye corazón." Melco 3950.

Beto Villa y su Orquesta. *Beto Villa*. Falcón FLP 108 (LP).

———. *Father of Orquesta Tejana*. Arhoolie Productions CD/C 364.

———. "Mi cafetal"/"Adiós muchachos." Ideal 700 (78 RPM).

———. "Palco de honor"/"Victoria Polka." Ideal 777 (78 RPM).

———. *Saludamos a Texas*. Ideal 104 (LP).

Beto Villa y su Orquesta, with Narciso Martínez. "Rosita Vals"/"Madre Mía." Ideal R-149 (78 RPM).

Don Tosti. "Palito de tendedera"/"Noches de Mazatlán." Combo 500 (78 RPM).

Don Tosti and Cuarteto Martínez. "Chicano Boogie." Taxco RS-303. (78 RPM).

Isidro López y su Orquesta. "La bicicleta"/"La hiedra." Ideal 45-1810 (45 RPM).

———. "Mala cara." Ideal 1585 (78 RPM).

———. "Sufriendo y penando"/"Tu nueva vida." Ideal 1775 (78 RPM).

Jimmy Edward [Treviño]. *My Special Album*. Texas Best Records TXB-LP-1001.

———. *Romántico*. Scorpio Productions, Inc. SRP-209 (LP).

Latin Breed. *Power Drive*. Guerra Company Productions GCPLP-124.

Little Joe and the Latinaires. *Amor bonito*. El Zarape ZLP 1008 (LP).

———. *Por un amor*. El Zarape ZLP 1002 (LP)

———. *The Best of Little Joe*. El Zarape ZLP 1012 (LP).

Little Joe y la Familia. *La voz de Aztlán*. Leona Record Corp. LRC 007 (LP).

———. *Para la gente*. BSR 1038 (LP).

———. *Sea la paz la fuerza*. Leona Record Corp. LRC 019 (LP).

———. *Total*. BSR 1041 (LP).

Ramón Márquez y su Orquesta. "Rumba Swing." Taxco TX-1100 (78 RPM).

Sammy Mendoza and His Mambo Kings. "Pennies from Heaven"/"No hay como tú." Taxco TX-1311 (78 RPM).

Sunny and the Sunliners. *Amor de mis amores*. Key-Loc Records KL 3030 (LP).

————. *Grande, grande, grande.* Key-Loc Records KL 3028 (LP).

————. *Los enamorados.* Key-Loc Records KL 3020 (LP).

Tejano Roots: Orquestas Tejanas. Manuel Peña, ed. Arhoolie Productions CD/C 368.

Texas-Mexican Border Music: The String Bands. Chris Strachwits, ed. Folkyric/Arhoolie Records 9007 (LP).

Tortilla Factory. *Mis favoritas.* Falcon Records GLP-011 (LP).

References Cited

Acuña, Rodolfo. 1981. *Occupied America*. San Francisco: Canfield Press.

Agger, Ben. 1992. *The Discourse of Domination: From the Frankfurt School to Postmodernism*. Evanston, Ill.: Northwestern University Press.

Allen, Robert L. 1990. *Black Awakening in Capitalist America*. Trenton, N.J.: Africa World Press.

Allsup, Carl. 1982. *The American G.I. Forum: Origins and Evolution*. Austin: Center for Mexican American Studies (University of Texas).

Alurista. 1972. Poem in Lieu of Preface. In *Aztlán: An Anthology of Mexican American Literature*, ed. Luis Valdez and Stan Steiner, pp. 332–333. New York: Vintage Books.

Alvarez, Rodolfo. 1973. The Psychohistorical and Socioeconomic Development of the Chicano Community in the United States. *Social Science Quarterly* 53 (4): 920–942.

Amastae, Jon, and Lucía Elías-Olivares, eds. 1982. *Spanish in the United States: Sociolinguistic Aspects*. Cambridge: Cambridge University Press.

Anaya, Rudolfo, and Francisco Lomelí, eds. 1989. *Aztlán: Essays on the Chicano Homeland*. Albuquerque: Academia/El Norte Publications.

Arnold, Charles A. 1928. Folklore, Manners and Customs of the Mexicans in San Antonio, Texas. Master's thesis, The University of Texas at Austin.

Bakhtin, M. M. 1986. *Speech Genres and Other Late Essays*, trans. Vern W. McGee. Austin: University of Texas Press.

Balibar, Etienne. 1994. *Masses, Classes, Ideas: Studies on Politics and Philosophy Before and After Marx*. New York: Routledge.

Ballaert, William. 1956. *William Ballaert's Texas*. Norman: University of Oklahoma Press.

Bancroft, Hubert H. 1888. *California Pastoral, 1769–1848*. San Francisco: History Company Publication.

Bandini, Helen. 1908. *History of California*. New York: American Book Company.

Baqueiro Foster, Gerónimo. 1964. *La música en el período independiente*. Mexico City: Fondo de Cultura Económica.

Barrera, Mario. 1979. *Race and Class in the Southwest: A Theory of Racial Inequality.* Notre Dame: University of Notre Dame Press.

———. 1988. *Beyond Aztlán: Ethnic Autonomy in Comparative Perspective.* New York: Praeger.

Barthes, Roland. 1972. *Mythologies.* New York: Hill and Wang.

———. 1983. *The Fashion System.* New York: Hill and Wang.

Bateson, Gregory. 1972. *Steps to an Ecology of Mind.* San Francisco: Chandler Publishing.

Baudrillard, Jean. 1975. *The Mirror of Production.* St. Louis: Telos Press.

———. 1981. *For a Critique of the Political Economy of the Sign.* St. Louis: Telos Press.

Bauman, Richard. 1972. Differential Identity and the Social Base of Folklore. In *Toward New Perspectives in Folklore,* ed. Américo Paredes and Richard Bauman, pp. 31–41. Austin: University of Texas Press.

Bauman, Richard, and Joel Sherzer, eds. 1974. *Explorations in the Ethnography of Speaking.* London: Cambridge University Press.

Bell, Daniel. 1960. *The End of Ideology.* Glencoe, Ill.: The Free Press.

Bell, Horace. 1927. *Reminiscences of a Ranger.* Santa Barbara: Wallace Hibberd.

———. 1930. *On the Old West Coast.* New York: William Morrow.

Birnbaum, Larry. 1994. Ancient Roots, Fresh Tendrils: A Musical Garden Rich with the Spices of Life. *Pulse* (August): 55–59.

Blacking, John. 1974. Ethnomusicology as a Key Subject in the Social Sciences. In *Memoriam, Antonio Jorge Diaz,* pp. 71–93. Lisbon: Instituto de Alta Cultura.

Blom, Jan Petter, and John J. Gumperz. 1972. Social Meaning and Linguistic Structures: Code-Switching in Norway. In *Directions in Sociolinguistics: The Ethnography of Communication,* ed. John J. Gumperz and Dell Hymes, pp. 407–434. New York: Holt, Rinehart and Winston.

Bluestein, Gene. 1972. *The Voice of the Folk.* Amherst, Mass.: University of Massachusetts Press.

Breen, Marcus. 1992. Desert Dreams, Media and Intervention in Reality: Australian Aboriginal Music. In *Rocking the Boat: Mass Music and Mass Movements,* ed. Reebee Garofalo, pp. 149–170. Boston: South End Press.

Briones, Brígida. 1971. A Glimpse of Domestic Life in 1828. In *Sketches of Early California,* ed. Donald de Nevi. San Francisco: Chronicle Books.

Browning, Harley L., and Rodolfo de la Garza, eds. 1986. *Mexican Immigrants and Mexican Americans: An Evolving Relation.* Austin: Center for Mexican American Studies (University of Texas).

Bureau of the Census. 1970. *Characteristics of the Population: California* 1 (6): 1.

Burns, E. Bradford. 1980. *The Poverty of Progress: Latin America in the Nineteenth Century.* Berkeley: University of California Press.

Burr, Ramiro. 1994. Banda. *Pulse* (August): 59.

Callinicos, Alex. 1989. *Against Postmodernism: A Marxist Critique.* New York: St. Martin's Press.

Camarillo, Albert. 1979. *Chicanos in a Changing Society.* Cambridge, Mass.: Harvard University Press.

Carmichael, Stokely, and Charles V. Hamilton. 1968. *Black Power: The Politics of Liberation in America.* New York: Random House.

Chabram-Dernersesian, Angie. 1992. I Throw Punches for My Race, but I Don't Want to Be a Man: Writing Us—Chica-nos (Girls, Us)/Chicanas—into the Movement Script. In *Cultural Studies,* ed. Lawrence Grossberg, et al., pp. 81–95. New York: Routledge.

Chapple, Eliot, and Carleton S. Coon. 1942. *Principles of Anthropology.* New York: Holt.

Chatfield, W. H. 1893. *The Twin Cities of the Border.* New Orleans: E. P. Brandon.

Cleland, Robert G. 1964. *The Cattle on a Thousand Hills.* San Marino, Calif.: The Huntington Library.

Clifford, James. 1986. Introduction: Partial Truths. In *Writing Culture: The Poetics and Politics of Ethnography,* ed. James Clifford and George E. Marcus, pp. 1–26. Berkeley: University of California Press.

Clifford, James, and George E. Marcus, eds. 1986. *Writing Culture: The Poetics and Politics of Ethnography.* Berkeley: University of California Press.

Clopper, J. C. 1929. J. C. Clopper's Journal and Book of Memoranda. *Texas Historical Association Quarterly* 13: 1 (July): 44–80.

Crisp, James E. 1976. Anglo-Texan Attitudes Toward the Mexican, 1821–1845. Ph.D. diss., Yale University.

Cumberland, Charles C. 1968. *Mexico: The Struggle for Modernity.* London: Oxford University Press.

Curtis, Albert. 1955. *Fabulous San Antonio.* San Antonio: The Naylor Company.

Czarnowski, Lucille K. 1971. *Dances of Early California Days.* Palo Alto, Calif.: Pacific Books.

Dana, Richard Henry. 1964. *Two Years Before the Mast: A Personal Narrative of Life at Sea.* Los Angeles: Ward Ritchie Press.

Davis, William W. H. [1857] 1973. *El Gringo; or New Mexico and Her People.* New York: Arno Press.

De la Teja, Jesús Francisco. 1988. Land and Society in Eighteenth-Century San Antonio de Bexar, a Community in New Spain's Northern Frontier. Ph.D. diss., The University of Texas at Austin.

De la Teja, Jesús Francisco, and John Wheat. 1991. Bexar: Profile of a Tejano Community, 1820–1832. In *Tejano Origins in Eighteenth-Century San Antonio,* ed. Gerald E. Poyo and Gilberto M. Hinojosa, pp. 1–24. Austin: University of Texas Press.

De la Torre, Chito. 1993. A Taste of Tejas. *Hispanic* 6: 1 (March): 22–26.

De León, Arnoldo. 1982. *The Tejano Community, 1835–1900.* Albuquerque: University of New Mexico Press.

———. 1983. *They Called Them Greasers.* Austin: University of Texas Press.

Deleuze, Gilles, and Felix Guattari. 1977. *The Anti-Oedipus: Capitalism and Schizophrenia.* New York: Viking Books.

DeNevi, Donald, ed. 1971. *Sketches of Early California*. San Francisco: Chronicle Publishing.

Dinger, Adele. 1972. *Folklife and Folklore of the Mexican Border*. Edinburg, Tex.: Hidalgo County Historical Museum.

Downs, Fane. 1971. The History of Mexicans in Texas, 1820–1845. Ph.D. diss., Texas Tech University.

Eco, Umberto. 1976. *A Theory of Semiotics*. Bloomington: University of Indiana Press.

Erving, Susan, and Charles E. Osgood. 1954. Second Language Learning and Bilingualism. In *Psycholinguistics*, ed. Charles E. Osgood and Thomas A. Sebeok, pp. 139–146. Bloomington: University of Indiana Press.

Escobar, Edward J. 1993. The Dialectics of Repression: The Los Angeles Police Department and the Chicano Movement, 1968–1971. *The Journal of American History* 79 (4): 1483–1514.

Feld, Steven. 1988. Notes on World Beat. *Public Culture* 1 (1): 31–37.

———. 1994. From Schizophonia to Schizmogenesis: On the Discourses and Commodification Practices of "World Music" and "World Beat." In Charles Keil and Steven Feld, *Music Grooves: Essays and Dialogues,* pp. 257–289. Chicago: University of Chicago Press.

Fiske, John. 1989. *Understanding Popular Culture*. Boston: Unwin Hyman.

Flores, Richard R. 1992. The "Corrido" and the Emergence of Texas-Mexican Social Identity. *Journal of American Folklore* 105 (416): 166–173.

Foley, Douglas E. 1988a. *From Peones to Politicos: Class and Ethnicity in a South Texas Town, 1900–1987*. Austin: Center for Mexican American Studies (University of Texas).

———. 1988b. The Legacy of the *Partido Raza Unida* in South Texas: A Class Analysis. *Ethnic Affairs* 1 (2): 47–73.

———. 1990. *Learning Capitalist Culture: Deep in the Heart of Tejas*. Philadelphia: University of Pennsylvania Press.

Foster, George M. 1953. What Is Folk Culture? *American Anthropologist* 55: 159–173.

Foucault, Michel. 1980. *Power/Knowledge: Selected Interviews and Other Writings,* ed. and trans. Colin Gordon. New York: Pantheon Books.

Franco, Jean. 1970. *The Modern Culture of Latin America*. Baltimore: Penguin Books.

Fraser, Nancy, and Linda Nicholson. 1988. Social Criticism Without Philosophy: An Encounter Between Feminism and Postmodernism. In *Universal Abandon? The Politics of Postmodernism,* ed. Andrew Ross, pp. 83–104. Minneapolis: University of Minnesota Press.

Frith, Simon. 1981. *Sound Effects: Youth, Leisure and the Politics of Rock'n'Roll*. New York: Pantheon Books.

———. 1988. Art, Ideology and Pop Practice. In *Marxism and the Interpretation of Culture,* ed. Cary Nelson and Lawrence Grossberg, pp. 461–475. Urbana: University of Illinois Press.

Gabler, Neal. 1994. Owners Win Public Sentiment Battle. In "Vision," *The Fresno Bee,* August 14, B9.

Gamio, Manuel. 1971. *Mexican Immigration to the United States: A Study of Human Migration and Adjustment.* New York: Dover Publications.

García, Ignacio. n.d. A Short History of the Beto Villa Band. Unpublished manuscript.

García, James E. 1994. Selena: Glorious Madonna? In "Onward" [entertainment supplement], *Austin American-Statesman,* May 5, 5.

García, Mario T. 1981. *Desert Immigrants: The Mexicans of El Paso, 1880–1920.* New Haven: Yale University Press.

———. *La Frontera:* The Border as Symbol and Reality in Mexican-American Thought. *Mexican Studies/Estudios Mexicanos* 1 (2): 195–225.

———. 1989. *Mexican Americans: Leadership, Ideology and Identity.* New Haven: Yale University Press.

———. 1992. Review of The Lost Land: The Chicano Image of the Southwest (John Chávez). In *Chicano Discourse,* ed. Tatcho Mindiola and Emilio Zamora, pp. 164–174. Houston: Mexican American Publications (University of Houston).

García, Richard A. 1983. The Mexican American Mind: A Product of the 1930s. In *History, Culture and Society: Chicano Studies in the 1980s,* ed. Mario T. García, et al., pp. 67–93. Ypsilanti, Mich.: Bilingual Press.

———. 1991. *The Rise of the Mexican American Middle Class: San Antonio, 1929–1941.* College Station: Texas A&M Press.

García Canclini, Néstor. 1993. *Transforming Modernity: Popular Culture in Mexico.* Austin: University of Texas Press.

Geertz, Clifford. 1973. *The Interpretation of Cultures.* New York: Basic Books.

Goetzmann, William H. 1985. Anglo-American Dreams: Keep the White Lights Shining. *The Texas Humanist* 7 (3): 30–32.

Goldman, Shifra. 1982. Mexican Muralism: Its Social-Educative Roles in Latin America and the United States. *Aztlán* 13 (1 & 2): 111–133.

Goldman, Shifra, and Tomás Ybarra-Frausto. 1991. The Political and Social Contexts of Chicano Art. In *Chicano Art: Resistance and Affirmation, 1965–1985,* ed. Richard Griswold del Castillo et al., pp. 83–95. Los Angeles: Wright Art Gallery (University of California, Los Angeles).

Gómez-Quiñones, Juan. 1990. *Chicano Politics: Reality and Promise, 1940–1990.* Albuquerque: University of New Mexico Press.

González, Jovita. 1930. Social Life in Cameron, Starr, and Zapata Counties. Master's thesis, The University of Texas at Austin.

González, Nancie L. 1969. *The Spanish-Americans of New Mexico.* Albuquerque: University of New Mexico Press.

Gordon, Milton M. 1964. *Assimilation in American Life.* New York: Oxford University Press.

Gramsci, Antonio. 1971. *Selections from the Prison Notebooks.* Trans. and ed. Quintin Hoare and Geoffrey Noel Smith. New York: International Publishers.

Gregg, Josiah. [1844] 1954. *Commerce of the Prairies*. Norman: University of Oklahoma Press.

Griswold del Castillo, Richard. 1979. *The Los Angeles Barrio, 1850–1890: A Social History*. Berkeley: University of California Press.

Grosjean, François, and Carlos Soares. 1986. Processing Mixed Language: Some Preliminary Findings. In *Language Processing in Bilinguals: Psycholinguistic and Neuropsychological Perspectives*, ed. Jyotsna Vaid, pp. 145–179. Hillsdale, N.J.: Lawrence Erlbaum Associates.

Grossberg, Lawrence. 1992. *We Gotta Get Out of This Place: Popular Conservatism and Postmodern Culture*. New York: Routledge.

Gumperz, John J., and Dell Hymes, eds. 1972. *Directions in Sociolinguistics: The Ethnography of Communication*. New York: Holt, Rinehart and Winston.

Gutiérrez, Ramón A. 1989. Aztlán, Montezuma, and New Mexico: The Political Uses of American Indian Mythology. In *Aztlán: Essays on the Chicano Homeland*, ed. Rudolfo A. Anaya and Francisco A. Lomelí, pp. 172–190. Albuquerque: Academia/El Norte Publications.

———. 1991. *When Jesus Came, the Corn Mothers Went Away*. Stanford, Calif.: Stanford University Press.

Habermas, Jurgen. 1970. *Toward a Rational Society: Student Protest, Science and Politics*. Boston: Beacon Press.

———. 1975. *Legitimation Crisis*. Boston: Beacon Press.

Hall, Stuart. 1988. The Toad in the Garden: Thatcherism Among the Theorists. In *Marxism and the Interpretation of Culture*, ed. Cary Nelson and Lawrence Grossberg, pp. 35–73. Urbana: University of Illinois Press.

Harris, James K. 1927. A Sociological Study of a Mexican School in San Antonio, Texas. Master's thesis, The University of Texas at Austin.

Hebdige, Dick. 1979. *Subculture: The Meaning of Style*. London: Methuen.

Hernández-Chávez, Eduardo, Andrew D. Cohen, and Anthony F. Beltramo, eds. 1975. *El lenguaje de los Chicanos: Regional and Social Characteristics of Language Used by Mexican Americans*. Arlington, Va.: Center for Applied Linguistics.

Herrera-Sobek, María. 1993. *Northward Bound: The Mexican Immigrant Experience in Ballad and Song*. Bloomington: University of Indiana Press.

Hittell, Theodore H. 1898. *History of California*. Vol. 2. San Francisco: N. J. Stone.

Horkheimer, Max, and Theodore W. Adorno. 1972. *Dialectic of Enlightenment*. New York: Herder and Herder.

———. 1993. The Culture Industry: Enlightenment as Mass Deception. In *The Cultural Studies Reader*, ed. Simon During, pp. 29–43. London: Routledge.

Howard, Raymond G. 1952. Acculturation and Social Mobility Among Latin Americans in Resaca City. Master's thesis, The University of Texas at Austin.

Huizinga, Johan. 1950. *Homo Ludens: A Study in the Play Element in Culture*. Boston: Beacon Press.

Israel, Joachim. 1979. *Alienation from Marx to Modern Sociology*. New Jersey: Humanities Press.

Jacobson, Rodolfo. 1978. The Social Implications of Intra-Sentential Code-Switching. In *New Directions in Chicano Scholarship*, ed. Ricardo Romo and Raymund Paredes, pp. 227–256. La Jolla, Calif.: University of California at San Diego.

Jameson, Fredric. 1981. *The Political Unconscious: Narrative as a Socially Symbolic Act*. Ithaca, N.Y.: Cornell University Press.

———. 1984. Foreword to *The Postmodern Condition*, by Jean-François Lyotard, pp. vii–xxi. Minneapolis: University of Minnesota Press.

Jansen, William H. 1965. The Esoteric-Exoteric Factor in Folklore. In *The Study of Folklore*, ed. Alan Dundes, pp. 43–51. Englewood Cliffs, N.J.: Prentice-Hall.

Jáuregui, Jesús. 1990. *El mariachi: Símbolo musical de México*. Mexico City: Banpais.

Jordan, Rosan A. 1972. Language Loyalty and Folklore Studies: The Mexican American. *Western Folklore* 31 (2): 77–86.

———. 1981. Tension and Speech Play in Mexican-American Folklore. In *"And Other Neighborly Names": Social Process and Cultural Image in Texas Folklore*, ed. Richard Bauman and Roger D. Abrahams, pp. 252–265. Austin: University of Texas Press.

Keil, Charles, and Angeliki V. Keil. 1992. *Polka Happiness*. Philadelphia: Temple University Press.

Kellner, Douglas, ed. 1994. *Baudrillard: A Critical Reader*. Oxford: Blackwell Publishers.

Kendall, George W. 1935. *Narrative of the Texan Santa Fe Expedition*. Vol 1. Austin: The Steck Company.

Kenneson, Susan K. 1978. Through the Looking Glass: History of Anglo-American Attitudes Toward the Spanish-Americans and Indians of New Mexico. Ph.D. diss., Yale University.

Kottack, Conrad. 1992. *Anthropology: The Exploration of Human Diversity*. New York: McGraw-Hill.

LaCappra, Dominick. 1983. *Rethinking Intellectual History: Texts, Contexts, Language*. Ithaca, N.Y.: Cornell University Press.

Lafaye, Jacques. 1976. *Quetzalcoatl and Guadalupe: The Formation of Mexican National Consciousness, 1531–1818*. Chicago: University of Chicago Press.

Lambert, Wallace. 1978. Some Cognitive and Sociocultural Consequences of Being Bilingual. In *International Dimensions of Bilingual Education*, ed. James E. Alatis, pp. 214–229. Washington, D.C.: Georgetown University Press.

Leach, Edmund R. 1972. Ritualization in Man in Relation to Conceptual and Social Development. In *Reader in Comparative Religion: An Anthropological Approach*, ed. William A. Lessa and Evon Z. Vogt, pp. 333–337. New York: Harper & Row.

León-Portilla, Miguel. 1972. The Norteño Variety of Mexican Culture: An Ethno-historical Approach. In *Plural Society of the Southwest*, ed. Edward H. Spicer and Raymond Thompson, pp. 77–114. Albuquerque: University of New Mexico Press.

Lévi-Strauss, Claude. 1963. *Structural Anthropology*. New York: Basic Books.

———. 1969. *The Elementary Structures of Kinship*. Boston: Beacon Press.

———. 1974. *From Honey to Ashes*. New York: Harper & Row.

———. 1983. *The Raw and the Cooked*. Chicago: University of Chicago Press.

Lewis, Glyn. 1972. *Multilingualism in the Soviet Union*. The Hague: Mouton.

Limón, Jose E. 1974. El Primer Congreso Mexicanista de 1911: A Precursor to Contemporary Chicanismo. *Aztlán: Chicano Journal of the Social Sciences and the Arts* 5: 85–107.

———. 1978. *Agringado* Joking in Texas-Mexican Society: Folklore and Differential Identity. In *New Directions in Chicano Scholarship*, ed. Ricardo Romo and Raymund Paredes, pp. 33–50. La Jolla, Calif.: University of California, San Diego.

———. 1983. Folklore, Social Conflict and the United States–Mexico Border. In *Handbook of American Folklore*, ed. Richard M. Dorson, pp. 216–226. Bloomington: University of Indiana Press.

———. 1994. *Dancing with the Devil: Society and Cultural Poetics in Mexican-American South Texas*. Madison: University of Wisconsin Press.

Little Joe: Personal and Musical History Outline. n.d. Unpublished biography.

Loza, Steven. 1993. *Barrio Rhythm: Mexican American Music in East Los Angeles*. Urbana: University of Illinois Press.

Lucero-White, Aurora. 1940. *Folk-Dances of the Spanish Colonials of New Mexico*. Silver City, N.M.: Western New Mexico University.

Lukács, Georg. 1971. *History and Class Consciousness: Studies in Marxist Dialectics*. Cambridge, Mass.: MIT Press.

Lummis, Charles F. 1905. Catching Our Archeology Alive. *Out West* 22, 1 (January): 35–45.

Lyotard, Jean-François. 1984. *The Postmodern Condition: A Report on Knowledge*. Minneapolis: University of Minnesota Press.

MacLachlan, Colin M., and Jaime E. Rodríguez O. 1980. *The Forging of the Cosmic Race: A Reinterpretation of Colonial Mexico*. Berkeley: University of California Press.

Madsen, William. 1964. *The Mexican-Americans of South Texas*. New York: Holt, Rinehart and Winston.

Manuel, Peter. 1988. *Popular Musics of the Non-Western World: An Introductory Survey*. New York: Oxford University Press.

Marcuse, Herbert. 1964. *One-Dimensional Man*. Boston: Beacon Press.

Marin, Marguerite V. 1991. *Social Protest in an Urban Barrio: A Study of the Chicano Movement, 1966–1974*. Lanham, Md.: University Press of America.

Márquez, Benjamin. 1993. *LULAC: The Evolution of a Mexican American Political Organization*. Austin: University of Texas Press.

Marx, Karl. 1977. *Capital.* Vols. 1 and 3. New York: Vintage.

Marx, Karl, and Frederick Engels. 1956. *The Holy Family, or Critique of Critical Critique.* Moscow: Foreign Languages Publishing House.

Mauss, Marcel. 1954. *The Gift,* trans. Ian Cunnison. London: Cohen & West.

Maverick, Mary A. [1921] 1989. *Memoirs of Mary A. Maverick,* ed. Rena Maverick Guen. Lincoln: University of Nebraska Press.

Mayer-Serra, Otto. 1941. *Panorama de la música mexicana.* Mexico City: Fondo de Cultura Económica.

Mazón, Mauricio. 1984. *The Zoot-Suit Riots: The Psychology of Symbolic Annihilation.* Austin: University of Texas Press.

McLeese, Don. 1994. Arista Sets Sights on Tejano. "Onward" [entertainment supplement], *Austin American-Statesman,* Thursday, May 5.

McLemore, S. Dale. 1980. *Racial and Ethnic Relations in America.* Boston: Allyn and Bacon.

McWilliams, Carey. [1948] 1968. *North From Mexico.* New York: Greenwood Press.

Melville, Margarita, ed. 1980. *Twice a Minority: Mexican American Women.* St. Louis: C. V. Mosby.

Menchaca, Martha. 1993. Chicano Indianism: A Historical Account of Racial Repression. *American Ethnologist* 20 (3): 583–603.

———. 1995. *The Mexican Outsiders: A Community History of Discrimination and Marginalization in California.* Austin: University of Texas Press.

Miliband, Ralph. 1969. *The State in Capitalist Society: An Analysis of the Western System of Power.* New York: Basic Books.

Montejano, David. 1987. *Anglos and Mexicans in the Making of Texas.* Austin: University of Texas Press.

Montoya, José. 1972. La Jefita. In *Aztlán: An Anthology of Mexican American Literature,* ed. Luis Valdez and Stan Steiner. New York: Vintage Books.

Montoya, Malaquías. 1980. A Critical Perspective on the State of Chicano Art. *Metamórfosis* 3 (1): 3–7.

Moore, Joan, and Harry Pachón. 1985. *Hispanics in the United States.* Englewood Cliffs, N.J.: Prentice-Hall.

Morner, Magnus, ed. 1970. *Race and Class in Latin America.* New York: Columbia University Press.

Muir, Andrew F. 1958. *Texas in 1837: An Anonymous Contemporary Narrative.* Austin: University of Texas Press.

Mukerji, Chandra, and Michael Schudson, eds. 1991. *Rethinking Popular Culture: Contemporary Perspectives in Cultural Studies.* Berkeley: University of California Press.

Muñoz, Carlos. 1989. *Youth, Identity, Power.* London: Verso Press.

Nájera-Ramírez, Olga. 1997. *Critical Encounters: Indigenous Perspectives in Festival Performance.* Albuquerque: University of New Mexico Press.

Navarro, Armando. 1975. The Evolution of Chicano Politics. *Aztlán* 5 (1 & 2): 57–84.

Nettl, Bruno. 1985. *The Western Impact on World Music: Change, Adaptation and Survival*. New York: Schirmer Books.

Newmark, Harris. 1930. *Sixty Years in Southern California, 1853–1913*. Boston: Houghton Mifflin.

Nicholson, Linda, ed. 1990. *Feminism /Postmodernism*. New York: Routledge.

Nishimura, Miwa. 1986. Intrasentential Code-Switching: The Case of Language Assignment. In *Language Processing in Bilinguals*, ed. Jyotsna Vaid, pp. 123–143. Hillsdale, N.J.: Lawrence Erlbaum Associates.

Orozco, Cynthia. 1992. The Origins of the League of United Latin American Citizens and the Mexican-American Civil Rights Movement in Texas with an Analysis of Women's Participation in a Gendered Context, 1910–1929. Ph.D. diss., University of California, Los Angeles.

Ortego, Philip D. 1970. The Chicano Renaissance. In *La Causa Chicana: The Movement for Justice*, ed. Margaret M. Mangold, pp. 42–64. New York: Family Service Association of America.

Ortner, Sherry. 1973. On Key Symbols. *American Anthropologist* 75: 1338–1346.

Padilla, Genaro. 1989. Myth and Comparative Cultural Nationalism: The Ideological Uses of Aztlán. In *Aztlán: Essays on the Chicano Homeland*, ed. Rudolfo A. Anaya and Francisco Lomelí, pp. 111–131. Albuquerque: Academia/El Norte Publications.

Paredes, Américo. 1958. *With His Pistol in His Hand*. Austin: University of Texas Press.

———. 1966. The Anglo-American in Mexican Folklore. In *New Voices in American Studies*, ed. Roy B. Browne and Donald H. Winkleman, pp. 113–127. Lafayette, Ind.: Purdue University Press.

———. 1968. Folk Medicine and the Intercultural Jest. In *Spanish-Speaking People in the United States*, ed. June Helm, pp. 104–119. Seattle: distributed by the University of Washington Press.

———. 1978. On Ethnographic Work Among Minority Groups: A Folklorist's Perspective. In *New Directions in Chicano Scholarship*, ed. Ricardo Romo and Raymund Paredes, pp. 1–32. La Jolla: University of California, San Diego.

———. 1993. *Folklore and Culture on the Texas-Mexican Border*. Austin: CMAS Books (The University of Texas).

———. 1995. *A Texas-Mexican Cancionero*. Austin: University of Texas Press.

Patterson, Tim. 1975. Notes on the Historical Application of Marxist Cultural Theory. *Science and Society* 34: 257–291.

Pattie, James O. [1831] 1930. *The Personal Narrative of James O. Pattie of Kentucky*. Chicago: R. R. Donnelly and Sons.

Peña, Manuel. 1980. Ritual Structure in a Chicano Dance. *Latin American Music Review* 1 (1): 47–73

———. 1981. The Emergence of Conjunto Music, 1935–1955. In *"And Other Neighborly Names": Social Process and Cultural Image in Texas Folklore*, ed. Richard Bauman and Roger D. Abrahams, pp. 280–299. Austin: University of Texas Press.

————. 1982. Folksong and Social Change: Two Corridos as Interpretive Sources. *Aztlán* 13 (1 & 2): 13–42.

————. 1985a. *The Texas-Mexican Conjunto: History of a Working-Class Music.* Austin: University of Texas Press.

————. 1985b. From Ranchero to Jaitón: Ethnicity and Class in Texas-Mexican Music (Two Styles in the Form of a Pair). *Ethnomusicology* 29 (1): 29–55.

————. 1987. Music for a Changing Community: Three Generations of a Chicano Family Orquesta. *Latin American Music Review* 8 (2): 230–245.

————. 1989. Notes Toward an Interpretive History of California-Mexican Music. In *From the Inside Out: Perspectives on Mexican and Mexican-American Folk Art,* ed. Karana Hattersley-Drayton, et al., pp. 64–76. San Francisco: The Mexican Museum.

————. 1993. Latino Music in the United States. In *The Hispanic Almanac,* ed. Nicolás Kanellos, pp. 595–620. Detroit: Gale Research.

Peñalosa, Fernando. 1973. Recent Changes Among the Chicanos. In *Chicano: The Evolution of a People,* ed. Renato Rosaldo et al., pp. 263–266. San Francisco: Rinehart Press.

————. 1980. *Chicano Sociolinguistics.* Rowley, Mass.: Newbury House Publishers.

Pitt, Leonard. 1966. *The Decline of the Californios: A Social History of the Spanish-Speaking Californians, 1848–1890.* Berkeley: University of California Press.

Poyo, Gerald S., and Gilberto M. Hinojosa. 1991. Introduction to *Tejano Origins in Eighteenth-Century San Antonio,* ed. Gerald S. Poyo and Gilberto M. Hinojosa, pp. ix–xxii. Austin: University of Texas Press.

Redfield, Robert. 1947. The Folk Society. *The American Journal of Sociology* 52: 293–308.

Reddy, Marlita A. 1993. *Statistical Record of Hispanic Americans.* Detroit: Gale Research.

Reisler, Mark. 1976. *By the Sweat of Their Brow: Mexican Immigrant Labor in the United States, 1900–1940.* Westport, Conn.: Greenwood Press.

Reyna, José. 1980. *Raza Humor.* San Antonio: Penca Books.

Robinson, Alfred. 1925. *Life in California Before the Conquest.* San Francisco: Thomas C. Russell.

Robinson, Cecil. 1977. *Mexico and the Hispanic Southwest in American Literature.* Norman: University of Oklahoma Press.

————. 1992. *No Short Journeys: The Interplay of Cultures in the History and Literature of the Borderlands.* Tucson: University of Arizona Press.

Robinson, Deanna Campbell, Elizabeth Buck, and Marlene Cuthbert. 1991. Industrial Roots. In *Music at the Margins: Popular Music and Global Cultural Diversity,* ed. Deanna Campbell Robinson, Elizabeth Buck, and Marlene Cuthbert, pp. 31–55. Newbury Park, N.J.: Sage.

Rodó, José Enrique. [1900] 1988. *Ariel.* Austin: University of Texas Press.

Rodríguez, Néstor, and Rogelio T. Núñez. 1986. An Exploration of Factors That

Contribute to the Differentiation Between Chicanos and Indocumentados. In *Mexican Immigrants and Mexican Americans: An Evolving Relation,* ed. Harley L. Browning and Rudolfo de la Garza, pp. 138–156. Austin: Center for Mexican American Studies (University of Texas Press).

Romo, Ricardo. 1983. *East Los Angeles: History of a Barrio.* Austin: University of Texas Press.

Rosen, Gerald Paul. 1975. *Political Ideology and the Chicano Movement.* San Francisco: R & E Research Associates.

Rosenbaum, Robert J. 1972. Mexicans vs. Americans: A Study of Hispanic-American Resistance to Anglo-American Control in New Mexico Territory, 1870–1900. Ph.D. diss., The University of Texas at Austin.

Rubel, Arthur J. 1966. *Across the Tracks: Mexican-Americans in a Texas City.* Austin: University of Texas Press.

Sánchez, Rosaura. 1978. Chicano Bilingualism. In *New Directions in Chicano Scholarship,* ed. Ricardo Romo and Raymund Paredes, pp. 209–225. La Jolla: University of California, San Diego.

San Miguel, Guadalupe. 1987. *Let All of Them Take Heed: Mexican Americans and the Quest for Educational Equality in Texas, 1918–1981.* Austin: University of Texas Press.

Santillán, Richard. 1979. The Dialectics of Chicano Political Development: A Political Economy Perspective. *Appeal to Reason* 5 (4): 51–66.

Sapir, Edward. 1949. Culture, Genuine and Spurious. In *Selected Writings of Edward Sapir,* ed. David G. Mandelbaum, pp. 308–331. Berkeley: University of California Press.

Saragoza, Alex M. 1980. *Fresno's Hispanic Heritage.* Fresno: San Diego Federal Savings and Loan Association.

———. 1987. The Significance of Recent Chicano-Related Historical Writings: An Appraisal. *Ethnic Affairs* 1 (1): 24–62.

———. n.d. *Mexican Media and the State: The Origins of Televisa, 1929–1972.* Forthcoming.

Schneider, Gretchen A. 1969. Pigeon Wings and Polkas: The Dances of the California Miners. *Dance Perspectives* 39 (Winter): 5–57.

Shay, Anthony. 1982. Fandangos and Bailes: Dancing and Dance Events in Early California. *Southern California Quarterly* 64 (2): 99–113.

Sheridan, Thomas E. 1986. *Los Tucsonenses: The Mexican Community in Tucson, 1854–1941.* Tucson: University of Arizona Press.

Simmons, Ozzie G. [1952] 1974. *Anglo Americans and Mexican Americans in South Texas: A Study in Dominant-Subordinate Group Relations.* New York: Arno Press.

Skerry, Peter. 1993. *Mexican Americans: The Ambivalent Minority.* New York: The Free Press.

Slobin, Mark. 1993. *Subcultural Sounds: Micromusics of the Western World.* Hanover, N.H.: Wesleyan University Press/University Press of New England.

Spottswood, Richard K. 1990. *Ethnic Music on Records: A Discography of Ethnic Recordings in the United States, 1893 to 1942.* Urbana: University of Illinois Press.

Stevenson, Robert. 1952. *Music in Mexico.* New York: Thomas Y. Crowell.

Stewart, Jack. 1991. The Mexican Band: Myth, Reality and Musical Impact; A Preliminary Investigation. *Jazz Archivist* 6 (2): 1–14.

Strachwitz, Chris, with Philip Sonnichsen. 1975. *Texas-Mexican Border Music.* Vols. 2 & 3 (Corridos, part 1 & 2). Berkeley: Arhoolie Records.

Swan, Howard. 1952. *Music in the Southwest, 1825–1950.* San Marino, Calif.: The Huntington Library.

Taussig, Michael T. 1980. *The Devil and Commodity Fetishism in South America.* Chapel Hill: University of North Carolina Press.

Taylor, Paul S. [1934] 1971. *An American-Mexican Frontier.* New York: Russell and Russell.

Todorov, Tzvetan. 1987. *The Conquest of America: The Question of the Other.* New York: Harper & Row.

Turner, Victor. 1969. *The Ritual Process.* Chicago: University of Chicago Press.

———. 1974. *Dramas, Fields, and Metaphor.* Ithaca, N.Y.: Cornell University Press.

———. 1977. Symbols in African Ritual. In *Symbolic Anthropology,* ed. Janet Dolgin, David S. Remnitzer, and David M. Schneider, pp. 183–194. New York: Columbia University Press.

Vaid, Jyotsna, ed. 1986. *Language Processing in Bilinguals: Psycholinguistic and Neuropsychological Perspectives.* Hillsdale, N.J.: Lawrence Erlbaum Associates.

Valdez, Luis. 1972. Introduction: La Plebe. In *Aztlán: An Anthology of Mexican-American Literature,* ed. Luis Valdez and Stan Steiner, pp. xiii–xxxiv. New York: Vintage Books.

Vallejo, Guadalupe. 1890. Ranch-Mission Days in Alta California. *The Century Magazine* 41 (2): 183–192.

Van de Grift Sánchez, Nellie. 1929. *Spanish Arcadia.* Los Angeles: Powell Publishing.

Van Gennep, Arnold. 1960. *The Rites of Passage.* Chicago: University of Chicago Press.

Vilar, Pierre. 1994. Marxist History, a History in the Making: Towards a Dialogue with Althusser. In *Althusser: A Critical Reader,* ed. Gregory Elliott, pp. 10–43. Oxford: Blackwell.

Weinburg, Meyer. 1977. *A Chance to Learn: A History of Race and Education in the United States.* Cambridge: Cambridge University Press.

Williams, Raymond. 1973. *The Country and the City.* Oxford: Oxford University Press.

———. 1977. *Marxism and Literature.* Oxford: Oxford University Press.

———. 1981. *The Sociology of Culture.* New York: Schocken Books.

Willis, Susan. 1991. *A Primer for Daily Life.* London: Routledge.

Wilson, William A. 1973. Herder, Folklore and Romantic Nationalism. *Journal of Popular Culture* 6: 819–835.

Zavalishin, Dmitry. 1973. California in 1824. *Southern California Quarterly* 55 (4): 369–412.

Zeleny, Carolyn. 1944. Relations Between Spanish-Americans and Anglo-Americans in New Mexico: A Study of Conflict and Accommodation in a Dual-Ethnic Situation. Ph.D. diss., Yale University.

Index

275, 320n; as *jaitón* performer, 149, 150, 158, 159, 188, 242
González, Jovita, 45, 54, 107
Great Depression, 21, 22; and Anglo-Mexican relations, 26, 27; effect of on capitalism, 21
Great Society, 27, 204, 205; and Anglo-Mexican relations, 27; and the dialectic of conflict, 310
grupos cumbieros, 229; as working-class expression, 229
grupos folklóricos, 216; and the Chicano movement, 30, 216; and *música norteña,* 219, 220
grupos tropicales, 228
Guerra, Manny, 255, 260–263, 267, 271–273, 276, 301, 304, 305, 310, 323n
Guerrero, Lalo, 85, 148, 149, 166, 167, 169, 183–188, 192–194, 275, 320n; and the Chicano boogie, 174
Guerrero, Tony "Ham," 227, 233, 236–239, 241, 242, 263, 267, 270, 303–305
Gutiérrez, Eugenio, 118, 139, 159, 160
Gutiérrez, José Angel, 218, 241
Gutiérrez, Ramón, 46, 209, 315n

Hall, Stuart, 8
Herder, Johann G., 208, 214, 221
Hermanas Padilla, 70, 135
Hermanos Areu, 70, 84
Hermanos Bañuelos, 60, 70
Hernández, Inez, 215
Hernández, Little Joe, 188, 227, 229, 233–235, 237, 238, 240–242, 255–257, 261, 263–267, 271, 272, 306, 322n, 323n; and bimusicality, 243, 244, 248, 250, 268, 285; as king of La Onda Chicana, 232, 241; y la Familia, 2, 170, 180, 220, 233, 238–240, 242, 255, 303; and the Latinaires, 235–239, 255, 265
Hernández, Oscar, 274

immigration, 58, 60, 183, 278, 324n; as catalyst, 57, 88; and class formation, 15; and interethnic conflict, 311; and interethnic relations, 15; and intraethnic relations, 15
indigenismo, 213; and the Chicano muralists, 213; and the myth of Aztlán, 321n
Infante, Pedro, 73
inorganic democracy, 13, 49
intrasentential code-switching, 119, 161; and bimusicality, 120, 161; and com-

pound bilingualism, 117; defined, 117. *See also* bilingualism

jaitón, lo, 2, 187, 322n; and orquesta, 142, 143, 149–152, 154, 157–159, 187, 192, 199, 203, 231, 232, 234, 242, 274–276, 280, 284, 323n; and the Chicano movement, 274; as master trope, 122, 290; versus *lo ranchero,* 2, 121–123, 125, 152, 169, 182, 188, 198, 217, 220, 225, 231, 233, 257, 264, 266, 267, 273
Jameson, Fredric, 5–7, 266, 289, 290, 314n, 324n; on the political unconscious, 6, 287, 288; on postmodernism, 7, 9, 311
jarabe, 50, 316n; "Tapatio," 131
Jiménez, José Alfredo, 263
Jiménez, Santiago, 73, 78, 136, 159
Jimmy Edward [Treviño], 262, 265, 268, 270
Jordan, Rosan, 23, 97, 108–111, 114, 216, 225

Kenton, Stan, 1, 179

Landín, María Luisa, 74
Lara, Agustín, 186
Las nubes, 2, 243, 258, 285, 286, 295, 297, 302; and bimusicality, 243, 244, 248, 257
late capitalism, 6, 309, 324n; and music, 68; and postmodernism, 6, 9, 309
Latin Breed, the, 220, 256, 260, 265, 268, 270, 271
Lawson, Oscar, 118, 250, 255, 256, 263
Lévi-Strauss, Claude, 265, 319n
Limón, José, 59, 108, 110, 111, 225, 296, 314n
Lobos, Los, 71, 125, 325n
López, Isidro, 116–120, 149, 158–160, 163, 165, 187, 188, 194, 225, 230, 236, 242, 243, 255, 263, 318n, 320n, 323n
López, Manny, 167, 180, 181
LULAC (League of United Latin American Citizens), 24, 207, 321n; aims of, 104, 105; and biculturalism, 106, 108, 207; and the Chicano Generation, 223; and the Mexican American Generation, 24, 29, 98; as middle-class organization, 102–104, 106, 107; and orquesta, 275, 276
Lummis, Charles, 57, 59

machismo, 3
Madrugadores, los, 70, 316n
Mafia, la, 273, 304, 305, 307, 322n

mambo, 180, 186, 194, 268; "Doña Chona," 194

MAPA (Mexican American Political Association), 24, 207; and the Chicano Generation, 223; in Fresno, 277, 324 n; and the middle class, 321 n

mariachis, 82, 228

Marroquín, Armando, 74–76, 122, 125, 134, 140, 142, 149, 159, 160, 167, 192–194, 317 n, 319 n; as cultural mediator, 76; as regional promoter, 133, 135, 137, 138, 142

Martínez, Freddie, 263, 323 n

Martínez, Narciso, 64, 72, 73, 78, 135, 159, 163, 219, 273, 316 n, 319 n

Marx, Karl, 5, 65, 67, 95, 288, 313 n

Marxian-Hegelian theory, 5, 95

Marxism, 1, 3, 9, 288, 313 n, 314 n, 320 n; and dialectical materialism, 3, 5; and postmodernism, 6–8, 314 n

Marxist dialectic, 3

Mazz, 273, 305, 307, 310, 322 n

McWilliams, Carey, 20–22

Meaux, Huey, 260

Mendoza, Lydia, 70, 72, 135, 153, 316 n

Mexican American Generation, 9, 21, 47, 93, 97, 98, 136, 204, 218, 223, 229, 285; and acculturation, 128, 130; and biculturalism, 27, 99, 108, 121, 139, 198; and bilingualism, 113, 114, 116; and bimusicality, 132; and class conflict, 26; and cultural citizenship, 23–26, 104, 105; and cultural contradiction, 127, 142, 188, 199, 203, 231, 232; and cultural synthesis, 225; and dialectic of conflict, 25, 187; and ideology of biculturalism, 98; and interethnic conflict, 26, 106, 111; and LULAC, 105, 106; and música ranchera, 125; and orquesta, 89, 93, 100, 108, 136, 142, 150, 151, 199; and upward mobility, 26, 94; versus the Chicano Generation, 28, 31. See also social class

Mexican American Music, 56, 69, 132, 149; commercialization of, 69, 75, 76; and cultural change, 87, 302; and exchange-value, 65; and use-value, 65, 86

Mexican Revolution, 13, 15, 82, 134, 198; and romantic nationalism, 123

Mexican Social Club, 43, 54

Mexican War, 12, 17

Migrant Generation, 9, 25

Montoya, José, 215, 225

Montoya, Malaquías, 213, 214

movimiento, el, 212

MTV, 301, 304; and La Onda Chicana, 303; and the post-Chicano Generation, 301, 302

música jaitona, 2, 125, 232

música moderna, 228, 229. See also música jaitona

música norteña, 71, 77, 170, 172, 228, 278; and the Chicano movement, 219; as ethnic symbol, 220; as working-class expression, 30, 279

música ranchera, 2, 85, 124–126, 138, 142, 154, 156, 176, 178, 243, 280, 282–285. See also lo jaitón; música jaitona; lo ranchero

mutualistas, 55, 56, 131, 278, 318 n

Myth of Aztlán, 28; and the Chicano Generation, 28. See also Chicano movement; indigenismo; romantic nationalism

National Heritage Award, 320 n

nationalism, 29, 82, 205, 206, 211, 220, 321 n

Navaira, Emilio, 125, 307, 322 n

Negrete, Jorge, 73

La Onda Chicana, 2, 165, 194, 198, 209, 219, 220, 226, 227, 230, 232, 236, 262, 276, 281, 310; and bilingualism, 250, 255; and bimusicality, 174, 232, 244, 248, 259, 268, 270, 325 n; and Chicano Generation, 228, 232, 239, 285, 287; and the Chicano movement, 165, 241, 262; as compound bimusicality, 244; and cultural synthesis, 233, 241, 244, 256, 265, 266, 268, 285; decline of, 301, 303, 304, 311; and dialectic of conflict, 310; influence of rock on, 256; and MTV, 303; as pinnacle of orquesta tradition, 203; and romantic nationalism, 220; as symbolic sleight-of-hand, 263, 264; versus major record labels, 229, 230; versus Tejano, 304, 305, 308

Ornelas, René, 305

orquesta, 1, 55, 83, 84, 118, 198, 230, 271, 275; and American big bands, 118, 129, 130, 139; and ballroom dance, 275; and biculturalism, 160; and bilingualism, 27, 114, 115, 120, 250; and bimusicality, 27, 119, 194; and brass band, 78, 79; and the Chicano Generation, 31, 203, 232, 239; and the Chicano movement, 30,